Leading Diversity in the 21st Century

Leading Diversity in the 21st Century

edited by

Terri A. Scandura
University of Miami

Edwin Mouriño-Ruiz
Rollins College

INFORMATION AGE PUBLISHING, INC.
Charlotte, NC • www.infoagepub.com

Library of Congress Cataloging-in-Publication Data

A CIP record for this book is available from the Library of Congress
http://www.loc.gov

ISBN: 978-1-68123-876-0 (Paperback)
       978-1-68123-877-7 (Hardcover)
       978-1-68123-878-4 (ebook)

Copyright © 2017 Information Age Publishing Inc.

All rights reserved. No part of this publication may be reproduced, stored in a retrieval system, or transmitted, in any form or by any means, electronic, mechanical, photocopying, microfilming, recording or otherwise, without written permission from the publisher.

Printed in the United States of America

CONTENTS

Introduction: Leading Diversity in the 21st Century:
Developing High-Quality Connections 1
Terri A. Scandura and Edwin Mouriño-Ruiz

SECTION I
WOMEN AND MINORITIES

1 Gender as a Deep-Level, Communicated, and Interactional
   Construct: Implications for Leaders, Subordinates, and
   Teammates 27
   Frankie J. Weinberg and A. O'Shea Cleveland

2 Mentors, Sponsors, and Diversity in Work Organizations:
   Who Helps Whom and What Difference Does It Make? 55
   Nancy DiTomaso and Catrina Palmer

3 Leadership Diversity in Africa and the African Diaspora 85
   *Clive M. Mukanzi, Terri R. Lituchy, Betty Jane Punnett,
   Bella L. Galperin, Thomas A. Senaji, Elham K. Metwally,
   Lemayon Melyoki, Courtney A. Henderson, Vincent Bagire,
   Cynthia A. Bulley, and Noble Osei-Bonsu*

4 Managing the Hispanic Workforce in the Context of Values,
   Acculturation, and Identity 111
   Carolina Gomez and Patricia G. Martínez

v

5 Leading Women: Unique Challenges and Suggestions
   for Moving Forward 137
   Caren Goldberg, Lucy Gilson, and Sarah Nesci

SECTION II
AGE AND GENERATIONS

6 The Leader–Member Exchange (LMX) Approach
   to Age Diversity 161
   Jacqueline H. Stephenson

7 Leader–member Relations in an Aging Workforce 191
   Barbara A. Fritzsche and Ghada Baz

8 Some of My Best Friends at Work Are Millennials: Leader–
   Member Exchange in the Face of Evolving Generational
   Diversity in the Workplace 221
   Daniel P. Gullifor, Lori L. Tribble, and Claudia C. Cogliser

9 Myths and Misconceptions About Leading Generations:
   Setting the Record Straight 243
   Cort W. Rudolph and Hannes Zacher

SECTION III
EMERGING TRENDS

10 LMX and Autism: Effective Working Relationships 281
    Amy E. Hurley-Hanson and Cristina M. Giannantonio

11 Trans Formational: LMX, Cisgenderism, and Building
    Inclusive Workplaces 303
    Manuel J. Tejeda

12 Social Media, Innovation, and Diversity in the 21st Century 327
    Pamela McCauley and Edwin Nassiff

About the Contributors 357

INTRODUCTION

LEADING DIVERSITY IN THE 21ST CENTURY

Developing High-Quality Connections

Terri A. Scandura
University of Miami

Edwin Mouriño-Ruiz
Rollins College

ABSTRACT

This chapter reviews current leadership research and practice, noting that despite the increase in studies of leadership, attention to diversity in the literature remains piecemeal and sparse. This persists despite the challenges faced by leaders in the development of quality relationships with diverse followers. Key workforce trends are highlighted, and the implications for leading diversity in the 21st century are noted. There is a need for new perspectives on diversity given these trends. To provide an overview of this edited volume, a unifying framework based upon the development of high-quality connections (HQCs) from the perspective of positive organizational scholarship is discussed. Key perspectives from positive organizational scholarship (POS) including exchange, identity, growth, and learning are presented, noting how HQCs might enhance leaders' ability to connect with diverse followers from each of these four perspectives. Next, the role of how HQCs can help leaders shape positive identities for followers is discussed, noting recent research on multiple identities and identity negotiation. An overview of the edited volume is presented, noting the contributions of each chapter to the development of HQCs. In conclusion, considerations and recommendations for practice are presented.

LEADERSHIP THEORY AND PRACTICE: CURRENT STATUS

Key Workforce Trends

When diversity was in the early stages from a business perspective, Dr. Roosevelt Thomas wrote that diversity was beyond just race and gender (Thomas, 1992). Over time, this title could not have been more predictive of what was going to come. Today and into the future, when we speak of diversity, workforce, organizational, and leadership implications it is better to think of it from a broader and more systemic perspective. The following trends highlight and accentuate how diversity has evolved and how organizational leaders need to think of the topic from a broader perspective and changing paradigm.

These trends include the need for organizational change due to the technological explosion, the educational challenges and opportunities, an aging workforce, four generations in the workplace, an increasing diverse (particularly Latino) workforce, the changing demands of the 21st century workforce, and the challenges and opportunities for organizational leaders and leadership development (Mouriño, 2014).

Organizational change is partly being driven by business models that did not exist probably as recently 5 years ago as represented by organizations like Uber, Lyft, and Airbnb. Where organization that were written about in books like *Good to Great* for their excellent qualities, like Circuit City (Collins, 2001), either did not adapt or change fast enough and now do not exist. These organizational shifts of companies being created and/or disappearing is not new since in the span from 1955 through 2011, 87% of Fortune 500 firms have disappeared (Chew, 2012).

Other causes of these changes in addition to globalization is the trend regarding the technological shift created by growth in this area. An example to put things in perspective is that it took the radio 38 years to reach 50 million people. Today it is estimated that there are more than 9 billion mobile devices and that is expected to grow to 12 billion by 2018 (Radicatti, 2014). These devices in union with advancing apps have enabled more than 3 billion users on the Internet (James, 2015). The continual evolution of technology has also enabled 3D printing, smart luggage, and smart homes, and due to the obsession we seem to have with texting and not looking where we're going, some countries are beginning to create laws and signs to ensure everyone's safety. Presently, "45% of tasks performed by U.S. workers can be automated by currently existing technology" (Fortune, 2016).

These technological changes, in turn, affect what is needed from the current and future educational system. The challenge is that the United States ranks 26th out of 34 countries in math and 38% of PhDs in science in the United States are held by foreign born individuals (Augustine, 2007). By 2018, it is expected that 63% of U.S. jobs will require a postsecondary education, and presently we only have 40% (Schroeder, 2015). While this highlights the need for technological skills, the top 10 skills needed for workers in 2020 include people and interpersonal skills like critical thinking, people management, emotional intelligence, and creativity, among others (Gray, 2016).

At the same time, we have an aging world and workplace. In the future demographic world map, only two countries—Mexico and India—look to have enough of a workforce for the future where most do not meet the minimum 2.1 number, which includes immigration, emigration, births, and deaths (Shervani, 2015). This is further highlighted in a 2014 TED Talk regarding the global aging workforce crisis (Strack, 2014). All of this will only make it more important to attract and retain an engaged workforce as competition increases for an aging workforce. This is particularly relevant when most workers crave meaning and purpose in life and few find this at work, or most organizations do not provide the type of workplace that most wish for (Mackey & Sisodia, 2014).

While there is an aging workforce in the 21st century, it is also time for four generations in the workplace, with baby boomers beginning to retire and Millennials as two of the major generations in the workplace. These two generations approach work differently, with the baby boomers known for being dedicated, expecting face time, increasingly working for a purpose (Hesselbein & Goldsmith, 2009), while Millennials are interested in collaboration, recognition, innovation, and relationships (Tapscott, 2008). These four generations provide a richness for a diverse workforce, especially as both older and younger staff members get promoted into leadership roles. The diversity of generations in the workplace will provide both opportunities and challenges in leader–member relationships.

While this generational change is taking place, there is also an increasing Latino demographic who are part of the growing Millennial workforce. There are presently 53 million Latinos in the United States, which make the United States the second largest country with the most Latinos in the world and also the second largest Spanish speaking country with an average age of 27 compared to 40 years old in the Anglo demographic (Rodriguez, 2007). Presently, in the Millennial potential workforce, the Latino portion make up 44% or the largest demographic segment of the Millennials (Krogstad, Lopez, López, Passel, & Patten, 2016). Latinos will make up 74% of labor force growth by 2020, which makes this group both an important part of the present workforce and client base for organizations in the United States. This too will present challenges and opportunities for organizations from a variety of perspectives. From a leader–employee relations perspective, this will be key to understanding how to relate to this growing demographic segment. Considering the potential for leadership development, this demographic will be a crucial one to keep in mind, especially with its younger age individuals as potential leaders.

With all of these changing demographics that include an aging workforce, four generations, and a growing Latino workforce, they all have one thing in common: an increasing need for employee engagement. When an organization has an engaged workforce, there is a tendency for higher productivity, fewer accidents, employees who are less inclined to leave an organization, and higher customer satisfaction (Friedman, 2015).

What these trends call for is leaders to be more engaged and sensitive to the changing needs of their workforce and attune to the changing diversity of the 21st century workplace, which includes an aging workforce, increasing technology, a global presence; and a need for a more educated workforce. Competition will be stiffer for the changing workforce, and helping to reduce turnover will be a challenge. This is a challenge that can be addressed by hiring good leaders who in turn retain more top talent (Besi & Glatzhofer, 2016), and are better equipped to ensure success within their organizations and with their workforce.

THE U.S. WORKFORCE AND ABROAD

Challenges for Leaders

The problem has been that for a while and still today organizations continue to promote or hire leaders with great analytical skills and poor social skills (Rock, 2013). This will not be adequate for the workforce in the 21st century and for the success of organizations. The key skills for today and going forward will be the social skills, so that workers and their leaders can work effectively as teams, which will mean organizations will increasingly need workers and leaders with relationship skills (Colvin, 2016). The skills needed in 2020 will consists primarily of people management skills that include emotional intelligence, coordinating with others, service orientation, and creativity, as examples (Gray, 2016). These "people skills" will be needed in organizations today and into tomorrow to engage an increasingly diverse workforce.

Despite these needs, or possibly due to these needs, some organizations have given up on managers and have gone without managers, like Zappos and W. L. Gore (Morgan, 2014). These organizations possibly did this due to their lack of belief and support of their management teams. So while some organizations have gone this route, most organizations are still developing their leaders and trying to make a difference. The challenges ahead are not just for the United States, but globally, including a diversity of countries such as India, China, Egypt, and Spain. Some of these challenges include leading a team, guiding change, developing employees, inspiring others, and in essence managerial effectiveness among others (Gentry, Eckert, Stawiski, & Zhao, 2016). All of these trends will have implications on leader and employee relations, particularly with the increasingly diverse workforce. This workforce is expecting more than just jobs, and craves meaning in the current context of work.

New Perspectives Needed

For the reasons previously mentioned and more, we believe this book is needed. We have not found many resources that take a comprehensive view regarding the evolving and increasing importance of diversity in the 21st century for organizations, its leaders, and its employees. In addition, the increasingly important need of organizations and its leadership development will continue to be a strategic need and imperative for organizations. This is continuing to grow in importance with an aging baby boomer workforce, where workers tend to leave organizations due to poor management, and most employees don't feel they are recognized even though recognition topped a global survey for job seekers (Strack, 2014). This book looks at leadership and diversity from a variety of perspectives, including a global view and different workforce, such as one with more autistic employees. This sets the stage for the importance of connections between leaders and their subordinates irrespective of their differences, and the need for creating a positive organizational environment with an engaged workforce, while maximizing the changing diversity in the workplace. We next turn to positive organizational scholarship perspectives on high-quality connections at work to develop a unifying theme for this book.

HIGH-QUALITY CONNECTIONS AS A UNIFYING THEME

Dutton and Heaphy (2003) define the quality of the connection between individuals in organizations by focusing on the degree to which the "connective tissue" between individuals gives life or depletes it. Thus, high-quality connections (HQCs) reflect positive scholarship (to be discussed) because they explain how and why leaders may influence the well-being, positive work attitudes, and ability of followers to thrive. HQCs have been studied as leader–member exchange (LMX) and mentoring at work, but are not limited to these connections. HQCs can be characterized in terms of the strength of the tie between individuals, the subjective experience of the connection, and the physiological experience (e.g., lower blood pressure).

Positive Organizational Scholarship

Positive organizational scholarship (POS) focuses on the dynamics leading to the development of human strength that produces resilience and restoration, and fosters vitality and ultimately enhances performance. According to Cameron and Caza (2004), "POS investigates positive deviance, or the ways in which organizations and their members flourish and prosper in especially affirmative ways" (p. 731). These authors unpack the term POS and explain that positive refers to an affirmative bias focused on processes in organizations that elevate individuals working in organizations. Organizational refers to the processes, conditions, and contexts in organizations. Scholarship refers to scientific, theoretically based, research that investigates positive processes in organizations. POS has roots in positive psychology, which started with an influential presidential address to the American Psychological Asssociation (APA) in 1998 (Seligman, 1999). Rather than focusing on pathology, Seligman called upon psychologists to focus on what is good and fulfilling in the lives of healthy people. This approach focuses on concepts such as optimism and hope, and starts with different assumptions regarding human nature. With the publication of an influential edited book (Cameron, Dutton, & Quinn, 2003), and the Center for Positive Organizations at the University of Michigan (http://positiveorgs.bus.umich.edu/), themes from positive psychology have been transported into organizational theory and behavior. POS provides new perspectives through which organizational phenomena may be viewed, and focuses on theory, research, and the practice of how individual strengths can be best manifested in the work context. Examples of the influence of POS on current theory and research include positive professional identities (Roberts, Cha, Hewlin, & Settles, 2009) and mentoring relationships (Ragins, 2009), The POS lens can increase our understanding of leader–member exchange (LMX) mentoring, and the development of positive identities for diverse followers. Indeed, Graen and Scandura (1987) defined the LMX relationship by articulating the equally important aspects of relationship quality and the coupling of behaviors. Consistent with the POS perspective, such understanding can explain the dynamics of interpersonal relationships that create the conditions under which individuals can thrive, which is the joint experience of learning and vitality (Spreitzer, Sutcliffe, Dutton, Sonenshein, & Grant, 2005).

The POS perspective sheds light on four broad perspectives central to understanding high-quality connections (Dutton & Heaphy, 2003). These perspectives will be reviewed in what follows noting the importance of each for understanding the development of HQCs with diverse followers. Following this review, the role of how leaders can facilitate positive work identities through HQCs will be discussed.

Exchange Perspective

Based upon the exchange theories of Thibaut and Kelley (1959) and Homans (1958), the premise of exchange theory is that people exchange commodities of value. The commodities may involve money, but may also include nonmonetary exchanges, such as social support and loyalty. Dutton and Heaphy (2003) specifically refer to the LMX theory of leadership development as an example of how relationships are negotiated over time as leaders and followers exchange "currencies" of exchange. The authors note, "The building of HQCs improves the flow and rate of valued resource exchange, which further cements and deepens the dyadic connection" (p. 270). While LMX theory and research predate research on POS by more than 30 years (cf. Graen, Orris & Johnson, 1973), it is clear that the LMX theory informs the emergent work on HQCs through the exchange lens.

Mentoring relationships have also been examined using a social exchange perspective. For example, Ensher, Thomas, and Murphy (2001) applied social exchange theory as a conceptual framework to understand how different types of mentors and support on protégés' related to mentor satisfaction and perceived career success. This study of 142 ethnically diverse protégés in informal mentoring relationship found that reciprocity related to protégés' satisfaction with their mentors. Young and Perrewe (2000) reviewed the mentoring literature and applied a social exchange framework, concluding that exchange explains why some mentoring relationships develop and others do not.

In sum, the exchange lens of POS offers a great deal of insight into the development of HQCs. Particularly in the early phases of relationship development, exchange of valued economic and social resources may help explain why some leaders are able to reach diverse followers and develop positive and productive work relationships. Exchange perspectives are premised on the idea that each follower is a unique individual and that different exchanges will occur with each individual. Troester and van Knippenberg (2012) found that relational demography effects are likely more positive when leaders are more similar to team members, or high on openness. It appears that the key is for the leader to show openness and listening skills so that the appropriate resources are matched to each follower's particular needs.

Identity Perspective

Work identities are developed, in part, through interactions with others. HQCs may have a powerful influence on how individuals see their roles at work and how this becomes part of their overall identity. Fletcher and Ragins (2007) propose that the mentoring interactions may enhance one's acceptance of one's identity. Through mentoring, a junior person grows into acceptance of a professional identity over time. Also mentor and protégé develop and identify in relationship to one another. This is considered separate from individual identity and is known as a relational identity, which is "the nature of one's role-relationship, such as manager-subordinate and coworker-coworker. It is how role occupants enact their respective roles vis-a`-vis each other" (Sluss & Ashforth, 2007). These authors further suggest that relational identity integrates person- and role-based identities, and thus individual, interpersonal, and collective levels of self as reflected in social identity (Hogg & Terry, 2000). Thus, the development of an HQC with a leader or mentor may help reduce the salience of the in-group bias found in research on social identity theory (SIT; Tajfel & Turner, 1986). In-group bias results when a person evaluates members of their own group more favorably than a designated out-group (Bettencourt, Charlton, Dorr, & Hume, 2001). Out-groups in organizations are often women and minorities who are not part of the power networks (Ibarra, 1995, 1997). Thus, leaders can have a positive influence on the reduction of the salience of out-group membership by reducing the influence of social identity on individual identity and emphasizing the importance of a diverse follower's relationship to them. However, research has indicated that leaders should allow the subgroup identity to be expressed rather than to force assimilation (Hornsby & Hogg, 2000). The creation of a superordinate identity (for example, "We are all on the same team") may be helpful.

Growth and Development Perspective

From this lens, followers thrive when they are able to grow and learn as a result of working. This is, in part, enabled by HQCs with leaders and others at work. This perspective builds on the attachment theory (Bowlby, 1969), which focuses on the relationship systems in early life that contribute to a person's growth, development, and sense of purpose. Attachment theory suggests that there are two adult attachment dimensions: anxiety and avoidance (Brennan, Clark, & Shaver, 1998). The anxiety dimension is associated with a negative self-identity and a higher need for approval from others. The insecure-avoidant attachment style manifests as self-reliance and emotional distancing, or detachment in day-to-day interpersonal relations. Bowlby argued that individuals strive to create attachments to others because they generate a sense of security; this is termed the secure attachment style. This greater level of security within an interpersonal relationship allows the person to experiment and learn new things. Research in the area of mentoring supports the importance of attachment styles to HQCs. Allen, Shockley, & Poteat (2010) found that a protégé's anxious attachment was associated with less feedback seeking and less feedback acceptance. Protégé feedback acceptance was associated with both the quality and frequency of feedback provided by the mentor. In a study of matched mentor-protégé pairs, Wang, Noe, Wang, and Greenberger (2009) found that avoidance and anxiety attachment styles had a significant influence on the willingness to mentor in the future. Thus, mentor and protégé attachment styles may influence both the HQC and the outcomes of the mentoring relationship. Despite the interesting findings from attachment theory and mentoring, less is known about how individuals with diverse backgrounds might differ in how the effects of anxiety and avoidance might play out in the development of HQCs.

Learning Perspective

According to Dutton and Heaphy (2003), HQCs "enable people to expand their knowledge about the self, the relationship, and the world" (p. 273). By creating environments of empathy that allow for concerns to be voiced, leaders and mentors can enhance the learning of their followers. For example, mentoring interactions create personal learning (Lankau & Scandura, 2002), and as such, mentoring relates to this perspective. Personal learning comprises relational job learning and personal skill development. Both having a mentor and mentoring functions (vocational, social support and role modeling) were found to be antecedents of personal learning. Personal learning enhanced the relationship of mentoring to outcomes of job satisfaction, role ambiguity, turnover intentions, and actual turnover. Fletcher (1999) describes the process of "empathic teaching" in which the teacher considers the emotional context as well as the intellectual context to create a learning environment characterized by respect. It seems that a similar approach to empathic leading and mentoring would enhance the development of HQCs.

Thus, learning appears to be part of a HQC and relates to personal and organizational outcomes. That said, there is a paucity of theory and research on how diversity may influence the learning process in the context of organizational relationships. A notable exception is a study by Gersick, Bartunek, and Dutton (2000) that examined the role of personal relationships in the development of professional identities. In this interview study, the top reasons why interviewees selected their "top two most important professional relationships" were collegiality, admiration for the other person, positive mentoring, and support. These findings are consistent with the literature on mentoring. However, the analysis also revealed gender differences with respect to the impact of personal relationships. Men were more likely to tell stories about the relationships that described career help. Women, on the other hand, were more likely to tell stories that described harm. These harming stories described either marginalization in the work environment or refusal of resources needed to complete work. This research underscores the importance of HQCs for the enablement of learning in a relationship, but also a potential "dark side" of relationships that must be addressed, particularly in the context of diversity.

HIGH-QUALITY CONNECTIONS AND IDENTITY

In considering the four lenses provided by POS (exchange, identity, growth, and learning), it seems that one way to examine the influence of diversity is to consider the influence of HQCs and the emergence of identity. As noted previously, identity is nested and comprises individual, relational, and social identities. For the relational identity to merge with the individual and social identity, there needs to be a recognition of three important aspects of identity. First, psychological safety must be present within the connection so that the diverse follower is willing to trust, take risks, and self-disclose. Second, there must be a recognition that followers have multiple identities, and that the leader needs to learn about the follower. Third, research on identity negotiation has shown that the revelation of identity is a process that unfolds over time. These three key themes in understanding now HQCs relate to identity will be discussed next.

HQCs and Psychological Safety

One of the most important aspects of having HQCs is that these bonds create a climate of psychological safety. This is particularly important for women and minorities, since they may be reluctant to trust and share personal information. In a longitudinal study, Carmeli, Brueller and Dutton (2009) found that high-quality relationships predicted psychological safety. As noted previously from the learning perspective, psychological safety predicted increased learning. Their study also found that HQCs were both directly and indirectly related to learning through psychological safety. In another study, Carmeli and Gittel (2009) found HQCs generate relational dimensions of relational coordination (shared goals, shared knowledge, and mutual respect), and this fostered psychological safety. Because of this, respondents reported that they were better able to learn from their failures. In other words, psychological safety plays a pivotal role in understanding how HQCs relate to outcomes, such as learning on the job. This study underscores the importance of having HQCs in the workplace for creating environments that are supportive and psychologically safe. This is important for women and minorities due to invisible and visible stigma associated with their social identities.

An employee may have an "invisible stigma" that the individual feels uncomfortable disclosing to their leader or mentor. Ragins, Singh and Cornwall (2007) found that the disclosure of gay identity at work invoked fear for those that had not disclosed. However, employees reported less fear and more disclosure when they worked in a group that was perceived as supportive and sharing their stigma. The fear of disclosure was related to lower work attitudes, such as job satisfaction and increased psychological strain. Other invisible stigmas include disabilities such as epilepsy, alcoholism, drug abuse, cancer, HIV/AIDS, stroke, mental disability, and mental illness (Ragins, 2008). Ragins discusses the key role of "supportive and ally relationships," which can alleviate identity disconnects and make it safe for an employee to disclose their invisible stigma. In addition to invisible stigmas, the negative workplace impact of visible stigmas such as age and disability may be alleviated by a supportive and/or transformational leader (Boehm & Dwertmann, 2015). Their analysis points out that age and disability are correlated, and thus any given employee may be a member of multiple groups and thus have multiple identities. In other words, an employee might be disabled, African American, and/or a union member. All of these identities influence how they may view themselves, their role at work, and their relationship with leaders, mentors, and coworkers.

Multiple Identities

Subordinates have an influence on the development of the HQC by providing valued resources for leaders, mentors, and coworkers. Creary, Caza, and Roberts (2015) have articulated a theory of how multiple identities are managed within the manager-subordinate relationship. However, their analysis is relevant for mentoring and coworker relationships as well. They employ LMX theory and relational cultural theory to explain how an employee's management of multiple identities in the workplace may affect the HQC with the manager. They define multiple identities as "two or more meanings that individuals attach to themselves as a function of their multiple social group memberships (i.e., social identities)" (p. 539). By recognizing that identities are multifaceted, leaders are better able to create conditions of psychological safety that encourage followers to disclose. This safety must communicate that multiple identities reflect diversity and are valued by the organization as important resources. To develop HQCs with all followers, leaders must understand identity dynamics, which describe the process through which identity unfolds. This is articulated in self-verification theory, also known as the identity negotiation process.

Identity Negotiation

Research on identity negotiation has demonstrated that individuals seek to self-verify by having others see them as they truly are. In other words, people are motivated to have others see them as they see themselves (Swann, 1983). Individuals need to reinforce their sense of identity, and this need exists even if the identity is negative (i.e., the person is a member of a minority or a stigmatized group) (Swann, 1987; Swann, Polzer, Seyle, & Ko, 2004). Individuals may join organizations that reflect their identity to maintain a sense of self (Swann, 1983). Once in the organization, Swann (2005) suggests that people next seek self-verification partners who they decide they will disclose their identity to. Interestingly, people with low self-esteem seek out others who will reinforce their negative self-views. However, when confronted with disconfirming evidence (i.e., being told they are dominant when they are not), people will defend their self-views (Swann & Hill, 1982). In follow-up studies, Swann and Ely (1984) found that this defending reaction only occurs when people are certain about their identities. Longitudinal research has demonstrated that individuals make attempts to bring others views of themselves into line with their own self-views (McNulty & Swann, 1994; Swann, Milton, & Polzer, 2000). In sum, research on this perspective demonstrates that identity unfolds over time. Individuals engage in self-disclosure with another person because they are driven to have their identity affirmed by others. People will protect their sense of identity, and will go to great lengths to do so.

As noted previously, psychological safety is essential for an employee to trust their coworkers to discuss multiple aspects of their identity, particularly if the individual is a member of a stigmatized group. People self-verify over time, and "test" out whether the environment is safe to divulge their multiple identities. Taken together, the processes of identity negotiation and the management of multiple identities within a climate of psychological safety helps explain what leaders can do to facilitate HCQs and the outcome of positive self-worth through affirming followers' identities.

CHAPTER NOTES

Women and Minorities

No book on leading diversity in the 21st century would be complete without inclusion of chapters on women and minorities. In the first section of this book, six chapters address this topic. Weinberg and Cleveland (Chapter 1) describe gendered communication styles (GCOM) as a form of deep-level diversity that has important organizational implications. The authors introduce a useful typology of GCOM and articulate implications of these communicative orientations for leaders, managers, and their subordinates. This chapter may be viewed as a deep-level analysis of how communication may facilitate self-disclosure and supportive HQCs when one party to the dyad is female.

To follow up this chapter, DiTomaso and Palmer discuss the roles of mentors and sponsors and their helping behaviors for women (Chapter 2). This chapter provides a critical review of the mentoring literature, clarifies the difference between mentor and sponsor, and raises new questions that have not been given sufficient attention in the research literature about who helps whom in the labor force and to what effect. The chapter ends with a discussion of how employees who may be at a disadvantage in gaining access to supportive relationships in the workplace can improve their chances of positive outcomes. This chapter focuses on mentoring as a HQC, to which women have had less access, and discusses recommendations for future practice.

Chapter 3 provides a fascinating overview of leadership diversity in Africa and the African diaspora (Mukanzi et al.). The chapter reviews results of a large-scale research project in Kenya, Uganda, Tanzania, Ghana, Egypt, the Caribbean, the United States, and Canada. The authors provide insight into leadership diversity in countries that are among the most ethnically, religiously, and culturally diverse in the world. Leadership in these regions reflects ethnic groups split into multiple states having different languages, cultures, and ethnic compositions. This chapter underscores the need for in-depth, deep-level research into understanding the nuances of identity in Africa and the African diaspora, and provides useful guidance for managers operating in these cultures.

Chapter 4 (Gomez & Martinez) focuses on managing the Hispanic workforce, considering cultural values, acculturation, and identity. Their review and analysis suggests that Hispanic employees view leadership differently than other groups due to culturally-embedded assumptions, which suggest the need for the development of HQCs due to Hispanics having a relational perspective. The chapter highlights paternalistic leadership and interactional justice as recommendations for practicing leaders to develop HQCs with Hispanics. These practices must acknowledge employees' Hispanic identity, noting that some are more acculturated and have weaker ethnic identification and may be more similar to U.S. majority members.

The final chapter in this section, Chapter 5 by Goldberg, Gilson, and Nesci, provides an excellent summary of theory and research on leading women and minorities. The chapter addresses unique challenges faced by women and minorities in the workplace, including the role of stereotypes. Their recommendations for moving forward include training to address these challenges, as well as to provide guidelines for managers to develop HQCs with diverse followers. Recognition of hiring practices is also discussed including token hiring, creating larger pools of women and minorities, and creating affinity groups within organizations. By creating critical mass in organizations, these practices will enable greater psychological safety for women and minorities, which is essential for them to thrive at work. This chapter provides an excellent summary for many of the themes from the first section of the book, and provides very specific practice guidelines for leaders to create climates of inclusion that develop HQCs.

Age and Generations

The second section of the book addresses trends that have been noted for some years related to age and generations at work. Chapter 6 (Stephanson) discusses the leader–member exchange (LMX) approach and how it can address the issues of age diversity in the workplace. This chapter examines the persistent stereotypes and discrimination of older workers, rather than viewing them as having unique skills and talents. The LMX approach is suggested as a remedy due to its focus on the uniqueness of each individual. Stereotypes are a challenge for the identity negotiation process, and leaders must be sensitive to them to develop HCQs with older workers. The key roles of leaders and human resource practitioners are highlighted in changing the work environment and provide needed support to older workers. Clear practice implications to develop trust, fairness, and ultimately enhanced productivity for older workers are presented.

The chapter by Fritzsche and Baz (Chapter 7) continues the discussion of leader–member relations in an aging workforce. This chapter examines challenges brought by the aging workforce, while focusing on the roles of a leader of all ages in developing HQCs with older subordinates. The chapter first reviews the research related to leader behaviors and age, including LMX relationships when the supervisor is younger than the subordinate. The role of workplace ageism is discussed, followed by a discussion of the challenges and opportunities associated with an aging workforce. Finally, evidence-based recommendations for building HQCs with older workers are presented. Taken together, Chapters 6 and 7 provide a comprehensive overview of the micro- and macro-organizational issues related to identity as an aging worker, and how leaders can develop high-quality relationships with older subordinates.

Chapter 8 by Guilfor, Tribble, and Cogliser reports results of a qualitative study of LMX across generations. This research was based upon social identity theory and fits with the theme of the book with respect to the role of leaders in negotiating identity at work. The authors suggest that individuals engage in behaviors that are congruent with salient aspects of their identities, but higher levels of organizational identification are necessary for them to thrive. The research examines whether views of HQCs are consistent across generations (baby boomers, Gen X, and Millennials). Generational differences in approaches to developing connections are explored, noting how the identities of the different generations might clash, but may also complement one another. Since Millennials now comprise the largest group in the U.S. workforce, understanding these differences is essential knowledge for leaders and mentors.

The final chapter in the section on age and generations is by Rudolph and Zacher (Chapter 9). This chapter "sets the record straight" by debunking several common myths and misconceptions about generations at work. Next, a lifespan developmental perspective is presented that addresses the process of leading workers of different ages. This approach is consistent with the POS lens of growth and development, and the authors argue that this approach is more useful for leading an age-diverse workforce than the model of generational differences. The chapter concludes with best practice recommendations based on this lifespan perspective.

Emerging Trends

The final section of the book addresses recent and emerging trends in leading diversity. First, the chapter on LMX and autism by Hurley-Hanson and Ginnantonio addresses one of the stigmas that has been discussed in the identity literature. The authors note that over the next decade, close to half a million people with autism spectrum disorder (ASD) will reach adulthood and enter the workforce (Chapter 10), yet, there is almost no research on the work experiences of employees with ASD and how they may develop HQCs. Leaders play an important role in the success of ASD followers, and several relevant leadership theories are reviewed commenting on how they may be employed to create effective working relationships between leaders and their employees with ASD. The authors conclude by urging leaders to consider practices to support ASD employees, including diversity and inclusion training for coworkers, managers, and supervisors; understanding the costs of accommodating employees with ASD as well as the benefits; encouraging leaders to develop empathy; developing mentoring programs for employees with ASD; and examining all the company's human resource programs and policies toward attention to this group.

Chapter 11 discusses the emerging trend of building inclusive workplaces for transgendered employees (Tejeda). This stigmatized identity group faces challenges at the workplaces that are not yet well understood. This chapter is a breakthrough work that explores how workforces maintain gender essentialism and reinforce stereotypical representations that restrain gender identity and expression. A useful typology of gender identity and expression is presented that focuses predominantly on transgender issues in the workplace. The chapter then explores how the development of HQCs may provide a mechanism for dismantling the coded privilege within the workplace and promote inclusivity. Recommendations and considerations for organizations and leaders to promote such inclusiveness are presented.

The final chapter discusses how dynamic changes in technology can be leveraged to enhance diversity initiatives (Chapter 12). This chapter focuses on the scientific communities' response to social media and the importance of diversity for innovation. Specific details are provided about a social media platform to connect scientists for the purposes of increasing representation of diverse groups in the innovation process. The role of social media as an influence on our world cannot be understated, and this chapter offers a cutting-edge view of how it can be harnessed as a positive force for creating HQCs and change.

IMPLICATIONS FOR ORGANIZATIONS, LEADERS, LEADERSHIP DEVELOPMENT, AND LEADING DIVERSITY

Diversity has been associated with many organizational benefits, including being more innovative, and some organizations can have up to 95% higher return on equity if they have a more diverse executive board (Grillo, 2014). Diversity provides everyone involved a broader view of issues and problems as well as different approaches to consider. Creativity and innovation are fundamentally important for organizations to reinvent themselves in these constantly changing times, and diversity enables organizations to be more broadly creative and innovative. If organizations can capitalize on diversity from a strategic perspective, it enables the organization, its leadership, and workforce to have a more creative, innovative, and customer-focused approach to success.

Yet diversity efforts have continued to fail, as exemplified by the millions of dollars paid out by corporations due to discrimination, and partly due to using old approaches to solving 21st century challenges (Dobbin & Kalev, 2016). Organizations and their leadership need to look at diversity from a systemic and holistic perspective while providing the leadership commitment and support, and not just lip service. An example is for an organization to have employee resources groups (ERG) that are one piece of a bigger organizational commitment. However, it does not help the organization and hinders leadership's credibility if they claim to have ERGs for women, Latinos, and other minority groups, but have minimal leader representation at the organizational level of these groups.

Taking a systemic and organizational change approach will position organizations better for success. First, organizations need to ensure they have a clear vision of why the organization wants to be a leader on diversity, this will help articulate "where" the organization is headed and minimize confusion. The organization needs to ensure its leadership team and workforce overall have the right skills in order to work in an increasingly diverse workforce, which will help minimize anxiety as to why the change is happening. Everyone from top to bottom in an organization needs to have an incentive to accept being a diverse organization to minimize resistance by implementing gradual change. All employees need to be provided with the resources to work effectively in a changing diverse workforce to minimize frustration. Finally, leaders and their workforce need to have an action plan in order to achieve change and diversity and to minimize false starts.

Many organizations and their leadership claim to be diversity friendly and recognize that diversity is not only good for business, but a good moral issue to embrace. It not only helps organizations but society overall. Organizations have to take a proactive and systemic approach to diversity and treat it as a major change effort to minimize resistance. Most employees resist change because they don't like it, don't understand it, or don't like the deliverer of change (Maurer, 2010). This can be seen as progressive IT companies like Twitter and Pinterest struggle with aligning diversity and strategic efforts in the 21st century (Wells, 2016).

Trying the same thing and expecting different results has been defined as insanity. And while eliminating bias is a noble cause, it seems to have not worked as extensively as most would like. All one has to do is watch the 5 o'clock news or read various Internet articles to see what still occurs in society, along with the constant news of companies getting sued for discrimination. What some suggest is that a better approach would go beyond the focus on reducing biases and also focus on changing the way leaders recruit and promote (Morse, 2016). It is important to note that different audiences look at the topic of diversity differently. For example, Millennials consider diversity to be about inclusion and valuing varying employee perspectives, while older workers tend to believe diversity is about equitable representation and assimilation (Burrell, 2016). This raises the issue of ensuring there is a similar understanding regarding what the organization and its leadership mean by diversity. The top management team must communicate that diversity goes beyond race and gender and Affirmative Action and Equal Employment Opportunities (EEO). Organizations cannot skim past these fundamental and legal issues since studies continue to find discrepancies linked to race, gender, and ethnicity in job interviews (Burrell, 2016). What organizations need to consider is a new approach to diversity for its leaders, leadership development, and its changing workforce especially when tried ways from the past don't seem to be as effective.

Part of the leadership development process for organizations needs to be beyond leadership training development workshops. It needs to ensure that this process is part of a bigger systemic effort that includes accountability, rewards, and 360-degree feedback, and that the effort is transparent to all. This can enable an organization create an organizational culture that is healthy and helps the organizational brand by making an engaging workplace environment. Taking a holistic view and a systemic approach to engagement can help in this effort. This means an organization must ensure it has competent managers in order to minimize underperformance; that there are clear and contextual goals in order to minimize confusion and missed deadlines; that there are objective metrics to ensure minimizing a disgruntled workforce; that there are right and adequate resources so as to minimize frustration; and last, that there is an environment that enables autonomy in order to minimize the feeling of being micromanaged (Cardius, 2014).

How leaders treat a staff who is different than themselves will impact engagement and turnover (Jones & Harter, 2005). In addition, organizational leadership must not lose sight of the fact that engaged employees should have a strong connection with their organization, and that engagement serves as a driver for organizational success (Lockwood, 2007). How leaders treat their subordinates who have ethnic, gender, age differences, and other identities can create an engaged environment that can lead to success all the way around the organization. Leader effectiveness has been linked to diversity, particularly collectivism when using the LMX model (Herrera, Duncan, Ree, & Williams, 2013). So not only does an organization need to focus on its diversity strategic efforts, it must also focus on the leader–member relationships. This dual approach enhances the chances of success in the pursuit of diversity as a business imperative. One way to consider this is to take a three-pronged approach to engaging managers on the front end and throughout the journey, expose them to different groups, and encourage social accountability and change (Dobbin & Kellev, 2016).

Organizations need to learn to harness the power of diversity and take advantage of their growing diverse workforces, including Millennials of which the Latino Millennials make up a large segment of this new workforce (Coulombe & Gil, 2016). Diversity is not only both a moral and business imperative, it also helps the company brand gain free public relations by becoming a great place for a diverse workforce and a great organization to work for that is perceived as being a workplace of fairness, high morale, and inclusion (Fortune, 2016). The organizations that do not take this imperative will do so at their own peril, and this could lead to them being on the list of Fortune 500 organizations that won't exist in the future.

CONCLUSION

We have provided an overview of this much-needed book that updates theory, research, and practice on leading diversity. Our hope is that this book will not only provide additional insights from a global and more progressive view in the 21st century, but also will provide readers with more questions and considerations for implementation within their own or client organizations. Leadership and diversity are topics that keep evolving. This is partly due to changing times and changing demographics. Worker expectations are dramatically changing, and organizations and their leadership must adapt, evolve, and keep pace (Mackey & Sisodia, 2014). We have reached a point where diversity is definitely beyond race and gender, but it remains crucial as present and future leaders work to be more effective and create an engaged workforce, maximize diversity and inclusion, enable their respective organizations to be great places to work, and work to achieve organizational success in this new era of work, or as some have called it the fourth industrial revolution (Gray, 2016). Going forward, leaders must remember that everyone lights up a room, some when they walk in and others when they walk out. Which ones do they want to be? What will be their brand as a leader, and how effective will they be at leading a diverse, inclusive, and engaged workforce in the 21st century? Successful leaders of the future will need to be emotionally agile and focused on results while being transparent, accountable, and forward thinking. They must do so while ensuring they are making the workplace a positive experience and being more concerned about what employees do versus where they do it while maximizing diversity at work (Meister & Mulcahy, 2016). We hope this book provides some current insights and reflective points to consider in leading the workforce of the future.

REFERENCES

Augustine, N., Barrett, C., Cassell, G., Chu, S., Gates, R., Grasmick, N., . . . Zare, R. (2007). *Rising above the gathering storm: Energizing and employing America for a brighter economic future.* Washington, DC: National Academies Press.

Allen, T. D., Shockley, K. M., & Poteat, L. (2010). Protégé anxiety attachment and feedback in mentoring relationships. *Journal of Vocational Behavior, 77*(1), 73–80.

Besi, A., & Glatzhofer, P. (2016). Reducing turnover starts with hiring and developing great leaders (A white paper). Retrieved from: http://www.selectinternational.com/whitepaper-reducing-turnover-starts-with-hiring-and-developing-great-leaders

Bettencourt, B., Charlton, K., Dorr, N., & Hume, D. L. (2001). Status differences and in-group bias: A meta-analytic examination of the effects of status stability, status legitimacy, and group permeability. *Psychological Bulletin, 127*(4), 520–542.

Boehm, S. A., & Dwertmann, D. J. (2015). Forging a single-edged sword: Facilitating positive age and disability diversity effects in the workplace through leadership, positive climates, and HR practices. *Work, Aging and Retirement, 1*(1), 41–63.

Morse, G. (2016). Designing a bias-free organization: It's easier to change your processes than your people [An interview with Iris Bohnet]. *Harvard Business Review, July–August*, 62–67. Retrieved from https://hbr.org/2016/07/designing-a-bias-free-organization

Bowlby, J. (1973). *Attachment and loss: Separation, anxiety and anger* (Vol. 2). New York, NY: Basic Books.

Brennan, K. A., Clark, C. L., & Shaver, P. R. (1998). Self-report measurement of adult attachment. In J. A. Simpson & W. S. Rholes (Eds.), *Attachment theory and close relationships*. New York, NY: The Guilford Press.

Burrell, L. (2016). We just can't handle diversity: A research roundup. *Harvard Business Review*. Retrieved from https://hbr.org/2016/07/we-just-cant-handle-diversity

Cameron, K. S., & Caza, A. (2004). Introduction contributions to the discipline of positive organizational scholarship. *American Behavioral Scientist, 47*(6), 731–739.

Cameron, K., & Dutton, J. (Eds.). (2003). *Positive organizational scholarship: Foundations of a new discipline*. San Francisco, CA: Berrett-Koehler.

Cardius, M. (2014). *The five levers of employee engagement*. Retrieved from https://mikecardus.com/the-5-levers-of-employee-engagement-2/

Carmeli, A., & Gittell, J. H. (2009). High-quality relationships, psychological safety, and learning from failures in work organizations. *Journal of Organizational Behavior, 30*(6), 709–729.

Carmeli, A., Brueller, D., & Dutton, J. E. (2009). Learning behaviors in the workplace: The role of high-quality interpersonal relationships and psychological safety. *Systems Research and Behavioral Science, 26*(1), 81–98.

Chew, J. (January, 2012). *Fortune 500 extinction*. Retrieved from http://csinvesting.org/2012/01/06/fortune-500-extinction/

Collins, J. (2001). *Good to great: Why some companies make the leap*. New York, NY: HarperCollins.

Colvin, G. (2016). *Humans are underrated: What high achievers know that brilliant machines never will*. New York, NY: Penguin.

Coulombe, K., & Gil, W. (2016). *The changing U.S. workforce: The growing Hispanic demographic and the workplace*. Retrieved from https://www.shrm.org/hr-today/trends-and-forecasting/research-and-surveys/pages/chci-growing-hispanic-demographic-report.aspx

Creary, S. J., Caza, B. B., & Roberts, L. M. (2015). Out of the box? How managing a subordinate's multiple identities affects the quality of a manager–subordinate relationship. *Academy of Management Review, 40*(4), 538–562.

Cummings, & B. Staw. (Eds.). *Research in organizational behavior, 9*, 175–208. Greenwich, CT: JAI Press.

Dobbin, F., & Kalev, A. (2016). Why diversity programs fail. And what works better. Retrieved from https://hbr.org/2016/07/why-diversity-programs-fail

Dutton, J. E., & Heaphy, E. D. (2003). The power of high-quality connections. In K. S. Cameron, J. E. Dutton, & R. E. Quinn (Eds.), *Positive organizational scholarship: Foundations of a new discipline* (pp. 263–278). San Francisco, CA: BerrettKoehler.

Dutton, J. E., & Ragins, B. 2007. *Exploring positive relationships at work: Building a theoretical and research foundation.* Mahwah, NJ: Erlbaum.
Ensher, E. A., Thomas, C., & Murphy, S. E. (2001). Comparison of traditional, step-ahead, and peer mentoring on protégés' support, satisfaction, and perceptions of career success: A social exchange perspective. *Journal of Business and Psychology, 15*(3), 419–438.
Fletcher, J. K. (1999). *Disappearing acts.* Cambridge, MA: Massachusetts Institute of Technology.
Fletcher, J. K., & Ragins, B. R. (2007). Stone center relational cultural theory: A window on relational mentoring. In B. R. Ragins & K. E. Kram (Eds.), *The handbook of mentoring at work: Theory research and practice.* Thousand Oaks: CA. SAGE.
Fortune. (2016). *Best workplaces for diversity 2016.* Retrieved from: https://www.greatplacetowork.com/best-workplaces/diversity/2016/default
Fortune. (2016). *The future of work is.* Retrieved from http://fortune.com/future-work-jobs-industries/
Friedman, R. (2015). *The best place to work: The art and science of creating an extraordinary workplace.* New York, NY: Penguin.
Gentry, W., Eckert, R., Stawiski, S., & Zhao, S. (2016). *The challenges leaders face around the world: More similar than different* (White paper). Retrieved from http://insights.ccl.org/wpcontent/uploads/2015/04/ChallengesLeadersFace.pdf
Gersick, C. J., Dutton, J. E., & Bartunek, J. M. (2000). Learning from academia: The importance of relationships in professional life. *Academy of Management Journal, 43*(6), 1026–1044.
Graen, G. B., Orris, J. B., & Johnson, T. W. (1973). Role assimilation processes in a complex organization. *Journal of Vocational Behavior, 3,* 395–420.
Graen, G. B., & Scandura, T. A. (1987). Toward a psychology of dyadic organizing. In L. L. Cummings, & B. Staw (Eds.), *Research in organizational behavior, 9,* 175–208. Greenwich, CT: JAI Press.
Gray, A. (2016). *The 10 skills you need to thrive in the fourth industrial revolution.* Retrieved from https://www.weforum.org/agenda/2016/01/the-10-skills-you-need-to-thrive-in-the-fourth-industrial-revolution
Grillo, G. (2014). *Diverse workforces are more innovative.* Retrieved from https://www.theguardian.com/media-network/media-network-blog/2014/mar/27/diversity-innovation-startups-fortune-500-companies
Herrera, R., Duncan, P., Ree, M., & Williams, K. (2013). Diversity as a predictor of leadership effectiveness. *Journal of Diversity Management, 8*(1), 1–14.
Hesselbein, F., & Goldsmith, M. (Ed.). (2009). *The organization of the future 2: Visions, strategies, and insights on managing in a new era.* Hoboken, NJ: Wiley.
Hogg, M. A., & Terry, D. J. 2000. Social identity and self-categorization processes in organizational contexts. *Academy of Management Review, 25,* 121–140.
Homans, G. C. (1958). Social behavior as exchange. *American Journal of Sociology,* 597–606.
Hornsey, M. J., & Hogg, M. A. (2000). Assimilation and diversity: An integrative model of subgroup relations. *Personality and Social Psychology Review, 4*(2), 143–156.

Ibarra, H. (1995). Race, opportunity, and diversity of social circles in managerial networks. *Academy of Management Journal, 38*(3), 673–703.

Ibarra, H. (1997). Paving an alternative route: Gender differences in managerial networks. *Social Psychology Quarterly*, 91–102.

James, J. (2015). *Data never sleeps 3.0*. Retrieved from https://www.domo.com/blog/data-never-sleeps-3-0/

Jones, J., & Harter, J. (2005). Race effects on the employee engagement-turnover intention relationship. *Journal of Leadership and Organizational Studies, 11*(2), 78–88.

Krogstad, J. M., Lopez, M. H., López, G., Passel, J. S., & Patten, E. (2016). *Millennials make up almost half of Latino eligible voters in 2016: Youth, naturalizations drive number of Hispanic eligible voters to record 27.3 million*. Retrieved from http://www.pewhispanic.org/2016/01/19/millennials-make-up-almost-half-of-latino-eligible-voters-in-2016/

Lankau, M. J., & Scandura, T. A. (2002). An investigation of personal learning in mentoring relationships: Content, antecedents, and consequences. *Academy of Management Journal, 45*(4), 779–790.

Lockwood, N. (2007). *Leveraging employee engagement for competitive advantage: HR's strategic role*. Retrieved from https://www.shrm.org/india/hr-topics-and-strategy/employee-advocacy-relations-and-engagement/documents/07marresearch quarterly.pdf

Mackey, J., & Sisodia, R. (2014). *Conscious capitalism: Liberating the heroic spirit of business*. Boston, MA: Harvard Business School.

Maurer, R. (2010). *Beyond the wall of resistance*. Austin, TX: Bard Press.

McNulty, S. E., & Swann, W. B., Jr. (1994). Identity negotiation in roommate relationships: The self as architect and consequence of social reality. *Journal of Personality and Social Psychology, 67*, 1012–1023

Meister, J., & Mulcahy, K. (2017). *The future workplace experience: 10 rules for mastering disruption in recruiting and engaging employees*. New York, NY: McGraw Hill.

Morgan, J. (2014). *The future of work: Attract new talent, build better leaders, and create a competitive organization*. Hoboken, NJ: Wiley.

Mouriño, E. (2014). *The perfect human capital storm: Workplace challenges and opportunities in the 21st century*. North Charleston, SC: CreateSpace.

Radicati. S. (2014). *Mobile statistics report, 2014–2018*. Retrieved from http://www.radicati.com/wp/wp-content/uploads/2014/01/Mobile-Statistics-Report-2014-2018-Executive-Summary.pdf

Ragins, B. R. (2008). Disclosure disconnects: Antecedents and consequences of disclosing invisible stigmas across life domains. *Academy of Management Review, 33*(1), 194–215.

Ragins, B. (2009). Positive identities in action: A model of mentoring self-structures and the motivation to mentor. In L. M. Roberts & J. E. Dutton (Eds.), *Exploring positive identities and organizations: Building a theoretical and research foundation* (pp. 237–264). New York, NY: Routledge.

Ragins, B. R., Singh, R., & Cornwell, J. M. (2007). Making the invisible visible: Fear and disclosure of sexual orientation at work. *The Journal of Applied Psychology, 92*(4), 1103–1118.

Roberts, L. M., Cha, S. E., Hewlin, P. F., & Settles, I. H. (2009). Bringing the inside out: Enhancing authenticity and positive identity in organizations. In L. M. Roberts & J. E. Dutton (Eds.), *Exploring positive identities and organizations: Building a theoretical and research foundation* (pp. 149–170). New York, NY: Routledge.

Rock, D. (2013). Why organizations fail. *Fortune.* Retrieved from http://fortune.com/2013/10/23/why-organizations-fail/

Rodriguez, R. (2007). *Latino talent-effective strategies to recruit, retain, and develop hispanic professionals.* New York, NY: Wiley.

Schroeder, L. (2015). Redefining the college degree. *Chief Learning Officer Magazine.* Retrieved from http://www.clomedia.com/2015/11/23/redefining-the-college-degree/

Seligman, M. E. (1999). The president's address. *American Psychologist, 54*(8), 559–562.

Shervani, T. (2015). *The workforce of the future.* Retrieved from http://www.ey.com/Publication/vwLUAssets/ey-the-workforce-of-the-future/$FILE/ey-the-workforce-of-the-future.pdf

Sluss, D. M., & Ashforth, B. E. (2007). Relational identity and identification: Defining ourselves through work relationships. *Academy of Management Review, 32*(1), 9–32.

Spreitzer, G., Sutcliffe, K., Dutton, J., Sonenshein, S., & Grant, A. M. (2005). A socially embedded model of thriving at work. *Organization Science, 16*(5), 537–549.

Strack, R. (2014). *The workforce crisis of 2030 and how to start solving it now.* Retrieved from http://www.ted.com/talks/rainer_strack_the_surprising_workforce_crisis_of_2030_and_how_to_start_solving_it_now

Swann, W. B., Jr. (1983). Self-verification: Bringing social reality into harmony with the self. In J. Suls & A. G. Greenwald (Eds.), *Social psychological perspectives on the self* (Vol. 2; pp. 33–66). Hillsdale, NJ: Erlbaum.

Swann, W. B., Jr. (1987). Identity negotiation: Where two roads meet. *Journal of Personality and Social Psychology, 53,* 1038–1051.

Swann, W. B., Jr (2005). The self and identity negotiation. *Interaction Studies, 6*(1), 69–83.

Swann, W. B., Jr., & Ely, R. J. (1984). A battle of wills: Self-verification versus behavioral confirmation. *Journal of Personality and Social Psychology, 46,* 1287–1302.

Swann, W. B., Jr., & Hill, C. A. (1982). When our identities are mistaken: Reaffirming self- conceptions through social interaction. *Journal of Personality and Social Psychology, 43,* 59–66.

Swann, W. B., Jr., Milton, L. P., & Polzer, J. T. (2000). Should we create a niche or fall in line? Identity negotiation and small group effectiveness. *Journal of Personality and Social Psychology, 79,* 238–250.

Swann, W. B., Jr., Polzer, J. T., Seyle, D. C., & Ko, S. J. (2004). Finding value in diversity: Verification of personal and social self-views in diverse groups. *Academy of Management Review, 29,* 9–27.

Tajfel, H., & Turner, J. C. (1986). The social identity theory of intergroup behavior. In S. Worchel & W. G. Austin (Eds.), *Psychology of intergroup relations* (2nd ed.; pp. 7–24). Chicago, IL: Nelson-Hall.

Tapscott, D. (2008). *Grown up digital: How the net generation is changing your world.* New York, NY: McGraw-Hill.

Thibaut, J. W., & Kelley, H. H. (1959). *The social psychology of groups.* Oxford, England: John Wiley.
Thomas, R. (1992). *Beyond race and gender: Unleashing the power of your total workforce by managing diversity.* New York, NY: Amacom.
Troester, C., & van Knippenberg, D. (2012). Leader openness, nationality dissimilarity, and voice in multinational management teams. *Journal of International Business Studies, 43,* 591–613.
Wang, S., Noe, R. A., Wang, Z. M., & Greenberger, D. B. (2009). What affects willingness to mentor in the future? An investigation of attachment styles and mentoring experiences. *Journal of Vocational Behavior, 74*(3), 245–256.
Wells, G. (2016). *Tech companies delay diversity reports to rethink goals.* Retrieved from http://www.wsj.com/articles/tech-companies-delay-diversity-reports-to-rethink-goals-1480933984
Young, A. M., & Perrewé, P. L. (2000). The exchange relationship between mentors and protégés: The development of a framework. *Human Resource Management Review, 10*(2), 177–209.

SECTION I
WOMEN AND MINORITIES

CHAPTER 1

GENDER AS A DEEP-LEVEL, COMMUNICATED, AND INTERACTIONAL CONSTRUCT

Implications for Leaders, Subordinates, and Teammates

Frankie J. Weinberg
Loyola University

A. O'Shea Cleveland
Louisiana State University

ABSTRACT

Although variance among individuals' communication styles is considered by the Society of Human Resource Management (SHRM, n.d.) to contribute to organizational diversity as a unique individual characteristic, there remains little guidance on how workforce practitioners may effectively lead efforts associated with this form of deep-level, interactional diversity. This chapter will describe gendered communication styles (GCOM) as a form of deep-level diversity that has important organizational implications. The authors will initially introduce a typology of GCOM congruent with gender schema theory (Bem, 1974) and discuss the various multilevel influences that inspire GCOM styles in the workplace. Building on these models, a series of taxonomies will be presented in which GCOM is considered a social process that manifests as a variety of communicative orientations. The implications of these communicative orientations are discussed in terms of interactional effectiveness between two or more individuals, and several suggestions for leaders, managers, and their subordinates are offered.

GENDER AS A DEEP-LEVEL DIVERSITY CHARACTERISTIC

In the interest of inclusivity and to embrace ongoing societal and cultural changes, many organizations have recognized the importance of fostering an expanded definition of diversity that moves beyond visible or surface-level differences to include "an infinite range of individuals' unique characteristics and experiences, including communication styles" (Society for Human Resource Management, n.d.). Communication is considered a dynamic and systemic process that at once reflects both content (literal meaning) and relationship (the communicator's self-attribution and perceptions, and metaperceptions referent to the intended recipient[s]) (Shectman & Kenny, 1994; Wood, 2013). In other words, one's communication style encompasses (a) *what* the communicator is saying, (b) how the communicator perceives *herself*, (c) how the communicator perceives the intended *recipient*, and (d) the communicator's perception of what the recipient thinks about her. As a result, one's communication style serves as a manifestation of deep-level (less readily apparent, attitudinal) diversity, which is understood to have a substantial effect on functioning of workplace relationships (Harrison, Price, & Bell, 1998; Harrison, Price, Gavin, & Florey, 2002; Phillips, Northcraft, & Neale, 2006; Riordan, 2000; Tepper, Moss, & Duffy, 2011).

One form of communication practice that has been shown to have important organizational implications is gendered communication styles (GCOM) among employees. Referent to the sex-typed (male/female) binary and congruent with gender schema theory's concept of gender as a socially constructed performance (Bem, 1974; Mumby, 2006), GCOM represents the externalized enactment of gender along stereotypical masculine and feminine dimensions. Drawing on discourse-driven theories of socially-constructed gender, Weinberg, Treviño, and Cleveland (2015) deducted and organized several characteristics that previous research had used to describe masculine communication (MCOM) and feminine communication (FCOM) styles. Specifically, MCOM encompasses assertive, egocentric, abstract, and instrumental facets, while FCOM encompasses egalitarian, compassionate, concrete, and relational facets (for a comprehensive review, see Weinberg et al., 2015).

Consideration of gender as a communicated, deep-level characteristic enables us to strengthen our conceptualization of the gender construct by expanding beyond some of the boundaries associated with sex-typed categorizing. As elaborated by Cañas and Sondak (2014), "Diversity affiliations are often portrayed as absolute and clearly distinct;" yet this type of essentialist thinking reduces our capacity to consider diversity as a "fluid, continuous, and indefinite" concept necessary to encompass the expanded definition of diversity (p. 12). Importantly, as displayed in Figure 1.1, GCOM maintains consideration of the gendered binary, but shifts the majority focus of the conversation from male-female to masculine-feminine. This focus acknowledges the importance of enacted gender as emergent from social situations, and serves to legitimize the fundamental gender division present in today's society (West & Zimmerman, 2003). In so doing, it enables a more elaborate understanding of masculine and feminine styles as a two-dimensional paradigm, rather than as two ends of a single continuum (Bem, 1974; Wood, 2013).

The purpose of this chapter is to draw on the multifaceted GCOM construct to consider the important role that communicative interaction within the binary plays in organizational life. Specifically, the objectives of this chapter are as follows:

- to introduce the reader to an expanded conceptualization of organizational diversity that includes gender as a deep-level, socially constructed, and communicated performance,
- to outline several influences in the organizational environment that shape expectations for and motivations to engage in gendered communication, and
- to describe how gendered communication manifests as a social process that influences interactional effectiveness in organizations.

In order to realize these objectives, we must begin by visualizing gendered communication as a two-dimensional paradigm.

As evidenced in Figure 1.1, the masculine and feminine dimensions of gendered communication are orthogonal; that is, they are statistically independent from one another, but not mutually exclusive (Leaper & Ayres, 2007; Palomares, 2016). Thus, any expressed communication could be categorized simultaneously along the masculine and feminine dimensions, such that the placement of any uttered communication onto this two-dimensional map will depend on both the degrees to which the communication is characterized as high/low masculine and high/low feminine. For instance, a statement such as, "I need to meet with you right now," which

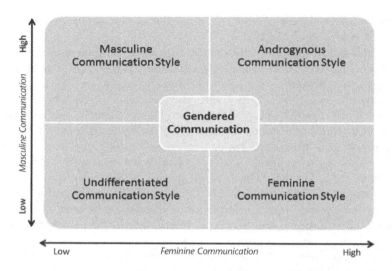

Figure 1.1 Gendered communication style as a two-dimensional paradigm.

expresses largely egocentric and assertive connotations, would fall into the masculine (high masculine, low feminine) quadrant. On the other hand, the expression "I need to meet with you as soon as possible to share ideas, if you have time" retains some of the assertiveness and egocentric nature (referent to the communicator, "I"), while referring to collaborative idea sharing and inviting the recipient to participate in the decision to meet. Accordingly, this latter statement could be categorized in the androgynous (high masculine, high feminine) quadrant in Figure 1.1. It is important to recognize that although the terms masculine and feminine refer to stereotypic attributes of men and women respectively, these gendered communication categorizations remain independent from one's biological sex. Further, it is possible that although individuals may each have a preferred communication style, men and women both may employ varying gendered communication styles to meet the needs of different situations and contexts. For these reasons, current research has, for the most part, withdrawn from asking essentialist questions

> regarding women's versus men's workplace communication styles [and] has largely given way to the idea that gendered organizational identities are socially constructed, and that these processes of construction are political, routine, and at the very core of the dialectics of power and resistance that characterize organizational life. (Mumby, 2006, p. 94)

CURRENT STATE OF GENDERED COMMUNICATION APPLICATION AND RESEARCH

Although gendered communication has a long and rich history within the field of feminist communicology (cf. Ashcraft & Mumby, 2004; Ashcraft, 2014), we will focus this section on the application of gendered communication styles in workplace-specific interactions. It is worth noting that despite the recognized distinction between men/masculinity and women/femininity, the authors have encountered a considerable number of missteps whereby even academics trained in diversity research neglect to properly distinguish sex from gender. This is complicated further by the existence of an ongoing stream of inquiry surrounding differences between men and women in the workplace, and alternative types of diversity research such as gender identity and sexual orientation. As recently elaborated by President Barack Obama, "Gender stereotypes affect all of us, regardless of our gender, gender identity, or sexual orientation" (2016). Throughout the remainder of this chapter, it is important that the reader put aside expectations of sex-based differences and similarities, and focus on employees' gendered communication styles and preferences above and beyond consideration of their biological sex or identification. That is not to say that sex-based differences are irrelevant; indeed, research suggests that the interaction of one's biological sex and enacted gender roles may have important implications for several organizational outcomes, including career advancement and leadership effectiveness (Johnson, Murphy, Zewdie, & Reichardt, 2008; Smith, Weinberg, & Treviño, 2014).

While scholarly thinking has increased in complexity and has simultaneously advanced to represent shifts in individual and societal attitudes over the years, several basic components of gendered communication theory have remained relatively stable. Specifically, (a) gender is a socially constructed and performed/communicated construct separate from one's biological sex and ranging along the binary depicted in Figure 1.1; (b) there exist gendered norms regarding expectations for behavior and deviations from those norms; (c) gendered communication is relevant to meaning-making; and (d) the way in which gendered communication is interpreted and perceived are situationally and culturally bound.

Early research "sought to expose and challenge biased perceptions that block women from climbing the hierarchy," focusing largely on similarities between men and women, and making the case that training standardization could encourage equal treatment between the sexes (Ashcraft, 2014, p. 128). The influence of this early focus has been far reaching: For over four decades, literature on advancement, gender, and communication has called for training employees to use a masculine communication style consistent with a *think leader, think male* stereotype (Dow & Wood, 2006). These suggestions stem largely from Lakoff's (1975) study of women's language in which she concludes: "If we [women] are aware of what we're doing, why we're doing it, and the effects our actions have on ourselves and everyone else, we will have the power to change" (p. 83). Her conclusion "inspired classes and workshops that encouraged women to learn to be more assertive, strong communicators (i.e., to speak more like men)" (Wood, 2006, p. 3). Naturally, this type of training and associated expectations prompted the "endorsement of agentic and task-oriented leadership characteristics for women" (Duehr & Bono, 2006, p. 815). Such workshops remain commonplace today; in fact, a 2016 Google search for the term "workshop and speak and assertively" yields approximately 1.4 million results. The prevalence of this type of training, however, lends to the tacit assumption that assertive communication styles typically associated with men are superior to those typically expressed by women (Wood, 2013). Whether this preference for masculine-dominant organizational communication is an appropriate default has begun to be brought to question.

The controversy regarding universal applicability of gender role theory and appropriateness of masculine communication at work has been summarized recently by Anne-Marie Slaughter, formerly the director of policy planning at the State Department and dean of Princeton's Woodrow Wilson School of Public and International Affairs:

> I continually push the young women in my classes to speak more. They must gain the confidence to value their own insights and questions, and to present them readily. My husband agrees, but he actually tries to get the young men in his classes to act more like the women—to speak less and listen more. If women are ever to achieve real equality as leaders, then we have to stop accepting male behavior and male choices as the default and the ideal. (Slaughter, 2012, p. 102)

This focus may be described as a different but equal versus a different but superior framing; a framing that has resulted in myriad studies that began to consider the politicization of gender at work, power relations among organizational members, and restoration of the value of things associated with women and femininity (Ashcraft, 2006, 2014). Indeed, some research has begun to offer an alternative perspective that femininity may offer advantages in the workplace. Building on this stream of thought, organizational studies of gender differences have started to unravel the think manager, think masculine/male mindset, and have postulated that deviance from the masculine norm could at times be construed as positive. These studies have found that employees often prefer feminine qualities in their leaders (Elsesser & Lever, 2011), that effective leadership often incorporates elements of both feminine and masculine communication behaviors (Eagly & Carli, 2007; Eagly, Johannesen-Schmidt, & van Engen, 2003; Fletcher, 1999), and that both masculine and feminine communication styles are uniquely related to positive career outcomes (Weinberg et al., 2015). From this stream of research, it is clear that both styles of communication are necessary toward effectiveness in organizations and their teams (Wood, 2013).

While gender difference studies focus almost entirely on the individual as the unit of analysis, research with its basis in systems theory has begun to take a more macrolevel, embedded approach to the discussion of enacted gender at work. Beginning with standpoint theory, which incorporates consideration of contextual factors, researchers (e.g., Allen, 1996; Dougherty, 1999) have begun to view organizing as a fundamentally communicative phenomenon. Such research suggests that "our ways of knowing and communicating are influenced by our contexts...as our contexts change, so might our ways of thinking, communicating, and performing...gender" (Wood, 2013, p. 244). Building on this consideration of context as an influential factor, Smith et al. (2014) recently found considerable variance in the effectiveness of masculine and feminine communication styles by male and female employees when the two styles are used in organizational contexts characterized as either male or female dominated. This follows a mode of thought that organizations produce gender differences as a product of their formal processes and structures (Acker, 1990; Trethewey, Scott, & LeGreco, 2006). Therefore, studies that examine gender performance in organizations benefit from considering not only the individual actor's characteristics, but also the organizational context. Communication styles are learned (rather than innate; Wood, 2013), and men and women have demonstrated the ability to develop new communicative proficiencies to serve effectively in their jobs (Buzzanell & Lucas, 2006). This suggests the potential for organizational members to influence the effectiveness of their interactions by performing gender through managed and locally situated gendered communication practices (Ashcraft, 2014; West & Zimmerman, 2003).

ORGANIZATIONAL RELEVANCE

Most discussions of gender and communication in organizations take one of three perspectives: (a) societal expectations frame gendered expectations at work (gender as shaped by societal influences); (b) organizations as gendered discourse communities (gender at the organizationally-referent level); or (c) gender identity shapes communication habits (gender at the intrapersonal level). In this chapter, we acknowledge all of these respective influences on gendered communication while building the case that GCOM is often influenced by and determined (in)effective largely within, group and dyadic interactions. As displayed in Figure 1.2, several forces

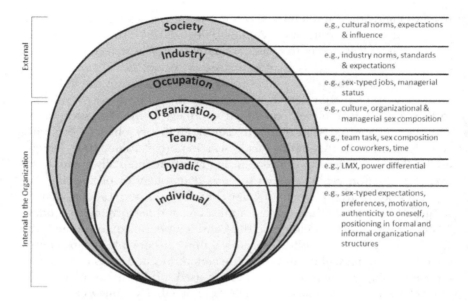

Figure 1.2 Multilevel influences on gendered communication styles at work.

both internal and external to the organization serve to influence expectations for and motivation to engage in masculine or feminine GCOM styles.

External Influences on Gendered Communication Styles

The outermost layers in Figure 1.2 (society and industry) represent the more macrolevel influences on GCOM. Whereas societal perceptions inform gender and gendered expectations (Ashcraft & Mumby, 2004), societal changes serve important pivotal roles in stimulating changing expectations. For instance, emerging evidence suggests that today's younger-generation workers tend to prefer using communication styles that are higher in FCOM and lower in MCOM than their older colleagues (Weinberg et al., 2015). Further, given that differing global societies tend to value high and low masculinity to varying degrees (House et al., 2004), these differences are likely to play an important role in setting expectations for gendered communication styles in contemporary multinational and virtual teams. Finally, standards and expectations for GCOM expression may vary by industry, though one study suggests that inter-industry variance in GCOM styles may not be as substantial as expected (Weinberg et al., 2015). Occupational influence refers to an individual's specific job, and while it is likely that there exists some level of standardized GCOM preferences within a profession, organizational context may also play a role in dictating this. Thus, even within one particular occupation, there may be considerable instances of variation among communicative expectations given that culture "conditions attitudes toward communication and communication processes," including both the creation of messages and interpretation of those messages (Brown & Starkey, 1994, p. 811).

For instance, whereas feminine styles of communication may be characteristic of salespeople, who could benefit from building even temporary relationships and rapport with potential clients (relationship marketing, cf. Oly Ndubisi, 2004). This would likely be exacerbated in an organizational culture that encourages cooperation and discourages competition among sales force members. In a more competitive climate (for example, one in which sales commissions are based on relative rank compared to average sales or when communication is more oriented toward a one-time payout as opposed to developing a longer-term working relationship), this may set the stage for a tournament-like setting in which salespeople may be expected to employ more assertive communication strategies with clients/customers (Verbeke, Bagozzi, & Belschak, 2016). This climate could also inspire egocentric communication styles among sales force members/competitors when communicating with one another. Another example draws on the potentially considerable differences in communicative tasks that may be asked of a professional in one setting as compared to another; for instance, in the nursing profession, a school nurse, pediatric nurse, or geriatric care nurse might be expected to communicate in a more compassionate and relational manner in their jobs due to their continual interactions and ongoing relationships with patients. Alternatively, an operating room nurse who communicates primarily with other medical practitioners in a high-risk setting could be expected to communicate in a more instrumental and necessarily assertive manner to meet the unique demands of this job, though one study found evidence of a structured disposition of operating room nurse silence that "may reflect an actualization of structured power dynamics" among operating room teams (Gardezi et al., 2009, p. 1397). By suggesting that team dynamics and occupational characteristics could clash, this complication serves as an example of the potential for cross-level effects among the various embedded levels indicated in Figure 1.2.

Internal Influences on Gendered Communication Styles

Figure 1.2 also displays several factors that are likely to influence GCOM expectations that are internal to the organizational environment, including: (a) organization-level influencers such as institutionalized meanings, identity, and power relations owing to organizational culture and the sex composition of managers; (b) team-level influencers such as team task, the sex composition of team members, and the amount of time members have spent working together; (c) interpersonal influencers at the one-on-one (dyadic) level, including power differential, sex composition of the dyad, time together and the state of relationships between leaders and each member (i.e., leader–member exchange, LMX); and (d) intrapersonal influencers such as sex-based attributions, authenticity to oneself, the communicator's personal motivation to engage in communication, and the communicator's formal and informal organizational positioning. In keeping with this volume's focus on leader–employee relationships, we will focus the remainder of this chapter largely on interpersonal communication in team and dyadic relationships.

Relevance to the Contemporary and Future Workplace

Several aspects of today's changing workplace lend value to the proposition that consideration of GCOM styles is becoming increasingly important. For instance, as there are more women entering the workforce than ever before, this implies that while these new female employees are working their way into more senior positions there will likely exist several opportunities for opposite-sex leader-follower and mentor-protégé relationships (Weinberg & Lankau, 2011). Further, the popularity of team-based and flatter organizational structures has permeated contemporary thought on workplace organizing. Together, these organizational changes may be contributing to a preference among U.S. workers for more feminized leadership that may be described as a desire to work for a strong, sensitive leader (Elsesser & Lever, 2011; Johnson et al., 2008). Given that people select and enact gendered communication styles in response to the contexts in which they are situated (Wood, 2013), two common forms of organizational context are worth elaborating on with regard to the impact that they could have on GCOM utilization in the workplace: dyads and teams. Thus, as gendered communication is an interactional and interpersonal phenomenon (West & Zimmerman, 2003), GCOM styles play a particularly important role at the team and dyadic levels, those contexts in which employees communicate throughout their daily work interactions.

Dyadic Influences on Gendered Communication

Dyads are clusters consisting of two members interacting with one another, these could include a leader and a follower, a mentor and a protégé, two coworkers, or any combination of two individuals. Dyadic relationships create the backbone for patterns of communication throughout an organization and accordingly are the unit of analysis at which studies of entire social networks are analyzed. Several characteristics of a dyad could influence the manner in which gendered communication is enacted within each two-person relationship. First, aligning with the notion of gender as an externalized performance (e.g., Butler, 2004), people are often driven to communicate in a way that they believe the other member would expect them to perform (for a review of how this may play out with regard to expectations for gendered communication at work, see Smith et al., 2014). The purpose of the relationship will also play an important role: In mentoring relationships, for instance, the relationship serves two general purposes: career development and sponsorship. While feminine components of relational and compassionate communication styles could be effective toward these purposes (i.e., in expressing empathy and enabling others to feel safe, or to display openness to personal development), masculine, instrumental communication could also serve an important instructional function. Even in a developmental dyadic relationship, each member could be motivated to communicate in egocentric, assertive manners at times in order to emphasize their authority over a specific subject matter. Mentors or leaders, for instance, could apply this communicative tactic early in the relationship to gain leadership status in the eyes of the follower who would attribute subject matter expertise to the leader (Chiu, Balkundi, & Weinberg, 2017). Alternatively, a dyad could involve two members who are in competition with one another in which case the relationship would likely foster enactment of low feminine and high masculine communication, particularly in regards to the egocentric facet.

Sex differential within a dyad is also likely to affect communication among the members, especially as the relationship develops in its earliest stages (Weinberg & Lankau, 2011). Stereotype activation is defined as "the increased accessibility of the constellation of attributes that are believed to characterize members of a given social category" (Wheeler & Petty, 2001, p. 797), and gender serves to affect stereotype activation (Correll & Ridgeway, 2006). This bias is particularly salient in instances where male members are the observers (Koenig, Eagly, Mitchell, & Ristikari, 2011). Further, women (men) when interacting with other women (men) may choose to communicate in a manner that is congruent with their biological sex in order to avoid negative reactions stemming from a presumed lack of femininity (masculinity). This could result from a desire to encourage perceptions of similarity in the dyad. Further, in instances where one member has greater authority than the other, a high extent of power differential between the two parties could encourage these members to enact gender strategically as a political act (Ashcraft & Mumby, 2004). For instance, one might be inclined to use masculine forms of communication such as dominating the conversation or interrupting the other member, as these methods are associated with improved status and influence (Farley, 2008); hence, members could attempt to influence decisions in the dyad by emulating the masculine stereotype in this manner.

Team Influences on Gendered Communication

Likewise, team characteristics are likely to influence the styles of gendered communication enacted by team members. In the early stages of team development, the relationship-building, collegial and affiliative characteristics associated with feminine communication could relay one's availability and willingness to work as a team player, and could consequently serve to help the team members form an understanding of how they will work together. Here, clear communication of concrete reasoning (also associated with feminine communication) will help to cultivate personal connections (Wood, 2013). Beyond the foundational stages of team development, however, as with any work-related environment, teams tend to develop certain norms as members begin working together functionally (Allen, 1995); norms inherent to the group serve as tacit guidelines for behavior, including the style of communication that is generally fostered and accepted. In this sense, teams may act as speech communities in which shared communicative norms result from a system of shared symbolisms, meanings, and experiences (Labov, 1972; Wood, 2013). Similarly, other cultural features of the team environment could influence the ways in which members communicate with one another; for instance, whether there exists a team culture of support, competitiveness, or indifference toward other members. Group norms and perceptions of those norms are also likely to be linked to the sex composition within the team, such that acting in a manner that is stereotypically linked to the dominant sex group is a tactic that members may choose to employ to gain favor (Tharenou, 1997).

Further, the purpose of the team will play a role in influencing members' communication styles. For instance, if the team faces shared goals for which all members expect to be collectively rewarded, members are more likely to employ feminine, egalitarian communication that relinquishes control, empowers others, and encourages productive discourse toward navigating dilemmas more so than in instances where the team goal is not entirely shared (Ashcraft, 2000). Also, if the team's purpose is to follow specified rules to accomplish a set task, masculine communication could be called for; however, if the team's purpose centers on collaborative problem solving or creative outcomes or presents an opportunity to create rules, feminine communication would be welcomed and considered useful. In a similar vein, team leadership style would play an important role in determining which communication styles are welcomed; for instance, even when a team leader chooses to employ a style in which each member has the opportunity to build on other members' opinions and suggestions (i.e., egalitarian, feminine communication), this process could be conducted with varying degrees of group interaction, and could potentially result in advice-giving behaviors and/or competition for the leader's or other members' attention (i.e., egocentric masculine communication). Finally, team structuring itself is often associated with a flattened organizational hierarchy (Ahuja & Carley, 1998) in which case feminine communication, which is associated with nonhierarchical career success (Weinberg et al., 2015), may be a preferred mode of communication.

Again, when discussing team-level influence on GCOM, it is worth noting potential complexities associated with potential cross-level effects referent to the levels of influence outlined in Figure 1.2. Specifically, various configurations of dyadic relationships within the team, and the development of subgroups within the team could affect the degree to which overall team-level characteristics influence the emergence of members' GCOM styles. For instance, members undergo strong psychological pressure to agree with others who they consider to be close personal friends, and "this pressure becomes [more] powerful as soon as a dyadic interaction (between two people) expands to include three people" (Balkundi & Kilduff, 2006, p. 429). Under such coalition-like conditions, two possible GCOM-related outcomes could come about: On one hand, it is possible that a member who relies upon a clique of teammate-colluders for support may be more likely to assert the coalition's shared ideas by using a bold MCOM style. But on the other hand, if this individual is simultaneously embedded within several sets of mutually discrepant cliques, as happens in complex organizational environments (Balkundi & Kilduff, 2006), she might feel pressure to remain impartial by employing a more egalitarian FCOM style.

Toward Dyadic and Team Effectiveness

It goes without saying that gender and communication diversity can have an enormous effect on dyadic and team functioning (cf. Mulac, Wiemann, Widenmann, & Gibson, 1988; Savicki, Kelley, & Lingenfelter, 1997). However, research to date has barely scratched the surface of possibilities with regard to the ways in which the gendered communication binary may be drawn on in organizational discourse to enact a variety of goals. Specifically, by restricting research questions to only the two binary dimensions of masculine and feminine communication, extant studies have limited our capacity to imagine the possibilities of multiplex communication patterns among employees. The purpose of this section is to take a deeper look at underlying facets of MCOM and FCOM styles to provide a more nuanced examination of the ways in which various overlapping forms of communicative gender performance (i.e., GCOM) can be utilized to influence the interactive functioning of organizational teams and dyadic relationships.

Communicative Orientations Emerging From Gendered Communication

Building on several key facets of the gendered communication construct presented by Weinberg et al., 2015, we have developed a number of communicative orientations through which GCOM is viewed as a social process. These communicative orientations are displayed through a series of taxonomic classifications in Figures 1.3a-1.3c.

Relationship-Building and Instrumentality

As displayed in Figure 1.3a, the intersection of instrumental and relationship-building communication styles produce diverse communicative orientations dependent on the relative strengths of each style. Task orientation, represented in the upper-left quadrant, characterizes a highly instrumental and low relationship-building style. Long touted as a positive approach to conflict in teams (Amason, 1996), meta-analytic evidence suggests that this may not always be the case (De Dreu & Weingart, 2003). Task-oriented communication is clarity-focused, concentrating on such issues as policies, requirements, interpretation of the assigned task, and other aspects related to how members should approach getting the job done. Accordingly, it has a reduced focus on interactional rules and interpersonal relationships (i.e., issues of power dynamics, trust, and emotional states among members). A socializing orientation, on the other hand, involves friendly chatting without serving any instrumental purpose. In so doing, socializing-oriented communication promotes a sense of togetherness within a group and can encourage psychosocial bonding among members.

Quiescence refers to a state of inactivity or dormancy. Accordingly, quiescent-oriented communication, characterized as neither highly instrumental nor relationship-building, involves a passive style that maintains the status quo without complicating issues. This passive communication style can be useful at times, especially when tensions in the group may be running high or if members have recently entered a state of agreement. Unlike quiescent-oriented communication's dormant characteristics, a dynamics-oriented communication style tends to be more action-driven. This type of communication helps to produce processes (i.e., norms, roles, and action plans) that simultaneously represent the group's common goal(s) and the individual characteristics and preferences of each member. Thus dynamics-oriented communication, high on both instrumental and relationship-building focus, can help to set the stage for a state of functional interdependence among members. Finally, a networking orientation, characterized as somewhat instrumental oriented and somewhat relationship-building-oriented, helps to build relationships that serve a purpose. Networking-oriented communication can at once be both self-serving (for instance, positioning

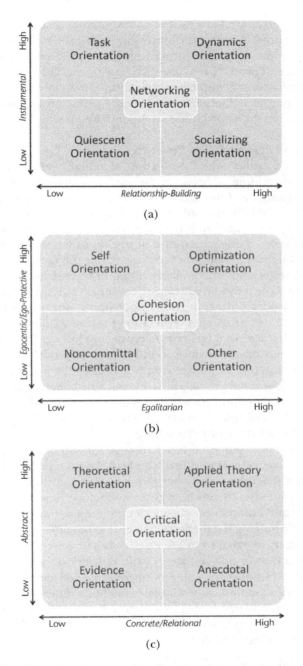

Figure 1.3 Two-dimensional taxonomies of gendered communication as a social process: (a) Network Orientation, (b) Cohesion Orientation, (c) Critical Orientation.

oneself in a more central position of an important social group) and helpful toward group efficiency, as it encourages an exchange of information that could produce improved intragroup transactive memory systems and a denser advice network (Cross, Borgatti, & Parker, 2001); that is, networking orientation within group communication can enable members to have a better idea of who knows what and be more prepared to acquire relevant information from the appropriate members when needed.

Egalitarian and Egocentric/Ego-Protective

Figure 1.3b considers the intersection of a highly egocentric/ego-protective communication style (characterized as self-oriented individuals) with highly egalitarian (other-oriented) communication style. Self-orientation can be helpful in both dyadic and team settings for several reasons. For instance, such an orientation is necessary when negotiating one's position, focusing attention to one's strengths, or in circumstances where a member is highly confident that her approach to a task is the most effective or otherwise appropriate solution. Similarly, an other-oriented standpoint can be equally useful toward dyadic or team effectiveness as it can serve to provide support for another's ideas, provide opportunities for others to be heard, and can contribute to expeditious decision-making. While a noncommittal orientation (characterized by low egocentric and low egalitarian communication styles) may on the surface sound like an unproductive or impractical approach, this, too, can serve team functioning. By not communicating the merit of each member's submitted ideas, nor believing that one's own initial thoughts about an idea are necessarily correct or even defendable, noncommittally oriented members may enable a critical dialogue to unfold naturally within a dyadic or team setting.

Opposite the noncommittal orientation resides an optimization orientation, characteristic of an individual who both favors equality while heartily proposing and defending his or her own viewpoints. Although this may initially appear somewhat oxymoronic, this combination depicts a member who at once elicits and enforces equal consideration of each member's proffered ideas, but upon judging the merits of one idea to be superior will aggressively encourage others to agree to this selected idea's veracity. This orientation is optimization-driven in that it inspires swift, efficient decision making while encouraging full team participation, but could be considered off-putting to a less egocentric communicator who favors either a different idea or the opportunity to continue developing new alternatives. Finally, a cohesion orientation refers to communication that falls in the middle of the egocentric/ego-protective and egalitarian model. A member who enacts cohesion-oriented communication may avoid the pitfalls of sharing too little (noncommittal orientation), administering too much (self-orientation), heavily weighting other members' viewpoints (other-orientation) or putting one's own weight behind a single idea (optimization orientation) and could accordingly serve the purpose of discursively shaping the team into a united whole.

Concrete/Relational and Abstract

Although it is generally agreed that gendered communication has two unique dimensions (i.e., masculine and feminine) rather than existing along a single continuum, the one set of facets that may be considered potentially the most opposite from one another are those related to concrete versus abstract communication. Concrete communication refers to disclosure of details and concrete reasoning, which aids in cultivating a close and personal connection (Ashcraft & Mumby, 2004; Hall & Langellier, 1988) and sharing oneself via disclosure of personal details in a conversation (Johnson, 1996; Weinberg & Locander, 2014). Therefore, concrete communication is highly related to relational discourse, in which one communicates with the purpose of creating and maintaining relationships (Wood, 2013). Communicatively, this style emerges as having an anecdotal orientation, characterized by storytelling involving oneself and one's own experiences, and in so doing, enables a more tangible connection between communicator and recipient(s). Abstract communication, on the other hand, involves the use of impersonal, general terms that serve to distance the communication from personal experiences and feelings (Newman, Groom, Handelman, & Pennebaker, 2008). The theoretical orientation associated with highly abstract (and low concrete) communication can come across as somewhat detached from reality. While this type of communication may encourage innovative thinking by leaving open a range of possible interpretations, the intangible nature of heavily abstract communication could make it difficult for some members to digest.

Yet, despite the surface opposition between abstract and concrete styles, we view these styles as having a potentially very useful role in organizational communication when applied jointly in conjunction with one another. Referred to in Figure 1.3c as relating to an applied theory orientation, this hybrid style of communicative positioning serves to bridge theory and reality and accordingly serves the important purpose of translating abstract ideas into practical lessons digestible to a wide audience of members whose backgrounds and perceptions may vary. The potential importance of this translating role cannot be overstated; in the words of Werner Heisenberg, theoretical physicist and pioneer of quantum mechanics, "Even for the physicist the description in plain language will be a criterion of the degree of understanding that has been reached" (Heisenberg, 1958, p. 168). Opposite to an applied theory orientation is an evidence orientation, characterized by low abstract and low concrete/relational communication. A member with an evidence-oriented communication style would likely default to inputs involving best-available known alternatives and draw on the advice of experts when contributing to the conversation. Finally, a critical orientation is characterized as falling within the midpoint of the abstract-concrete/relational model without prescribing to either ideological approach. A critical approach is pragmatically integrative and as a result, someone who leans toward a critical orientation would likely view communication as an opportunity to at once express the merits and potential faults associated with a line of reasoning, and could be well-suited to serve as devil's advocate in a decision-making process. By harmoniously integrating personal case-study examples with more removed theoretical considerations, a member with this orientation could serve as a communicative bridge between analytically minded teammates and those more inclined toward less systematic or more emotional or artfully constructed decision processes.

Communicative Orientations: Key Points and Emerging Issues

The discussion of communicative orientations serves several purposes: First, it enables us to effectively draw on the two-dimensional gendered communication binary to create unique communicative patterns that serve varying purposes in workplace interactions. In so doing, it illuminates how the use of different GCOM styles along the binary can work together to produce a series of communicative purposes. Further, it depicts no one style or combination of styles as necessarily superior to another; rather, we can draw on this set of communicative orientations to achieve effectiveness based on characteristics of the communicator, the intended audience, the situation in which the communicator and audience are embedded and the outcomes of interest.

The communication orientations presented in Figure 1.3 represent merely a sampling of taxonomical configurations that could result through the compounding of various facets of masculine and feminine communication. Other potentially notable configurations could include within-gender taxonomies that consider; for instance, the degree to which one communicates in both an egocentric and assertive masculine manner as compared to communication that focuses on only one of these MCOM facets. The study of such nuances within masculine and feminine communication styles could promote a greater understanding of which components of MCOM and FCOM could be serviceably applied to meet different desired outcomes. Future work is needed to flesh out the potential effects that contextual variables such as communicator sex and the sex composition of the communicator's workplace, could have on the effectiveness of each of these GCOM orientations.

IMPLICATIONS FOR LEADERS AND ORGANIZATIONS

This final section covers some ways that organizational leaders may incorporate knowledge of gendered communication styles to ensure that their organizations and teams benefit, while simultaneously ensuring that individuals succeed. These will be discussed as a process that considers both challenges and opportunities for leader–member relations and considers both the leaders' and members' perspectives. Briefly, this process involves assessment and education, followed by facilitation.

Assessment

Understanding deep-level and performed gender differences can help organizational members relate to each other. And this begins with assessment. Assessment is a co-created process that incorporates a mutuality perspective (Dobrow, Chandler, Murphy, & Kram, 2012; Weinberg & Locander, 2014). That is, leaders must inspire members to assess their own styles and those of their coworkers and their leader, while the leader herself concurrently engages in self-assessment. Thus, before a leader may begin to make inferences regarding the appropriateness or effectiveness of different communicative orientations for a given situation, she must initially find out what kinds of GCOM styles the members have and understand her own styles as well.

To lead members through assessment requires a leader to listen to the employees, encouraging them to reflect upon and describe their own communicative preferences. In order to ensure that the assessment focuses on deep-level diversity and performance so that it can ultimately be viewed through a GCOM lens, the leader could ask members to consider organizational communication from the perspective of roles they enact on the job and their perceived expectations of various stakeholders and more generally of society. Further, assessment involves both the leader and members considering the various multilevel contexts in which these communicative roles are played out (see Figure 1.2) and the influences that each of these embedded contexts may have on their own GCOM styles and effectiveness. This involves analyzing the structural elements of the organization and its external environment and the communicative arrangement of coworkers and supervisors.

Assessment must precede facilitation, and we suggest that it precede education as well. First, members are likely to be more receptive to feedback and to new ways of knowing once they have become aware of their own communicative styles and attributions. Further, following assessment, subsequent conversations are more likely to proceed in a way that is centered on interactive communication styles, rather than on the people, their ideas, or their own personal needs; that is, the members would be oriented toward deep-level (as opposed to surface-level) communicative diversity.

Education

Once employees have had the opportunity to assess organizational communication through a masculine- and feminine-typed lens, the leader's next step is to ensure that members are sufficiently introduced to principles of gendered communication so that they may begin to organize these assessments around the GCOM binary. Importantly, this education should include a discussion of the historical context of gender and sex-typed attributions and expectations so that employees can begin to recognize the deeply sociological nature of gender performance. The concept of gender as a socially-learned and performed construct can be one that remains difficult for many individuals to conceptualize, and accordingly this must be clarified and given appropriate focus.

Education enables members to know the various styles of communication arranged along the gender binary and to begin to recognize some of the more nuanced communicative orientations that stem from this binary. Mapping their own communication assessments onto the GCOM taxonomical map would allow members to become aware of how they communicate and teach them about different ways they and others around them could communicate. Being aware of such distinctions is important toward creating change. To this end, it is equally important to recognize that communication styles are dynamic and can change (Buzzanell & Lucas, 2006). Learning about how referent others communicate and how you yourself communicate could help to prompt not only a greater mutual understanding, but also change when necessary.

Facilitation

Leading Facilitation

The purpose of GCOM facilitation is to provide tools to better understand how to approach and solve interpersonal dilemmas in a way that draws on performed gender diversity to create a more cohesive work environment. It is worth noting that we refer to this stage as facilitation as opposed to training. Whereas training involves content matter expert(s) presenting predetermined known lessons to an audience, facilitation does not necessitate that the leader is a gendered communication expert; moreover, it does not require there to exist a known desired outcome; rather, facilitation involves assisting an engaged group through a process by which the members themselves leverage their own perceptions and expertise to communicatively discover previously unknown knowledge and understanding.

Before the member-centric facilitation process begins, the leader could encourage members to focus the discussion by asking questions such as, what are our goals, which styles of communication could help us to achieve them, where are we now with our preferred communication styles, what types of communicative gaps might be creating challenges for us, and how could we overcome these challenges? After opening with a topic-and-communication-centric introduction, the leader could then facilitate a member-centric discovery process. For facilitation to be effective, both listening and clear communication are key. Consider, for instance, a scenario where members have not been meeting productivity goals. The session could involve discussion of how the various member-assessed communication elements might be hindering productivity; in this way, the understanding that had arisen at the assessment and education stages can be applied such that connections between communication styles and productivity are better understood. In this scenario, the leader could facilitate this by asking employees why they don't feel they are achieving their goals and when necessary (re)focus the conversation on the communicative differences/difficulties that come up.

Leader–Member Relations During Facilitation and Beyond

A leader may draw on different GCOM styles to improve communication between herself and members as well as communication among members. For instance, understanding members' unique communication styles can help guide a leader to determine the best way to approach each subordinate when introducing a topic. Also, assigning tasks that are best suited to members' communication styles could work with each member's strengths and abilities, ultimately helping to improve efficiency and strengthen communication among members. Thus, it is important that the leader attempt to develop strong exchange relationships with each member in order to better understand the members' communicative styles and preferences. With that said, it is worth recognizing the aforementioned contemporary trend whereby employees, on average, have begun to express preference for a more feminized style of leadership. Thus, understanding not only subordinates' personal communication preferences, but also the type of communication each member expects from and respects in a leader, could go a long way toward influencing whether an individual is viewed as a leader by her subordinates.

Further, the arrangement of power within a relationship could also dictate the degree to which MCOM and FCOM could be differentially effective. Formality designates hierarchy, and therefore masculine forms of communication may be more accepted of leaders in formal relationships. In cases of informal leadership, however, asserting one's individuality and communicating egotistically without considering others' ideas may be less accepted, as individuals tend to dislike being told what to do by those to whom they do not officially report. Paradoxically, it is just this type of communication style that may help to bolster an individual to gain informal leadership status; again, it is a matter of individual differences that could be remedied by knowing who the members are in terms of their individual GCOM preferences. From the nonleader member's perspective, gendered communication could be leveraged to influence the relationship between this individual and the leader. For instance, asserting one's support for a leader's initiatives could serve to gain favor with the leader; alternatively, a follower who communicates concrete details could be viewed as humble, a characteristic that could also serve to gain the leader's favor (Castiglioni, 1528/1976).

Lastly, several team-referent factors could influence the effectiveness and desirability of different GCOM styles between leaders and members. In early stages of team formation, a leader's balance of egocentric and egalitarian communication (identified taxonomically as either having a cohesion or optimization orientation) could enable team members to more clearly understand their respective roles and responsibilities, while opening the opportunity for teammates to get to know one another and begin working together. Strong masculine communication from a team leader could prove particularly helpful when there exists a deep divide among group members, as it would serve to avoid the situation typically associated with having "too many cooks in the kitchen." This could also be useful if time-urgent decisiveness and quick decision making are a factor. On the other hand, strong feminine communication by the leader could prove most helpful when encouraging members to share ideas. The comfortable and open communicative environment produced by egalitarian and compassionate (feminine) leader communication could potentially enable members to feel safe to speak their minds without fear of negative repercussion (a concept referred to as *psychological safety*).

Leading Through the Unknown

It goes without saying that there is still very much presently left unknown about the effects of GCOM in various organizational circumstances, particularly toward more macro organizationally relevant outcomes. As we suggested earlier, uncovering the broader effects of GCOM styles in organizations will entail consideration of members' communicative orientations across various organizational and relational contexts. Further, there currently exists little to no guidance with regard to how masculine and feminine communication can respectively be leveraged by executives to improve organizational performance and drive change. We suspect that as with leader–member and team relations, the relationship between GCOM and organizational outcomes could be complex: Factors such as conflicting stakeholder demands and expectations, executive managers' social power among those various sets of stakeholders, and contingencies such as the firm's current position on the organizational life cycle and competitiveness of the organization's market could all play a part in determining which styles could be effectively employed by top organizational leaders.

Finally, it is worth noting two important boundary conditions that currently limit the extent to which we can predict the effectiveness of gendered communication in the global contemporary workplace. The first is that the overwhelming majority of theory and empirical evidence connecting GCOM to organizationally relevant consequences is U.S.-centric; hence, the degree to which suggestions presented in this chapter would generalize outside the United States or in multicultural teams is largely unknown. Second, although studies have begun to establish a predictable pattern of relationships between GCOM and workplace outcomes, it is not yet entirely understood whether the effectiveness of this relationship wanes if it is used politically as a type of influence tactic as opposed to applied in a more authentic manner. This topic was tangentially touched upon by President Obama in a recent op-ed:

> It's easy to absorb all kinds of messages from society about masculinity and come to believe that there's a right way and a wrong way to be a man. But as I got older, I realized that my ideas about being a tough guy or cool guy just weren't me. They were a manifestation of my youth and insecurity. Life became a lot easier when I simply started being myself. (Obama, 2016)

Adding to this, limited empirical evidence appears to suggest that those individuals who retain a single, identifiable GCOM style may benefit from stronger personal outcomes (Weinberg et al., 2015). With this in mind, until the relationship between authenticity and GCOM are better established, we caution practitioners to continually assess their potentially shifting GCOM preferences, and consider how to best employ their preferred style to meet situational expectations and demands.

A Caveat

It is important to recognize that, by drawing attention to how communication may be dichotomized based on gendered styles (following the way in which extant theory draws on language referent to stereotypical expectations of males and females, e.g., Dow & Wood, 2006; Wood, 2013), this work and enactment based on it "also renders the social arrangements based on sex category accountable as normal and natural, that is legitimate ways of organizing social life" (West & Zimmerman, 2003, p. 71). That is, by referring to communication as having masculine- and feminine-typed facets, we are training ourselves to execute aspects of assertiveness, egalitarianism, and other sex-category-attributed performances, and as a result are contributing to the reification of a gendered differential, thereby rendering sex-typed distinctions as legitimate. In so doing, the binary model "risks essentializing both men and women, thus largely preserving extant relations of institutional power" (Ashcraft & Mumby, 2004, p. 41).

CONCLUSION

When the authors first began working to expand gendered communication research into the field of quantitative organizational science, we were asked by a prominent organizational psychologist why we chose to use what sounded to him as somewhat archaic terminology in describing the communication styles as masculine and feminine. Our answer was twofold: (a) so doing serves to build conceptually on currently existing diversity theory that draws on this binary classification, and (b) a failure to do so would prejudicially ignore the important role that changing sex stereotypes and expectations and sex-typed organizing and biases continue to play in today's global society. It is our sincere hope that continued work in this area will serve to illuminate further ways in which organizations, their teams, and members may benefit from the potent opportunities associated with deep-level gender diversity.

REFERENCES

Acker, J. (1990). Hierarchies, jobs, bodies: A theory of gendered organization. *Gender & Society, 4*, 139–158.
Ahuja, M. K., & Carley, K. M. (1998). Network structures in virtual organizations. *Organization Science, 10*, 741–757.
Allen, B. J. (1996). Feminist standpoint theory: A black woman's (re)view of organizational socialization. *Communication Studies, 47*, 257–277.
Allen, M. W. (1995). Communication concepts related to perceived organizational support. *Western Journal of Communication, 59*, 326–346.
Amason, A. C. (1996). Distinguishing the effects of functional and dysfunctional conflict on strategic decision making: Resolving a paradox for top management groups. *Academy of Management Journal, 39*, 123–148.
Ashcraft, K. L. (2000). Empowering "professional" relationships: Organizational communication meets feminist practice. *Management Communication Quarterly, 13*, 347–392.
Ashcraft, K. L. (2006). Sights/sites of difference in gender and organizational communication studies. In B. J. Dow & J. T. Wood (Eds.), *The SAGE handbook of gender and communication* (pp. 97–122). Thousand Oaks, CA: SAGE.
Ashcraft, K. L. (2014). Feminist theory. In L. L. Putnam & D. K. Mumby (Eds.), *The SAGE handbook of organizational communication* (3rd ed., pp. 127–150). Thousand Oaks, CA: SAGE.

Ashcraft, K. L., & Mumby, D. K. (2004). *Reworking gender: A feminist communicology of organization*. Thousand Oaks, CA: SAGE.

Balkundi, P., & Kilduff, M. (2006). The ties that lead: A social network approach to leadership. *The Leadership Quarterly, 17*, 419–439.

Bem, S. L. (1974). The measurement of psychological androgyny. *Journal of Consulting and Clinical Psychology, 42*, 155–162.

Brown, A. D., & Starkey, K. (1994). The effect of organizational culture on communication and information. *Journal of Management Studies, 31*, 807–828.

Butler, J. (2004). *Undoing gender*. London, England: Routledge.

Buzzanell, P. M., & Lucas, K. (2006). Gendered stories of career: Unfolding discourses of time, space, and identity. In B. J. Dow & J. T. Wood (Eds.), *The SAGE handbook of gender and communication* (pp. 161–178). Thousand Oaks, CA: SAGE.

Cañas, K., & Sondak, H. (2010). Challenging and improving the teaching of diversity management. *International Journal of Diversity in Organisations, Communities & Nations, 10*, 139–158.

Castiglioni, B. (1976). *The book of the courtier* (G. Bull, Trans.). London, England: Penguin. Originally published in 1528.

Chiu, C. Y., Balkundi, P., & Weinberg, F. J. (2017). When managers become leaders: The role of manager network centralities, social power, and followers' perception of leadership. *The Leadership Quarterly, 28*(2), 334–348. doi:10.1016/j.leaqua.2016.05.004

Correll, S. J., & Ridgeway, C. L. (2006). Expectation states theory. In J. Delamater (Ed.), *Handbook of Social Psychology* (pp. 29–51). New York, NY: Springer.

Cross, R., Borgatti, S. P., & Parker, A. (2001). Beyond answers: Dimensions of the advice network. *Social Networks, 23*(3), 215–235.

De Dreu, C. K., & Weingart, L. R. (2003). Task versus relationship conflict, team performance, and team member satisfaction: a meta-analysis. *Journal of Applied Psychology, 88*, 741–749.

Dobrow, S. R., Chandler, D. E., Murphy, W. M., & Kram, K. E. (2012). A review of developmental networks: Incorporating a mutuality perspective. *Journal of Management, 38*, 210–242.

Dougherty, D. S. (1999). Dialogue through standpoint: Understanding men's and women's standpoints of sexual harassment. *Management Communication Quarterly, 12*, 436–468.

Dow, B. J., & Wood, J. T. (2006). The evolution of gender and communication research: Intersections of theory, politics, and scholarship. In B. J. Dow and J. T. Wood (Eds.), *The SAGE handbook of gender and communication* (pp. ix–xxiv). Thousand Oaks, CA: SAGE.

Duehr, E. E., & Bono, J. E. (2006). Men, women, and managers: Are stereotypes finally changing? *Personnel Psychology, 59*, 815–846.

Eagly, A. H., & Carli, L. L. (2007). *Through the labyrinth: The truth about how women become leaders*. Boston, MA: Harvard Business School Press.

Eagly, A. H., Johannesen-Schmidt, M. C., & van Engen, M. L. (2003). Transformational, transactional, and laissez-faire leadership styles: A meta-analysis comparing women and men. *Psychological Bulletin, 108*, 233–256.

Elsesser, K. M., & Lever, J. (2011). Does gender bias against female leaders persist? Quantitative and qualitative data from a large-scale survey. *Human Relations, 64*, 1555–1578.

Farley, S. D. (2008). Attaining status at the expense of likeability: Pilfering power through conversational interruption. *Journal of Nonverbal Behavior, 32*, 241–260.

Fletcher, J. (1999). *Disappearing acts: Gender, power and relational practice at work.* Cambridge, MA: MIT Press.

Gardezi, F., Lingard, L., Espin, S., Whyte, S., Orser, B., & Baker, G. R. (2009). Silence, power and communication in the operating room. *Journal of Advanced Nursing, 65*, 1390–1399.

Hall, D., & Langellier, K. (1988). Storytelling strategies in mother-daughter communication. In B. Bate & A. Taylor (Eds.), *Women Communicating: Studies of women's talk* (pp. 107–126). Norwood, NJ: Ablex.

Harrison, D. A., Price, K. H., & Bell, M. P. (1998). Beyond relational demography: Time and the effects of surface-and deep-level diversity on work group cohesion. *Academy of Management Journal, 41*, 96–107.

Harrison, D. A., Price, K. H., Gavin, J. H., & Florey, A. T. (2002). Time, teams, and task performance: Changing effects of surface-and deep-level diversity on group functioning. *Academy of Management Journal, 45*, 1029–1045.

Heisenberg, W. (1958). *Physics and philosophy.* New York, NY: Harper& Row.

House, R. J., Hanges, P. J., Javidan, M., Dorfman, P. W., & Gupta, V. (Eds.). (2004). *Culture, leadership, and organizations: The GLOBE study of 62 societies.* Thousand Oaks, CA: SAGE.

Johnson, F. (1996). Friendship among women: Closeness in dialogue. In J. T. Wood (Ed.), *Gendered relationships: A reader* (pp. 301–316). Fairfax, VA: George Mason University Press.

Johnson, S. K., Murphy, S. E., Zewdie, S., & Reichard, R. J. (2008). The strong, sensitive type: Effects of gender stereotypes and leadership prototypes on the evaluation of male and female leaders. *Organizational Behavior and Human Decision Processes, 106*, 39–60.

Koenig, A. M., Eagly, A. H., Mitchell, A. A., & Ristikari, T. (2011). Are leader stereotypes masculine? A meta-analysis of three research paradigms. *Psychological Bulletin, 137*, 616–642.

Labov, W. (1972). *Sociolinguistic patterns.* Philadelphia, PA: University of Pennsylvania Press.

Lakoff, R. T. (1975). *Language and woman's place.* New York, NY: Harper & Row.

Leaper, C., & Ayres, M. M. (2007). A meta-analytic review of gender variations in adults' language use: Talkativeness, affiliative speech, and assertive speech. *Personality and Social Psychology Review, 11*, 328–363.

Mulac, A., Wiemann, J. M., Widenmann, S. J., & Gibson, T. W. (1988). Male/female language differences and effects in same-sex and mixed-sex dyads: The gender-linked language effect. *Communications Monographs, 55*, 315–335.

Mumby, D. K. (2006). Gender and communication in organizational contexts: Introduction. In B. J. Dow & J. T. Wood (Eds.), *The SAGE handbook of gender and communication* (pp. 89–95). Thousand Oaks, CA: SAGE.

Newman, M. L., Groom, C. J., Handelman, L. D., & Pennebaker, J. W. (2008). Gender differences in language use: An analysis of 14,000 text samples. *Discourse Processes, 45*, 211–236.
Obama, B. (2016, August 4). Glamour exclusive: President Barack Obama says, "This is what a feminist looks like." *Glamour*. Retrieved from http://www.glamour.com/story/glamour-exclusive-president-barack-obama-says-this-is-what-a-feminist-looks-like
Oly Ndubisi, N. (2004). Understanding the salience of cultural dimensions on relationship marketing, its underpinnings and aftermaths. *Cross Cultural Management: An International Journal, 11*, 70–89.
Palomares, N. A. (2016). Language and gender. In C. R. Berger & M. E. Roloff (Eds.), *The international encyclopedia of interpersonal communication* (pp. 965–976). West Sussex, England: Wiley.
Phillips, K. W., Northcraft, G. B., & Neale, M. A. (2006). Surface-level diversity and decision-making in groups: When does deep-level similarity help? *Group Processes & Intergroup Relations, 9*(4), 467–482.
Riordan, C. M. (2000). Relational demography within groups: Past developments, contradictions, and new directions. *Research in Personnel and Human Resources Management, 19*, 131–174.
Savicki, V., Kelley, M., & Lingenfelter, D. (1997). Gender, group composition, and task type in small task groups using computer-mediated communication. *Computers in Human Behavior, 12*, 549–565.
Shectman, Z., & Kenny, D. A. (1994). Metaperception accuracy: An Israeli study. *Basic and Applied Social Psychology, 15*, 451–465.
Slaughter, A-M. (2012, July/August). Why women still can't have it all. *The Atlantic Magazine*. Retrieved from http://www.theatlantic.com/magazine/archive/2012/07/why-women-still-cant-have-it-all/309020/?single_page=true
Smith, C., Weinberg, F. J., and Treviño, L. J. (2014, November). *The effects of gendered communication and gender composition on objective indicators of career success*. Paper presented at the Southern Management Association Annual Meeting, Savannah, Georgia.
Society for Human Resource Management (SHRM). (n.d.). *Defining diversity*. Retrieved from: htt.p://hrasm.shrm.org/defining-diversity
Tepper, B. J., Moss, S. E., & Duffy, M. K. (2011). Predictors of abusive supervision: Supervisor perceptions of deep-level dissimilarity, relationship conflict, and subordinate performance. *Academy of Management Journal, 54*, 279–294.
Tharenou, P. (1997). Explanations of managerial career advancement. *Australian Psychologist, 32*, 19–28.
Trethewey, A., Scott, C., & LeGreco, M. (2006). Constructing embodied organizational identities: Commodifying, securing, and servicing professional bodies. *The SAGE handbook of gender and communication* (pp. 123–141). Thousand Oaks, CA: SAGE.
Verbeke, W., Bagozzi, R. P., & Belschak, F. D. (2016). The role of status and leadership style in sales contests: A natural field experiment. *Journal of Business Research, 69*, 4112–4120.
Weinberg, F. J., & Lankau, M. J. (2011). Formal mentoring programs: A mentor-centric and longitudinal analysis. *Journal of Management, 37*, 1527–1557.

Weinberg, F. J., & Locander, W. B. (2014). Advancing workplace spiritual development: A dyadic mentoring approach. *The Leadership Quarterly, 25*, 391–408.
Weinberg, F. J., Treviño, L. J., & Cleveland, A. O. (2015). Gendered communication and career outcomes: A construct validation and prediction of hierarchical advancement and non-hierarchical rewards. *Communication Research*, doi: 10.1177/0093650215590605
West, C., & Zimmerman, D. H. (2003). Doing gender. In R. J. Ely, E. G. Foldy, & M. A. Scully (Eds.), *Reader in gender, work, and organization* (pp. 62–74). Malden, MA: Blackwell.
Wheeler, S. C., & Petty, R. E. (2001). The effects of stereotype activation on behavior: a review of possible mechanisms. *Psychological Bulletin, 127*, 797–826.
Wood, J. T. (2006). Introduction to part I: Gender and communication in interpersonal contexts. In B. J. Dow and J. T. Wood (Eds.), *The SAGE handbook of gender and communication* (pp. 1–8). Thousand Oaks, CA: SAGE.
Wood, J. T. (2013). *Gendered lives: Communication, gender, and culture* (10th ed.). Boston, MA: Wadsworth Cengage Learning.

CHAPTER 2

MENTORS, SPONSORS, AND DIVERSITY IN WORK ORGANIZATIONS

Who Helps Whom and What Difference Does It Make?

Nancy DiTomaso and Catrina Palmer
Rutgers Business School

ABSTRACT

A major theme in the literature on diversity in the labor force is the importance of mentors for those who get ahead in their careers. Noting that women and minority employees are less likely to have mentors who can provide advice and help compared to White men, women and minority employees have been urged to find mentors, and companies have been urged to provide them, sometimes in formal programs and sometimes informally. More recently, a distinction has been made between a mentor who can give advice and a sponsor who can give more substantive help, although the focus on mentors who give advice still predominates in discussions about career needs for women and minority employees. In this paper we will make three contributions: (a) we provide an overview of the research with regard to mentoring; (b) we reinforce and clarify the distinctions between the roles of mentors and sponsors, along with the related roles of coaches, role models, and networks; and (c) we raise critical questions that have not been given sufficient attention in the research literature about who helps whom in the labor force and to what effect. We end with a discussion of how employees who may be at a disadvantage in gaining access to supportive relationships in the workplace can improve their chances of positive outcomes.

After years of research documenting the importance of getting help from colleagues and others for career success, it has now become common wisdom that having supportive relationships in the workplace makes a difference in terms of career outcomes (Fagenson, 1989; Hewlett, 2013; Kram, 1985; Lunding, Clements, & Perkins, 1979; Scandura, 1992; Thomas, 1989). Such relationships take different forms, and include in various studies the roles of mentors, sponsors, coaches, role models, and networks. While these roles overlap and are sometimes discussed together in the many studies on workplace supportive relationships, there are some distinctions that should be preserved in order to understand what issues need to be addressed in fostering better career outcomes, especially for women and minority employees.

Although most discussions of workplace supportive relationships have been under the label of mentors who give advice, more recent attention has been given to the role of sponsors who are thought to play a more substantive role in career assistance (Hewlett, Peraino, Sherbin, & Sumberg, 2011; Smith, 2005; Thomas, 1990). Workplace supportive relationships have both instrumental and socioemotional functions (Ibarra, 1993, 1995; Kram, 1985; Scandura, 1992). Such relationships can be beneficial to those employees who gain access to them as well as to those providing assistance and to the employing organizations. In this paper we make three contributions: (a) we provide an overview of the research with regard to mentoring; (b) we reinforce and clarify the distinctions between the roles of mentors and sponsors, along with the related roles of coaches, role models, and networks; and (c) we raise critical questions that have not received sufficient attention in the research literature about who helps whom in the labor force and to what effect. In our analyses, we place the discussion of mentors and sponsors in the larger literature on diversity and inequality (DiTomaso, Post, & Parks-Yancy, 2007).

The focus on workplace supportive relationships in the management literature emerged, in part, because of the recognition that women and minority employees have had less access to and receive less favorable outcomes from such relationships than do White men (Ibarra, 1993, 1995; Ragins, 1997; Thomas, 1990, 2001). A number of explanations have been given for this discrepancy, including the characteristics of women and minority employees themselves (Hennig & Jardim, 1977), the difficulties inherent in cross-sex and cross-race relationships (Hunt & Michael, 1983; Ragins, 1997; Thomas, 1989, 1990) and the lower status positions held disproportionately by women and minority employees compared to White men in most organizations (McGuire, 2000; McGuire & Reskin, 1993). Despite these challenges, women and minority employees have been urged to find mentors, while organizations have been urged to provide them through formal programs or to encourage them informally (Chun, Sosik, & Yi, 2012; Hewlett, 2013; Hewlett, Peraino, Sherbin, & Sumberg, 2011).

In the first part of this paper, we will discuss the different types of workplace supportive relationships, giving special attention to the distinctions between mentors and sponsors. We then discuss how career progression might be affected by workplace supportive relationships in order to highlight the different outcomes that are likely from mentors versus sponsors. In our discussion, we pose a key question about how mentors and sponsors interact with their protégés, and we ask specifically whether women and minority group members are more likely to receive advice that has a modest effect on career outcomes, while White males are more likely to be given opportunities, which can have a substantial and positive impact on their careers (DiTomaso, Post, Smith, Farris, & Cordero, 2007). Further, we argue that inattention to the varied patterns by which workplace supportive relationships are often enacted contributes to the unequal outcomes that have been frequently noted for women and minority employees (DiTomaso, 2015). In the final part of the paper, we outline ways that women and minority employees can use this information to improve the likelihood that they can form relationships on the job that will provide them with opportunity as well as advice. In our discussion, we challenge companies to take note of how opportunities get shared within their companies and to change policies and practices if they want to foster a more diverse workforce.

WORKPLACE SUPPORTIVE RELATIONSHIPS

Mentors, sponsors, coaches, role models, and networks each have been found to affect workplace outcomes, but there are important differences across these roles and in how they contribute to those who have access to them. Although the research literature often mixes the specific functions for each of these roles and indeed the functions overlap in any given relationship, the most basic definitions suggest that mentors primarily give advice, sponsors provide opportunity, coaches help improve skills, role models provide inspiration and often a vision of what might be possible and networks, although inherent in each of the other roles, are especially valuable as a form of social capital that links employees to others who might be able to provide information, influence, or opportunity, depending on the nature of the relationship (Adler & Kwon, 2002).

Mentors

In Greek mythology, Mentor is a friend of Odysseus who asked Mentor to take charge of his son, Telemachus, when Odysseus left for the Trojan War. In modern usage, being a mentor means to provide wisdom and advice, and that is the way that it has been used most often in the management literature. Mentoring is characterized as a developmental relationship in which a more experienced and knowledgeable person offers both career and psychosocial support to a protégé, who is usually younger and less experienced (Kram, 1985). Career support includes giving advice, enhancing visibility for the protégé and assisting with the navigation of the political environment. Psychosocial support includes offering both friendship and an emotional connection for the protégé (Kram, 1985). Although mentoring relationships often develop naturally (i.e., informally) for White men in organizations, women and minority employees are less likely to gain access to mentors through informal processes than are White men (Chao, Walz, & Gardner, 1992; Ragins & Cotton, 1999). When the relationships are informal, protégés receive more career-related support and higher salaries than protégés in formal relationships (Chao et al., 1992; Ragins & Cotton, 1999). Thus, informal mentoring processes tend to favor White men. Formal mentoring relationships, however, have been found to provide more access to mentors for women and minorities than they might be able to obtain on their own (K. E. O'Brien, Biga, Kessler, & Allen, 2010).

Mentoring relationships are reciprocal (Ragins, 1997), in that both the mentors and the protégés potentially gain benefits from mentoring relationships that work well. Having a mentor is assumed to benefit protégés because gaining the advice and support from a more experienced and often higher status colleague can help protégés understand the culture of the organization, the political landscape, how to best present themselves to others in the workplace, how to map out a career path and ways to address developmental needs. Not all mentors are equally capable of providing such benefits, and not all protégés are equally capable of productively using the advice that they receive. Thus, the quality of the mentoring relationship often depends on the career success of the mentor, the warmth of the relationship between the mentor and protégé, the duration of the relationship and the savviness of the mentor both with regard to the organization and in his or her own career. Most mentoring relationships do not last over time, both because of the growth of the protégé and the changes in the circumstances of the mentor including job changes and otherwise. Those who have studied mentoring relationships note that most last approximately 3 years, so it is important for protégés to know both how to enter a mentoring relationship and also how to end or transition out of one (Hill & Kamprath, 1991). Given the fragility and temporality of mentoring relationships, employees are encouraged to have more than one mentor, especially over time and to draw from mentors what each individual mentor can best offer.

Mentors may be internal to the protégé's organization or external to it. Some have suggested that internal mentors are likely to provide more instrumental advice, whereas those from other organizations can provide more socioemotional support (Ibarra, 1993, 1995). Due to proximity, internal mentors may be more physically accessible than external mentors, and they also may have better insight into navigating political turmoil and adversities within the workplace (Chao et al., 1992). Internal mentors are also better positioned to use influence on behalf of their mentees when opportunities come along and, in that regard, serve the role of sponsors (Ragins, 1997, p. 484). External mentors, in contrast, are typically in a better position to provide their protégés with "long-range career interventions and lateral career transitions" (Ragins, 1997, p. 485).

Because of the assumption that the higher the status position held by the mentor, the better for the mentee, women and minority employees are at a disadvantage in finding mentors who match their demographic characteristics, because both women and minority employees are less well represented among those in higher status positions in most organizations. Although higher status mentors may be able to provide protégés more support, for example in controversial situations (McGuire, 2000) and help them gain greater visibility as well as "reflected power" (Kanter, 1989; Ragins, 1997, p. 487), women and minority employees in relatively low status positions who find mentors who hold higher status positions may also face additional complications associated with cross-sex and cross-race mentoring relationships (Cohen, Steele, & Ross, 1999; Ensher & Murphy, 1997; Gibbons, 1993; Thomas, 1989, 1990). Such relationships often pose additional challenges for both mentors and mentees who are not matched by gender or race/ethnicity. Because of the paucity of women and minorities in high status corporate positions, junior level women may prefer to have male mentors and junior level minority employees may prefer to have White mentors, especially for internal mentoring relationships (Ibarra, 1993, 1995). For junior level women, cross-sex mentoring relationships may be fraught with sexual innuendos or tensions that cause both the mentor and the mentee to hesitate in their engagement in the relationship (Hewlett et al., 2011). For junior level minority employees, cross-race relationships may impede communication openness and the ability to gain reliable feedback (Thomas, 1989, 1990).

There are benefits for mentors who provide advice and support for less experienced protégés. Mentors may gain satisfaction and fulfillment from the professional and personal development of their protégés (Ragins & Scandura, 1994). Mentors may also themselves gain recognition from the support that they provide, especially if their mentees demonstrate competence and capability that benefits the organization (Ragins & Scandura, 1994). A protégé's performance can reflect on the reputation of the mentor, and thus, high-performing mentees can enhance their mentor's organizational role (Kram, 1985). Research has shown, however, that women are less likely to receive the same favorable recognition as men while serving as mentors (McGuire, 2000). Even in high status positions, women may experience greater visibility and performance pressures when they are in the minority (Kanter, 1977, 1979). Mentoring relationships can amplify both successes and failures (Ragins & Scandura, 1994). Thus, if the protégés do not perform well, female mentors may risk their own reputations. Female mentors may also be subject to accusations of favoritism if they try to help female mentees (Ragins & Sundstrom, 1989).

Although mentoring relationships are thought to be beneficial primarily to those involved in the relationships, employing organizations gain benefits as well. In the context of what has often been called the "war for talent" or talent management, companies have been encouraged to either create formal programs or to encourage and facilitate workplace supportive relationships within their organizations targeted especially to women and minority employees, because both continue to be less well represented in top level management and on boards of directors (Joecks, Pull, & Vetter, 2013; Post & Byron, 2015). Some companies have responded by creating formal mentoring programs, while others have provided mechanisms to make networking and connections more likely among their employees. Although research finds that such programs may extend access, they also have very little effect overall in terms of improving the career prospects for women and minority employees (Burke & McKeen, 1997; K. E. O'Brien et al., 2010). Because neither formal nor informal mentoring programs have had the effects promised, recent research has argued that women and minority employees need more than the advice given by mentors. They instead need sponsors who will actively look out for their career interests (Hewlett, 2013; Hewlett et al., 2011).

Sponsors

Unlike mentors who give advice and share information, sponsors are likely to help with career advancement (Cable & Murray, 1999; DiTomaso, Post, Smith et al., 2007; Thomas, 1990; Turner, 1960). Sponsors actively advocate for their protégés in meetings when opportunities are available (Ibarra, Carter, & Silva, 2010). Sponsors also both enhance visibility of their protégés and try to provide them with opportunities that will be valuable for their careers. Furthermore, sponsors help their protégés make connections with people who can help them, and they look out for the interests of their protégés. In other words, sponsors often take an active role in guiding the career steps of their protégés, whereas in mentoring relationships, it is often the mentee who has to take the initiative to ask for help and to keep the relationship active (Hewlett et al., 2011, p. 5).

Thus, despite the emphasis within the career literature on the importance of mentors, inequality by gender and race/ethnicity still exists in the workplace with men earning more; holding positions with greater authority; and having greater opportunity for assignments that develop skills, provide visibility, and position the protégés for more responsibility and promotion opportunities. Not surprisingly, therefore, past research has found that men are more likely than women to have access to sponsors in the workplace, although for both men and women only a small proportion have people who can sponsor their upward mobility. Hewlett et al. (2011, p. 8), for example, found that only 19% of men in their study had sponsors, but even fewer women, 13%, did.

In a corporate environment where White men disproportionately hold top level managerial positions, it is quite likely that White men will have disproportionate access to both mentors and sponsors (DiTomaso, 2015). Further, White men who are in positions to pass along opportunities and resources will do so primarily to other White men (DiTomaso, 2015). Such connections follow the principles of homophily (McPherson, Smith-Lovin, & Cook, 2001) in that people tend to gravitate to similar others. The in-group favoritism associated with homophily also leads to the belief that those who are in the normative in-group (usually U.S. born White men) are both more competent and trustworthy as well as more likable than those from outgroups (Fiske, Cuddy, Glick, & Xu, 2002; Hogg, 2001; Hogg & Terry, 2000; Hogg & Turner, 1985; McPherson et al., 2001; Ridgeway, Boyle, Kuipers, & Robinson, 1998; Ridgeway & Erickson, 2000).

Progressive organizations are taking more of an active role in creating formal sponsorship programs; however, the majority of relationships are created informally. In the informal environment, high-performing employees who embody the organizational culture and values are sought after by key executives. There are notable attributes that the sponsor evaluates to determine whether or not a protégé is worth his or her investment, such as an exceptional work ethic and trustworthiness (Hewlett, 2013). Essentially, the sponsor has to be confident in promoting an individual who not only delivers superb results and exudes an executive presence, but also an individual with whom the sponsor shares similar values and attitudes, which often notably will be those from the same demographic groups as the sponsor. Similarly, effective mentoring relationships may transform into a sponsor and protégé relationship (Hewlett, 2013), but that is more likely when both sponsors and their protégés are White men.

Like mentorship, sponsorship relationships are also reciprocal (Hewlett, 2013) in that there can be positive gains for the protégé, sponsor, and the organization. Protégés may be offered visibility, good job assignments, or new positions by high-status, seasoned executives who share their limited time and abundant resources with the selected junior-level employees they choose to help (Hewlett, 2013; Hewlett et al., 2011). As a result of these connections, protégés may enhance their intangible skills, such as managing the organizational political landscape and having the opportunity to form interpersonal relationships with key executives. Sponsors may also benefit from their protégé relationships. These benefits include having their brand extended through a promising, junior employee whom they believe embodies their work ethic, values, and philosophy (Hewlett, 2013). Additionally, the sponsor's reputation is augmented for identifying the protégé's potential and grooming him/her for successful leadership. Lastly, organizations benefit from the pipeline of talented employees who are groomed for success. As long as White men are disproportionately represented in managerial positions and as long as they choose protégés who are like them, then naturally forming sponsor-protégé relationships will reproduce inequality in organizations.

Under current circumstances, women and minorities are less likely to benefit from sponsorship relationships to the same extent as White men. In a recent study, Hewlett (2013, pp. 75–76) found that women and minorities do not seem to understand the differences between mentors and sponsors. This is critical, as the individuals who some women and minorities identify as sponsors are not truly advocating and championing on their behalf. Furthermore, similar to mentoring relationships, some studies suggest that cross-race (Thomas, 2001) and cross-sex (Hewlett et al., 2011) relationships tend to hinder women and minorities from accessing effective sponsorship. With White men historically being placed in positions of authority and power and having greater access to sponsors, it is not surprising that White men are still disproportionately represented in organizational leadership positions.

Even when women are able to gain access to sponsors, they do not seem to develop the relationship capital that is expected of such connections (Hewlett et al., 2011). Research has shown that women and men cultivate relationships differently (Babcock & Laschever, 2003; Fels, 2004; Hewlett, 2013; Hewlett et al., 2011). Women participate in less negotiating and quid pro quo transactions than do their male counterparts, who engage in self-promotion more than do women. According to Babcock and Laschever

(2003), women are more likely than men to believe that their hard work and exceptional performance speak for themselves, and thus women expect others to notice and certify their contributions. Hewlett et al. (2011) attribute these behaviors to the socialization of women compared to men. Women's inclinations are reinforced through social and cultural expectations of them as more concerned about others than for themselves.

Women face further barriers in their efforts to find sponsors and mentors because they are evaluated differently for the same behaviors exhibited by men. A number of studies have found, for example, that the characteristics associated with being a leader overlap the characteristics associated with being masculine, which has sometimes been translated into the phrase, "think manager, think male" (Eagly, Makhijani, Mona, & Klonsky, 1992; Fiske et al., 2002; Rudman, 2001; Ryan & Haslam, 2007; Schein, 1973). This implicit association, which is held by both men and women, can lead to what is called a "double bind" for women (Eagly & Carli, 2007), in which they face a trade-off between being thought of as competent as leaders and being thought of as sufficiently feminine (Fiske et al., 2002). Women who show their competence as leaders are often perceived as not being friendly or warm, (i.e., as not being feminine enough), while women who come across as friendly and warm are often thought of as not especially competent. In either situation, women can be thought of as not meeting expectations. Men do not face the same trade-off. They can be perceived as both competent and friendly or warm when enacting leadership roles.

Coaches

The primary purpose of a coach is to assist an employee with skill acquisition (Fournies, 1978; Hackman & Wageman, 2005). The coach facilitates learning by training an individual within a specific domain in which he or she is known to be an expert. A coach can assist with the development of hard technical skills or soft relational skills. Unlike a mentor or sponsor, a coach is not necessarily someone in a higher status position (Feldman, 2001). Skills can be learned from peers, from senior-level employees and even from subordinates. The defining characteristic of a coach is someone who helps with the acquisition of specific skills that can enhance development and potential mobility for employees who have access to coaches (Fournies, 1978). Coaching relationships are typically shorter than those of mentors or sponsors, lasting perhaps three to six months (Feldman, 2001; Thach & Heinselman, 1999).

The use of executive or career coaches have become more prevalent in the last two decades (Feldman, 2001; Hall, Otazo, & Hollenbeck, 1999; Thach & Heinselman, 1999). Coaching relationships are usually narrowly focused. The main objective of such relationships is for the coach to assist the improvement of skills (Feldman, 2001). A coach may be asked to help with the development of soft skills such as improving emotional intelligence, or verbal and nonverbal communication, which can benefit the organization by improving employee interactions and customer relations. A coach may also be asked to teach specific hard skills, such as how to use a new system or piece of technology.

The success and effectiveness of a coaching relationship depends on the communication and trust that is built between the coach and the client (Ianiro, Lehmann-Willenbrock, & Kauffeld, 2015; Thach & Heinselman, 1999). How easily communication and trust are built between the two parties can be affected by whether the coach is internal to the organization or external. External coaches may be preferred when dealing with an issue that is highly sensitive and requires confidentiality, while internal coaches may be preferred for issues that require immediate resolution and insight into the organizational culture, policies, and practices (Feldman, 2001; Hall et al., 1999).

A coaching relationship is mostly one-directional in that the employee being coached develops a new competency, while the coach provides a service. Internal coaches, though, have the opportunity to reap the benefits of their client's improved behavior or skillset. As with a mentor or sponsor, a coach's reputation may be enhanced if he or she is effective in helping the development of others. Organizations also benefit from the coach and client relationship. By investing in their human capital, organizations can reap long-term benefits, such as employee retention, improved performance, and increased satisfaction that outweighs short-term performance and cost (Feldman, 2001).

Because White men are disproportionately represented in managerial and especially in leadership positions in most companies, they are likely to get more training and assistance from coaches than are women and minority employees (Duncan & Hoffman, 1979; Evertsson, 2004; Tomaskovic-Devey & Skaggs, 2002). In fact, the lack of access to training is one of the key factors that contribute to disadvantages for women and minority employees in the labor market. Even when training is available, women and minority employees may not gain the same benefit from it as do White men (Evertsson, 2004). Further evidence suggests that women and minority employees also get less feedback and less honest feedback (Harber, 1998). Some evidence also suggests that women and presumably minority employees, may get too much help or not enough, often leading to their inability to develop and present themselves as competent in work settings (Kanter, 1979).

Role Models

Role models also play an integral part in individuals' professional development by potentially shaping their career path (Buunk, 2007). Though role models and mentors share similar attributes, they differ in their utilization. Drawing upon social learning theory and cognitive development theory (Bandura, 1969), role models exemplify a level of success that can be emulated by others. Individuals typically select role models with whom they are able to identify, often because of shared demographic and social characteristics. Further, individuals must perceive the role model's level of success as challenging, yet attainable (Gibson, 2003, p. 592). Hence, role models can possibly enhance one's confidence and provide a template of how to achieve his or her desired career goals.

Selecting role models are especially important for women and minorities, who want to improve in their careers. Especially for out-group members, role models become a reference for defining an individual's sense of self. Positive role models can enhance performance and reduce stereotype threat (Steele & Aronson, 1995). Marx, Ko, and Friedman (2009), for example, found that President Obama served as a role model for Black students, and as such reduced the performance gap between Black and White students. They (Marx et al., 2009, pp. 953–954) argue that role models can provide such benefits to negatively stereotyped groups when the role model is perceived as competent, thought of as an in-group member, and when the role model demonstrates competence in areas about which negative stereotypes of the in-group would otherwise be expected.

The primary beneficiary of role models is the individual who selects the role model. For example, when race and gender are salient, selecting a role model can increase both inspiration and motivation to break barriers and can reinforce beliefs that the individual can accomplish his or her goals by adopting similar leadership traits and styles (Marx et al., 2009). The effects of role models are complicated; however, under some circumstances they can counter negative stereotypes and improve performance, but under other circumstances, they can reinforce stereotypes or induce stereotype threat (Bages, Vernies, & Martino, 2015; Cheryan, Siy, Vichayapai, Drury, & Kim, 2011; Marx & Goff, 2005: O'Brien et al., 2016; Singh, Vinnicombe, & James, 2006; Taylor, Lord, McIntyre, & Paulson, 2011; Young, Rudman, Buettner, & McLean, 2013). Role models who counter negative stereotypes are likely to be more inspiring to both women and minority employees, but role models who reinforce negative stereotypes or who present images that seem unattainable can be demotivating. Unlike a mentor, sponsor, or coach, a role model does not need to be in close proximity to have influence on and benefit targets (Marx et al., 2009; Taylor et al., 2011). Role models can be helpful even from a distance.

Especially within organizations, role models may be harder to find for women and minority employees, because they are less likely to be represented in leadership positions. Although women and minority employees can look to people from outside their organizations for inspiration, to do so requires that they are able to relate the experiences of those they think of as role models to their own situations. When employees do not have role models whom they can emulate, it may undermine or limit their motivation and sense of self-efficacy, but role models have to meet conditions that reinforce competence and counter negative stereotypes in order to serve the intended function for women and minority employees. These kinds of conditions are less likely to affect Whites and males in the workplace.

Networks

Embedded in the larger conversation of workplace supportive relationships are networks, which consist of mentors and sponsors, along with family, friends, and acquaintances. Networks are a means by which individuals look to gain career-related information and a key vehicle that employers utilize to access potential job candidates. Relying less on the formal labor market, insider referral contacts are favored informal tools that employers use to obtain information about potential job candidates (Elliot, 2001). Insider referrals are obtained through an individual's social network that typically consists of friends, kin, and acquaintances who may evolve into mentors or sponsors. Accordingly, social networks play a dual role by (a) assisting individuals in gaining timely insider information that may not be available to others, thus increasing their chances of career advancement (Elliott, 2001, p. 403), and (b) providing employers with a means to match people to jobs (DiTomaso, 2013, 2015; Elliott, 2001).

The structure of social networks, such as whether or not the relationship is created formally or informally, has implications for determining career advancement outcomes (Ibarra, 1993; McGuire, 2000, p. 503). Formal relationships are typically initiated by the organization with the goal of completing a specified task or project. With formal networking, an individual's interactions may be limited to work-related purposes with defined boundaries on how to interact (Ibarra, 1993, p. 58; McGuire, 2000, p. 503). Informal relationships are more discretionary and contain broader scope, often consisting of work, social, and personal interactions and goals (McGuire, 2000, p. 503). These relationships tend to form organically through shared interests or on the basis of social and demographic similarities. Social networks can affect who gains access to distributed resources within an organization. While formal network ties may shift when job positions change, informal ties are likely to continue over time (Podolny & Baron, 1997, p. 677).

Networks vary in terms of both the strength of ties and the composition, which affect what is likely to be gained from such social relationships. Strong ties are "close, stable, and binding relative to weaker, more superficial links lacking in emotional investment" (Ibarra, 1993, p. 62). A lot of network literature focuses on the instrumental value gained from the information available from weak ties, because it is assumed that weak ties will have knowledge of jobs not known to strong ties (Burt, 1992; Granovetter, 1973, 1995). In contrast, strong ties tend to bond people who have similar attributes and a close relationship, typically including family and friends (Burt, 1992; Granovetter, 1973, 1995; Ibarra, 1993). With close ties among people who share the same background and who feel an obligation to each other, it is assumed that information about jobs will be shared and thus will also be redundant compared to what can be learned from those with whom one may have a more distant relationship and who is involved in networks with people with whom one is not already connected (Burt, 1992; Granovetter, 1973, 1995; Ibarra, 1993).

Research findings indicate that gender and race are significant factors in the formation of networks (Ibarra, 1993; Moore, 1990; Stoloff, Glanville, & Bienenstock, 1999). Women are more likely to develop supportive relationships through the strong ties of family and friends because of the roles they occupy within their families and because of their greater relational skills (Moore, 1990). Men, in contrast, are likely to have more nonkinship, job-related ties that consist of more instrumental interactions than are women (Hewlett et al., 2011; Moore, 1990). Additionally, White males have more access to high-status network connections than do women and minority employees. As such, White men are more likely than are women or minority employees to gain information that is valuable for promotion and advancement. According to McGuire (2000), the structural positions of White men versus women and minority employees in organizations is the primary factor that determine the outcomes of valuable social networks. High-status organizational members can provide those with whom they form networks with valuable resources, including information, influence, and opportunities (Adler & Kwon, 2002; McGuire, 2000).

Thus, while social networks are instrumental in connecting employees to valuable social and organizational resources and providing employers with an efficient process for matching candidates to opportunities and jobs, the use of social networks for distributing such resources appears to be more favorable for White men than for women and racial minorities (McPherson et al., 2001; Trimble & Kmec, 2011). Accordingly, over the last several decades, scholars have examined the access to and use of social networks to better explain inequality in who gains access to which jobs and how valuable social resources are distributed (DiTomaso, 2013, 2015; Elliott, 2001; Mouw, 2003; Petersen, Saporta, & Seidel, 2000). Since White men have historically been more likely to occupy high-status positions of authority (Stainback & Tomaskovic-Devey, 2012), they are likely to have greater access to social connections that can help them in the labor market. The homophily that is inherent in social network formation not only reproduces advantage through the exchange of valuable social resources, but such networks are reinforced as well by the perceptions that those who fit the prototype of those already in positions of authority are likely to be more competent and trustworthy (Haslam, Oakes, Reynolds, & Turner, 1999; Hogg & Ridgeway, 2003; Hogg & Terry, 2000; Ridgeway, 2001). In order for women and minority employees to gain similar opportunities, they usually need to seek out and form ties with those in higher status positions than their own and likely with White men from whom they can "borrow" social capital (Burt, 1997, 1998; Ibarra, 1993, 1995; Stoloff et al., 1999). Of course, because White men disproportionately hold high-status positions in many organizations and given the tendency toward homophily in the formation of social networks, women and minority employees are at a disadvantage in terms of developing the social network ties that might be most beneficial to their careers (McGuire, 2000; Stoloff et al., 1999; Trimble & Kmec, 2011).

Those who have access to each of these types of workplace supportive relationships are better able to enhance their career outcomes than those who have limited access to such assistance. The inequality that results from the differential access to such relationships overlays the existing inequality in which White men are more likely to hold positions of power, authority, and influence. While women and minority employees who are disproportionately found in lower level or lower status positions in most organizations can seek to form beneficial relationships with peers or even with subordinates and with those outside their organizations, their access to supportive relationships that might enhance their career outcomes are more limited and more challenging than is the case for White males, in general. Even when women and minority employees are able to find mentors or sponsors among those who hold higher status positions, in many cases these relationships are more likely to include cross-sex and cross-race characteristics, which as noted, may impede a sense of openness and cause hesitation in full engagement in the relationship on the part of either or both parties. While some organizations have tried to overcome this potential barrier to the success of women and minority employees by creating formal programs to assign mentors or sponsors, such programs have not transformed the unequal outcomes that continue to get reproduced in most organizations over time. To understand both the limits and the promise of workplace supportive relationships as a means to enhance inclusiveness in the labor force, we would like to look more closely at the roles of mentors versus sponsors and to consider ways that women and minority employees might use such relationships to better effect than has often been found to be the case.

THE STRUCTURE OF CAREER DEVELOPMENT AND GAINING ACCESS TO CAREER ASSISTANCE

In order to understand the role that workplace supportive relationships can play in the career development of women and minority employees, as well as for White men, we should give some attention to how the labor market is structured and the usual progression that is necessary in order for one to achieve career success in terms of obtaining positions of power, authority, and influence. In terms of formal theory in economics and sociology, the assumption is that people obtain employment through a process of matching people to jobs (Elliott, 2000; Goldberg, Finkelstein, Perry, & Konrad, 2004; Handel, 2003). In most cases, there is an assumption that this process is an open one in which jobs are made available and potential candidates seek out an opportunity to be chosen for jobs for which they are qualified. In such conceptions of the labor market, there is recognition that some potential job candidates may have better credentials, more motivation, and may make more effort in order to be recognized and selected for desirable job positions. Similarly, there is understanding that some jobs and some employers provide better opportunities for job growth and career success. Those who are selected for jobs for which their skills are matched, then enter organizations for which there is an internal process of job matching that might lead over time to promotions to higher level positions, or in some cases to opportunities with other organizations for which one is able to compete and move up through changes in either jobs or employers (Cao, 2001; Ibarra et al., 2010; James, 2000; Smith, 2005).

Career success, then, is a process of continually being on the lookout for new opportunities in which one can develop or utilize skills in ways that enable new responsibilities and potentially greater rewards (Burt, 2000, 2001; Lin, Cook, & Burt, 2001). Although the literature often speaks of careers as if there are defined paths to follow, in most cases there is a labyrinth through which job seekers must find a way forward, often going around obstacles and often doing so by recognizing or creating their own opportunities (Benko & Anderson, 2010; Eagly & Carli, 2007). In the career literature, job seekers are encouraged to create personal brands and to enhance their marketability through continual learning. Given the importance of the job matching process throughout one's career, it is also important to extend information about new opportunities on an ongoing basis by networking both with those with whom one has a close personal relationship and through the development of more distant relationships with people who have links to other sources of information and connections (Baker, 2000; Brass, Galaskiewicz, Greve, & Wenpin, 2004; Fernandez & Fernandez-Mateo, 2006; Marsden & Gorman, 2001; McGuire, 2000; Seidel, Polzer, & Stewart, 2000).

We know from the extensive research on career development that having friends and supporters in the labor market helps, because they can provide information about new opportunities, can use influence to ease one's access to being selected for desirable positions and often can provide or make opportunities known that can give one an inside edge (Adler & Kwon, 2002; de Janasz, Sullivan, Whiting, & Biech, 2003; Hewlett, 2013; Scandura, 1992; Seibert, Kraimer, & Liden, 2001). In this general process of using connections to enhance career outcomes, knowing lots of people and being known by them matters in terms of career success. Further, job seekers with high aspirations are often advised to recognize that some assignments matter more than others and that some jobs are better gateways to upward mobility than are others. Moving ahead requires finding the right pathway and doing so often requires developing relationships with people who can provide valuable assistance (Baker, 2000). Relationship building is an investment that career seekers are told to undertake, but they are also told that some investments in networking pay off more than others, so one should seek to develop those relationships that will be more instrumental for his or her own career development and where he or she can make the most contributions. As one seeks to develop his or her own career pathway, one can also enhance their networking position by acting as a broker for others (Burt, 1992). Being able to provide others with information, influence, or opportunity is a way to enhance one's own power with reference to others and doing so can also lead those with similar kinds of valuable social resources to reciprocate.

Against this ideal conception of the functioning of the job market, there has, of course, been recognition that sometimes discrimination takes place and that it may disadvantage some potential applicants over others, but understanding the extent and nature of such discriminatory processes has been the subject of disagreement in the labor force literature (Aigner & Cain, 1977; Becker, 1957; Bendrick, Jackson, & Reinoso, 1994; Blau & Ferber, 1987; Reskin, 2000; Sturm, 2001). Some believe that the labor force, in general, functions as expected, but that there are isolated pockets of discrimination that take place because of the ill will of a few gatekeepers in a few organizations. Others believe that discrimination is more widespread and systemic and that to curtail discriminatory actions requires regulations and close monitoring that restrain the ability of those who might want to discriminate to act on their preferences.

In either case, however, the focus has been on discrimination in terms of negative actions toward disadvantaged groups, for example, of Whites toward non-Whites or men toward women (DiTomaso, 2015; Greenwald & Pettigrew, 2014). The assumption in such analyses is that the mechanism that leads to inequality is a process of exclusion of disadvantaged groups from full access to opportunities. In the discussion of the roles of mentors and sponsors, the same kind of focus on exclusion has been the norm. When the issue of the need for mentors or sponsors is raised, the problem is framed in terms of the lack of such relationships for women and minority employees, rather than, for example, the overabundance of mentors and sponsors that White males seem to have available to them. We believe that to fully understand the structure of the labor market, including the role of workplace supportive relationships like those of mentors and sponsors, that we should turn this framework around and think more about advantage than about discrimination and about the inclusion that takes place within and among dominant groups more so than about the exclusion of women and minorities (DiTomaso, 2015).

Specifically, we argue that it may not be what Whites do to or against Blacks or other non-Whites that reproduces inequality in the labor force as much as what Whites do for each other (DiTomaso, 2013, 2015; Greenwald & Pettigrew, 2014). In other words, White men often act, both consciously and subconsciously, to give preference to other White men (DiTomaso, 2015; Stainback & Tomaskovic-Devey, 2012). White men are more often offered opportunities and are chosen for important assignments or jobs, and these processes of inclusion are what contribute most to the reproduction of inequality in the labor force and throughout careers. We know from the research on processes of homophily and in-group favoritism that under most circumstances, we give preferences to those who are like ourselves (Brewer, 1999; McPherson et al., 2001; Tajfel & Turner, 1986). Thus, when there is unequal representation across organizations in terms of who holds positions of authority, power, and decision making, with White men overrepresented as one moves from lower to higher status levels, then the enactment of homophily and in-group favoritism contributes to the reproduction of an already unequal system (Brewer, 1998; Ibarra, 1992, 1995; McPherson et al., 2001). The research evidence suggests that when inequality is long term and there is a dominant in-group, such as the position held by White men in the United States that they become associated with prototypes or schema that suggest that they will be evaluated as more competent, more likeable, more trustworthy, and importantly, that when resources are available to distribute, members of the dominant in-group members will be favored (Cuddy, Fiske, & Glick, 2008; Fiske et al., 2002; Stainback & Tomaskovic-Devey, 2012; Tilly, 1998). Despite these well documented patterns in the labor force and career literature, our theoretical models still focus on discrimination and racism or sexism against women and minority employees more so than on advantage and favoritism that benefits White men as the drivers of career outcomes.

Advice Versus Opportunity From Workplace Supportive Relationships

In this context, we want to raise questions about how the roles of mentors versus sponsors have been understood, and we want to challenge organizational leaders to consider more carefully how opportunities are accessed and distributed within their organizations. In prior research on the performance evaluations of scientists and engineers, we considered the relative importance of having mentors versus being given favorable working conditions that facilitate performance (DiTomaso, Post, Smith et al., 2007). With data from more than 3,000 scientists and engineers from 24 large, U.S. based companies, we found that both White and Black women were more likely to say that they had mentors, but White men were more likely to say that they had "technical control," meaning that they had a strong say in deciding the projects on which they worked. Importantly, we found as well that having a mentor had no effect on how the scientists and engineers were evaluated by their managers, but having technical control contributed significantly to improved evaluation of performance on both innovativeness (i.e., technical skills) and promotability into management. We interpreted these results to mean that women were getting advice, while men were getting opportunity. These results led us to consider more carefully what the role of mentors are for career success and what outcomes might be likely from the growth of programs to encourage more mentors for women and minority employees, whether formally assigned or informally encouraged.

Two issues became evident as we explored more fully the role of mentors as a solution to workforce inequality for women and minority employees. First, if one does a basic Internet search of the term mentor, most of the definitions zero in on giving advice or imparting wisdom. The notion that what mentors do is primarily give advice, of course, is inconsistent with how the issue of mentoring arose in the first place. It was through the recognition that most people who get ahead, meaning those who rise to positions of power and authority, do so with the help of others who led early proponents of mentoring to argue that in order to succeed, women and minority employees would need people to help them. But the kind of help that those who have been successful have gotten has not been so much getting advice from those who have themselves succeeded, as much as it has been being offered opportunities, in the form of access, visibility, rewards, and most importantly good jobs and good job assignments (Fagenson, 1989; Hewlett, 2013; Kram, 1985). In this regard, it is not advice that women and minority employees need. Rather it is someone to sponsor their advancement and to do so by being in a position to make sure that they get opportunities when they are available (Hewlett, 2013). Also necessary is someone to help them get the right training, to meet the right people, to have the right job assignments and to have the resources necessary to get the job done well. That is not the role that most mentors assume they are taking on and in many cases, those who serve as mentors for women and minority employees are not necessarily themselves in a position to offer such advantages to those to whom they are giving advice. Therefore, with growing attention to the distinctions between the roles of mentors and sponsors, there has been more recognition of the need for more substantive assistance than advice, but even in this conversation, there has been little discussion of how such roles are likely to work in an organizational system that is both hierarchical and unequal at the outset, and one in which White men are disproportionately in charge. Further, White men have not been held accountable in most organizations for how they distribute resources and opportunities on an everyday basis.

That is the second issue that we believe is important to consider when thinking about workplace supportive relationships. Because the focus on diversity and inclusion and more specifically on workplace inequality has been on discrimination in terms of a negative framing of Whites and men excluding non-Whites and women from job opportunities, there has been much less attention to the way that White men take steps to include, i.e., to look out for the interests of people like themselves (DiTomaso, 2015). It is not that they do so consciously or purposely, but because of the kind of ingroup favoritism that is pervasive in which we tend to think of people who are like ourselves as more competent and worthy, when opportunities come along, those who are likely to come to mind and who are likely thought to be especially well suited to new opportunities are likely to be similar others, especially in terms of gender and race/ethnicity. The evidence for this kind of favoritism is rather clear in the evidence (Reskin, 2003; Stainback & Tomaskovic-Devey, 2012). Even from the initial hire, White men are paid more, promoted sooner, and provided with more resources to do the job. Over time, they are found disproportionately at higher levels of authority, at higher income levels, and with more options available to them well before they have demonstrated performance. As Stainback and Tomaskovic-Devey (2012) found in their study using data from the Equal Employment Opportunity Commission from 1966 through 2005, White men retained their over representation in the best jobs, the jobs with the most authority, and the jobs with the most training associated with them. Thus, despite legislation to protect against discrimination, over a 50-year period since the passage of the Civil Rights Act, White men are as well situated in the labor market as ever before, and in fact in some sectors, they have expanded their representation. As long as companies look only to prevent discrimination against women and minorities, but do not pay attention to the opportunities that are preferentially offered to White men, then the structure of existing inequality will be reproduced over time, as it has been for decades.

In this context, what is it that mentors, whether formal or informal, are likely to do? They can give advice to their protégés, but unless they also consciously look out for their interests, pass along information, use influence, and offer opportunity as well, then the effects of the mentoring relationship may be modest at best. In an organizational system that is already unequal in terms of who is distributed into which sorts of positions and in which there is no attention to or salience of how opportunities are distributed and who gets considered first for advancement and rewards, then it is quite likely that even in well-meaning organizations who claim their commitment to diversity, women and minority employees will continue to get advice, while White men get opportunity. With a higher proportion of those who themselves have the capacity to offer meaningful opportunity being White men in most organizations, one might wonder if those who serve as "mentors" might offer advice to those who are not like themselves, but opportunity to those who are. In other words, they serve as mentors for women and minority employees, but as sponsors for other White men.

PRACTICAL IMPLICATIONS FOR BOTH MENTORS AND MENTEES

Broadening the Role for Mentors: More Than Advice

By calling attention to the way that favoritism, advantage, and privilege works in organizations that focus only on processes of discrimination, we hope to challenge the usual assumptions about why women and minorities, for example, may need "mentors," and importantly what mentors and/or sponsors should undertake in their efforts to provide workplace support. Certainly, our intention is to argue that meaningful support in the workplace requires more than offering advice or imparting wisdom. Those who want to make a difference and help change the outcomes over time should also champion, open doors, and connect their protégés with opportunities that will enhance their visibility, strengthen their skills, and position them for potential advancement. Mentors should, as has been assumed in past literature, teach leadership skills, suggest ways to develop competencies and provide recommended pathways for dealing with difficult situations. But mentors should also take on the role of sponsors who broker, influence, and actively engage where it is possible for them to do so in ways that might provide substantive opportunity for those they are trying to support.

Too often the discussion about mentors—and even discussions about mentors being sponsors—has not confronted head on the reality that taking on a role to help others get ahead is, on its face, a system of unequal influence in which some will benefit more than others. What would it mean in organizations if everyone had a mentor or sponsor? Presumably if it means that the organization is actively taking an interest in making sure that all employees have the resources they need and the developmental opportunities to enhance their skills and their contributions to the organization, then one would expect a better environment for employees and an overall better performance for the organization. But instead, such a system of workplace supportive relationships is uneven. Some have more access than others, some mentors are more powerful or better placed to be helpful than are others, and some protégés stand out as fitting the prototype of the competent employee more so than others. In that environment, when the point is to get an inside edge against potential competition, then mentors and sponsors both contribute to what might be perceived by some in the organization as a system that is unfair. By not paying attention overall to how opportunities are passed along, to whether there is favoritism or preference given, especially for already advantaged groups more so than for others and to whether managers accept a responsibility to assist the development and advancement of all of their employees, then inequality will be reproduced in the company and it is likely that women and minority employees will continue to get less benefit from a system of mentoring, or even sponsorship, than the literature suggests that they should.

How Mentees Can Help Their Mentors Open Doors for Them

In raising these issues about mentoring and inequality, however, we would be remiss if we did not also consider ways that women and minority employees, or White men for that matter, can improve their experiences with those with whom they form relationships in the workplace and, in doing so, also gain more substantive outcomes (Hill & Kamprath, 1991; Humberd & Rouse, 2015; Scandura, 1992; Wellington & Spence, 2001). As already mentioned, mentoring relationships rarely last more than three years, because people change positions, organizations, and take on other responsibilities. It is good advice for all employees, therefore, to foster good workplace relationships with a number of people, across multiple positions, and across time. Because any given relationship takes time and effort to develop and maintain, there are limits to what one can do in developing such relationships, but there are ways that one can be the type of person in an organization who others want to know and help, and that is one of the primary goals (Hill & Kamprath, 1991). Those mentees who help mentors help them will likely receive more benefit from a given relationship. First, being someone whom others will want to be around, to reach out to help and to be associated with helps in building meaningful mentor-protégé relationships. In other words, if you are someone who makes your mentor look good because of the association with you, there will be more incentive for your mentor to act more like a sponsor and to look out for your interests. One can be the type of person whom others want to help by taking initiative, standing out for doing a good job, taking on difficult assignments, demonstrating competence, and being a person of ideas and good will. Mentoring is not a one-way relationship. The mentee can help the mentor, as well as the other way around, even in terms of things like extending their networks and helping them understand what is going on in other parts of the organization. When a protégé has multiple mentors and actively pursues relationships across functions and both inside and outside the organization, then he or she can act as a bridge to new sources of knowledge that can be beneficial to the mentor as well as to oneself. The relationship of mentor and protégé should be one where both parties grow and change with the relationship, so that when the time comes that the relationships take a new path, both are grateful for the experience and ready to move forward. These, of course, are ideal representations of the kinds of relationships that would be most beneficial to both employees and to those who might help them and to the organization as well.

CONCLUSIONS

In this paper, we have tried to review briefly the research on different types of workplace supportive relationships, with special attention to the concepts of mentors versus sponsors. In doing so, we have raised questions about the seemingly overemphasis given to mentors, who are people who give advice, rather than to those who can provide more substantive help by looking out for the interests of those who are being helped and providing them with opportunities that will enhance their skills, their potential for advancement and their rewards. We have discussed why White men have been the beneficiaries of such relationships, whether mentors, sponsors, coaches, role models, or networks, and we have especially noted the inattention to the ways that White men are favored in the distribution of such social resources in most organizations. Rather than focusing policy concerns primarily on discrimination and exclusion of women and minorities, it seems that more organizations should recognize and make more visible the advantage, preference, and favoritism that are often provided to White men, who more easily form relationships with those in positions of power, authority, and influence, because of the already existing inequality that exists in many organizations, with White men disproportionately in higher status positions. Programs that try to expand the access of women and minority employees to mentors, or even to sponsors, but which do not also address more broadly the way social resources are shared and distributed across the organizations on an everyday basis are not likely to have major effects in reducing inequality or changing who is likely to end up in charge.

The issues that we raise are large ones and not ones that are easy to address in most organizations. Most organizations are hierarchical, unequal, and do not have much of a mandate to change those characteristics. Unless there is more of a commitment for outcomes and not just process, it is unlikely that programs of amelioration, focused on what women and minority employees lack or how they are excluded, are not going to lead to major change. But, there are things that women and minority employees can do to better position themselves for organizational success, including for forming relationships with potential mentors and sponsors. Understanding the nature of such relationships, the importance of being actively involved in fostering them and also recognizing that one has to be someone who others will want to know and help may shift the conversation about how to be successful in organizations. Knowing that taking initiative, accepting challenges, acting as a broker, and generally being someone who other people like (which is a skill that can be learned like other leadership behaviors) can enable women and minority employees to understand ways to stand out and stand up and in doing so can also enhance both their confidence and capabilities in ways that may make a difference over time.

REFERENCES

Adler, P. S., & Kwon, S.-W. (2002). Social capital: Prospects for a new concept. *Academy of Management Review, 27*(1), 17–40.

Aigner, D. J., & Cain, G. C. (1977). Statistical theories of discrimination in labor markets. *Industrial and Labor Relations Review, 30*, 175–187.

Babcock, L., & Laschever, S. (2003). *Women don't ask: Negotiation and the gender divide.* Princeton, NJ: Princeton University Press.

Bages, C., Vernies, C., & Martino, D. (2015). Virtures of a hardworking role model to improve girls' mathematics performance. *40*(1), 55–64.

Baker, W. E. (2000). *Achieving success through social capital: Tapping the hidden resources in your personal and business networks.* San Francisco, CA: Jossey-Bass.

Bandura, A. (1969). A social learning theory of identification process. Handbook of Socialization Theory and Research. Chicago: Rand McNally.

Becker, G. S. (1957). *The economics of discrimination* (1st ed.). Chicago, IL: University of Chicago Press.

Bendrick, M., Jr., Jackson, C. W., & Reinoso, V. A. (1994, Summer). Measuring employment discrimination through controlled experiments. *The Review of Black Political Economy, 23*, 25–48.

Benko, C., & Anderson, M. (2010). *Lattice ways to work: How companies can reconfigure when, where, and how work happens.* Boston, MA: Harvard Business Review Press.

Blau, F. D., & Ferber, M. A. (1987). Discrimination: Empirical evidence from the United States. *American Economic Review, 77*(2), 316–320.

Brass, D. J., Galaskiewicz, J., Greve, H. R., & Wenpin, T. (2004). Taking stock of networks and organizations: A multilevel perspective. *Academy of Management Journal, 47*(6), 795–817.

Brewer, M. B. (1998). In-group favoritism: The subtle side of intergroup discrimination. In D. Messick & A. Tenbrunsel (Eds.), *Codes of conduct: Behavioral research and business ethic* (pp. 160–170). New York, NY: Russell Sage Foundation.

Brewer, M. B. (1999). The psychology of prejudice: Ingroup love or outgroup hate? *Journal of Social Issues, 55*(3), 429–444.

Burke, R. J., & McKeen, C. A. (1997). Not every managerial woman who makes it has a mentor. *Women in Management Review, 12,* 136–139.

Burt, R. S. (1992). *Structural holes: The social structure of competition.* Cambridge, MA: Harvard University Press.

Burt, R. S. (1997). The contingent value of social capital. *Administrative Science Quarterly, 42,* 339–365.

Burt, R. S. (1998). The gender of social capital. *Rationality and Society, 10,* 5–36.

Burt, R. S. (2000). The network structure of social capital. *Research in Organizational Behavior, 22,* 345–423.

Burt, R. S. (2001). Structural holes versus network closure as social capital. In N. Lin, K. Cook, & R. Burt (Eds.), *Social capital: Theory and research* (pp. 31–56). New York, NY: Aldine De Gruyter.

Buunk, A. P., Peiró, J. M., & Griffioen, C. (2007). A positive role model may stimulate career-oriented behavior. *Journal of Applied Social Psychology, 37*(7), 1489–1500.

Cable, D. M., & Murray, B. (1999). Tournaments versus sponsored mobility as determinants of job search success. *The Academy of Management Journal, 42*(4), 439–449.

Cao, Y. (2001). Careers inside organizations: A comparative study of promotion determination in reforming China. *Social Forces, 80*(2), 683–711.

Chao, G. T., Walz, P. M., & Gardner, P. D. (1992). Formal and informal mentorships: A comparison on mentoring functions and contrast with nonmentored counterparts. *Personnel Psychology, 45*(3), 619–636.

Cheryan, S., Siy, J. O., Vichayapai, M., Drury, B. J., & Kim, S. (2011). Do female and male role models who embody STEM stereotypes hinder women's anticipated success in STEM? *Social Psychological and Personality Science, 2*(6), 656–664.

Chun, J. U., Sosik, J. J., & Yi, Y. N. (2012). A longitudinal study of mentor and protege outcomes in formal mentoring relationships. *Journal of Organizational Behavior, 33*(8), 1071–1094.

Cohen, G. L., Steele, C. M., & Ross, L. D. (1999). The mentor's dilemma: Providing critical feedback across the racial divide. *Personal and Social Psychology Bulletin, 25,* 1302–1318.

Cuddy, A. J. C., Fiske, S. T., & Glick, P. (2008). Warmth and competence as universal dimensions of social perception: The stereotype content model and the bias map. *Advances in Experimental Social Psychology, 40,* 61–137.

de Janasz, S. C., Sullivan, S. E., Whiting, V., & Biech, E. (2003). Mentor networks and career success: Lessons for turbulent times. *The Academy of Management Executive, 17*(4), 78–93.

DiTomaso, N. (2013). *The American non-dilemma: Racial inequality without racism.* New York, NY: Russell Sage Foundation.

DiTomaso, N. (2015). Racism and discrimination versus advantage and favoritism: Bias for versus bias against. *Research in Organizational Behavior, 35*, 57–77.

DiTomaso, N., Post, C., & Parks-Yancy, R. (2007). Workforce diversity and inequality: Power, status, and numbers. *Annual Review of Sociology, 33*(1), 473–501.

DiTomaso, N., Post, C., Smith, D. R., Farris, G. F., & Cordero, R. (2007). Effects of structural position on allocation and evaluation decisions for scientists and engineers. *Administrative Science Quarterly, 52*(2), 175–207.

Duncan, G. J., & Hoffman, S. (1979). On-the-job training and earnings differences by race and sex. *Review of Economics and Statistics, 61*, 594–603.

Eagly, A. H., & Carli, L. L. (2007, September). Women and the labyrinth of leadership. *Harvard Business Review*, 62–71.

Eagly, A. H., Makhijani, Mona G., & Klonsky, B. (1992). Gender and the evaluation of leaders: A meta-analysis. *Psychological Bulletin, 111*(1), 3–22.

Elliott, J. R. (2000). Class, race, and job matching in contemporary urban labor markets. *Social Science Quarterly, 81*(4), 1036–1052.

Elliott, J. R. (2001). Referral hiring and ethnically homogeneous jobs: How prevalent is the connection and for whom? *Social Science Research, 30*, 401–425.

Ensher, E. A., & Murphy, S. E. (1997). Effects of race, gender, perceived similarity, and contact on mentoring relationships. *Journal of Vocational Behavior, 50*, 460–481.

Evertsson, M. (2004). Formal on-the-job training: A gender-typed experience and wage-related advantage? *European Sociological Review, 20*(1), 79–94.

Fagenson, E. A. (1989). The mentor advantage: Perceived career/job experiences of protégés versus non-protégés. *Journal of Organizational Behavior, 10*(4), 309–320.

Feldman, D. C. (2001). Career coaching: What HR professionals and managers need to know. *People and Strategy, 24*(2), 26–35.

Fels, A. (2004, April). Do women lack ambition? *Harvard Business Review, 82*(4), 50–56, 58–60.

Fernandez, R. M., & Fernandez-Mateo, I. (2006). Network, race, and hiring. *American Sociological Review, 71*, 41–71.

Fiske, S. T., Cuddy, A. J. C., Glick, P., & Xu, J. (2002). A model of (often mixed) stereotype content: Competence and warmth respectively follow from perceived status and competition. *Journal of Personality and Social Psychology, 82*(6), 878–902.

Fournies, F. F. (1978). *Coaching for improved work performances.* Bridgewater, NJ: Van Nostran Reinhold.

Gibbons, A. (1993). White men can mentor: Help from the majority. *Science, 262*(5136), 1130–1134.

Gibson, D. E. (2003). Developing the professional self-concept: Role modelconstruals in early, middle, and late career stages. *Organization Science, 14*(5), 591–610.

Goldberg, C. B., Finkelstein, L. M., Perry, E. L., & Konrad, A. M. (2004). Job and industry fit: The effects of age and gender matches on career progress outcomes. *Journal of Organizational Behavior, 25*(7), 807–829.

Granovetter, M. (1973). The strength of weak ties. *American Journal of Sociology, 78,* 1360–1380.

Granovetter, M. (1995). *Getting a job: A study of contacts and careers* (2nd ed.). Chicago, IL: University of Chicago Press.

Greenwald, A. G., & Pettigrew, T. F. (2014). With malice toward none and charity for some. *American Psychologist, 69*(7), 669–684.

Hackman, J. R., & Wageman, R. (2005). A theory of team coaching. *Academy of Management Review, 30*(2), 269–287.

Hall, D. T., Otazo, K. L., & Hollenbeck, G. P. (1999). Beyond closed doors: What really happens in executive coaching. *Organizational Dynamics, 27*(3), 39–53.

Handel, M. J. (2003). Skills mismatch in the labor market. *Annual Review of Sociology, 29*(1), 135–165.

Harber, K. D. (1998). Feedback to minorities: Evidence of a positive bias. *Journal of Personality and Social Pscyhology, 74*(3), 622–628.

Haslam, S. A., Oakes, P., Reynolds, K. J., & Turner, J. C. (1999). Social identity salience and the emergence of stereotype consensus. *Personality and Social Psychology Bulletin, 25,* 809–818.

Hennig, M., & Jardim, A. (1977). *The managerial woman.* Garden City, NY: Anchor Press/Doubleday.

Hewlett, S. A. (2013). *Forget a mentor, find a sponsor: The new way to fast–track your career.* Boston, MA: Harvard Business Review Press.

Hewlett, S. A., Peraino, K., Sherbin, L., & Sumberg, K. (2011). The sponsor effect: Breaking through the last glass ceiling *Harvard Business Review.* Boston, MA.

Hill, L., & Kamprath, N. (1991). *Beyond the myth of the perfect mentor: Building a network of developmental relationships.*(Product #491096). Boston, MA: Harvard Business School Press.

Hogg, M. A. (2001). A social identity theory of leadership. *Personality and Social Psychology Review, 5*(3), 184–200.

Hogg, M. A., & Ridgeway, C. L. (2003). Social identity: Sociological and social psychological perspectives. *Social Psychology Quarterly, 66,* 97–100.

Hogg, M. A., & Terry, D. J. (2000). Social identity and self-categorization processes in organizational contexts. *Academy of Management Review, 25*(1), 121–140.

Hogg, M. A., & Turner, J. C. (1985). Interpersonal attraction, social identification, and psychological group function. *European Journal of Social Psychology, 15,* 51–66.

Humberd, B. K., & Rouse, E. D. (2015). Seeing you in me and me in you: Personal identification in the phases of mentoring relationships. *Academy of Management Review, 41*(3), 435–455.

Hunt, D. M., & Michael, C. (1983). Mentorship: A career training and development tool. *Academy of Management Review, 8*(3), 475–485.

Ianiro, P., Lehmann-Willenbrock, N., & Kauffeld, S. (2015). Coaches and Clients in action: A sequential analysis of interpersonal coach and client behavior. *Journal of Business and Psychology, 30*(3), 435–456.

Ibarra, H. (1992). Homophily and differential returns: Sex differences in network structures and access in an advertising firm. *Administrative Science Quarterly, 37*, 422–438.

Ibarra, H. (1993). Personal networks of women and minorities in management: A conceptual framework. *Academy of Management Review, 18*, 56–87.

Ibarra, H. (1995). Race, opportunity, and diversity of social circles in managerial networks. *Academy of Management Journal, 38*(3), 673–703.

Ibarra, H., Carter, N. M., & Silva, C. (2010). Why men still get more promotions than women. *Harvard Business Review, 88*(9), 80–85.

James, E. H. (2000). Race-related differences in promotions and support: Underlying effects of human and social capital. *Organization Science, 11*(5), 493–508.

Joecks, J., Pull, K., & Vetter, K. (2013). Gender diversity in the boardroom and firm performance: What exactly constitutes a "critical mass?" *Journal of Business Ethics, 118*, 61–72.

Kanter, R. M. (1977). *Men and women of the corporation.* New York, NY: Basic Books.

Kanter, R. M. (1979). Power failure in management circuits. *Harvard Business Review, 57*(4), 65–75.

Kanter, R. M. (1989). The new managerial work. *Harvard Business Review, 67*(6), 85–92.

Kram, K. E. (1985). *Mentoring at work: Developmental relationships in organizational life.* Glenview, IL: Scott Foresman.

Lin, N., Cook, K. S., & Burt, R. S. (Eds.). (2001). *Social capital: Theory and research.* New York, NY: Aldine de Gruyter.

Lunding, F. S., Clements, C. E., & Perkins, D. S. (1979). Everyone who makes it has a mentor. *Harvard Business Review, 56*, 89–101.

Marsden, P. V., & Gorman, E. H. (2001). Social networks, job changes, and recruitment. In I. Berg & A. L. Kalleberg (Eds.), *Sourcebook on labor markets: Evolving structures and processes* (pp. 467–502). New York, NY: Kluwer Academic/Plenum.

Marx, D. M., & Goff, P. A. (2005). Clearing the air: The effect of experimenter race on targets' test performance and subjective experience. *British Journal of Social Psychology, 44*, 645–657.

Marx, D. M., Ko, S. J., & Friedman, R. A. (2009). The "Obama effect": How a salient role model reduces race-based performance differences. *Journal of Experimental Social Psychology, 45*(4), 953–956.

McGuire, G. M. (2000). Gender, race, ethnicity, and networks: The factors affecting the status of employees' network members. *Work & Occupations, 27*, 500–523.

McGuire, G. M., & Reskin, B. (1993). Authority hierarchies at work: The impacts of race and sex. *Gender and Society, 7*(4), 487–506.

McPherson, J. M., Smith-Lovin, L., & Cook, J. M. (2001). Birds of a feather: Homophily in social networks. *Annual Review of Sociology, 27*, 415–444.

Moore, G. (1990). Structural determinants of men's and women's personal networks. *American Sociological Review, 55*, 726–735.

Mouw, T. (2003). Social capital and finding a job: Do contacts matter? *American Sociological Review, 68*, 868–898.

O'Brien, K. E., Biga, A., Kessler, S. R., & Allen, T. D. (2010). A meta-analytic investigation of gender differences in mentoring. *Journal of Management, 36*(2), 537–553.

O'Brien, L. T., Hitti, A., Shaffer, E., Van Camp, A. R., Henry, D., & Gilbert, P. N. (2016, October). Improving girls' sense of fit in science: Increasing the impact of role models. *Social Psychological and Personality Science Online First.* URL: journals.sagepub.com/doi/abs/10.1177/1948550616671997

Petersen, T., Saporta, I., & Seidel, M.-D. L. (2000). Offering a job: Meritocracy and social networks. *American Journal of Sociology, 106*(3), 763–816.

Podolny, J. M., & Baron, J. N. (1997). Resources and relationships: Social networks and mobility in the workplace. *American Sociological Review, 62*(5), 673–693.

Post, C., & Byron, K. (2015). Women on boards and firm financial performance: A meta-analysis. *Academy of Management Journal, 58*(5), 1546–1571.

Ragins, B. R. (1997). Diversified mentoring relationships in organizations: A power perspective. *Academy of Management Review, 22*(2), 482–521.

Ragins, B. R., & Cotton, J. L. (1999). Mentor functions and outcomes: A comparison of men and women in formal and informal mentoring relationships. *Journal of Applied Psychology, 84*(4), 529–550.

Ragins, B. R., & Scandura, T. A. (1994). Gender differences in expected outcomes of mentoring relationships. *The Academy of Management Journal, 37*(4), 957–971.

Ragins, B. R., & Sundstrom, E. (1989). Gender and power in organizations: A longitudinal perspective. *Psychological Bulletin, 105*(1), 51–88.

Reskin, B. F. (2000). The proximate causes of employment discrimination. *Contemporary Sociology, 29*(2), 319–328.

Reskin, B. F. (2003). Modeling ascriptive inequality: From motives to mechanisms. *American Sociological Review, 68*(1), 1–21.

Ridgeway, C. L. (2001). The emergence of status beliefs: From structural inequality to legitimizing ideology. In J. T. Jost & B. Major (Eds.), *The psychology of legitimacy* (pp. 257–277). Cambridge, England: Cambridge University Press.

Ridgeway, C. L., & Erickson, K. G. (2000). Creating and spreading status beliefs. *American Journal of Sociology, 106*(3), 579–615.

Ridgeway, C. L., Boyle, E. H., Kuipers, K. J., & Robinson, D. T. (1998). How do status beliefs develop? The role of resources and interactional experiences. *American Sociological Review, 63*(3), 331–350.

Rudman, L. A., & P. Glick. (2001). Prescriptive gender stereotypes and backlash toward agentic women. *Journal of Social Issues, 57*, 743–762.

Ryan, M. K., & Haslam, S. A. (2007). The glass cliff: Exploring the dynamics surrounding the appointment of women to precarious leadership positions. *Academy of Management Review, 32*(2), 549–572.

Scandura, T. A. (1992). Mentorship and career mobility: An empirical investigation. *Journal of Organizational Behavior, 13*(2), 169–174.

Schein, V. E. (1973). The relationship between sex role stereotypes and requisite management characteristics. *Journal of Applied Psychology, 57*(2), 95–100.

Seibert, S. E., Kraimer, M. L., & Liden, R. C. (2001). A social capital theory of career success. *Academy of Management Journal, 44*(2), 219–237.

Seidel, M.-D., Polzer, J. T., & Stewart, K. J. (2000). Friends in high places: The effects of social networks on discrimination in salary negotiations. *Administrative Science Quarterly, 45*(1), 1–24

Singh, V., Vinnicombe, S., & James, K. (2006). Constructing a professional identity: How young female managers use role models. *Women in Management Review, 21*(1), 67–81.

Smith, R. A. (2005). Do the determinants of promotion differ for white men versus women and minorities: An exploration of intersectionalism through sponsored and contest mobility processes. *American Behavioral Scientist, 48*(9), 1157–1181.

Stainback, K., & Tomaskovic-Devey, D. (2012). *Documenting desegregation: Racial and gender segregation in private-sector employment since the Civil Rights Act.* New York, NY: Russell Sage Foundation.

Steele, C. M., & Aronson, J. (1995). Stereotype threat and the intellectual test of performance of African-Americans. *Journal of Personality and Social Psychology, 69,* 797–811.

Stoloff, J. A., Glanville, J. L., & Bienenstock, E. J. (1999). Women's participation in the labor force: The role of social networks. *Social Networks, 21*(1), 91–108.

Sturm, S. (2001). Second generation employment discrimination: A structural approach. *Columbia Law Review, 458*(101).

Tajfel, H., & Turner, J. C. (1986). The social identity theory of intergroup behaviour. In S. Austin & W. Worchel (Ed.), *The social psychology of intergroup relations* (pp. 7–24). Chicago, IL: Nelson Hall.

Taylor, C. A., Lord, C. G., McIntyre, R. B., & Paulson, R. M. (2011). The Hillary Clinton effect: When the same role model inspires or fails to inspire improved performance under stereotype threat. *Group Processes & Intergroup Relations, 14*(4), 447–459.

Thach, L., & Heinselman, T. (1999). Executive coaching defined. *Training & Development, 53*(3), 34–39.

Thomas, D. A. (1989). Mentoring and irrationality: The role of racial taboos. *Human Resource Management, 28,* 279–290.

Thomas, D. A. (1990). The impact of race on managers' experiences of developmental relationships (mentoring and sponsorship): An intra-organizational study. *Journal of Organizational Behavior, 11*(6), 479–492.

Thomas, D. A. (2001, April). The truth about mentoring minorities: Race matters. *Harvard Business Review, 79*(4), 99–107.

Tilly, C. (1998). *Durable inequality.* Berkeley, CA: University of California Press.

Tomaskovic-Devey, D., & Skaggs, S. (2002). Sex segregation, labor process organization, and gender earnings inequality. *American Journal of Sociology, 108*(1), 102–128.

Trimble, L. B., & Kmec, J. A. (2011). The role of social networks in getting a job. *Sociology Compass, 5*(2), 165–178.

Turner, R. H. (1960). Sponsored and contest mobility and the school system. *American Sociological Review, 25*(6), 855–867.

Wellington, S., & Spence, B. (2001). *Be your own mentor: Strategies from top women on the secrets of success.* New York, NY: Random House.

Young, D. M., Rudman, L. A., Buettner, H., & McLean, M. C. (2013). The influence of female role models on women's implicit science cognitions. *Psychology of Women Quarterly, 37*(3), 283–292.

CHAPTER 3

LEADERSHIP DIVERSITY IN AFRICA AND THE AFRICAN DIASPORA

Clive M. Mukanzi
Jomo Kenyatta University of Agriculture and Technology, Kenya

Terri R. Lituchy
CETYS Universidad, Mexico

Betty Jane Punnett
University of the West Indies, Barbados

Bella L. Galperin
University of Tampa

Thomas A. Senaji
Kenya Methodist University, Kenya

Elham K. Metwally
American University in Cairo, Egypt

Lemayon Melyoki
University of Dar es Salaam Business School, Tanzania

Courtney A. Henderson
Berkeley College

Vincent Bagire
Makerere University Business School, Uganda

Cynthia A. Bulley
Central University, Ghana

Noble Osei-Bonsu
Central University, Ghana

ABSTRACT

The motivation for this chapter is to demonstrate how leadership is diverse in Africa and the African diaspora. The chapter summarizes the findings from the LEAD (Leadership Effectiveness in Africa and the Diaspora) research project. The chapter incorporates the findings of the LEAD research in Kenya, Uganda, Tanzania, Ghana, Egypt, the Caribbean, the United States, and Canada. This is made possible by an analysis of the results from Delphi Technique and focus groups discussion used in the LEAD project. Using these techniques, we have been able to develop a greater understanding of leadership diversity in Africa and the African diaspora. African countries are among the most ethnically, religiously, and culturally diverse in the world with many ethnic groups split into multiple states that are different in terms of language, culture, and ethnic composition. The study found that some aspects of leadership diversity are not included in the popular Western measures and concepts as found in the extant literature. For example is the case of the big men, Ubuntu, religion and spirituality. It is important to recognize that the LEAD results took place in selected African countries, but more countries have been included for future research. The chapter provides a broader understanding of how leadership is diverse in Africa and the African diaspora.

Africa is the fastest growing region of the world. A large number of companies from China, Japan, the United States, Britain, and India are investing in the continent (*The Economist*, 2011). The World Economic Forum report listed several African countries with the highest index in terms of ease of doing business in 2015–2016 (World Economic Forum, 2015). African countries are among the most ethnically and culturally diverse in the world with many ethnic groups split into multiple states (Robinson, 2014) that are different in terms of language and religion (e.g., Bodomo, Anderson, & Dzahene-Quarshie, 2009; Lupke, 2009; Phinney, 1996). Posner (2004) noted that African countries are ethnically diverse, and the ethnic heterogeneity and linguistic diversity can be linked to the way leadership is perceived in the continent. Africa has approximately 2,000 of the 6,000 languages of the world (Lupke, 2009). Many of the languages are spoken by millions of people making the continent the epicenter of linguistic and cultural diversity in the world. For example, Ghana has 85 ethnic communities and more than 87 languages (Agbedor, 1996; Bodomo, 1996, 1997; Dolphyne & Kropp-Dakubu, 1988; Gordon & Grimes, 2005), while Kenya has 42 ethnic communities with more than 70 languages (Ongechi, 2003).

The Caribbean on other hand is seen as a blend of African influences with European colonial practices (Punnett, Singh, & Williams, 1994). This has influenced the way leadership is perceived (Galperin, Lituchy, Acquaah, Bewaji, & Ford, 2014) in the region. Nettleford (1978) noted that as a result of the colonial influence, Caribbean natives remain pressured by institutions, mechanisms, processes, or psychological pressures to liberate themselves in the service of values and norms of an outside power and culture. In connection with what defines modern Caribbean leadership and culture, Thomas (1988) believed that the resulting interrelationship of class and ethnicity, sex, color, religion, rural/urban, and language divisions in the region made the social structure and culture even more difficult to analyze. The influence of the colonial cultures mixed with that of the imported cultures results in a culturally plural place.

Management scholars have called for more management research in underresearched countries (Lituchy, Ford, & Punnett, 2013; Punnett, Dick-Forde, & Robinson, 2006), other scholars have pointed to the fact that management knowledge is severely biased toward Western perspectives (Lituchy & Punnett, 2014; Bruton, 2010; Zoogah & Nkomo, 2013). Zhang et al. (2012) admit that almost all leadership studies and theories have been developed based on the Western context therefore making them very limited in their applicability to different economies and cultures. Lituchy, Ford, and Punnett (2013) and Lituchy, Punnett, and Puplampu (2013) as well as Zoogah and Nkomo (2013) have discussed the limited management research in Africa. Lituchy and Punnett (2014) acknowledge that little is known of Caribbean people's views on their own culture or of their beliefs regarding leadership. Only a few researchers have looked at the role and impact of culture on leadership diversity in Africa (Jackson, Amaeshi, & Yavuz, 2008; Wanasika, Howell, Littrell, & Dorfman, 2011) or at indigenous concepts such as Ubuntu (Brubaker, 2013; Mbigi, 2000), big man, (James, 2008) and Tree of Talking (Wambu, 2007). A paper by Lituchy, Punnett, Ford and Jonsson (2009) found that there is leadership diversity in countries across Africa, the Caribbean, and North America that is brought about by cultural differences that exist between developed (North America) and developing countries (Africa and the Caribbean). For example, Africans in the United States and Canada have different conceptions and perceptions of what leadership is compared with their counterparts in the Caribbean.

The United States has the largest African diaspora living in any single country of the world accounting for about 12% of the total American population (The World Factbook, 2012). Canada, on the other hand, has a relatively small African diaspora with around 800,000 people accounting for around 2.7% of the population (Statistics Canada, 2010). Researchers have suggested that the African diaspora can play an important role in influencing democratic leadership and social processes, such as religious networks and political institutions, in African countries (Mohan & Zack-Williams, 2002). Kaba (2011) has argued that African immigrants with relatively high incomes in developed countries have contributed to the increase in remittances to family members remaining in Africa. The establishment of the World Bank's African Diaspora Program has further facilitated the human and financial capital contributions of the African diaspora to the economic development of their home countries (Lituchy, Galperin, & Punnett, 2016). The program seeks to leverage diaspora skills for development in Africa by better utilizing the abilities and knowledge of millions of people of African descent.

Despite these developments, research on leadership diversity in Africa and the African diaspora are largely invisible in mainstream management literature (Lituchy, Punnett, Ford & Jonsson, 2009; Nkomo, 2011) with Western literature tending to ignore the dynamics that shape Africa's leadership differences (Mangaliso, 2001). A number of scholars in management are critical of the Western perspectives of understanding leadership in Africa and the African diaspora (Zoogah & Nkomo, 2013; Lituchy & Punnett, 2014). Others have acknowledged that leadership in divergent parts of the world should be looked at within specific cultural contexts (Tsui, 2004; Wanasika, Howell, Littrell & Dorfman, 2011). A host of these authors have advocated for an increase in research in the African continent (Lituchy, Punnett, Ford & Jonsson, 2009; Zoogah & Nkomo, 2013; Nkomo, 2011). Additionally, the management scholars have found that Western theories have failed to address the leadership diversity issues in Africa and the African diaspora (Lituchy, Punnett & Puplampu, 2013; Lituchy & Punnett, 2014).

We believe that the lack of knowledge about leadership diversity in non-Western countries and developing countries means that very little is known about leadership diversity from a more global perspective. We hope that this chapter will help scholars and practitioners to appreciate the leadership diversity in Africa and the African diaspora by highlighting differences among various groups and the effect on peoples and institutions. This book chapter is important as it incorporates the concepts of religion and spirituality, belief in ancestry, Ubuntu, and the Big Man theory when discussing leadership diversity in Africa as well as what is considered morality, wisdom, serving others, visionary, inspirational, caring, and accountable leadership for the African diaspora. In this chapter, we will review the current literature on leadership diversity experiences in multinational companies and the African culture so as to build a model of the diversity in leadership. We conclude by supporting the Delphi Technique and focus group discussion to understand leadership diversity in Africa and the African diaspora, and we also propose further areas of investigation.

WHY LEADERSHIP DIVERSITY IN AFRICA AND THE AFRICAN DIASPORA?

This chapter demonstrates how leadership is diverse in the context of Africa and the African diaspora (Canada, United States, and the Caribbean). This is significant from a theoretical perspective to understanding leadership differences in unfamiliar contexts. It is relevant to the management of enterprises, especially in the under-researched countries, groups, and regions of the world, which today are being considered to be the fast growing regions of the world. Management researchers have carried out cross-cultural studies and cross-national studies, and have come up with a basis of understanding national and cultural similarities and differences. For example, a study by Hofstede (1981) on culture demonstrated that different countries have different cultural values that impact the way leadership is viewed. Cross-country research (Hale & Fields, 2009; Lituchy & Punnett, 2014; Lituchy, Ford, & Punnett, 2013; Morrison, 2000) has highlighted some similarities and differences in perceptions of leaders in various countries, their characteristics, and the relationship between culture and leadership behaviors. GLOBE studies by Waldman et al. (2006) on cultural and leadership predictors of corporate social responsibility values of top management in 15 countries; Koopman, Den Hartog, and Konrad (2009) on national culture and leadership profiles in Europe in 21 European countries; and House, Hanges, Javidan, Dorfman, and Gupta's (2004) study involving 62 societies around the world provide important insight demonstrating diversity in leadership in various regions. Therefore those studies are relevant to this context. Such large studies remain relatively rare, and certain regions and groups of the world continue to be largely ignored. Similarly, the African diaspora has been essentially ignored in most studies. This is of concern because the perception of effective leadership differs among cultures (Den Hartog, House, Hanges, Ruiz-Quintanilla, & Dorfman, 1999). This gap must be addressed especially in those areas identified as under-researched. Addressing this gap, while important for academic knowledge, is particularly so from a practical perspective as managers and executives conducting business in different parts of the world can draw on the knowledge.

Leadership Diversity

Diversity is created by group members who on the basis of their different social identities categorize others as similar or dissimilar (Mazur, 2010). "A group is diverse if it is composed of individuals who differ on a characteristic on which they base their own social identity" (O'Reilly, Williams, & Barsade, 1998, p. 186). Leadership diversity is all about leaders having multiple, overlapping identities and using those identities to ensure that the community prospers. Leadership diversity alludes to the different forms, styles, and characterizations that exist among different groups. Diversity basically encompasses all the many characteristics and cultural norms and traits that differentiate one leader from the other. Certainly cultural characteristics might influence how a leader behaves. However, despite the various leadership theories, comparative research in these areas is not extensive (Morrison,

2000; Suutari, 2002) with a limited number of studies (Galperin et al., 2014; Graham, 1994; Parker, 1996) that focus on Africa and the African diaspora.

Leadership Diversity in Africa

One review of 17 papers dealing with management in Africa (Lituchy, Punnett, Ford, & Jonsson, 2009) found that three dealt with Africa in general, another with southern Africa, and the other with western Africa. Further, much of this management literature from Africa and African diaspora was conceptual rather than empirical. Empirical literature shows that there is diversity leadership in Africa. For example, James (2008) described the traditional concept of leadership as encompassing the "Big Man" who is all-powerful, fearsome, all-knowing, and an infallible multifaceted problem solver in Africa. The Big Man (always a male) is the head of the community and enjoys fanatical support from the community. He is also a political leader whose leadership is eternal. The leaders' main function is focused on representing the community to the outside, resolving disagreements, and providing protection to the community, and successful warrior and gains cattle (wealth) through raids, which later serve to benefit the community (Wandibba, 2004). The Big Man status rests on certain characteristics that distinguish him from his fellows: wealth, eloquence, generosity, physical fitness, bravery, and supernatural powers. Men are considered big men because they have certain personalities. They amass resources during their own lifetime and they did not inherit their wealth or position. The Big Man personality at the organization level helps in the development of careers, particularly at high managerial levels, which depend on accumulation of power as the vehicle for transforming individual interests into activities that influence other people.

Servant Leaders

Nelson (2003) described servant leaders as leaders with a focus on the good of their followers. Servant leader constructs are virtues, including a good moral quality, the general quality of goodness, and moral excellence. A servant leader serves diligently and selflessly, and always puts the needs of people first. While Ekundayo (2013) described a servant leader as one capable of showing clear sensibility and feelings to lead others in time of crisis. His influence is not necessarily exerted by the personal authority of the leader, but by being the servant of the community he leads (Smith, 2002) focused on spirituality, which is seen as eternal, and who acknowledges the importance of ancestors along with a connection to the ancestors' world, the land, and communalism. Smith concluded that decisions are holistic and collective in spiritual leadership, while Wellman, Perkins, and Wellman (2009) suggested that spirituality is the core of effective leadership in Africa, and it guides the way leaders behave and interact with others. Spirituality leadership includes three subcategories of caring for others in the society: transcendence and seeking goodness, being truthful, and forgiving others for their bad deeds.

Mangaliso (2001) considered Ubuntu leadership as demonstrating compassion, dignity, respect, and a humanistic concern for relationships. Mbigi and Maree (1995) described Ubuntu as a sense of brotherhood among marginalized groups combined with spiritualism. Blunt and Jones (1997) suggested that in Africa the effective leadership styles are more paternalistic than the effective leadership styles in the West, and that in Africa interpersonal relations are placed higher than individual achievement. Leaders bestow favor and expect to receive obeisance or deference. Consensus is highly valued and decision making within levels can therefore take a long time. Between levels (downwards) observance of hierarchy means that consensus can be achieved relatively quickly (Blunt & Jones, 1997). Hale (2004) thought that the transformational leadership model was not the most effective leadership model in the African perspective. He found West Africa high on hierarchy with leaders expected to be powerful and to make decisions. He proposed an effective leadership model for Africa as a blending of transformational leadership theory with servant leadership, the components of which include egalitarianism, moral integrity, empowering, empathy, and humility (Mittal & Dorfman, 2012). Walumbwa, Orwa, Wang, and Lawler (2005) compared the relationship of transformational leadership to organizational commitment and job satisfaction in the United States and Kenya. They identified African leadership as authoritarian due to high power distance and hypothesized that this may negate the positive impact of transformational leadership. They found that respondents from the United States rated transformational leadership and satisfaction higher than Kenyan respondents; however, they found that in both cultures the relationship between transformational leadership and commitment and satisfaction was positive.

Leadership Diversity in African Diaspora (Canada, United States)

The African diaspora is simply defined as "having African roots," (Ford & Miller, 2014, p. 270), and therefore inclusion of respondents of African descent from the United States and Canada is important in the understanding leadership diversity across national boundaries. Research suggests that cultural characteristics influence differences in leadership across cultures

(Aimar & Stough, 2007; Galperin, Lituchy, Acquaah, Bewaji & Ford 2014; Lanik, Thornton, & Hoskovcova, 2009). Furthermore, empirical literature in the field of cultural psychology suggests that African Americans have a different cultural identity than other ethnic groups, which influences the way they view what leadership is all about (Galperin et al., 2014). Zaff, Blount, Phillips, and Cohen (2002) found that African American students scored significantly higher on ethnic identity compared to Caucasian American students. In Pierce, Hudson, and Singleton's (2011) examination of the ethnic identities of various groups from the African diaspora, they found a high ethnic identity among all three African diaspora groups: (a) native born—African Americans born in the United States to parents born in the United States; (b) first generation—those born in the United States with at least one parent born outside the United States; and, (c) Black immigrants—those not born in the United States with parents not born in the United States.

Studies on leadership in Canada have only focused on a single culture at a time (e.g., Arnold & Loughlin, 2010; Block, 2003; St-Onge, Morin, Bellehumeur, & Dupuis, 2009). For example, Arnold and Loughlin's (2010) study on leadership (examining five provinces within the country) found that leaders were more likely to engage in supportive rather than developmental, individually considerate, and transformational leadership behavior. Block (2003) used a sample from a North American organization wherein she combined Western Canadian and American participants. Block (2003) found that employees who rated their supervisors high in transformational leadership were more likely to view their organizational culture in positive terms.

Leadership Diversity in the African Diaspora (Caribbean)

The Caribbean comprises 26 states with a population of about 41.6 million in 2010 (ILO, 2011; United Nations, 2010). The people of the Caribbean are largely of sub-Saharan African descent representing around 73% of the total population (Central Intelligence Agency, 2013). Descendants of African slaves brought to the Caribbean during the slave trade have lived in the Caribbean for generations, and the culture in the Commonwealth Caribbean is seen as a blend of African influences with European colonial practices (Punnett, Singh, & Williams, 1994; Holder, Knight, Punnet & Charrles, 2014). Thomas (1988) found that leadership in the Caribbean is influenced by the interrelationship of class, ethnicity, sex, color, religion, and language divisions. In most Caribbean countries, African descendants make up the majority of the population; however, some countries also have a large Indian descended population (notably Guyana, Trinidad, and Tobago) and there is a substantial number of individuals with a Chinese background in many islands, while European descendants represent smaller numbers (Central Intelligence Agency, 2013). Research in the Caribbean has mainly focused on the historic experiences of the African and Indian descendants and the racial divides in the region (Johnson, 1998) with little management research.

The Caribbean culture tends to be analyzed through the class structures that emerged after the gaining of independence. The result of the colonial and postcolonial periods was an enhanced class consciousness in the region. Bolland (2001) suggested that the resulting class structure had its roots in the late 19th century when the middle class was comprised of educated professionals whose roles were teachers, doctors, lawyers, and civil servants. Bolland asserted that during this period of change class consciousness, which coincided with racial-consciousness, manifested itself in various forms of class struggle (strikes/protests) resulting in the emergence of a broader middle class. The postcolonial class structure remains very complex (Thomas, 1988) in that the region's ruling class has found the ways and means of ensuring its continued influence thus inevitably continuing to complicate and affect the social relations and the structure of the Caribbean states. Thomas (1988) found that this influence reached as far as creating divisions within the working class along sexual, ethnic, and religious lines.

Some recent cultural research based on Hofstede's Value Survey concepts suggested that people in the English-speaking Caribbean are low on hierarchy/power distance, moderate on individualism, and high on uncertainty avoidance preferring certainty and avoiding risk (Punnett & Greenidge, 2009; Punnett et al., 2006). Nurse and Punnett (2002) also noted the importance of religion and spirituality in the Caribbean context. Punnett, Singh, and Williams (1994) argued that the Caribbean cultural profile reflected both African and European roots. This research found that respondents were high on both individualism and collectivism, which were measured separately, and were relatively high on thinking/controlling and relatively low on doing/action.

Method

This chapter summarizes the findings from the LEAD (Leadership Effectiveness in Africa and the Diaspora) research project. The chapter incorporates the findings of the LEAD research in Kenya, Uganda, Tanzania, Ghana, Nigeria, Egypt, the Caribbean, the USA and Canada. This is made possible by analysis of the results from Delphi Technique and focus groups used in the LEAD project. Using these techniques, we have been able to develop a greater understanding of leadership diversity in Africa and the African diaspora.

The key question for the LEAD research project is: How do cultural differences effect the perception of effective leadership for people in the Caribbean, United States, Canada, and Africa?

Delphi Technique

The LEAD project began with an emic approach involving the Delphi Technique (Linstone & Turoff, 1975). The emic approach is used to investigate how the local people think, perceive, and categorize the world around them and how they imagine and explain things around them (Kottak, 2006). The emic strives to understand the culture of people from a native's/local point of view (Ludwig, 1997). While the emic links cultural practices to external forces or factors such as economic and ecological conditions that may not be salient to the cultural practices of the locals (Harris, 1979). Why the Delphi Technique? This technique was important in the research because we wanted to find out how participants in Africa and the African diaspora understood the concept of leadership and to compare the leadership diversity that is being brought out. The Delphi Technique method for achieving convergence of opinion concerning real-world knowledge solicited from experts within certain topic areas. The Delphi Technique is designed as a group communication process that aims at conducting detailed examinations and discussions of a specific issue for the purpose of goal setting, policy investigation, or predicting the occurrence of future events (Ludwig, 1997; Turoff & Hiltz, 1996).

The Delphi Technique is a means and a method for consensus building by using a series of questionnaires to collect data from a panel of selected subjects and to analyze and provide feedback (Young & Jamieson, 2001). This provides the opportunity for individuals to revise their judgments on the basis of feedback. The participants in the Delphi Technique held various leadership positions in various organizations in five countries in Africa (Egypt, Ghana, Kenya, Nigeria, Uganda), three Caribbean countries (Barbados, Trinidad and Tobago, St. Vincent and the Grenadines), Canada and the United States. The leaders were identified from the following groups: (a) academics, (b) private sector, (c) public sector, and (d) other (religious leaders, leaders in non-governmental and charitable organizations, and community leaders). Following the Delphi Technique, data was also collected from people not considered as experts by use of focus group discussion. The purpose of the focus groups was to find out if responses to the same questions from nonleaders would support the Delphi Techniques' findings. The method is useful for exploring people's knowledge and experiences (Kitzinger, 1995) and can be used to examine what people think, how they think, and why they think that way. In round one, participants were asked a series of seven open-ended questions regarding culture, leadership, and motivation that included: (a) What three to five words best describe your ethnic or cultural background? (b) What words/terms would you use to describe an effective leader? (c) What does an effective leader do? (d) What motivates leaders to succeed? (e) What motivates people (other than leaders) to work hard? (f) Name three to five people, men or women, who you consider to be, or to have been, effective leaders (they can be local, national, or international) and why each is effective? and (g) How would you describe "your culture"? With round two, respondents were asked to rate the most common responses that emerged in round one on a 5-point Likert scale in terms of their importance. A total of 86 participants were involved in the Delphi process distributed across the countries as follows: Egypt (21), Ghana (12), Kenya (15), Nigeria (10), Uganda (16), Barbados (7), Trinidad and Tobago (3), and St. Vincent and the Grenadines (2). Knowledgeable people were identified from the following groups: (a) academics, (b) private sector, (c) public sector, and (d) other (religious leaders, leaders in non-governmental and charitable organizations, and community leaders). For example the Barbados, Trinidad and Tobago, and St. Vincent and the Grenadines's 12 respondents (7 males and 5 females) 4 of whom were born in Barbados, 3 in Trinidad and Tobago, 2 in St. Vincent and the Grenadines, with the remaining 3 born in Britain and St. Lucia but living in Barbados for 32, 44, and 46 years, respectively. Their ages ranged from 28 to 56 years with an average of 47.3 years. Of the 12 respondents, 8 had postgraduate degrees, 3 had undergraduate degrees, and 1 had a college diploma. All were in leadership positions in their respective organizations. For a more detailed overview of the Delphi process that was used in the LEAD project see Lituchy and Punnett (2014). For the results of the Delphi Technique used in the United States and Canada see Ford, Lituchy, Punnett, Puplampu, and Sejjaaka (2013) and Lituchy, Ford, and Punnett (2013). For a more detailed overview of the Delphi process used in the LEAD project see Lituchy and Punnett (2014).

Focus Groups

Focus group sessions utilized the same questions from the two rounds of the Delphi Technique. Several focus groups were conducted across the countries of interest to further explore and refine the Delphi findings. In focus group sessions, comfortable settings were arranged, refreshments provided, and participants were encouraged to sit around in a circle, which helped to establish the right atmosphere. The groups were from four to eight participants. The sessions took one to two hours but sometimes extend into a whole afternoon. The lead facilitator explained the aim of the focus groups and encouraged each participant to talk. Participants were assured that the results and their information would remain confidential. Each focus group participant was provided with paper and a pen for taking notes. The lead facilitator encouraged a discussion of each question and recorded the responses. The focus group participants were not leaders or leadership experts but lower level managers, supervisors, and employees in followership roles. The focus groups were conducted by two facilitators, and the discussion culminated with each participant being asked to rank the top five responses that emerged for each question. A total of 119 participants, all of whom were of African descent, took part in focus groups distributed across the countries as follows: United States, 29; Canada, 27; Ghana, 7; Kenya, 6; Nigeria, 20; Barbados, 15; and Trinidad and Tobago, 15 (Lituchy & Punnett, 2014).

Focus group discussions enhance the group process, which can help people to explore and clarify their views in ways that would be less easily accessible in a one-on-one interview. Focus group discussion is particularly appropriate when the interviewer has a series of open-ended questions and wishes to encourage research participants to explore the issues of importance to them (in their own vocabulary) generating their own questions and pursuing their own priorities. Similar to the Delphi Technique, focus groups prevent researchers from imposing their own ideas and ensure that the results reflect the thinking of the participants (Lituchy & Punnet, 2014). We believe that the two approaches provide a valuable design for a research project in under-researched areas as it is particularly important to avoid introducing a Western researcher's bias into these concepts, as cautioned by other researchers (Nkomo, 2011; Lituchy & Punnet, 2014).

RESULTS OF DELPHI AND FOCUS GROUPS

Leadership Diversity in Africa Results

The results from the Delphi Technique and focus groups conducted across multiple countries highlight some of the diversity within and between visible minority groups. The perceptions of the effectiveness and motivation of leaders across several countries in Africa (Ghana, Egypt, Kenya, Nigeria, and Uganda) and across the African diaspora in the Caribbean (Barbados and Trinidad and Tobago), the United States, and Canada were varied in some regards. The African paper by Senaji, Metwally, Sejjaaka, Puplampu, Michaud, and Adedoyin-Rasaq (2014) showed the result from five African countries (Ghana, Egypt, Kenya, Nigeria, and Uganda). The authors found that the majority of participants agreed that there is leadership diversity across the five countries. Fairness/impartiality, commitment/

dedication, honesty/trustworthiness, and being knowledgeable were descriptors of effective leadership. Focus group respondents from Ghana, Kenya, and Nigeria agreed that effective leaders were visionary, charismatic, intelligent, and innovative. Some interesting variance emerged in the data from the respondents in Africa on leadership effectiveness. For example, in Kenya respondents considered "assertiveness" as an attribute of effective leadership; whereas in Nigeria, respondents mentioned "modesty" or "unassuming" as an effective leader trait; and in Egypt respondents mentioned "enthusiastic." On effective leadership behavior, the respondents across all samples indicated effective leaders "lead by example," "inspire and influence others," "motivate and encourage others," and "delegate." Differences in responses by country that emerged were such that in Uganda, Kenya, and Nigeria respondents stressed "caring and empathetic" behaviors as being effective leader behaviors. Additionally, in Uganda and Ghana respondents indicated effective leaders should "innovate."

Leadership Diversity in African Diaspora Results (Canada, United States)

For the paper by Galperin, Lituchy, Acquaah, Bewaji, and Ford (2014), 10 focus groups were conducted in the United States and Canada. There was agreement that visionary, effective communicator, honest/trustworthy, and wise/knowledgeable described an effective leader. In terms of motivation, participants in both countries described the need to support, monetary rewards, and nonmonetary rewards as factors that motivated leaders to succeed. All participants saw security, potential rewards, and recognition as important motivators for people who were not in leadership positions. Differences in words and phrases used to describe an effective leader were such that in Canada respondents also mentioned decisiveness. In the United States, respondents additionally believed effective leaders should be empowering. Differences in responses to leadership behavior emerged in the United States and Canada. In the United States, respondents expected leaders to demonstrate competence, in Canada effective leaders were expected to build consensus.

Leadership Diversity in the African Diaspora Results (Caribbean)

In the Caribbean paper by Holder, Knight, Punnett, and Charles (2014), the authors presented the results of both the Delphi Technique and focus groups to examine diversity in leadership. The authors stated that in most

Caribbean countries the African diaspora made up a majority of the population. They found that effective leaders were charismatic, visionary, and results oriented. They motivated others, led by example, and developed visions and goals. The leaders believed that they were motivated by "making a difference." Nonleaders were perceived as being motivated primarily by financial rewards.

Discussion

The objective of this book chapter was to demonstrate leadership diversity in Africa and the African diaspora. The results of this emic research (Delph technique and focus group) show that there is leadership diversity across the different groups, countries, and cultures. Using an emic approach the respondents were allowed to define and describe the characteristics of effective leadership, what effective leaders do, and what motivates leaders to succeed. Overall, the findings suggest that there is leadership diversity regarding the way people from African and the African diaspora perceive effective leadership and what motivates leaders to succeed. Participants in the United States revealed that effective leaders are involved in executing plans, inspiring others to take action, leading by example, mentoring, and grooming others to lead; while the Canadian participants revealed that effective leaders focus on encouraging others, developing vision, goals, objectives and planning ahead, and living up to demands of their followers. Therefore, one can relate these findings to the Hierarchical Taxonomy of Leadership Behavior (Yukl, Gordon, & Taber, 2002; Yukl, 2012), which categorizes leader behavior in three groupings: task behavior, relations behavior, and change behavior.

To show that leadership diversity was expressed in leaders' behavior in the United States, our findings suggest that effective leaders engaged in a wide range of relations behavior including inspiring others to take action, leading by example, motivating, and listening. Nevertheless executing a plan, which represents task behavior in the taxonomy, received the highest average ranking. In the Canadian sample, the response "encourages," which falls under relations behavior in the taxonomy, received the highest ranking. Other relations behaviors in our sample included: motivator, communicates, and delegates responsibilities. Task behaviors in our sample included: setting a vision, lives up to demands takes control, and adaptively executes. Finally, the response "leads" may include both task and relations behaviors. Interestingly, different aspects of relations and task behaviors were represented in our United States and Canadian samples.

In terms of leadership diversity qualities, United States participants suggested that effective leaders exhibited qualities including being a visionary, inspirational, caring and showing unwavering morals and ethics, as well as being selfless, hardworking, and accountable. Interestingly, the three most important characteristics (charisma, wise/knowledgeable, and humility) of effective leaders in the United States were not mentioned by the Canadian sample. Canadian participants stated that effective leaders exhibited unwavering morals and ethics and believed in a cause, which were not mentioned as part of the most important characteristics of a leader (inspirational, wise/knowledgeable, and motivated) in an earlier question. These findings reveal that the ideal leadership characteristics preferred by the African diaspora (United States and Canada) for effective leaders are different from the leadership qualities they identify with and the attributes they assign to effective leaders. Moreover, the list of effective leaders and the reasons provided for their effectiveness clearly show that the African diaspora (United States and Canada) considers leaders who are visionaries, strong, and decisive, as well as caring, selfless, and ethical.

The participants of the African diaspora (Caribbean) identified effective leaders as charismatic, visionary, and results oriented. This is quite different in comparison to respondents from Africa, the United States, and Canada. Therefore, it seems clear that the idea of charisma, inspiration, and vision are seen as important in a good leader and along with this so are good management abilities such as goal orientation, ability to create a team, competence, and communication. These are all words that are reflective of current Western thinking on leadership, where transformational leadership has come to be thought of as effective leadership. These characteristics are similar to those that would flow from Western definitions of leadership; thus, we suggest that these characteristics may be seen as effective across different cultures similarly (House et al., 2004), and results suggest that charismatic leadership, including visionary, performance oriented, and integrity were preferred in all countries. There are other words or phrases in our findings that have different implications; for example, phrases like wise, moral, serving others, mentorship, and compassion. The second set of characteristics might be interpreted in overall terms as servant leadership, leadership incorporating morality, wisdom, serving others, and compassion. Dennis and Bocarnea (2005) described Servant Leaders as leaders with a focus on the good of their followers. Servant Leader constructs were virtues, including a good moral quality, the general quality of goodness, and moral excellence. The Delphi results also suggested wise, moral, and servanthood as components of effective leaders of the Caribbean group. These attributes are all somewhat different from what we might expect from Western theories.

Leadership diversity in the Caribbean is also expressed in what effective leaders do. Here responses included motivating and inspiring others, leading by example, developing a vision and goals, and attracting people. This was quite different from the Africa result. The Delphi responses and those from the focus group were in agreement on the main ideas. These ideas were also consistent with Western concepts of what leaders do and again support the findings of House et al. (2004) that certain ideals are universal. These support the characteristics that leaders in the Caribbean should exhibit to be effective. Leaders appear to see their motivation as most importantly coming from an "other" orientation, which would support the concept of servant leadership seen in the responses to what describes an effective leader. Interestingly, respondents from the first Delphi round in the Caribbean mentioned self-fulfillment and financial security only twice compared to five times on the desire to help others. A desire to help others was the favored answer for Delphi respondents, while in the focus groups self-interest was indicated as more important to leaders; specifically, self-fulfillment was indicated in the Barbados and financial rewards were indicated in Trinidad and Tobago. This suggests that the experts, who were in fact leaders in their fields, see themselves quite differently from those who are not in leadership positions. This difference in perceptions is particularly interesting because the leaders see themselves as "other" oriented, while they are perceived by nonleaders as being self-oriented.

We examined leadership diversity in Africa by carrying out LEAD research in Kenya, Uganda, Tanzania, Ghana, Nigeria, and Egypt and looked at characteristics pertaining to effective leadership, culture, and motivation in order to expand the literature on the personal characteristics, behaviors, and motivations of effective leaders that had been largely based on Western cultures, beliefs, and values (Steers, Sanchez-Runde, & Nardon, 2010). Overall, the findings suggested that factors that motivate leaders to work hard (extrinsic factors such as money and intrinsic factors such as need to succeed) can be applied in African countries. Further, both leaders and nonleaders placed importance on both extrinsic and intrinsic motivators, which has important implications for policy around the compensation of leaders in Africa. Of particular interest were notions of what motivates leaders (involvement with people, respect of subordinates, involvement with society, etc.) and what constitutes engagement of the human spirit in the work place (May, Gilson, & Harter, 2004).

In the Africa study, it was suggested that effective leaders motivate people, are involved in activities of society, and show vigor, passion, and dedication in all issues around them. This confirms Puplampu's (2010) notion of leadership as a process of engagement. There has been much scholarly writing about the limitations and deficit of leadership in Africa (Agulanna, 2006). It is therefore interesting to note that issues around justice, helping others, and service are considered important drivers for leaders' motivations. Therefore, one may suggest that where leaders engage with the aspirations of the community, they find a greater synchronization or mutuality of purpose, which may prove a powerful tool for change. We also found that participant perceptions of effective leaders included focus on maintaining discipline, giving hope/inspiration, setting goals, and delegating to others.

Implications for Research

The LEAD research study increased our knowledge and understanding of leadership diversity in Africa, the Caribbean, the United States, and Canada. It informed us about the perceptions people have on effective leadership and what motivates leaders to behave or succeed. Our unique attention to Africa and the African diaspora makes a valuable contribution to international management and cross-cultural literatures, which has been criticized for putting a lot of emphasis on Western theories. Our study provides a greater understanding of the complex and multidimensional approach to leadership and motivation among Africans in Africa and the African diaspora in the Caribbean, the United States, and Canada. Moreover, our study contributes to a better understanding of leadership theories in a cross-cultural context. For example, according to implicit leadership theory (ILT; Epitropaki & Martin, 2004) people's beliefs, assumptions, and convictions regarding attributes and behaviors of leaders comprise their ILT, and these persons' ILTs, in turn, influence the values they attribute to leadership and the values they place on selected leader behaviors (House, Hanges, Javidan, Dorfman, & Gupta, 2004). From the findings, we acknowledge that personal characteristics such as charisma, influence, and empowerment fell under the dynamism category. Thus, this finding suggests that a leader who develops strong interpersonal relationships is important (Newenham-Kahindi, 2009). The most important characteristics that were used to describe an effective leader by the participants in Africa and the African diaspora were charismatic, visionary, inspirational, wise/knowledgeable, honest and trustworthy, and humble, which are related to the same construct of transformational leadership (Avolio & Bass, 1988).

This paper also contributes to our understanding of what motivates leaders to succeed. The LEAD results seem to suggest that leaders largely ascribe to intrinsic motivation and self-determination motivation theory (Ryan & Deci, 2000). That is motivation that is driven by an interest or enjoyment in the task itself and which exists within the individual rather than relying on external pressures or a desire for reward. Need theories of motivation (cf. Maslow, 1943; McClelland, 1961) explain what drives behavior based on what we observe day to day in many leaders' behaviors. In line with Maslow's need hierarchy theory, participants from the Caribbean, the United States, and Canada stated that leaders were motivated to succeed by lower-level needs such as safety, as well as by higher-level needs such as esteem; while participants from Africa suggested that leaders were motivated by the extrinsic rewards of money and financial gain, which possibly helped to satisfy some leaders' basic physiological and safety needs (Maslow, 1943). We believe the intrinsic and self-determination motivation theories offer promise for further examining the findings related to motivation, which may not have been so prominent in other studies of leadership.

The findings also highlight the diversity among the people in Africa and the African diaspora in terms of what motivates leaders to succeed. Although participants described support, monetary rewards, and nonmonetary rewards as factors that motivated leaders to succeed, the United States's participants placed more emphasis on support and nonmonetary rewards, with the top three as desire for the best, supporting others, and passion for people and country. Canadian participants emphasized task completion and monetary rewards with the most important being desire to complete a task, empathy, and monetary or financial compensation. In the Caribbean, leaders were motivated by making a difference, and nonleaders were motivated primarily by financial rewards. In Africa, leaders were motivated by the need to achieve, serve others, and get recognition.

The findings offer some practical implications for leadership research into Africa and the African diaspora. Our results underline the importance of understanding leadership diversity within organizations. Managerial processes should be sensitive to normative differences that may exist within Africa and the African diaspora. While similarities were found between the perceptions of effective leadership and motivation in Africa and the African diaspora, differences also emerged between Africa and the African diaspora, pointing to the importance of cross-cultural differences between the Africa countries, the Caribbean, the United States, and Canada. Our findings can help companies better manage diversity within their organizations. Managers will be more equipped to effectively lead and motivate their diverse employees. This study contributes improved approaches toward development of leaders in Africa and the African diaspora by informing the content and philosophy of such development programs. It also lends a dialogue on how effective leaders behave and how such practices may be promoted.

Although there are some universal characteristics about leadership across cultures, transformational leadership characteristics—such as inspirational, visionary, charismatic, and motivational—were found to be important to Africa and the African diaspora. There was also a focus on characteristics based on the vestiges of the African cultural value system, such as spirituality or godliness along with collectivist and autocratic characteristics. Some phronetic leaders from the African diaspora may use their knowledge and cultural ties to Africa to help in better understanding a culturally distinct perspective of leadership and motivation in the African diaspora and Africa.

The findings also support the importance for practitioners to better understand the diversity within their organizations and their countries, and the role of national culture in determining what motivates employees and determines perceptions of what behaviors constitute effective leader behaviors. Finally, the empirical findings reported in the special issue papers could potentially translate into better and more realistic leader development training programs and HR systems for managing employees in the countries studied by informing the content and philosophy of such programs.

Turning our attention to the extant research specifically focused on sub-Saharan Africa, researchers have shown that in southern and eastern Africa there is a prevalence of the Ubuntu philosophy, which is a humanistic approach to African management with an emphasis on respect, human dignity, compassion, relationship building, personal interaction, and mutual respect (Wanasika, Howell, Littrell, & Dorfman, 2011). For example, Newenham-Kahindi (2009) found that several South African multinational corporations exhibited cross-cultural human resource management practices that incorporated humanistic traditions. Ncube's (2010) illustration of the Ubuntu leadership philosophy enumerates six steps to this philosophy, which are similar to some of the finding of the LEAD research in Africa:

1. Setting the example and modeling the way
2. Inspiring a shared vision among followers
3. Searching for opportunities to initiate change through people and the use of consensus decision making
4. Building relationships with others that foster interconnectedness and interdependency
5. Having a collectivist mentality that encourages teamwork and a noncompetitive environment
6. Cultivating innovation and empowering others through continuous development of human potential, mentoring, and building relationships

The Ubuntu leadership philosophy shows how Ubuntu can be applied practically as a leadership model as demonstrated by the data from the LEAD project results.

Limitations and Future Research Direction

There are a number of limitations that came from Africa; for example, in Kenya male participants dominated the second Delphi round and therefore appropriate levels of gender representation and balance need to be considered in future studies. Also, this research used a rather small sample size for the Delphi process. We recognize that with the continent's huge population and diverse in-country demographics, capturing the African reality requires sampling decisions that cover both the depth and representation of countries within Africa. Larger samples from many more countries are needed in order to generate more robust results. The research was conducted in English because all countries included in the study were English speaking, despite indigenous African languages such as Kikuyu and Luo for Kenya, Yoruba and Igbo for Nigeria, Akan and Ewe for Ghana, and Ganda and Muganda for Uganda. It is possible that the research may have missed nuances peculiar to those languages. The research did not use samples from French- and Portuguese-speaking Africa.

The United States and Canadian study also had limitations. First, while focus groups were conducted in various locations across the United States and Canada in order to achieve a representative sample of the African diaspora in the two countries, future studies should conduct focus groups in areas where more comparisons can be drawn. For example, as the focus groups were conducted in both English-speaking and French-speaking Canada, it would be interesting to conduct focus groups in the English- and French-speaking United States. The state of Louisiana has strong historical ties with France and would allow such comparisons. While all other U.S. states' legal systems are based on common law, Louisiana's legal system is based on the Napoleonic civil code. In addition, the state has a large concentration of people from one region of Africa that strongly shaped the Louisiana Creole culture (Hall, 1992). Due to historical and administrative ties between France and Senegal, two-thirds of the slaves brought to Louisiana by the French slave trade came from Senegambia, which is the region between the Senegal and Gambia rivers. Participants in the United States and Canadian samples possessed a minimum of a high school diploma or were pursuing undergraduate or post-graduate degrees.

The Caribbean group had small sample sizes that were not randomly selected; rather, they were selected because of known characteristics and often because the respondents were known to the researchers. In addition, the Trinidad and Tobago group consisted entirely of women. This meant that there were likely biases in the responses reported. The result was also obtained from a limited number of Caribbean countries, and we would like to expand this sample to obtain a more truly Caribbean picture.

In conclusion, we note that the findings add to the call for contextualized research. We conclude that management and organizational research in Africa and the African diaspora requires significant use of methods that allow the voice of those sampled to be heard. Future research should examine the development of mass surveys that use the findings (such as those reported here) to construct survey items and interview questions. Such surveys need to answer specific questions such as what corporate leaders in Africa and the African diaspora actually do; how followers and interest groups perceive leader effectiveness; how leader behaviors influence employee motivation; and how leader/follower behaviors and aspirations construct and reconstruct leader behaviors in an iterative and social constructionist way. Future research should include participants from a broader demographic spectrum, including more women and greater representation from various African countries and the diaspora group. Future research should increase the number of focus groups in each city as well as increase the number of cities in each country to investigate possible differences within the countries. In addition, future research should empirically examine similarities and differences between Africa and the African diaspora.

REFERENCES

Agbedor, P. K. (1996) Educational language planning for development in Ghana: Problems and prospects. *Legon Journal of the Humanities, 9*, 25–56.

Agulanna, C. (2006). Democracy and the crisis of leadership in Africa. *The Journal of Social Political and Economic Studies, 31*(3), 255–264.

Aimar, C., & Stough, S. (2007). Leadership: Does culture matter? Comparative practices between Argentina and United States of America. *Academy of Educational Leadership Journal, 11*(3), 9–43.

Arnold, K. A., & Loughlin, C. (2010). Individually considerate transformational leadership behavior and self-sacrifice. *Leadership & Organization Development Journal, 31*, 670–686.

Avolio, B. A., & Bass, B. M. (1988). Transformational leadership, charisma and beyond. In J. G. Hunt, B. R. Balaga, H. P. Bachler, & C. Schriesheim (Eds.), *Emerging leadership vista* (pp. 29–50). Emsford, NY: Pergamon Press.

Block, L. (2003). The leadership-culture connection: An exploratory investigation. *Leadership & Organization Development Journal, 24*, 318–334.

Blunt, P., & Jones, M.L. (1992). *Managing organizations in Africa*. Berlin, Germany: Walter De Gruyter.

Bodomo, A. B. (1996). On language and development in sub-Saharan Africa: The case of Ghana. *Nordic Journal of African Studies, 5*(2), 31–53.

Bodomo, A. B. (1997). Linguistics, education, and politics: An interplay on Ghanaian languages. In R. Herbert (Ed.), *African linguistics at the crossroads: Papers from Kwaluseni* (pp. 469–484). Koln, Germany: Rudiger Koppe Verlag.

Bodomo, A., B., Anderson, J., & Dzahene-Quarshie, J. (2009). A Kente of many colors: Multilingualism and the complex ecology of language shift in Ghana. *Sociolinguistic Studies, 3*(3), 357–379.

Bolland, O. N. (2001). The *politics of labor in the British Caribbean: The social of authoritarianism and democracy in the Labor movement*. Kingston, Jamaica: Ian Randle.

Brubaker, T. A. (2013). Servant leadership, ubuntu, and leader effectiveness in Rwanda. *Emerging Leadership Journeys, 6*(1), 95–131.

Bruton, G. D. (2010). Business and the world's poorest billion: The need for an expanded examination by management scholars. *Academy of Management Perspectives, 24*(3), 6– 10.

Central Intelligence Agency. (2013). *The world factbook.* Retrieved October 30, 2016, from https://www.cia.gov/library/publications/resources/the-world-factbook/index.html

Den Hartog, D. N., House, R. J., Hanges, P. J., Ruiz-Quintanilla, S. A., & Dorfman, P.W. (1999). Culture specific and cross culturally generalizable implicit leadership theories: Are attributes of charismatic/transformational leadership universally endorsed? *The Leadership Quarterly, 10*(2), 219–256.

Dennis, R. S., & Bocarnea, M. (2005). Development of the servant leadership assessment instrument. *Leadership and Organizational Development Journal, 26*(8), 600–615.

Dolphyne, F. A., & Kropp-Dakubu, M. E. (1988). The volta-comoe languages. In M. E. Kropp-Dakubu (Ed.), *The languages of Ghana.* London, England: KPI.

Ekundayo, J. M. (2013). *Out of Africa: Fashola—Reinventing servant leadership to engender Nigeria's transformation.* Bloomington, IN: AuthorHouse.

Epitropaki, O., & Martin, R. (2004). Implicit leadership theories in applied settings: Factor structure, generalizability, and stability overtime. *Journal of Applied Psychology, 89*(2), 293–310.

Ford, D., Lituchy, T., Punnett, B. J., Puplampu, B., & Sejjaaka, S. (2013). Leadership in Africa and the diaspora. In T. Lituchy, B. J. Punnett, & B. Puplampu (Eds.), *Management in Africa: Macro and micro perspectives* (pp. 249–269). New York, NY: Routledge.

Ford, D. L., & Miller, C. D. (2014). Leadership and motivation in Africa and the African diaspora (LEAD): Summary and epilogue. *Canadian Journal of Administrative Sciences, 31*(4), 270–279.

Galperin, B., Lituchy, T., Acquaah, M., Bewaji, T., & Ford, D. (2014). Leadership and motivation in the African diaspora: The United States and Canada. *Canadian Journal of Administrative Sciences, 31*(4). doi:10.1002/CJAS.1296

Gordon, R. G, Jr., & Grimes, B. F. (2005). *Ethnologue: Languages of the world* (15th ed.). Dallas, TX: SIL International.

Graham, S. (1994). Motivations in African America. *Review of Educational Research, 64,* 55–117.

Hale, J. R. (2004, August). A contextualized model for cross-cultural leadership in West Africa. *Proceedings of the Servant Leadership Research Round*table. Retrieved from https://www.regent.edu/acad/global/publications/sl_proceedings/2004/hale_contextualized_model.pdf

Hale, J. R., & Fields, D. L. (2009). Exploring servant leadership across cultures: A study of followers in Ghana and the U.S.A. *Leadership, 3*(4), 397–416.

Hall, G. M. (1992). *Africans in colonial Louisiana: The development of Afro-Creole culture in the eighteenth century.* Baton Rouge: Louisiana State University.

Harris, M. (1979). *Cultural materialism.* New York, NY: Random House.

Hofstede, G. (1981). *Cultures consequences.* Thousand Oaks, CA: SAGE.

Holder, K., Knight, N., Punnet, B. J., & Charrles, R. (2014). Culture, leadership and motivation in two commonwealth Caribbean countries: One look at the African diaspora. *Canadian Journal of Administrative Sciences, 31,* 245–256

House, R., Hanges, P., Javidan, M., Dorfman, P., & Gupta, V. (2004). *Culture, leadership and organizations: The GLOBE study of 62 societies*. Thousand Oaks, CA: SAGE.

ILO Decent Work Team. (2011). *Caribbean countries and territories*. Retrieved from http://ilocarib.org.tt/index.php?option=com_content&view=article&id=1146&itemi.

Jackson, T., Amaeshi, K., & Yavuz, S. (2008). Untangling African Indigenous management: Multiple influences on the success of SMES in Kenya. *Journal of World Business, 43*(4), 400–416.

James, R. (2008). Leadership development inside-out in Africa. *Non Profit Management & Leadership, 18*(3), 359–375.

Johnson, H. (1998). White women and a West India fortune: Gender and wealth doing slavery. In H. Johnson & K. Watson (Eds.), *The white minority in the Caribbean* (pp. 1–16). Chicago, IL: James Currey.

Kaba, J. A. (2011). The status of Africa's emigration brain drain in the 21st century. *Western Journal of Black Studies, 35*, 187–207.

Kitzinger, J. (1995). Qualitative research: Introducing focus groups. *BMJ: British Medical Journal, 311*(7000), 299.

Koopman, P. L., Den Hartog, D. N., & Konrad, E. (1999). National culture and leadership profiles in Europe: Some results from the GLOBE study. *European Journal of Work and Organizational Psychology, 8*, 503–520.

Kottak, C. (2006). *Mirror for humanity*. New York, NY: McGraw Hill.

Lanik, M., Thornton, G., & Hoskovcova, S. (2009). A flat world? A comparative study of achievement motivation in the Czech Republic and the United States. *Studia Psychologica, 51*, 69–84.

Linstone, H., & Turoff, M. (1975). *The Delphi method: Techniques and applications*. Reading, MA: Addison-Wesley.

Lituchy, T. R., Ford, D., & Punnett, B. J. (2013). Leadership in Uganda, Barbados, Canada and the U.S.A: Exploratory perspectives. *African Journal of Economic and Management Studies, 4*(2), 201–222.

Lituchy T. R., & Punnett, B. J. (2014). Leadership effectiveness and motivation in Africa and the African diaspora (LEAD): An introduction. *Canadian Journal of Administrative Sciences, 31*, 221–227.

Lituchy, T. R., Punnett, B. J., Ford, D. L., & Jonsson. C. (2009, June). *Leadership effectiveness in Africa and the diaspora*. Eastern Academy of Management International Proceedings. Rio, Brazil.

Lituchy, T. R., Punnett, B. J., & Puplumpu, B. (2013). Introduction. In T. R. Lituchy, B. J. Punnett, & B. B. Puplampu (Eds.), *Management in Africa: Macro and micro perspectives* (pp. 1–8). London, England: Routledge.

Ludwig, B. (1997). Predicting the future: Have you considered using the Delphi methodology? *Journal of Extension, 35*(5), 1–4.

Lüpke, F. (2009). At the margin-African endangered languages in the context of global endangerment discourses. *African Research & Documentation*, (109), 15.

Mangaliso, M. P. (2001). Building competitive advantage from ubuntu: Management lessons from South Africa. *Academy of Management Executive, 15*(3), 23–32.

Maslow, A. H. (1943). A theory of human motivation. *Psychological Review, 50*, 370–396.

May, D., Gilson, R., & Harter, L. (2004). The psychological conditions of meaningfulness, safety and availability and the engagement of the human spirit at work. *Journal of Occupational and Organizational Psychology, 77*(1), 11–37.

Mazur, B. (2010). Cultural diversity in organizational theory and practice. *Journal of Intercultural Management, 2*(2), 5–15.

Mbigi, L. (2000). *In search of the African business renaissance: An African cultural perspective.* Randburg, South Africa: Knowledge Resources.

Mbigi, L., & Maree, J. (1995). *Ubuntu: The spirit of African transformation management.* Randburg, South Africa: Knowledge Resources.

McClelland, D. C. (1961). *The achieving society.* New York, NY: Free Press.

Mittal, R., & Dorfman, P. W. (2012). Servant leadership across cultures. *Journal of World Business, 47*(4), 555–570.

Mohan, G., & Zack-Williams, A. B. (2002). Globalization from below: Conceptualizing the role of the African diasporas in Africa's development. *Review of African Political Economy, 29*(92), 211–236.

Morrison, A. J. (2000). Developing a global leadership model. *Human Resource Management, 39*(2), 117–32.

Ncube, L. (2010). Ubuntu: A transformative leadership philosophy. *Journal of Leadership Studies, 4*(3), 77–82.

Nelson, L. (2003). *An exploratory study of the application and acceptance of servant leadership theory among black leaders in South Africa.* Retrieved from https://www.regent.edu/acad/global/publications/dissertations/nelson2003.cfm

Nettleford, R.M. (1978). *Caribbean Cultural identity: Caribbean cultural identity: The case of Jamaica.* Kingston, Jamaica: Herald Limited.

Newenham-Kahindi, A. (2009). The transfer of ubuntu and indaba business models abroad: A case of South African multinational banks and telecommunication services in Tanzania. *International Journal of Cross Cultural Management, 9*(1), 87–108.

Nkomo, S. M. (2011). A postcolonial and anti-colonial reading of 'African' leadership and management in organization studies: Tensions, contradictions and possibilities. *Organization, 18*(3), 365–386.

Nurse, L., & Punnett, B. J. (2002). A review of management research in the English speaking Caribbean. *Journal of Eastern Caribbean Studies, 27*(2), 1–37.

Ogechi, N. O. (2003). On language rights in Kenya. *Nordic Journal of African Studies, 12*(3), 277–295.

O'Reilly, C.A., III, Williams, K.Y., & Barsade, W. (1998). Group demography and innovation: Does diversity help? In D. Gruenfeld (Ed.), *Research on managing groups and teams* (pp. 183–207). St. Louis, MO: Elsevier.

Parker, P. S. (1996). Gender, culture, leadership: Toward a culturally distinct model of African American women executives' leadership strategies. *The Leadership Quarterly, 7*, 189–214.

Phinney, J. S. (1996). Understanding ethnic diversity. *The American Behavioral Scientist, 40*, 143–152.

Pierce, W. J., Hudson, R. E., & Singleton, S. M. (2011). Ethnic identity and propensity for practice among African descended MSW students. *Journal of Social Work Education, 47*, 403–421.

Posner, D. N. (2004). Measuring ethnic fractionalization in Africa. *American Journal of Political Science,* (48), 4

Punnett, B. J., Dick-Forde, E., & Robinson, J. (2006). Culture and management in the English speaking Caribbean. *Journal of Eastern Caribbean Studies, 31*(2), 44–57.

Punnett, B. J., & Greenidge, D. (2009). Culture, myth and leadership in the Caribbean. In E. H. Kessler & D. J. Wong-Mingji (Eds.), *Cultural mythology and global leadership* (pp. 65–78). Northhampton, MA: Edward Elgar.

Punnett, B. J., Singh, J. B., & Williams, G. (1994). The relative influence of economic development and anglo heritage on expressed values: Empirical evidence from a Caribbean country. *International Journal of Intercultural Relations, 18*(1), 99–115.

Puplampu, B. B. (2010). Leadership as engagement, leadership as systems development: A contextualized Ghanaian study. *European Business Review, 22*(6), 624–651.

Robinson, A. L. (2014). National versus ethnic identification in Africa: Modernization, colonial legacy, and the origins of territorial nationalism. *World Politics, 66*(4), 709–746.

Ryan, R., & Deci, E. (2000). Self-determination theory and the facilitation of intrinsic motivation, social development, and well-being. *American Psychologist, 55*(1), 68–78.

Senaji, T. A., Metwally, E., Sejjaaka, S., Puplampu, B. B., Michaud, J., & Adedoyin Rasaq, H. (2014). LEAD-leadership effectiveness, motivation, and culture in Africa: Lessons from Egypt, Ghana, Kenya, Nigeria, and Uganda. *Canadian Journal of Administrative Sciences, 31*(4), 228–244.

Smith, B. (2002). Worldview and culture: Leadership in sub-Saharan Africa. *New England Journal of Public Policy, 19*(1), 243–274.

Statistics Canada. (2010). *Visible minority population, by province and territory (2006 census).* Retrieved from http://www.statcan.gc.ca/tables-tableaux/sum-som/l01/cst01/demo52a-eng.htm

Steers, R. M., Sanchez-Runde, C. J., & Nardon, L. (2010). *Management across cultures: Challenges and strategies.* London, England: Cambridge University Press.

St-Onge, S., Morin, D., Bellehumeur, M., & Dupuis, F. (2009). Managers' motivation to evaluate subordinate performance. *Qualitative Research in Organizations and Management: An International Journal, 4,* 273–293.

Suutari, V. (2002). Global leader development: An emerging research agenda. *Career Development International, 7*(4), 218–233.

The Economist. (2011, December 3). *Africa rising.* Retrieved October 30, 2016, from http://www.economist.com/node/21541015

The World Factbook. (2012). *The United States.* Retrieved September 19, 2012, from https://www.cia.gov/library/publications/The-World-Factbook/Index.Html

Thomas, C. Y. (1988). *The poor and the powerless: Economic policy and change in the Caribbean.* London, England: Latin America Bureau (Research and Action) Limited.

Tsui, A. (2004). Contributing to global management knowledge: A case for high quality indigenous research. *Asia Pacific Journal of Management, 21,* 491–513.

Turoff, M., & Hiltz, S. R. (1996). Computer based Delphi process. In M. Adler, & E. Ziglio (Eds.), *Gazing into the oracle: The delphi method and its application to social policy and public health* (pp. 56–88). London, England: Jessica Kingsley.
United Nations. Department of Economic and Social Affairs, Population Division. Population Estimate and Projection Section. (2010). *World population prospects (2010 revision)*. New York, NY: Author.
Waldman, D. A., De Luque, M. S., Washburn, N., House, R. J., Adetoun, B., Barrasa, A., & Dorfman, P. (2006). Cultural and leadership predictors of corporate social responsibility values of top management: A GLOBE study of 15 countries. *Journal of International Business Studies, 37*(6), 823–837.
Walumbwa, F., Orwa, B., Wang, P., & Lawler, J. (2005). Transformational leadership, organizational commitment, and job satisfaction: A comparative study of Kenyan and U.S. financial firms. *Human Resource Development Quarterly, 16*(2), 235–256.
Wambu, O. (2007). *Under the tree of talking: Leadership for change in Africa*. London, England: Counterpoint.
Wanasika, I., Howell, J. P. Littrell, R. F., & Dorfman, P. (2011). Managerial leadership and culture in sub-Saharan Africa. *Journal of World Business, 46*(2), 234–241.
Wandibba, S. (2004). Kenyan cultures and our values. *Wajibu, 19*(1), 3–5.
Wellman, W., Perkins, G., & Wellman, N. (2009). Educational leadership: The relationship between spirituality and leadership practices. *Spirituality in Higher Education Newsletter, 7*, 1–6.
World Bank. (2014). *The African diaspora program*. Retrieved January 26, 2014, from http:www.worldbank.org/en/search?q=+The+African+Diaspora+Program.+&currentTab=1
World Economic Forum. (2015). *The global competitiveness report 2015–2016*. Geneva, Switzerland: Klaus Schwab.
Young, S. J., & Jamieson, L. M. (2001). Delivery methodology of the delphi: A comparison of two approaches. *Journal of Park & Recreation Administration, 19*(1).
Yukl, G. (2012, November). Effective leadership behavior: What we know and what questions need more attention. *Academy of Management Perspectives*, 66–85.
Yukl, G., Gordon, A., & Taber, T. (2002). A hierarchical taxonomy of leadership behavior: Integrating a half century of behavior research. *Journal of Leadership and Organizational Studies, 9*, 15–32.
Zaff, J. F., Blount, R. L., Phillips, L., & Cohen, L. (2002). The role of ethnic identity and self-construal in coping among African American and Caucasian American seventh graders: an exploratory analysis of within-group variance. *Adolescence, 37*, 751–773.
Zhang, X., Fu, P., Xi, Y., Li, L., Xu, L., Cao, C., & Ge, J. (2012). Understanding indigenous leadership research: Explication and Chinese examples. *The Leadership Quarterly, 23*(6), 1063–1079.
Zoogah, D. B., & Nkomo, S. (2013). Management research in Africa: Past, present and future. In T. R. Lituchy, B. J. Punnett, & B. B. Puplampu (Eds.), *Management in Africa: Macro and micro perspectives* (pp. 9–31). London, England: Routledge.

CHAPTER 4

MANAGING THE HISPANIC WORKFORCE IN THE CONTEXT OF VALUES, ACCULTURATION, AND IDENTITY

Carolina Gomez
Florida International University

Patricia G. Martínez
Loyola Marymount University

ABSTRACT

Discussions about leading the 21st century workforce must include Hispanics, the largest ethnic group who will account for 80% of the U.S. labor force growth in the next four decades. In today's multicultural context, leading Hispanic employees requires knowledge of cultural values and how these are related to social identity and acculturation. Within this context, we review research on how Hispanic employees may perceive leadership, organizational justice, teams, and the effect of job factors on motivation. Additionally, we discuss how culturally embedded leadership favors a relational perspective. Paternalistic leadership emphasizes such relational leadership as does the use of interactional justice. Furthermore, differences in attribution styles need to be noted so as to minimize conflict between managers and Hispanic employees. Research also suggests that in teams, Hispanics will emphasize the importance of team maintenance behaviors as well as potentially providing special treatment to in-group members. Finally, extrinsic job factors such as colleagues, benefits, company reputation, and managers will be related to motivation. Nevertheless, all of these factors need to be taken in the context of employees' levels of acculturation and identification with Hispanic ethnicity and values. As employees are more acculturated and have weaker ethnic identification, Hispanics will display cultural values, job characteristic and leadership preferences which are more similar to U.S. majority members. We conclude with a discussion of several managerial implications.

Any discussion of workforce trends in the 21st century must include a discussion of the Hispanic workforce, which is projected to increase from 14.8% of workers in 2010 to 18.6% in 2020 (Bureau of Labor Statistics, 2012). As the largest ethnic group in the country, currently 55 million (U.S. Census Bureau, 2014) and projected to represent about 80% of the total growth in the U.S. labor force over the next four decades, Aguinis and Joo (2014) argue that future research on Hispanics and Latin Americans is likely to have important social implications. Hispanic culture reflects values that may differ from the mainstream U.S. culture, and these important cultural differences may lead to differences in workplace preferences and behaviors. In this chapter we discuss Hispanics' perceptions of leadership, organizational justice, the group context, and motivation, and how their levels of acculturation and social identity may further affect these important organizational issues.

HISPANIC CULTURAL VALUES

First and foremost it is important to note that when we refer to Hispanics, we are referring to those whose origin is Spain or the Spanish-speaking countries of Latin America. While such a definition comprises people from many different countries, research on cultural values (Hofstede, 1980; House, Hanges, Javidan, Dorfman & Gupta, 2004) supports that individuals with these origins have a common set of cultural values. Blancero and Stone (2014) argue that cultural similarities arise from a common religion, the mestizaje (mixing) of races, more than 400 years of shared history and other factors that influence attitudes and behaviors. For example, without a doubt, Hofstede's (1980) research found that Latin American countries are collectivistic cultures. Furthermore, Marin and Triandis (1985) note that Hispanics in the United States also are collectivistic. This collectivistic orientation is important because individuals with such values tend to emphasize group solidarity and obligations (Triandis, 1994a). Moreover, individuals from collectivistic cultures tend to belong to a select few in-groups, such as families and friendship circles (Triandis, Bontempo, Villareal, Asai, & Lucca, 1988). These in-groups tend to be stable over time (Triandis et al., 1988) and collectivists favor members from their in-group.

Collectivism has been studied extensively as it seems to affect many behaviors, such as cooperation (Cox, Lobel, & McLeod, 1991) and social loafing (Earley, 1989). Interestingly, Early found that while collectivists worked better in groups compared to individualists, their performance was lower when they thought they were working alone or in an out-group. Thus the relationship was moderated by who comprised the group (in-group or out-group members). Other research has shown how collectivists will be more generous in their rewards toward team members who they believe to be part of their in-group (Gomez, Kirkman, & Shapiro, 2000). These results confirm the importance of in-group members to individuals with a collectivist orientation. In addition, Gomez et al. (2000) also found that collectivists seemed to value group maintenance contributions, while individualists valued task contributions.

Research also supports important differences in attributional biases between collectivists and individualists. Markus and Kitayama (1991) discuss how individualists' independent view and collectivists' interdependent view affects their cognition, emotions, and motivations. A collectivistic view leads people to make more external attributions (e.g., the environment or luck), while a more individualistic view is associated with more internal attributions (effort or ability). Choi, Nisbett, and Norenzayan (1999) note that research across a diverse set of collectivistic cultures supports collectivists' tendency to make external situational attributions. The interdependent view of the self-results in Hispanics (Betancourt & Weiner, 1982; Newman, 1991), as well as other collectivist cultures, reflect a tendency toward more external attributions. Individuals with a collectivist culture will make internal attributions, but appear to be more sensitive to the contextual variables, which may better explain behavior and phenomena. Therefore, collectivism, a value that characterizes the Hispanic culture, seems to have a strong impact on employee perceptions and behaviors.

Related to the collectivist orientation, Hispanics place great importance on the family (Marin & Marin, 1991). Familialism is defined as individuals' strong identification and attachment with their families, both nuclear and extended, and strong feelings of loyalty, reciprocity and solidarity among members of the same family (Triandis, Marín, Betancourt, Lisansky & Chang, 1982). Despite differences in country of origin, Mexican Central and Cuban Americans reported similar attitudes toward the family indicating that familism is a core characteristic in the Hispanic culture (Marín, Sabogal, Otero-Sabogal, Vanoss Marín, Perez-Stable, 1987). Three basic dimensions of familism include familial obligations, perceived support from the family, and family as referents.

Another common value across Hispanic groups is an acceptance of power differences (referred to by Hofstede as power distance). That is, Hispanic groups tend to accept differences among individuals in terms of power (Hofstede, 1980). This value is related to a respect for titles and hierarchy. Indeed research has shown that a more authoritarian management style has a stronger negative effect on employees' organizational commitment when these individuals are from the United States and thus generally exhibit low power distance; nevertheless, when individuals accept power differences, lack of participation does not have the same detrimental effect on their level of organizational commitment (Brockner et al., 2001).

In addition, the Latin American countries tended to score high on uncertainty avoidance (Hofstede, 1980), thus Hispanics prefer more rules, procedures, and overall structure in their workplace. They also have a present orientation and accept traditional gender roles (Marin & Marin, 1991), and Hispanics value *simpatia*, a word that emphasizes social behavior that focuses on harmony in relationships (Triandis, Marin, Lisansky, & Betancourt, 1984). Overall, it appears that the Hispanic culture has a strong emphasis on relations and acceptance of hierarchy and traditional gender roles as well as an emphasis on the present (Guerrero & Posthuma, 2014). However, as Guerrero and Posthuma (2014) argue, there are important differences among Hispanic nationalities on values, where some countries may be higher or lower on a given value (for example, Colombia is lower on power distances) and thus researchers have cautioned against assuming that these commonalities apply to all groups (Triandis, 1994; Stone-Romero, Stone & Salas, 2003). Other factors that may affect the extent to which one can make generalizations about the behavior of Hispanic employees, include gender, education, socioeconomic status, and religion (Blancero & Stone, 2014). Nevertheless, there is a common set of values that tends to differentiate Hispanics from other ethnic groups. These values in turn can provide insight into how Hispanic employees may perceive and respond to different forms of supervision and leadership, perceive justice differently, behave in teams differently, and be motivated by different job factors.

The Role of Acculturation and Ethnic Identity

While these cultural values are important considerations for supervisors and managers working with Hispanic employees, it is critical to take into account individuals' degree of acculturation as well as their ethnic identity. The process of acculturation involves a change in people's activities, thinking patterns, values, and self-identification (Berry, 1997). Thus for Hispanics born outside of the United States, as they spend time in the mainstream U.S. culture, they may change their values and identification to be more reflective of the U.S. culture. Researchers have proposed two different models of acculturation and according to Phinney (1996) one model proposes a linear model whereby as individuals develop stronger ties with the mainstream culture, their ethnic ties tend to weaken. A second model proposes that individuals can have strong or weak ties and identifications with both their ethnic culture as well as the mainstream culture. With either model we expect the degree of acculturation to have an effect on an individual's values, attitudes, and ultimately their behavior. Indeed, Berry (1997) noted that without measuring acculturation, researchers may arrive at inappropriate conclusions regarding the effect of ethnicity. Thus, Hispanic employees with low levels of acculturation may exhibit more of the values typically related to Hispanic culture, e.g., collectivism, familialism, power distance, which as we outline in this chapter and they may affect their job characteristic preferences, their preferred leadership style, and how they behave in teams.

In contrast, Hispanic employees with high levels of acculturation or a weak ethnic identity may have similar preferences as their Anglo-American counterparts. For example, Guerrero and Posthuma (2014) noted that gender roles expectations within the Hispanic community are affected by acculturation, with low acculturation associated with more traditional gender role expectations. Thus, it may be misleading for researchers to assume that Hispanic employee research participants will exhibit traditional gender role values.

It is important to note that "Hispanic" does not constitute a race, but rather a distinct ethnic group (Stone, Johnson, Stone-Romero, & Hartman, 2006). The reality is that some Hispanics may identify as White, some identify as Black and some may identify as having a mixed race (Gallegos & Ferdman, 2007). In contrast, ethnicity has been defined as the "subjective symbolic or emblematic use of any aspect of culture [by a group], in order to differentiate themselves from other groups" (DeVos, 1975). As a result, we know that individuals vary in the extent to which they ascribe identities to themselves, such as ethnicity. These categorizations provide a basis for an individual's self-concept, and next we discuss the role of social identities in the self-concept.

Social identity theory proposes that through the process of self-categorization (Tajfel & Turner, 1979; Turner & Oakes, 1986), individuals assign membership within social categories, such as gender and ethnicity, to themselves and to others. Thus, social identity consists of those social groups with which an individual identifies. These identities are indeed tied to values (as noted elsewhere), attitudes, and needs, which then can translate to behaviors (Folger, Konovsky, & Cropanzano, 1992; Markus & Wurf, 1987).

The extent to which social identities guide behaviors and attitudes will depend upon the centrality and the salience of that identity within a given context. Individuals vary in their ethnic identity centrality, which is the importance they place on their ethnic identities (Ethier & Deaux, 1990). Thus an individual with a central career identity may be more willing to exert more effort at work than those who may have more salient family identities (Lobel & St. Clair, 1992). Ethnicity is one of the potential self-identities that an individual can ascribe to themselves that will then affect their attitudes, perceptions, and behavior. Given the complexity involved in ethnic identity, Phinney (1996) recommends that researchers measure and confirm the values of an ethnic group, assessing differences within the group and assessing how these values affect attitudes and behaviors. These ideas are consistent with early critiques of social demography research (e.g., Lawrence, 1997), which noted the importance of researchers confirming that when they ascribed individuals a particular social identity, such as Hispanic, these individuals indeed included this social category within their social identity. For example, in a study of U.S. Hispanic business professionals' perceptions of discrimination, DelCampo, Jacobson, Van Buren, and Blancero (2010) found that immigrants had higher levels of Hispanic identity as compared to U.S.-born Hispanics.

With these cultural values and the concepts of identity and acculturation as a backdrop, we will explore several topics central to Hispanics in the workplace; mainly, some key findings related to leadership, teams and collaboration in groups, and motivation.

LEADING HISPANIC EMPLOYEES

Leadership involves behaviors that are contextually and culturally endorsed. Inevitably, the cultural context will influence followers' expectations of leadership behaviors (Bass, 1991, 1997). As such, it is essential to consider the collectivistic nature of employees' countries of origin in order to understand why Hispanics may value, and often expect a leadership style that emphasizes concern for the individual. One can look to initial research on paternalism, a leadership style that is prevalent in Latin American countries (Martínez, 2003; 2005; Elvira & Dávila, 2005; Pellegrini & Scandura, 2006; Uhl-Bien, Tierney, Graen & Wakabayashi, 1990). Paternalism is a leadership style that combines decision-making control with benevolence and concern for individuals' welfare (Martínez, 2003, 2005); it relies on social bonds based on reciprocity and stresses workers' expectations (Dávila & Elvira, 2012). However, this merging of care with control makes this form of leadership difficult for Western scholars to understand, such that paternalism is often viewed as an anachronism (Padavic & Earnest, 1994), with Americans typically regarding it as a system where employees become dependent upon the organization (Uhl-Bien et al., 1990).

A collectivistic society, where mutual obligations are embedded within society, is conducive to paternalism (Jackson, 2015), such that subordinates may expect leaders to be aware of and involved in their lives, thus providing care and protection. In contrast, in an individualistic society, this may be viewed as an invasion of privacy. (Aycan, 2006; Jackson, 2015). Pellegrini, Scandura and Jayaraman (2010) noted that from a leadership perspective, while paternal benevolence may correspond to "individualized consideration" (e.g., Bass, 1985), it consists of a longer-term, relational aspect that extends to subordinates' personal lives.

A discussion of the historical roots of paternalism within the colonial hacienda system helps to frame paternalism in Latin America (Martínez, 2003, 2005). Hacienda studies discuss the evolution of an agricultural model into a commercial model, describing the management style of the *hacendados*, the owners, as paternalistic (e.g., Diaz-Saenz & Witherspoon, 2004; Guerra, 1988). Although the hacienda system (the basis of the agrarian sector of contemporary Latin America) began its decline during the 19th century, it continued well into the 20th century. Over time this seemingly feudal hacienda system evolved to include elements of free enterprise and capitalism, where workers typically had rights, freedom, compensation, and perquisites (Gibson, 1964; Miller, 1990). Many of the late 19th century textile mills were established in haciendas and as a result, paternalistic relations between mill owners and employees had deep roots (Boyer, 2000). As Mexico's hacienda agricultural model began to evolve, several "benevolent" paternalistic practices continued, providing for a number of basic needs for workers and, often, their families.

A similar evolution, driven by the need to meet the competitive demands of a global market, is illustrated in recent studies of contemporary organizations in Latin America. In a recent review of the psychological, sociological, and historical explanations underlying leadership styles in Latin America, Davila and Elvira (2012) argued that humanistic leadership (emphasizing compassion) is typical in Latin America. This leadership approach includes an interest in workers beyond the employment relationship.

One example of leadership research within the Latin American context is a recent comparative study of management and delegation where Liberman (2014) found that as expected, delegation was higher in the United States compared to Chile, while paternalism was higher in Chile. However in the United States, paternalism had a stronger relationship with job satisfaction and organizational commitment than did delegation. Liberman noted that nearly one-quarter of his U.S. sample was Hispanic and considers that this demographic is likely related to the strong, unexpected positive relationships between paternalism and job attitudes in the U.S. context.

Similarly, in a recent qualitative case study of a Mexican-owned multinational corporation, Brumley (2014) found a "hybrid organizational logic," which is characterized by paternalism within a competitive work culture that evolved in response to global forces. The paternalistic work culture was characterized by deference, loyalty, and traditional work and family roles.

In yet another study, Darío Rodríguez and Ríos (2009) argue that while Chile finds its labor relations in a transitional state, moving to a more formalistic, industrialized, Western form, human resource management practices should consider that paternalism is present as an employee expectation. Furthermore, the researchers argue that despite an organization's modernized appearance, paternalism can still pervade administrative activities and practices. Finally, it is important to reinforce that while some dimensions of followers' leadership expectations may vary across Latin American countries, recent studies support the idea that the region still shares elements of paternalism. In a detailed analysis of the Latin American region for the GLOBE Project, Castaño et al., (2015) argue that their results suggest that in Latin America, charismatic/value-based and team-oriented leadership is desirable. Furthermore, they state that these leadership behaviors may be indicative of "paternalism theory" where charismatic corresponds to person-centered and team-oriented to a relational style.

As is apparent in the contemporary organizational studies discussed previously, in response to a global competitive landscape, the organizational culture, structures and practices in Latin American organizations have often imported Western management practices (e.g., Davila & Elvira, 2012; Liberman, 2014). Similarly, within the U.S. context, it is necessary to consider that while individuals who are immigrant or first-generation may be more comfortable with and potentially expect a more paternalistic style of leadership (e.g., Martínez, 2003; Martínez, 2005), it is important to consider acculturation. As individuals adopt more U.S. individualistic values, they may perceive this type of leadership as anachronistic, irrelevant, and ineffective.

ORGANIZATIONAL JUSTICE AND FAIRNESS PERCEPTIONS

Related to employees' expectations of leaders, exploratory research in Mexico also suggests that Hispanics may differ in what matters to them as related to organizational justice, which consists of distributive justice, the fairness of the distribution of outcomes (Greenberg, 1990); procedural justice, or the perceived fairness of the policies and procedures used to make the outcome decisions (Greenberg, 1990); and interactional justice, the perceived interpersonal treatment that an individual receives during the enactment of organizational procedures (Bies & Moag, 1986). Studies in a variety of empirical studies within the U.S. context suggest that procedural justice is related to organizational commitment (Brockner et al., 2001; Brockner, Tyler, & Cooper-Schneider, 1992; Folger & Konovsky, 1989; McFarlin & Sweeney, 1992). As an example, perceptions of procedural justice increase when employees have a greater voice or participate more in decisions (Lind & Tyler, 1988). Thus procedural justice has been shown to affect organizational-level outcomes. As far as interactional justice, it is a significant predictor of job satisfaction and organizational citizenship behaviors (Moorman, 1991). Nevertheless, interactional justice in the United States is often not distinguishable from procedural justice. Indeed as noted by Cropanzano, Prehar, and Chen (2002), while initial research treated them as separate concepts, more recent research has viewed them as part of the process used to make decisions, hence the high correlation between them. Nevertheless, they argue that social exchange theory helps distinguish them and their research shows that they have different correlates; procedural justice was related to trust in upper management and performance appraisal system satisfaction, whereas, interactional justice was related to the quality of the manager.

Interestingly, initial research in Mexico found that interactional justice, not procedural, related to affective commitment (Gomez & Kirkman, 2005). Moreover, in the Mexican context, distributive justice was related to normative commitment (i.e., a reflection that employees stay because they feel they ought to) as well as affective commitment. While this type of research needs to be confirmed in a larger, ideally comparative study, it makes sense that in a relational culture, an employee's emotional and normative attachment is highly influenced by the level of interactional justice (Gómez & Kirkman, 2005).

The concept of psychological contract fairness is another dimension of employees' perception of fair treatment. Psychological contracts have been defined as the individual's beliefs about mutual obligations between the employee and employer. These include the employees' expectations of what the organization has promised and what it expect from employees in return (Rousseau, 1995). In a longitudinal study of Hispanic business professionals, DelCampo & Blancero (2008) found a negative relationship between individuals' psychological contract fairness and perceptions of discrimination and a positive relationship between psychological contract fairness and autonomous status. In a later study, DelCampo, Rogers & Jacobson (2010) found a positive relationship between perceived discrimination and psychological contract breach, and this relationship was stronger for those with a higher level of Hispanic identity.

Volpone (2012) argues that organizations' failure to consider Hispanics' cultural values may shed light on why Hispanics' perceptions and behaviors in the workplace, such as turnover, differ from other racioethnic groups' perceptions and behaviors. Furthermore, she argues that a supportive diversity climate that incorporates Hispanic cultural values (collectivism, power-distance, masculinity, uncertainty avoidance, time orientation, trust *confianza*, ethnic pride) relates to improved retention through the fulfillment of psychological contracts. In contrast, when employees perceive that the organization does not honor their psychological contract, known as a psychological contract breach (e.g., Bal, De Lange, Jansen, & Van Der Velde, 2008; Deery, Iverson, & Walsh, 2006), they often experience negative outcomes, such as decreased organizational commitment, higher levels of intentions to quit, and higher levels of turnover.

An important element within a discussion of psychological contract fulfillment and breach is how and when employees form their psychological contract perceptions. Several theorists have argued that in large part human resource management (HRM) practices determine psychological contracts (Conway & Briner, 2005; Guzzo, Noonan, & Elron, 1994; Rousseau, 1995; Rousseau & Greller, 1994). More recent work has drawn from signaling theory (Spence, 1973; 1974) to argue that these HRM practices substantially determine psychological contracts (Suazo, Martínez, & Sandoval, 2009; Suazo, Martínez & Sandoval, 2011). For example, recruitment and selection practices, such as on-site job interviews, realistic job previews, job shadowing, and generous training and development programs may convey particular signals, such that prospective employees perceive that the organization devotes a generous amount of resources to employees' skill development and thus creates a long-term employment relationship.

We build on Volpone's (2012) argument that in managing psychological contracts, organizations need to consider Hispanics cultural values by noting that managers should also pay special attention to treating employees with respect and consideration, realizing it is the treatment more so than the procedures themselves that will result in committed employees. This is in alignment with Gomez and Kirkman's (2005) finding that interactional justice strongly affects organizational commitment in Mexican employees. Similarly, the importance of distributive justice is tied to the paternalistic leadership emphasis noted earlier (Gómez & Kirkman, 2005). Thus when there is distributive justice, employees are more committed to the organization as they perceive that the organization is taking care of them. Similarly, when the managers in an organization display interactional justice, organizational commitment increases with Hispanic employees. As with our other conclusions, it is important to note that the importance of interactional and distributive components will be critical to those Hispanics who are not highly acculturated to the U.S. culture. For those who have assimilated into the U.S. culture and who may identify strongly with the mainstream culture, procedural justice will be a more important driver to their commitment to the organization.

Another factor that may strongly affect the relationship between leaders and employees of different ethnic groups is the tendency to attribute performance to either internal or external factors. As noted earlier, there is a body of research suggesting that individuals of different cultures make significantly different causal attributions (e.g., Chiang & Birtch, 2007; Markus & Kitayama, 1991). In our discussion of cultural values, it was noted that due to collectivistic values, Hispanics tend to view the world in greater interdependent terms. Research supports that collectivists with this interdependent view make more external attributions, thus taking into account the context, the environment, even luck, in attributing why someone may have or may not have performed well (Markus & Kitayama, 1991). In contrast, individuals with a more individualistic orientation, tend to make internal attributions (e.g., effort, ability, skill). Martinko, Moss, and Harvey (2006) found that these differences in attributional tendencies can lead to lower quality relationships between leaders and members. Thus managers should be aware that Hispanic employees who are high in collectivism will consider the situation when attributing causation. If the manager is from an individualistic culture (such as the United States), the employee's attribution may conflict with the manager's tendency to make internal attributions, leading to significant conflict between managers and employees. Typically, research has supported a positive relationship between perceived supervisor support and perceived organizational support, such that employees view supervisors as acting on behalf of the organization. Drawing from Yan and Hunt (2005), who argue that collectivists attribute failure and success to group efforts rather than the efforts of an individual supervisor, Rhoades Shannock, Masuda, and Arboleda (2012) propose that their findings suggest that followers' cultural differences may influence the degree to which they attribute leaders' actions to the organization.

All in all, this body of research indicates that for those employees who identify with Hispanic cultural values, the focus within employment relationships and leadership should be much more relational in nature than is typical for the United States, individualistic-oriented context.

WORKING WITH OTHERS

According to Guerrero and Posthuma's (2014) review on Hispanic research, Hispanic employees place more value on interpersonal exchanges, thus leading to a sense of obligation toward friends in the organization. Sanchez-Burks, Nisbitt, and Ybarra (2000) note that compared to Anglo Americans, Mexican Americans viewed workgroups with a socioemotional orientation more favorably. Similarly, Gomez, Kirkman and Shapiro (2000) note that collectivists, such as Hispanics, value maintenance, relationship-oriented contributions more, while individualists value task contributions more.

When working in a team environment, Hispanic cultural values may also impact perceptions and behaviors that can affect the team culture and thus outcomes. Previously, we introduced organizational justice as an area where values could have a strong impact. A team environment often requires the distribution of rewards among team members and in a strong team environment, team members are often involved in allocating the distribution of rewards. This distribution can be affected by the collectivistic orientation. For example, research shows that Mexicans allow the distribution of rewards in teams to be affected by the status of the team member in terms of the individual's in-group status (Gómez, Kirkman, & Shapiro, 2000). They are more generous with in-group members regardless of their performance and this could influence reward distributions. Hispanic team members may take into account the status of a team member, whether they are part of their in-group or out-group, before deciding how generous to be with their rewards. Unintentionally, this may lead to a distributive justice issue with other team members and could potentially create conflict. Thus when implementing teams, reward/evaluation criteria should be spelled out in great detail such that it is clear what criteria should be taken into account when rewarding team members.

Nevertheless, when working in teams, conflict will arise and again, the collectivist mentality of Hispanics may lead to the use of different conflict resolutions strategies than their Anglo, more individualistic counterparts. Research with a Mexican sample noted that due to the level of collectivism, Mexicans appear to have a preference for both the use of social influence and negotiating when confronting a conflict (Gomez & Taylor, 2012). Gomez and Taylor (2012) found that when confronting a conflict with a coworker, Mexicans, compared to U.S. participants, had a preference for both the use of social influence and negotiating and that collectivism appeared to explain these preferences. Thus, even how Hispanic employees confront conflict with a team member may reflect their collectivistic values. They will try to use social influence and work through others to deal with conflict. Similarly, it appears that they will engage in negotiation to try to resolve conflict.

MOTIVATION

Assuming that job attributes are related to job satisfaction or increased motivation, cultural values should affect what Hispanics seek in employers. For example Stone et al. (2006) found that both Hispanics and non-Hispanics who held collectivist values rated relationships with coworkers as well as workplace diversity highly. In addition, those high on familialism rated time off from work higher. Finally, workers with higher power distance gave higher ratings to good company reputation and promotion opportunities. It is clear that Hispanic's cultural values drive their job preferences and preferences for their employer's policies.

Similarly, Gomez (2003) examined the relationship between acculturation, collectivism, and job attribute preferences. She found that levels of acculturation were related to collectivistic values; those Hispanics who were least acculturated held significantly higher levels of collectivism than those that were highly acculturated. The most acculturated Hispanics were similar in values to their Anglo American counterparts. Additionally she found that those with strong collectivistic values placed greater importance on contextual job attributes, such as working conditions and human relations. In contrast, those with stronger individualistic values had a stronger preference for task-related job attributes such as responsibility and autonomy. According to Gomez (2003), for collectivists the job characteristics such as affiliation and supervisor support may very well be more important than variety, autonomy, and task significance. Similarly, according to Hofstede (1980) collectivistic cultures placed greater emphasis on having training opportunities and good working conditions, while individualistic cultures placed emphasis on having freedom to perform the job according to the individual's preferences and having challenging work that gives a sense of accomplishment.

Indeed different studies have explored Hispanics' job attribute preferences. Dornbusch and Edwards (1991) found that Hispanics value role clarity, which is in alignment with Hofstede's finding that Latin American countries display higher levels of uncertainty avoidance (1980). Stone et al. (2006) noted Hispanics' preference for mentoring opportunities and opportunities to help others. Furthermore, Del Campo et al. (2011) found that Hispanic immigrants were significantly more likely to seek out mentors as opposed to their U.S.-born counterparts, while the latter were more likely to join affinity groups at work. The researchers note that immigrants may not want to engage in overt, public actions that might suggest that they are not assimilating, such as joining an affinity group, but instead they may be more willing to seek out a mentor, which is more discreet and consistent with a motivation to maintain a particular appearance. Blancero, DelCampo, and Marron (2007) argue that U.S.-born Hispanics may believe that workplace support from affinity groups is more important than any concerns about maintaining an outward appearance about assimilation or ethnic identity.

Given that Hispanics, regardless of country of origin, are high on familialism (Marín et al., 1987), this strong identification and attachment with members of the same family will likely impact how Hispanic employees perceive their interface between family and work. For example, within the Hispanic culture, high familialism can mean that perceived obligations to one's family may extend beyond the nuclear family to the extended family. Additionally, applying a collectivistic, generalized social exchange (Ekeh, 1974) view to this obligation would mean a reciprocal obligation for the extended family to, in turn, provide assistance with familial obligations and support. As a result, this is an important dimension for understanding Hispanic employees' work attitudes and behaviors.

Taylor, DelCampo and Blancero (2009) found that individuals who experience low work-to-family conflict and high facilitation in the direction of work-to-family are more likely to report their perception of the psychological contract to be fair. They also found a direct relationship between the availability of formal workplace supports, such as formal work–family policies, supervisor support, a work climate for family, job characteristics, and psychological contract fairness. Beutell & Schneer (2014) found that Hispanic women, as compared to men, reported the highest work-to-family conflict and work-family synergy (WFS) levels, However they found that job resources, such as job autonomy, schedule flexibility, supervisor and worker support, are negatively related to work-to-family conflict for Hispanic women but not Hispanic men. This suggests that these resources help Hispanic women to manage and decrease this conflict. Beutell and Scheer argue that gender role ideology and the increased demands that Hispanic women face from work and home may explain these findings; Hispanic men do not face the same gender role expectations and thus these resources are not helpful. It is important to note that the researchers did not measure cultural values, ethnic identity nor whether the individuals were born within or outside of the United States, thus they are assuming that respondents possessed traditional gender roles regardless of their level of acculturation.

Finally, in their study of working female students at community colleges in the United States and Mexico, Zhang, Gowan and Trevino (2014) found support for their prediction that country of origin would be related to career and parental role commitment, such that those born in Mexico would have greater career role commitment and lower parental role commitment than those born in the United States. Zhang and colleagues reason that first, a familialism orientation suggests that work may be integral to one's family role, which is supported by Yang, Chen, Choi and Zhou (2000), who found that collectivists (Mexicans/Hispanics) view work as a means of providing for family; whereas individualists (i.e., U.S. born/non-Hispanic whites) view the work and family domains as competing demands. Additionally, Zhang and colleagues argue that commitment to family does not need to interfere with commitment to work, particularly since Mexican nationals reported less compartmentalization between work and life activities as compared to individuals in the United States. Furthermore, Marin et al. (1987) previously argued that social support from the extended family, e.g., assisting with childcare obligations, may foster work/family enrichment, while DelCampo et al. (2011) suggest that Hispanics may view fulfilling work responsibilities as a primary channel to contribute to work and family.

THE IMPORTANCE OF SOCIAL IDENTITY AND ACCULTURATION

A recurring theme in this chapter is that in order for managers to better understand their Hispanic employees' job attitudes, motivation, preference for leadership style, job or employer preferences, and job attribute preferences, they need to consider their employees' degree of acculturation and ethnic identity. For example, the importance of the tie between values and job attribute preferences cannot be overlooked, because as noted from the beginning of this chapter, Hispanic's cultural values may change with the level of acculturation and social identity. Thus as Hispanic employees become more acculturated, their preferences may no longer differ, or not differ as much, from their majority counterpart employees. Nevertheless, for less acculturated Hispanics, it appears that the contextual factors of the job as well as time off, role clarity, and relationships are key factors for job satisfaction, leadership, teamwork, and motivation.

IMPLICATIONS FOR LEADERSHIP PRACTICE

As management research has gradually considered how demographic trends and the growth of ethnic groups within the workforce might affect workplace attitudes and behaviors, it is essential to consider how cultural values affect preference for leadership styles, perceptions of justice, and how these relationships are further impacted by acculturation and self-identity. Indeed this chapter points to some important managerial implications. In terms of leadership style, an emphasis on a relational style takes into account the employees' lives beyond work. Indeed, the emphasis on familialism would support an interest in the employees' families. Such a relational approach should affect the emphasis on interactional justice as well as distributive justice so that employees perceive that they are taken care of as well as receiving fair treatment.

It is important for supervisors and HR managers to understand the mechanisms by which the organization and individual managers create psychological contracts and that managers be aware of the messages that different elements of their HR practices, such as compensation and benefit policies (Suazo, Martínez, & Sandoval, 2009, 2011), can emit. One area to consider is the signaling value of HR practices and how the cultural value of familialism suggest that first, employees will perceive human resource management practices that assist them to meet family obligations (one dimension of familialism) as supportive organizational practices. Second, Hispanic employees who are high on familialism may view their work-life boundaries differently and perhaps more permeable, such that based upon the importance of a family situation, they may be more comfortable with allowing family to interfere with work. Thus what may appear to an individualist as out of the question, a request to leave work early for a family obligation may seem perfectly reasonable to a collectivist or an Hispanic employee high on familialism.

Additionally, Hispanic employees will be attracted to companies that focus on extrinsic job factors such as reputation and colleagues. In fact, Hispanics will value an organizational culture that allows for flexibility and values diversity, because familialism often creates individual conflict. This is not to be confused or misunderstood as a lack of interest in work. Research noted in this chapter has shown that for Hispanics, high familialism leads to a central role, viewing work and careers as critical in providing for their family. Furthermore, managers should not view family-related requests for time off as indicators of a low organizational commitment. When familialism is strong, employees will value mangers' efforts to support and facilitate their familial obligations. A social exchange perspective suggests that employees will reciprocate in their future job attitudes and performance.

Hispanic cultural values may lead to conflicts between Hispanic employees and their managers. Due to their collectivistic values they may tend to make external attributions that may lead to conflicts if their managers hold individualistic values and thus emphasize internal attributions. Furthermore, in working with others, Hispanics may tend to treat members of their in-group, i.e., close friends, differently. Thus in working in teams, very specific guidelines should be given in terms of how a company or a manager expects group rewards to be distributed, if the team members are involved in the distribution of these.

While we have previously noted the importance of considering Hispanic employees' levels of acculturation and social identity, it is also important to consider the salience of that identity at work. For example, Avery and McKay (2006) propose that when organizations publicize their sponsorship of minority causes, this will only impact minorities' perceptions that the organization values diversity only if this (minority) identity is salient. Additionally, Friedman and Craig (2004) found that social identity motivates minority employees to join network groups, such that those with greater group racial/ethnic identity are more likely to join. Furthermore, they also determined that minorities perform cost-benefit analyses and will join when the benefits of career advancement outweigh any potential negative effects of joining, such as backlash or stigma. As previously noted, for Hispanics considering whether or not to join an organization, organizational culture and a climate of inclusion may be key issues.

One way to create a climate of inclusion may come from a recent concept tied to organizational citizenship behavior, which is the potential of ethnic citizenship behaviors (Martínez, Randel, & Ramirez, 2011). These helping behaviors are similar to organizational citizenship behaviors (OCBs), discretionary behaviors that are not formal job duties and which do not directly result in a reward (Organ, 1998; Organ, Podsakoff, & MacKenzie, 2006), yet they are empirically distinct. OCBs, such as helping fellow employees are regarded and performing job duties with extra care (Moorman, Blakely, & Niehoff, 1998), inevitably contribute to organizations' long-term success by adding to the organization's bottom line (Konovsky & Pugh, 1994; Organ & Ryan, 1995). Ethnic citizenship behaviors are targeted toward one's ethnic group and include helping to recruit job candidates, orienting or mentoring fellow employees, and joining an employee interest/affinity group. The importance of these cooperative behaviors should be considered within the context of the value of employee affinity groups, which are designed to provide employees an avenue for working with and supporting similar others.

This idea is supported by Guerrero and Posthuma's review, (2014) where the researchers note that Hispanics indeed perceive receiving greater social support from Hispanic, rather than Anglo, coworkers. Similar to OCBs, these behaviors are likely beneficial for organizational functioning, particularly when these behaviors are extended to minority employees. Bolino, Turnley, and Bloodgood (2002) propose that OCBs facilitate the development of structural, relational and cognitive connections among employees, and that in part this is represented by trust, mutual identification and shared norms and perceived obligations. This proposition supports the idea that helping behaviors that are directed at one' ethnic group can lead to positive outcomes for both the employees and the organization. For example, minority employees often experience social isolation and less psychosocial support in cross-race mentoring relationships than majority employees (Ibarra, 1995; Thomas, 1990). Thus ethnic citizenship behaviors may help other ethnic minority members through supporting their organizational socialization and integration.

Initial analyses suggest that when ethnic identity is important (or central), individuals will enact helping behaviors toward similar others (Martínez et al., 2011). This underscores the idea that if an ethnic identity is not important and central to one's self-concept, it will not motivate helping behaviors to individuals of one's ethnic group. However in a recent analysis (Martínez & Gómez, 2016), we found that while possessing a central (and important) ethnic identity is strongly related to enacting ECBs. This relationship occurs entirely through the mediation of this identity's salience. In other words, when ethnic identity is highly salient and likely to be invoked in a particular situation or context (Hogg, Terry, & White, 1995), individuals are much more likely to enact these helping behaviors. This suggests that while ethnic identity may be central and important, when it is not salient in the work context, individuals will not likely enact ECBs. The more that a company encourages employees' unique identities to flourish and the more this identity leads to ECBs, the more likely it will result in a self-supporting climate of inclusion.

In closing, the U.S. workforce demographic changes that are unfolding at the beginning of the 21st century highlight the growing presence and influence of Hispanics across organizations. These changes suggest the importance of organizations learning about the Hispanics' cultural values and how these influence perceptions and preferences for leadership styles, justice, team work, and helping others, as well as job factors. Moreover, given the diversity in levels of acculturation and identity among Hispanic employees, managers must understand the level to which their employees identify with the Hispanic culture or the mainstream culture. To identify their employees' levels of acculturation/identity, managers can begin to understand the degree to which these employees listen to television, radio, and other such media outlets in their native tongue, Spanish. Some acculturation measures indeed consider the degree to which an individual listens to music, news, and television shows in Spanish, as well as the degree to which they use the Spanish language among their friends and family. In alignment with paternalistic leadership, managers may need to delve deeper into the lives of their employees to understand them and their preferences. While some managers may perceive that the uniqueness of the Hispanic culture may pose particular management challenges, we suggest that developing a familiarity with Hispanic employees and their cultural values is essential to developing organizational practices and programs and in carrying out decisions that can better integrate Hispanic employees and create more positive and productive workplaces.

REFERENCES

Aguinis, H., & Joo, H. (2014). Research on Hispanics benefits the field of management. *Journal of Managerial Psychology, 29,* 604–615.

Avery, D. R., & McKay, P. F. Target practice: An organizational impression management approach to attracting minority and female job applicants. *Personnel Psychology, 59,* 157–187.

Aycan, Z. (2001). Paternalistic leadership. In C. L. Cooper (Ed.), *Wiley encyclopedia of management.* Retrieved July 19, 2016, from http://onlinelibrary.wiley.com/doi/10.1002/9781118785317.weom060156/abstract

Bal, P. M., De Lange, A. H., Jansen, P. G. W., & Van Der Velde, M. E. G. (2008). Psychological contract breach and job attitudes: A meta-analysis of age as a moderator. *Journal of Vocational Behavior, 72,* 143–158.

Bass, B. M. (1985). *Leadership and performance beyond expectations.* New York, NY: The Free Press.

Bass, B. M. (1991). From transactional to transformational leadership: Learning to share the vision. *Organizational Dynamics, 18*(3), 19–31.

Bass, B. M. (1997). Does the transactional–transformational leadership paradigm transcend organizational and national boundaries? *American Psychologist, 52*(2), 130–139.

Berry, J. W. (1997). Immigration, acculturation, and adaptation. *Applied Psyhology, 46*, 5–34.

Betancourt, H., & Weiner, B. (1982). Attributions for achievement-related events, expectancy, and sentiments: A study of success and failure in Chile and the United States. *Journal of Cross Cultural Psychology, 13*, 362–374.

Beutell, N. J., & Schneer, J. A. (2014). Work-family conflict and synergy among Hispanics. *Journal of Managerial Psychology, 29*, 705–735.

Bies, R., & Moag, J. (1986). Interactional justice: Communication criteria of fairness. *Research on Negotiation in Organizations, 1*, 43–55.

Blancero, D. M., & DelCampo, R. G. (2012). *Hispanics at work: A collection of research, theory and application.* Hauppauge, NY: Nova Science.

Blancero, D. M., DelCampo, R. G., & Marron, G. F. (2007). Perception of fairness in psychological contracts by Hispanic business professionals: An empirical study in the United States. *International Journal of Management, 24*, 364–375.

Blancero, D. M., & Stone, D. (2014). Introduction to Hispanic and Latin American work issues. *Journal of Managerial Psychology, 29*(6).

Bolino, M. C., Turnley, W. H., & Bloodgood, J. M. (2002). Citizenship behavior and the creation of social capital in organizations. *Academy of Management Review, 27*, 505–522.

Boyer, C. R. (2000). The threads of class at La Virgen: Misrepresentation and identity at a Mexican textile mill, 1918–1935. *The American Historical Review, 105*, 1576–1598.

Brockner, J., Ackerman, G., Greenberg, J., Gelfand, M. J., Francesco, A. M., Chen, Z. X., ... Shapiro, D. L. (2001). Culture and procedural justice: The moderating influence of power distance on reactions to voice. *Journal of Experimental Social Psychology, 37*, 300–315.

Brockner, J., Tyler T. R., & Cooper-Schneider, R. (1992). The influence of prior commitment to an institution on reactions to perceived unfairness: The higher they are, the harder they fall. *Administrative Science Quarterly, 37*, 241–261.

Brumley, K. M. (2014). The gendered ideal worker narrative professional women's and men's work experiences in the new economy at a Mexican company. *Gender & Society, 28*, 799–823.

Bureau of Labor Statistics. (2012, February 3). *The employment situation—January 2012* [News Release USDL-12-0163]. Washington, DC: U.S. Department of Labor.

Castaño, N., de Luque, M. F. S., Wernsing, T., Ogliastri, E., Shemueli, R. G., Fuchs, R. M., & Robles-Flores, J. A. (2015). El jefe: Differences in expected leadership behaviors across Latin American countries. *Journal of World Business, 50*, 584–597.

Chiang, F. F., & Birtch, T. (2007). The transferability of management practices: Examining cross-national differences in reward preferences. *Human Relations, 60*, 1293–1330.

Choi, I., Nisbett, R.E., & Norenzayan, A. (1999). Causal attribution across cultures: Variation and universality. *Psychological Bulletin, 125*, 47–63.

Conway, N., & Briner, R. B. (2005). *Understanding psychological contracts at work: A critical evaluation of theory and research.* New York, NY: Oxford University Press.

Cox, T. H., Lobel, S. A., & McLeod, P. L. (1991). Effects of ethnic group cultural differences on cooperative and competitive behavior on a group task. *Academy of Management Journal, 34,* 827–847.

Cropanzano, R., Prehar, C. A., & Chen, P. Y. (2002). Using social exchange theory to distinguish procedural from interactional justice. *Group and Organizational Management, 27,* 324–351.

Darío Rodríguez, M., & René Ríos, F. (2009). Paternalism at a crossroads: Labor relations in Chile in transition. *Employee Relations, 3,* 322–333.

Dávila, A., & Elvira, M. M. (2005). Culture and human resource management in Latin America. In A. Davila & M. Elvira, *Managing human resources in Latin America* (pp. 3–24). London, England: Routledge.

Dávila, A., & Elvira, M. M. (2012). Humanistic leadership: Lessons from Latin America. *Journal of World Business, 47,* 548–554.

Deery, S. J., Iverson, R. D., & Walsh, J. T. (2006). Toward a better understanding of psychological contract breach: A study of customer service employees. *Journal of Applied Psychology, 91,* 166–175.

Delcampo, R. G., & Blancero, D. M. (2008). Perceptions of psychological contract fairness of Hispanic professionals. *Cross Cultural Management: An International Journal, 15,* 300–315.

DelCampo, R. G., Blancero, D. M., & Boudwin, K. M. (2008). Hispanic professionals after 11th September: A move toward "American" identification. *Cross Cultural Management: An International Journal, 15,* 20–29.

DelCampo, R. G., Jacobson, K. J., Van Buren III, H. J., & Blancero, D. M. (2011). Comparing immigrant and U.S. born Hispanic business professionals: Insights on discrimination. *Cross Cultural Management: An International Journal, 18*(3), 327–350.

DelCampo, R. G., Rogers, K. M., & Jacobson, K. J. (2010). Psychological contract breach, perceived discrimination, and ethnic identification in Hispanic business professionals. *Journal of Managerial Issues,* 220–238.

DeVos, G. (1975). Ethnic pluralism: Conflict and accommodation. In G. DeVo & L. Romanucci-Ross (Eds.), *Ethnic identity: Cultural continuities and change* (pp. 5–41). Palo Alto, CA: Mayfield.

Diaz-Saenz, H. R., & Witherspoon, P. D. (2004). Possessing a "sense of community": A study of employee perceptions in selected organizations in Mexico. *International and Multicultural Organizational Communication,* 145–169.

Dornbusch, R., & Edwards, S. (1991). The macroeconomics of populism. In *The Macroeconomics of populism in Latin America* (pp. 7–13). Chicago, IL: University of Chicago Press.

Earley, P. C. (1989). Social loafing and collectivism: A comparison of the United States and the People's Republic of China. *Administrative Science Quarterly, 34,* 565–581.

Ekeh, P. P. (1974). *Social exchange theory: The two traditions.* Cambridge, MA: Harvard University Press.

Elvira, M. M., & Dávila, A. (2005). Emergent directions for human resource management research in Latin America. *The International Journal of Human Resource Management, 16*, 2265–2282.
Ethier, K., & Deaux, K. (1990). Hispanics in ivy: Assessing identity and perceived threat. *Sex Roles, 22*, 427–440.
Folger, R., & Konovsky, M. (1989). Effects of procedural and distributive justice on reactions to pay raises. *Academy of Management Journal, 32*, 115–130.
Folger, R., Konovsky, M. A., & Cropanzano, R. (1992). A due process metaphor for performance appraisal. *Research in Organizational Behavior, 14*, 129–129.
Friedman, R. A., & Craig, K. M. (2004). Predicting joining and participating in minority employee network groups. *Industrial Relations, 43*, 793–816.
Gallegos, P. V., & Ferdman, B. M. (2007). Identity orientations of Latinos in the United States: Implications for leaders and organizations. *The Business Journal of Hispanic Research, 1*, 26–41.
Gibson, C. (1964). *The Aztecs under Spanish rule: A history of the Indians of the valley of Mexico, 1519–1810*. Redwood City, CA: Stanford University Press.
Gómez, C. (2003). The relationship between acculturation, individualism/collectivism, and job attribute preferences for Hispanic MBAs. *Journal of Management Studies, 40*, 1089–1105.
Gómez, C., & Kirkman, B. L. (2005, July). *Organizational justice: Its applicability and predictive power on employee commitment in Mexico*. Paper presented at the Academy of International Business conference, Quebec City, Canada.
Gómez, C., Kirkman, B. L., & Shapiro, D. L. (2000). The impact of collectivism and in-group/out-group membership on evaluation generosity. *Academy of Management Journal, 43*, 1097–2007.
Gómez, C., & Taylor, K. (2012, August). *Cultural differences in conflict resolution strategies: A U.S.-Mexico comparison*. Paper presented at the Academy of Management Annual Meeting, Boston, MA.
Greenberg, J. (1990). Organizational justice: Yesterday, today, and tomorrow. *Journal of Management, 16*, 399–432.
Guerra, F. X. (1988). Mexico: Del antiguo régimen a la revolución. *México: Fondo de cultura economica*.
Guerrero, L., & A. Posthuma, R. (2014). Perceptions and behaviors of Hispanic workers: A review. *Journal of Managerial Psychology, 29*, 616–643.
Guzzo, R. A., Noonan, K. A., & Elron, E. (1994). Expatriate managers and the psychological contract. *Journal of Applied Psychology, 79*, 617–626.
Hofstede, G. (1980). *Culture's consequences: International differences in work-related values*. Beverly Hills, CA: SAGE.
Hogg, M. A., Terry, D. J., & White, K. M. (1995). A tale of two theories: A critical comparison of identity theory with social identity theory. *Social Psychology Quarterly, 58*, 255–269.
House, R. J., Hanges, P. J., Javidan, M., Dorfman, P. W., & Gupta, V. (Eds.). (2004). *Culture, leadership, and organizations: The GLOBE study of 62 societies*. SAGE Publications.
Ibarra, H. (1995). Race, opportunity, and diversity of social circles in managerial networks. *Academy of Management Journal, 38*, 673–703.

Jackson, T. (2015). Is paternalistic leadership bad? A view from the other side of the fence. *Cross-cultural Management Studies*. Retrieved July 15, 2016, from https://terencejackson.net/2015/02/05/is-paternalistic-leadership-bad-a-view-from-the-other-side-of-the-fence/

Konovsky, M. A., & Pugh, S. D. (1994). Citizenship behavior and social exchange. *Academy of Management Journal, 37*, 656–669.

Liberman, L. (2014). The impact of a paternalistic style of management and delegation of authority on job satisfaction and organizational commitment in Chile and the U.S. *Innovar, 24*, 187–196.

Lind, E. A., & Tyler, T. R. (1988). *The social psychology of procedural justice.* New York, NY: Plenum.

Lobel, S. A., & Clair, L. S. (1992). Effects of family responsibilities, gender, and career identity salience on performance outcomes. *Academy of Management Journal, 35*, 1057–1069.

Marin, G., & Marin, B. V. (1991). *Research with Hispanic populations: Applied social research methods.* Newbury Park, CA: SAGE.

Marin, G., Sabogal, F., Marin, B. V., Otero-Sabogal, R., & Perez-Stable, E. J. (1987). Development of a short acculturation scale for Hispanics. *Hispanic Journal of Behavioral Sciences, 9*, 183–205.

Marin, G., & Triandis, H. C. (1985). Allocentrism as an important characteristic of the behavior of Latin Americans and Hispanics. In R. Diaz-Guerrero (Ed.), *Cross-cultural and national studies in social psychology, 69,* 80. Amsterdam, the Netherlands: North Holland.

Markus, H., & Kitayama, S. (1991). Culture and the self: Implications for cognition, emotion and motivation. *Psychological Review, 98,* 224–253.

Markus, H., & Wurf, E. (1987). The dynamic self-concept: A social psychological perspective. *Annual Review of Psychology, 38,* 299–337.

Martínez, P. G. (2003). Paternalism as a positive form of leader-subordinate exchange: Evidence from Mexico. *Management Research: Journal of the Iberoamerican Academy of Management, 1,* 227–242.

Martinez, P. G. (2005). Paternalism as a positive form of leadership in the Latin American context: Leader benevolence, decision-making control and human resource management practices. *Managing Human Resources in Latin America: An Agenda for International Leaders,* 75–93.

Martínez, P. G., & Gómez, C. G. (2016, August). *Ethnic identity salience & citizenship behaviors: Helping similar others.* Paper presented at the Academy of Management annual meeting, Anaheim, CA.

Martínez, P. G., Randel, A., & Ramirez, R. R. (2011, August). *An empirical test of the ethnic citizenship behaviors construct and its relationship with organizational citizenship behaviors and ethnic identity.* Presented at the Academy of Management Annual Meetings, Gender and Diversity Division Publishing Workshop, San Antonio, TX.

Martinko, M. J., Moss, S., & Harvey, P. (2006, August). *The effects of culture and attribution styles on leader–member relationships.* Presented at the 2006 Academy of Management conference. Atlanta, GA.

McFarlin, D., & Sweeney, P. (1992). Distributive and procedural justice as predictors of satisfaction with personal and organizational outcomes. *Academy of Management Journal, 35*, 626–637.

Miller, S. (1990). Mexican junkers and capitalist haciendas, 1810–1910: The arable estate and the transition to capitalism between the insurgency and the revolution. *Journal of Latin American Studies, 22*, 229–263.

Moorman, R.H. (1991). Relationship between organizational justice and organizational citizenship behaviors: Do fairness perceptions influence employee citizenship? *Journal of Applied Psychology, 76*, 845–855.

Moorman, R. H., Blakely, G. L., & Niehoff, B. P. (1998). Does perceived organizational support mediate the relationship between procedural justice and organizational citizenship behavior? *Academy of Management Journal, 41*, 351–357.

Newman, L. S. (1991). Why are traits inferred spontaneously? A developmental approach. *Social Cognition, 9*, 221.

Organ, D. W., & Foegen, J. H. (1998). Are managers losing control? *Business Horizons, 41*(2), 1–5.

Organ, D. W., Podsakoff, P. M., & MacKenzie, S. B. (2006). *Organizational citizenship behavior: Its nature, antecedents, and consequences.* Thousand Oaks, CA: SAGE.

Organ, D. W., & Ryan, K. (1995). A meta-analytic review of attitudinal and dispositional predictors of organizational citizenship behavior. *Personnel Psychology, 48*, 775–802.

Padavic, I., & Earnest, W. R. (1994). Paternalism as a component of managerial strategy. *The Social Science Journal, 31*, 389–405.

Pellegrini, E. K., & Scandura, T. A. (2006). Leader–member exchange (LMX), paternalism, and delegation in the Turkish business culture: An empirical investigation. *Journal of International Business Studies, 37*, 264–279.

Pellegrini, E. K., Scandura, T. A., & Jayaraman, V. (2010). Cross-cultural generalizability of paternalistic leadership: An expansion of leader–member exchange theory. *Group & Organization Management, 35*, 391– 420.

Phinney, J. S. (1996). When we talk about American ethnic groups, what do we mean? *American Psychologist, 51*, 918.

Rhoades Shanock, L., Masuda, A. D., & Arboleda, M. B. (2012). Supervisor and organizational support perceptions in Hispanics versus non-Hispanics. In D. M. Blancero & R. G. DelCampo (Eds.), *Hispanics at work: A collection of research, theory and application* (pp. 85–109). New York, NY: Nova Science.

Rousseau, D. (1995). *Psychological contracts in organizations: Understanding written and unwritten agreements.* Thousand Oaks, CA: SAGE.

Rousseau, D. M., & Greller, M. (1994). Human resource practices: Administrative contract makers. *Human Resource Management, 33*, 385–401.

Sanchez-Burks, J., Nisbett, R.E. and Ybarra, O. (2000). Cultural styles, relationship schemas, and prejudice against out-groups. *Journal of Personality and Social Psychology, 79*(2), 174–189.

Shanock, L., Masuda, A., & Arboleda, M. (2012). Supervisor and organizational support perceptions in Hispanics versus non-Hispanics. In D. M. Blancero & R. G. DelCampo (Eds.), *Hispanics at work: A collection of research, theory, and application.* (pp. 85–109). Hauppauge, NY: Nova.

Stone, D. L., Johnson, R. D., Stone-Romero, E. F., & Hartman, M. (2006). A comparative study of Hispanic-American and Anglo-American cultural values and job choice preferences. *Management Research: Journal of the Iberoamerican Academy of Management, 4*, 7–21.
Stone-Romero, E. F., Stone, D. L., & Salas, E. (2003). The role of culture on work-related scripts and role taking in organizations. *Applied Psychology: An International Review, 52*, 328–362.
Suazo, M., Martínez, P. G., & Sandoval, R. (2009). Creating psychological and legal contracts through human resource practices: A signaling theory perspective. *Human Resource Management Review, 19*, 154–166.
Suazo, M., Martínez, P.G & Sandoval, R. (2011). Creating psychological and legal contracts through HRM practices: A strength of signals perspective. *Employee Responsibilities and Rights Journal, 23*, 187–204.
Tajfel, H., & Turner, J. C. (1979). An integrative theory of intergroup conflict. *The Social Psychology of Intergroup Relations, 33*(47), 74.
Taylor, B. L., DelCampo, R. G., & Blancero, D. M. (2009). Work–family conflict/facilitation and the role of workplace supports for U.S. Hispanic professionals. *Journal of Organizational Behavior, 30*, 643–664.
Thomas, R. R. (1990). From affirmative action to affirming diversity. *Harvard Business Review, 68*(2), 107–117.
Triandis, H. C. (1994). *Culture and social behavior.* New York, NY: McGraw-Hill.
Triandis, H., Bontempo, R., Villareal, M., Asai, M., & Lucca, N. (1988). Individualism and collectivism: Cross-cultural perspectives on self-in-group relationships. *Journal of Personality and Social Psychology, 54*, 323–338.
Triandis, H. C., Marin, G., Betancourt, H., Lisansky, J., & Chang, B. (1982). *Dimensions of familialism among Hispanic and mainstream Navy recruits.* (Technical Report No. 14). Champaign, IL: University of Illinois, Department of Psychology.
Triandis, H. C., Marin, G., Lisansky, J., & Betancourt, H. (1984). Simpatia as a cultural script of Hispanics. *Journal of Personality and Social Psychology, 47*, 1363–1375.
Turner, J. C., & Oakes, P. J. (1986). The significance of the social identity concept for social psychology with reference to individualism, interactionism and social influence. *British Journal of Social Psychology, 25*, 237–252.
Uhl-Bien, M., Tierney, P. S., Graen, G. B., & Wakabayashi, M. (1990). Company paternalism and the hidden-investment process identification of the "right type" for line managers in leading Japanese organizations. *Group & Organization Management, 15*, 414–430.
United States Census Bureau. (2014). *Annual estimates of the resident population by sex, age, race, and Hispanic origin for the United States and States: April 1, 2010 to July 1, 2014.* Retrieved September 26, 2016, from https://factfinder.census.gov/faces/tableservices/jsf/pages/productview.xhtml?src=bkmk
Volpone, S. D. (2012). Es muy importante! Integrating Hispanics' cultural values in the workplace to influence the retention of Hispanic employees. In D. M. Blancero & R. G. DelCampo (Eds.), *Hispanics at work: A collection of research, theory, and application.* (pp. 39–64). Hauppauge, NY: Nova.
Yan, J. & Hunt, J. (2005). A cross cultural perspective on perceived leadership effectiveness. *International Journal of Cross Cultural Management, 5*, 49–66.

Yang, N., Chen, C.C., Choi, J., & Zou, Y. (2000). Sources of work-family conflict: A Sino–U.S. comparison of the effects of work and family demands. *Academy of Management Journal*, 43, 113–123.

Zhang, L., A. Gowan, M., & Treviño, M. (2014). Cross-cultural correlates of career and parental role commitment. *Journal of Managerial Psychology, 29*, 736–754.

CHAPTER 5

LEADING WOMEN

Unique Challenges and Suggestions for Moving Forward

Caren Goldberg
Bowie State University

Lucy Gilson and Sarah Nesci
University of Connecticut

ABSTRACT

The number of women graduating from college and entering the workforce continues to rise, and while research has examined women as leaders, much less attention has been given to leading women. In this chapter, we aim to start a conversation that looks to flip the conventional leadership discourse, by suggesting that an important component of effective leadership is understanding how to lead women. It is through this lens that we emphasize the importance of recognizing some of the differences and adaptations that leaders must make to effectively lead women. Specifically, we discuss some of the unique challenges faced by women employees, with an eye toward uncovering ways in which traditional leadership paradigms might need to shift in order to meet the needs of an increasingly heterogeneous workforce. We note, too, that while our primary focus is on women employees, some of these challenges parallel those experienced by racial-ethnic minority employees; thus, throughout the chapter we refer to the research on both groups. At the end of each section we offer a set of recommendations grounded in research and current events that we hope will add to the academic/practitioner conversation on how to more effectively lead women.

It is 2017, so we are happy to report that organizations have made great strides in the recruitment and selection of women and minorities. In the 50 years since the U.S. Equal Employment Opportunity Commission began tracking data, women's labor force participation rate has increased from 31.5% to 48.7%. Similarly, the labor force participation rate for African Americans has risen from 8.2% in to 14% over the same period. However, despite these gains in overall employment, less attention has been given to strategies that aim to retain, promote and facilitate the career progression of women and minorities. An example of this was recently highlighted in the mainstream media with Ursula Burns, CEO of Xerox, announcing that when the company splits by the end of 2016, she will no longer be at the helm, a role she has held since 2009. It is worth noting here, Catalyst (2016) reports that when she steps down, the number of women CEO's in the Fortune 500 will drop from 23 to 22, the number Black Fortune 500 CEO's will drop from five to four, and the sum total of Black women CEOs in the Fortune 500 will drop to zero, just as it was prior to 2009.

While much has been written about leadership, leadership styles, and the topic of women as leaders, much less is known about how to lead women. The scarcity of women and minorities in higher level positions suggests that traditional notions of what constitutes good leadership might not be working in the expected ways for women and/or minorities. Decades of research on leadership suggest that while there are individual differences in leadership ability (Gardner, Lowe, Moss, Mahoney & Cogliser, 2010), much of what constitutes "good leadership" is subordinate-specific. For example, the leader–member exchange (LMX) literature emphasizes that leadership is a function of the dyadic relationships between leaders and followers (Graen & Uhl-Bien, 1995; Graen & Scandura, 1987). More specifically, LMX theory proposes that leaders vary their styles based on who they are leading (subordinates), or in other words, subordinates can influence how leaders behave. The argument that leadership is based on the relationship and that subordinates can affect the leadership process further suggests that leadership is not unidirectional and that who is being led needs to be considered. Within this stream of literature, researchers have posited that compared to White male followers, women and minority followers experience greater difficulty establishing and maintaining high quality relationships with their (predominantly White and male) supervisors (Goldberg & McKay, 2015; Scandura & Lakau, 1996).

Decades of research supports the notion that leadership does not occur in a vacuum and thus leaders who consider the specific needs of their followers are deemed more effective than those who do not. For example, Bass's (1985) model of transformational leadership (and subsequent variations of it), which has been among the most popular individual-difference models of leadership in the past 30 years, emphasizes the importance of "individualized consideration" in overall leadership effectiveness. Like LMX, individualized consideration emphasizes the unique interactions that supervisors have with their subordinates. However, whereas LMX focuses on the dyad as the unit of observation, transformational leadership emphasizes the leaders' ability to see each follower as unique. Thus, whether one favors the dyadic approach or the individual difference perspective on effective leadership, it is clear that being able to understand and respond to the unique challenges faced by one's followers is an important component of effective leadership. It is through this lens that we emphasize the importance of recognizing some of the differences and adaptations that leaders must make, to effectively lead women. That is, to the extent that women face obstacles that are substantively different from those of their White and/or male counterparts, leaders who view their employees as individuals are apt to better perceive these differences and act accordingly. As a race-based example, consider the number of videos of unarmed Black men and women being treated as "guilty" by police officers in what appear to be routine traffic stops that have recently been posted on social media. These posts, in conjunction with the Black Lives Matter movement, cannot be isolated from the organizational experience of people of color. In support of this point, a recent *PBS Newshour* article (Downs, 2016) underscored the need for leaders to consider the impact of such events on Black employees. As noted in the article:

> According to Monnica Williams, clinical psychologist and director of the Center for Mental Health Disparities at the University of Louisville, graphic videos (which she calls vicarious trauma) combined with lived experiences of racism, can create severe psychological problems reminiscent of post-traumatic stress syndrome.

Thus, while it may feel like just another day at the office for White employees, leaders need to be sensitive to the impact that these events may have on their Black employees.

In this chapter, we will discuss some of the unique challenges faced by women and minority employees with an eye toward uncovering ways in which traditional leadership paradigms need to shift in order to meet the needs of the increasingly heterogeneous workforce. We begin with an overview of some of the research on diversity; we next discuss how leaders' speech patterns may affect how words are perceived by women; and move to a discussion of the role of technology in leadership and followership. We close by offering a set of recommendations grounded in research and current events, which we hope will add to the academic/practitioner conversation on how to more effectively lead women.

UNIQUE CHALLENGES FACED BY WOMEN EMPLOYEES

The Role of Stereotypes

As measures of diversity, sex and race have the longest and most thoroughly documented history (Williams & O'Reilly, 1998). Race and sex are both highly visible individual differences that, for the most part, enable one to make quick assessments on these characteristics after a very brief encounter. Demography research suggests that categories that are most visible and therefore easily accessible and salient across situations trigger immediate social categorization of oneself and others. In support of this, researchers have found that individuals use sex more than any other immediately apparent features in social categorization (Stangor, Lynch, Duan, & Glass, 1992). In addition, individuals working in groups or organizations of differing proportions of men and women have been found to report having different work experiences (Ely, 1994; Tsui et al., 1992). Consequently, sex remains a key segregating variable not only because it is easily detectable, but also because of the readily observable social differentiations associated with it as a category (Blau, 1977; Milliken & Martin, 1996).

Research on person perception suggests that competence and warmth are two primary attributes people use for categorizing others into groups (Fiske, Cuddy, Glick, & Xu, 2002; Wojciske, 2005). Notably, Whites are often perceived as higher in competence than Blacks (Cuddy, Fiske, & Glick, 2007; Fiske, Xu, Cuddy, & Glick, 1999; Fiske et al., 2002; Major & O'Brien, 2005), while women are generally perceived as higher in warmth. Decades of research suggests that women are frequently perceived as less suitable for leadership positions, as such roles are typically deemed as requiring more masculine, agentic traits (e.g., dominant, aggressive, self-confident; Eagly, Wood, & Diekman, 2000). While the effects of negative stereotypes may be particularly pronounced early in a relationship between leader and follower, they also are difficult to overcome. For instance, even when a woman or minority subordinate counters the negative competence stereotype—that is, they do well on a task or in a specific job—perceivers tend to recall stereotype-consistent information more readily than information that is inconsistent with or unrelated to a stereotype (Brewer & Miller, 1984). Consequently, the impact of initial expectations of competence may have a lasting effect and thus affect subsequent promotion opportunities often masking actual performance. For example, Jones and King (2016) recently noted that managers frequently assume they need to "protect" women from risky and/or more challenging work assignments, even when there are no differences in men's and women's interest in pursuing such assignments. The result of these acts of "benevolent sexism" are that women are less prepared to take on future leadership roles and are less apt to receive the constructive criticism, feedback, encouragement, mentoring, and support they need to improve their work performance and grow in leadership roles.

In addition to the effects that negative stereotypes have on leaders' perceptions of women and minorities, these stereotypes also can impact the women and minority employees themselves. Berger, Rosenholtz, and Zelditch (1980) noted that members of low-status groups tend to internalize the lower expectations that others have of them. Thus, a vicious cycle begins: Leaders' low expectations decrease followers' confidence; lack of confidence, in turn, results in fewer contributions to the group and decreased desire to stay at the organization. Work by Sabat, Goldberg, and King (2016) recently found that after controlling for new hires' initial self-efficacy, managers' efficacy beliefs in them had a significant effect on the new hires' later self-efficacy, which was related to turnover outcomes. This study suggested that the "leaky pipeline" (higher turnover among women and minorities) is partly attributable to a Pygmalion effect, whereby leaders' expectations of subordinates' competence influence subordinates' own sense of competence and ultimately their desire to stay at the organization. These findings are consistent with leader–member-exchange (LMX) research, which points to additional means through which stereotypes influence superior-subordinate work relationships. For example, Goldberg, McKay, and Zhang (2009) found that role clarity mediates the link between subordinates' initial perceptions of LMX and leaders' subsequent perceptions of LMX for Black newcomers, but not for White newcomers. This suggests that there may be fundamental differences in the ways in which demographically dissimilar dyads perceive the subordinate's role (and hence subsequent leader perceptions of how well the individual fulfills it), which may be overcome through role-clarifying efforts, such as the provision of constructive feedback, encouragement, and mentoring.

Suggestion for Moving Forward

Given the effects that stereotypes can have on the retention and career advancement of women and minorities, we offer several suggestions to mitigate these effects. While each of these suggestions addresses a different HR functions, all share the common thread of helping to build the female or minority employee's efficacy expectations (beliefs in their ability to do the job well), rather than chip away at them.

- Train leaders to be aware of stereotypes. Currently, the term "implicit bias" (Devine, Forscher, Austin, & Cox, 2012) is receiving a great deal of media attention, and many well-known companies (i.e., Google) are running diversity training programs to help employees become aware of their biases and blind spots. Training everyone is a good step, but more specific training needs to be targeted at organizational leaders. Many employers' appraisal systems "call out" a particular manager for not having promoted a substantive number of women or minority subordinates. Therefore, we suggest that training provide a broader message about the pervasiveness of stereotypes as a means of curbing defensiveness or denial on the part of individual managers, which might undermine effectiveness. For example, training aimed at openly discussing the stereotypes that exist with regard to women and minorities coupled with an understanding of the fact that stereotyping is a natural human tendency is less likely to lead to a defensive reaction on the part of leaders. It is important to allow managers time to reflect on their stereotypes or assumptions and in particular the instances where particular female and/or minority employees did not fit with the stereotype. Recollection and reflection may allow leaders to feel more comfortable discussing their own experiences and help them to identify possible pitfalls before they occur.
- Train and reinforce organizational decision makers to value the aspects of leadership that are more commonly associated with underrepresented groups. A great deal of empirical research supports the notion that "men fit cultural construals of leadership better than women do and thus have better access to leader roles and face fewer challenges in becoming successful in them" (Koenig, Eagly, Mitchell, & Ristikari, 2011, p. 637). Thus, rather than putting the onus on women to behave in what is traditioanlly considered to be a more masculine manner (e.g., dominant, assertive, self-confident), perhaps the burden should be shifted to emphasize the importance of feminine qualities in grooming employees for leadership roles (e.g., warmth, consideration, democratic decision making).
- Conduct employee training in positive error climates so they see mistakes as natural rather than as reflections of incompetence. Psychological safety research (Edmondson, 1999) finds that when climates allow individuals to take risks and try new things, employee creativity and performance is enhanced (Shalley & Gilson, 2004). In a similar vein, women and minority employees face a vexing prob-

lem and a vicious cycle when it comes to asking for help and seeking feedback, which are both ultimately related to creativity and performance. Employees need feedback to improve performance. However, there are differences in how requests for help are perceived. For example, when men ask for help, they are often perceived as trustworthy, because they are demonstrating a willingness to show their vulnerabilities. In contrast, women and minorities asking for help may serve to reinforce the negative competence stereotypes that they don't really know how to do their jobs without the help of others, stereotypes that are often attributed to employees who are considered to be different from oneself or from diverse race-ethnic groups (Steele, 1997). Employee training that occurs in a climate in which errors are expressly expected and indicated to be a natural part of learning (Baumgartner & Seifried, 2014), in other words "a psychologically safe work environment" (Edmondson, 1999), should help to alleviate the threat experienced by members of groups that are stereotyped as low in competence.

- Encourage leaders to establish rapport with subordinates early in the relationship so that they feel comfortable clarifying their roles. As with the previous recommendation, the emphasis here is on creating an environment where employees feel less reticent to actively seek clarification for fear of retribution (Edmondson, 1999) or confirmation of negative competence stereotypes (Roberson & Kulik, 2007). The earlier a leader establishes this rapport with a follower, the more trust there should be in the relationship allowing for feedback seeking, feedback giving and constructive criticism. In a similar vein, research on virtual teams finds that meeting at least once face-to-face allows team members to develop trust, foster stronger working relationships, and perform better on complex ambiguous tasks (Martins, Gilson, & Maynard, 2014 for a review). As noted elsewhere, this information is critical to the employee's performance and development, which in turn should affect that individual's subsequent promotion opportunities and retention within an organization.

Token Status

The effects of stereotypes are likely particularly pronounced in organizations where only a few token women or minorities are promoted. Kanter (1977) contended that being in an extreme minority (less than 15%) relegates one to token status. Because of their small numbers, token employees are more visible to leaders, which (a) makes group stereotypes more salient and (b) subjects them to greater pressures to perform their work to higher standards. Given that women and minorities are, in general, accorded lower status in society (Berger et al., 1980), their token status in an organization is apt to evoke particularly negative stereotypes (Fairhurst & Snavely, 1983a, 1983b).

In certain fields, women and/or minorities are in short supply, and this is apt to affect leaders' ability to hire more than a token number of individuals from underrepresented groups. For example, the racial divide in employment in STEM fields partly reflects the fact that Blacks and Hispanics are less likely than their White counterparts to pursue degrees in science, technology, math, or engineering. While average group investments in human capital may account for some of the disparities in employment, this is an overly simplistic view of investment/return ratios. In particular, it ignores the fact that the same investment made by individuals of different groups is not likely to yield the same return. Research suggests that Blacks and Hispanics with bachelor's and graduate level degrees have significantly lower odds of employment in high-tech jobs (Gatchair, 2013). This creates something of a vicious cycle. Given that their human capital investments are not likely to yield as high of a return, there is less incentive to make investments upfront, and because fewer investments are made, they yield lower returns.

Suggestions for Moving Forward

To minimize the likelihood of tokenizing women or minorities, we offer suggestions aimed at both increasing the numbers of individuals from underrepresented groups as well as creating more inclusive environments for those individuals. The key here is to move away from the "promote one and say done," mentality that may result in the token woman or minority feeling isolated, or worse, questioning whether their membership in the underrepresented category was the sole basis for having been promoted.

- Hire women and minorities in larger numbers. While employee selection is somewhat outside the scope of this chapter, it seems obvious that organizations that do not recruit and/or retain enough individuals from underrepresented groups to maintain a talent pool for subsequent promotions, will face greater challenges in effectively leading these individuals. In fields where there is an abundant supply, such as business where men and women claim an almost equal percentage of bachelor's degrees awarded annually, this should be a fairly straightforward task. In other areas, where there is a paucity of women and minority graduates this may involve more systemic efforts, such as scholarships aimed at increasing the number of individuals from underrepresented groups and consciously mentoring individuals once they are in these programs to encourage them to stay and complete their program of study. However such mentoring programs while often well-intentioned can also be controversial and receive a great deal of backlash. The University of Connecticut recently opened a learning community to Black male students. This dorm was supported (financially) by Black male alumni who wanted to give back to the university by mentoring and supporting young Black men, a population with one of the lowest graduation rates at many universities. While many saw this as a step forward, others criticized it as a form of segregation because dorm space had been created for Black males. Other programs such as Microsoft's scholarship program for Black high school students who plan to pursue college degrees in engineering, information systems, or computer science, and the PhD Project supported by KPMG, which helps minority students navigate the path to getting a doctoral degree in business, have been welcomed in their respective domains.

- Promote cohorts of women and minorities at various levels. In larger organizations, particularly those in industries that have a reasonable representation of women and minorities, it is wise to consider promoting multiple women and minorities at the same time. The presence of similar others serves to reduce one's perception of being the token minority/woman. In addition, it is an effective means of getting voice, particularly at higher levels of the organization where the representation of other women and minorities gets thinner. For example, Landsbaum (2016) recently highlighted an example from underrepresented women in the Obama administration:

    > Female staffers adopted a meeting strategy they called "amplification": When a woman made a key point, other women would repeat it, giving credit to its author. This forced the men in the room to recognize the contribution and denied them the chance to claim the idea as their own.

- Affinity groups are another means of minimizing the isolation that can be experienced by individuals who belong to underrepresented groups. Even the most effective leadership may not fully guard against a woman or minority employee's perceived isolation, particularly in organizations or industries where there remains a large imbalance. While we certainly encourage leaders to adopt the practice of promoting women and minorities in cohorts, such a policy may not be practical in smaller organizations where there aren't a sufficient number of openings to promote employees in groups or in fields where there aren't enough women or minorities at any given level (for example, many engineering fields) to expect them to be promoted in cohorts. In such situations, affinity groups may be particularly effective. Broadly speaking, affinity or network groups provide a forum for employees of similar backgrounds who are typically underrepresented in the organization to get together socially and share ideas outside of their work group. By creating a venue for employees from underrepresented groups to meet, affinity groups provide an atmosphere of inclusion to employees who might otherwise feel marginalized. Although the leader may not necessarily be a part of the affinity group (unless the individual is also a member of the underrepresented group), advocating for the creation of such groups or encouraging employees to participate in them if they already exist may go a long way in signaling an understanding to female or minority followers that the leader recognizes the employee may be experiencing feelings of isolation. For example, companies like ESPN have active women's leadership forums dedicated to promoting "diversity, inclusion and wellness" (https://espncareers.com/working-here/diversity-inclusion-wellness) in an industry that has traditionally been male-dominated. Tauriac, Kim, Sarinana, and Kahn (2013) also point out that affinity groups provide fertile ground for generating ideas about how to improve the organizational environment that may subsequently be shared with other groups as well as senior leadership, which is usually comprised of White males described as "pale, male, and stale" a term coined in the 1940s, but rose to prominence in 1992 when NASA administrator Daniel Goldin declared that the agency was too "pale, male, and stale." Affinity groups may increase inclusiveness in multiple ways. For example, a lone female engineer may feel more comfortable sharing ideas about improving the experience of women in the workplace in a group of other female engineers than with her leader. Likewise, given the psychological toll that police brutality toward Black civilians may have on Black employees that may go unnoticed by a Black employee's leader, an affinity group might provide a more comfortable space for Black employees to discuss how such events affect them personally.

When looking at the aforementioned recommendations holistically, one of the themes that starts to emerge is that successfully leading women and minorities requires that some conscious choices be made by leadership. In other words, the "if you build it they will come" mentality is not working. Leaders need to connect with their subordinates and be clear on what their needs are individually and collectively. Toward this end, an area of research that emphasizes the criticality of building connections and strengthening relationships is communication. In the next section, we will discuss the role of communication in leading women. This is not an exhaustive review on communication and there is a chapter in this book that covers this topic in more depth. However, in order to do justice to our topic and to transition to the role of technology in leading women, the topic of communication must first be addressed.

THE ROLE OF SPEECH PATTERNS IN LEADING WOMEN, AND WOMEN AS LEADERS

While men and women have differences that they are born with, which while no longer impossible are very hard to change (i.e., chromosomes, reproductive organs, and hormones), research suggests that communication styles are learned (Tannen, 1990, 1994). Deborah Tannen notes in a recent article "The Power of Talk: Who Gets Heard and Why" (2016) that people learn conversational rituals starting on the playground. In other words, women learn very early on and long before they are considering career choices, leadership style and how they want to be led, or who they want to lead them; the more they use inclusive pronouns like "we" as opposed to pronouns like "I" and "me," the more friends they will have.

Gendered Speech Patterns

While girls and boys develop different communication patterns from a very young age, the choice of words and their associated thought processes clearly transition into workplace communication. Here, research consistently finds that women talk in a more inclusive manner, seeking to engage and share through using terms like "we" more often than men, who are prone to speak in a more declarative manner where the goal is to win or solve a problem (Tannen, 1995). The flip side of this equation is that women who are looking to move up the corporate ladder and ensure that their voices get heard at work, often experience trouble building credibility because of the way they speak (Dominic, 2010). Note the example used earlier from the Obama cabinet: the women had to "band together" to ensure that their voices were heard (Landsbaum, 2016).

Women in the Obama cabinet came up with a successful strategy to get their voices heard; however, research suggests that the content of women's messages is more highly scrutinized than the content of men's messages. For example, small talk or polite conversation about unimportant and/or uncontroversial matters that is social in nature has been found to benefit men but not women. Research by Shaughnessy, Mislin, and Jones (2015) found that when men use small talk, they get up to an 8% boost in the overall impression others have of them with regard to trust, which can result in a positive foundation for future relationships. No such effects (positive or negative) were found for women who engage or use small talk. Taken together this could mean that assertive language can hurt women and small talk does not help—not a promising picture!

The question of whether women should change the way they talk in the workplace is one which, according to Evans (2016), is tightly coupled with issues related to power. Because assertive speech patterns are negatively received, women have been found to ask a lot of "tag-questions," questions that are framed so that the person being asked feels like he or she has equal or more authority than the person doing the asking (Dominic, 2010). For example, a female employee in a work group is more likely to say something like, "We should probably report this missing bank statement to accounting, shouldn't we?" In contrast, a male counterpart in the same work group might phrase the same request as, "Amy, can you send this missing statement over to accounting?" In the latter question, the choice of sentence structure makes the male appear to have the power in the conversation because he is not asking for input.

Gender and Filler Words

Along with these tag questions, female speech patterns include more filler words that are used as either compliments or apologies (Tannen, 1994). According to linguist Janet Holmes (1995), women compliment other women more than they compliment men and more than men compliment men. This research supports the idea that men talk to accomplish something whereas women talk to build rapport. If a female coworker asked another to give her feedback on a presentation, the response would likely include some form of compliment along with constructive feedback. Therefore, while the employee will hear of things she needs to improve upon, she also will get praise for how eloquently she spoke or the great points she made. In contrast, a male coworker who asked for input would be more likely to see this question as an opportunity to give criticism that he will perceive as helpful to his coworker and a means to help her present better the next time. These types of linguistic patterns can cause tension in the workplace between male and female coworkers when the expected response differs from the actual response. Apologies such as saying "sorry" even when there is nothing to apologize for also are commonly used by females, especially in phone and email conversations (Tannen, 1994). This type of filler is considered a way to restore a power balance to the conversation by women. Men however say "I'm sorry" less because they have learned that one-upping their partner is a means of achieving or maintaining a position of power in the conversation. The consequence of filler words is that women are often taken less seriously as leaders because they do not create a power position through their speech.

Gendered Speech Patterns

The relationship between power and leadership is well established and both are further connected to credibility. Two recently labeled phenomena "manterrupting" and "bropropriating" (Bennet, 2015) are being attributed to making it harder for women to be seen as credible in leadership positions. Manterrupting is defined by Bennet as "unnecessary interruption of a woman by a man." This common male communication pattern is a problem that reaches outside the borders of the office. Researchers from George Washington University conducted a study in which 20 male and 20 female volunteers engaged in one short conversation with a male volunteer and one short conversation with a female volunteer. The results showed that the male volunteers interrupted their female counterparts an average of 2.1 times per conversation, while females interrupted their male counterparts an average of one time per conversation (Hancock & Rubin, 2014).

The term bropropriating refers to "taking a woman's idea and getting credit for it." In her 1995 book *Talking 9 to 5,* Tannen provides multiple examples of how ideas raised by women are ultimately credited to men. She suggests that part of the reason for this is the question-tagging discussed previously. That is because women end sentences with a question or seek input as a way of gaining buy-in for their ideas, listeners may be less apt to give them credit for originating the idea. Bropropriating has significant implications for women's ability to move up in the ranks. Specifically, as ideas are not properly being attributed to the women who create them, these women may be perceived as less capable of contributing to upper level positions where such input is more often demanded.

Manterrupting and bropropriating are both newer terms that resonate with many Millennials entering the workforce for the first time. A similar trend within the Millennial generation is known as, "vocal fry." Vocal fry, also known as laryngealization or popcorning, is when the vocal cords compress and form a large vibrating mass that produces a low rattling sound when air passes through. When individuals use this speech pattern their voice drops at the end of sentences and a guttural sound ensues. While hard to describe, a video clip of vocal fry can be heard online (https://www.youtube.com/watch?v=YEqVgtLQ7qM). Vocal fry has been popularized by celebrities such as Kim Kardashian (Katz, 2014). A study done on the effects of vocal fry on women in the labor market found that women who exhibit vocal fry are perceived as less competent, less educated, less trustworthy and even less attractive than others in their mock interviews (Anderson, Klofstad, Mayew, & Venkatachalam, 2014). These findings suggest that while this is a popular trend, it may be hindering the employment and advancement opportunities of younger women.

In addition to vocal fry, general pitch and tone of voice affect the way that men and women are perceived in the workplace. Specifically, men speak louder than women and have lower voice tones that carry further and are easier to hear than are higher pitched tones. Therefore, while it might be more "natural" for men to speak louder and use more direct statements, when women try to employ these very same tactics their communicated message is less favorably received (Tannen, 1994). Instead of being considered assertive and knowledgeable, they are labeled "bossy" and worse their audience does not take them seriously. (Tannen, 1994).

Suggestions for Moving the Conversation Forward

While we cannot offer suggestions to change the biological attributes of speech, we do offer suggestions aimed at both improving the way women communicate as leaders and to their leaders. Because communication is learned through socialization, certain types of speech patterns that are inhibiting female growth and advancement can be unlearned. More masculine styles of language can be taught in their place and recognizing the differences in speech patterns can be used to the advantage of women.

- Understand the difference between assertive and aggressive communication. It behooves organizations to ensure that HR managers, leaders, and employees are all clear on the difference between assertive and aggressive communication. The dictionary definition states that aggression is a communication method that while expressing one's needs and desires does not take in to account the welfare of others. In contrast, assertive communication means expressing oneself effectively, standing up for a point of view while also respecting the rights and beliefs of others. The critical difference here is the respect for the beliefs of others. Because as a society we are still less accustomed to seeing women speak up, assertive communication is often labeled as aggressive, which really does a huge disservice to the communicator.
- Provide vocal training on projection and pitch. Theater students spend a great deal of time learning how to project their voices, change the timber or pitch of their monologue, and where to place emphasis for effect. Why can we not offer the same training to female leaders? Given that we know certain voice tones are more easily heard, organizations might want to invest in this sort of training for their employees.

- Train both men and women on taking and giving credit for ideas and suggestions. As we saw in the Obama cabinet example, awareness is often the first step.

The previous section focused on the importance of communication for leaders as well as leading others. However, the focus has been on what is now considered a traditional or even old-school communication modality: face-to-face talking. With the increase in technological capabilities, a great deal of communication today takes place via technology, and the topic of virtual teams and leading virtual teams has received a great deal of research attention over the last 15 years (see Martins et al., 2004; Gilson et al., 2014 for reviews). Accordingly, we close our chapter with a section in which we discuss the effects of technology on women as leaders and how technology can and is being used to lead others.

THE INFLUENCE OF TECHNOLOGY ON WOMEN LEADERS AND LEADING WOMEN

As work continues to become increasingly more geographically dispersed and reliance on technology assisted communication increases, we now turn our attention to the implications of this trend on women at work. The Millennial generation is believed to place a greater value on work-life balance (Carless & Wintle, 2007), and telework or flexible work arrangements allow for scheduling latitude and mobility that should align with their expectations of balance and outside of work responsibilities. In addition, the Millennial generation has grown up with technology so using it to communicate has become an expectation. Although the percentages have been shifting regarding family-role expectations, women still bear a much larger portion of the responsibility when it comes to caring for family and home life. This has led many to believe that virtual teams and telework should provide a great number of benefits to women. And indeed they do, in particular when it comes to scheduling and times at which work can be conducted. No longer is it necessary to physically be present in a specific location to work. In fact, work can often follow the employee or leader and be conducted 24/7 from virtually any location. However, technology is not the panacea that it was once hoped to be.

Being "Camera Ready" for Work

With an increased reliance on technology, there is also an increased expectation that employees will be always available and while they may not be physically present at the same place, they can always be reached or seen via technology. As we see frequently in the media, women are judged more harshly based on their physical appearance and technological presence. For example, whereas a manager may not think negatively of a male employee who participates in a video conference looking somewhat unkempt (i.e., having not shaved or wearing a baseball cap to disguise unclean hair), a woman who participates in a video conference without makeup is apt to be perceived in a negative light. Similarly, a male supervisor or subordinate who has a child with him while taking a conference call is apt to be regarded positively as, "He is helping take care of his family." In contrast, a woman in the same scenario will most likely be perceived as not giving her full attention to work. Therefore, while technology can be beneficial for women because it allows them to have more control over when and where they work, a double standard is emerging when it comes to being "camera ready" for work.

Leading Virtual Teams

One of the more encouraging findings with regard to developing female leaders comes from the research on leading virtual teams. In contrast to traditional face-to-face scenarios where masculine agentic characteristics signal the potential for leadership development, in a virtual environment, transformational leadership appears to arise from personality and (more importantly here) specific facets of leader communication (Balthazard, Waldman, & Warren, 2009). Specifically, a study by Ruggieri (2009) found that leaders of virtual teams who focused on relationships rather than task-based factors were perceived as more intelligent, creative, and original. Thus, rather than considering traditionally feminine communication characteristics such as relationship-building and inclusiveness as indicative of low leadership potential, as had traditionally been the case, within virtual teams these characteristics are rated as indicative of high leadership potential. The literature on leadership competencies needed in virtual teams (Malholtra, Majchrzak, & Rosen, 2007; Switzer, 2000) consistently lists characteristics such as enabling others, ensuring other members feel understood and appreciated, listening and including others as some of the most important qualities. In part, this is because members of virtual teams often feel isolated and that they don't *really* know who they are working with. Early research on virtual teams consistently found that while they were successful on simple additive tasks, once the task became more complex or ambiguous virtual teams were no longer as successful as their face-to-face counterparts (Martins et al., 2004). One suggestion for this finding was that virtual team members did not feel connected to one another, so when there was uncertainty no one was willing to show the necessary levels of vulnerability. Therefore, leaders who include everyone and make them feel a part of the team are more successful in a leaner communication environment. Hence, a less agentic communication style lends itself better to leading virtual teams. This finding is very similar to the work on LMX described in the opening of this chapter that highlighted the importance of individual consideration in building the strong relationships necessary to successfully lead women.

Technology and Anonymity

A potential advantage of working virtually or using technology to communicate has always been positioned as some level of anonymity. Being somewhat obscured from others should dampen several of the issues detailed as challenges encountered by women in face-to-face communication. Interestingly however, research by Gilson et al. (2013) found that one of the first things members of virtual teams try to do is ascertain who they are communicating with. In a study of college students across universities, the research team found that on receiving their team assignments the first thing the students did was to log into as many other electronic sources (i.e., Facebook, LinkedIn) as possible to "put a face to the name." When pressed as to why it mattered whether Chris from the University of XYZ was male or female, the answer was consistently that they needed to know who they were talking to so as to make talking easier! This response ties closely to research on demographic diversity and self-categorization theory (Tajfel & Turner, 1986). Self-categorization theory states that individuals seek to place themselves and others into groups based upon characteristics that are the most salient or easily observable. These groups are then used as the basis to promote a positive self-identity and categorize the self and like others as in-group members and those who are different as out-group members (Tajfel & Turner, 1986). What this suggests is that even when using technology our stereotypes and biases about working with others who are different from oneselves may persist. Further research is needed to determine whether virtual communication might weaken such effects. For example, much of the research on implicit biases relies on visual stimuli (i.e., subjects react to the presentation of a White/ Black or male/female photograph). If team members are aware of others' demographics but not visually prompted with this information, perhaps the effects and attributions might diminish.

Suggestions for Moving Forward

- When it comes to leading teams using technology the results for women are mixed. There is a lot that is positive, but some hurdles still exist that need to be considered moving forward.

- Ensure technology and task needs match. There is a wide range of technology available to organizations, teams, and individuals. However, employees and leaders are somewhat reluctant to change; hence, we tend to rely on the same technology for almost every task. Understanding the media-richness theory (Daft & Lengel, 1984) might be important here. Media richness theory discusses the extent to which a technology enables synchronous collaboration. For example, videoconferencing is relatively high in media richness and synchronicity, whereas email is low on both dimensions. Other technologies such as the telephone, websites, instant messaging, file- and application-sharing, all range with regard to their richness. Leaders need to be trained to think carefully about what technology they use and why because the unexpected consequences of certain technologies for women might be higher than expected. There are times when a rich media that allows team members to see each other is appropriate and necessary, but Skype video is not always necessary and awareness of what other options are available and what tasks they are best suited for is a useful leadership tool.
- Develop virtual team leadership training. While it appears women are already doing well in the sphere of virtual team leadership, as more and more teams rely on technology to communicate it will be beneficial to train leaders on the skills needed to lead virtual teams. What is interesting here is that leading virtual teams appears to be less about demonstrating task-relevant knowledge and more about individualized consideration and ensuring that other team members feel connected to each other. Communication frequency, tone, and modeling the way through encouragement as well as building on the suggestions of others are all important steps.

CONCLUSION

In conclusion, most current theories on leadership advocate for treating each subordinate or dyad as unique. In practice, however, organizations have often adopted a one-size-fits-all approach. In this chapter we have outlined some of the particular challenges faced by women and minority employees in an effort to help leaders recognize them and respond accordingly. In addition, we provide several recommendations for mangers who are looking for ways to more effectively lead women and minority employees.

REFERENCES

Anderson, R. C., Klofstad, C. A., Mayew, W. J., & Venkatachalam, M. (2014). Vocal fry may undermine the success of young women in the labor market. *PLoS ONE 9*(5), e97506. doi:10.1371/journal.pone.0097506

Balthazard, P. A., Waldman, D. A., & Warren, J. E. (2009). Predictors of the emergence of transformational leadership in virtual decision teams. *The Leadership Quarterly, 20*(5), 651–663.

Bass, B. M. (1985). *Leadership and performance.* New York, NY: Free Press.

Baumgartner, A., & Seifried, J. (2014). Error climate and how individuals deal with errors in the workplace. In C. Harteis, A. Rausch, & J. Seifried (Eds.). *Discourses on professional learning: On the boundary between learning and working.* Dordrecht, the Netherlands: Springer.

Bennet, J. (2015, January 14). How not to be "manterrupted" in meetings. *Time.*

Berger, J., Rosenholtz, S. J., & Zelditch, M. (1980). Status organizing processes. *Annual Review of Sociology, 6*, 479–508.

Blau, P. (1977). *Inequality and heterogeneity: A primitive theory of social structure.* New York, NY: Free Press.

Brewer, M. B., & Miller, N. (1984). Beyond the contact hypothesis: Theoretical perspectives on desegregation. In N. Miller & M. B. Brewer (Eds.), *Groups in contact: The psychology of desegregation* (pp. 281–302). Orlando, FL: Academic Press.

Carless, S. A., & Wintle, J. (2007). Applicant attraction: The role of recruiter function, work-life balance policies and career salience. *International Journal of Selection and Assessment, 15*(4), 394–404.

Catalyst. (2016). *Women CEOs of the S&P 500.* Retrieved from http://www.catalyst.org/knowledge/women-ceos-sp-500

Cuddy, A. J. C., Fiske, S. T., & Glick, P. (2007). The BIAS map: Behaviors from intergroup affect and stereotypes. *Journal Personality and Social Psychology, 92*, 631–648.

Daft, R. L., & Lengel, R. H. (1984). Information richness: A new approach to managerial behavior and organization design. *Research in Organizational Behavior, 6*, 191–233.

Devine, P. G., Forscher, P. S., Austin, A. J., & Cox, W. T. (2012). Long-term reduction in implicit race bias: A prejudice habit-breaking intervention. *Journal of Experimental Social Psychology, 48*, 1267–1278.

Dominic, L. (2010). Snips and snails and puppy dog tails: Does what we're made of make a difference in the courtroom? *The Jury Expert, 22*(5), 15–22.

Downs, K. (2016). *When Black death goes viral, it can trigger PTSD-like trauma.* Retrieved November 30, 2016, from http://www.pbs.org/newshour/rundown/black-pain-gone-viral-racism-graphic-videos-can-create-ptsd-like-trauma/

Eagly, A. H., Wood, W., & Diekman, A. (2000). Social role theory of sex differences and similarities: A current appraisal. In T. Eckes & H. M. Trautner (Eds.). *The developmental social psychology of gender* (pp. 123–174). Mahwah, NJ: Erlbaum.

Edmondson, A. (1999). Psychological safety and learning behavior in work teams. *Administrative Science Quarterly, 44*, 350–383.

Ely, R. J. (1994). The effects of organizational demographics and the dynamics of relationships among professional women. *Administrative Science Quarterly, 39,* 203–238.

Evans, D., (2016). Should women change the way they talk in the workplace? *New York Magazine.* Retrieved from http://nymag.com/thecut/2016/06/womens-speech-patterns-coaching.html

Fairhurst, G. T., & Snavely, B. K. (1983a). Majority and token minority group relationships: Power acquisition and communication. *Academy of Management Review, 8,* 292–300.

Fairhurst, G. T., & Snavely, B. K. (1983b). A test of the social isolation of male tokens. *Academy of Management Journal, 26,* 353–361.

Fiske, S. T., Cuddy, A. J. C., Glick, P., & Xu, J. (2002). A model of (often mixed) stereotype content: Competence and warmth respectively follow from perceived status and competition. *Journal of Personality and Social Psychology, 82,* 878–902.

Fiske, S. T., Xu, J., Cuddy, A. J. C., & Glick, P. (1999). (Dis)respecting versus (dis)liking: Status and interdependence predict ambivalent stereotypes of competence and warmth. *Journal of Social Issues, 55,* 473–489.

Gardner, W. L., Lowe, K. B., Moss, T. W., Mahoney, K. T., & Cogliser, C. C. (2010). Scholarly leadership of the study of leadership: A review of The Leadership Quarterly's second decade, 2000–2009. *The Leadership Quarterly, 21*(6), 922–958.

Gatchair, S. (2013). Race/ethnicity and education effects on employment in high technology industries and occupations in the U.S., 1992–2002. *Review of Black Political Economy, 40,* 357–370.

Gilson, L. L., Maynard, M. T., & Bergiel, E. B. (2013). Virtual team effectiveness: An experiential activity. *Small Group Research, 44*(4), 412–427.

Gilson, L. L., Maynard, M. T., Jones Young, N. C., Vartiainen, M., & Hakonen, M. (2015, July). *Virtual teams research: 10 years, 10 themes, and 10 opportunities.* Retrieved from http://journals.sagepub.com/doi/pdf/10.1177/0149206314559946

Goldberg, C. B., McKay, P. F., & Zhang, L. (2009, August). *A second chance to make a first impression? A longitudinal examination of changes in Black and White newcomers' leader–member exchange and career future.* Presented at the Academy of Management Conference, Chicago, IL.

Goldberg, C., & McKay, P. (2015). Diversity and LMX development. In T. Bauer & B. Erdogan (Eds.), *The Oxford handbook of leader–member exchange.* Oxford, England: Oxford University Press.

Graen, G. B., & Scandrua, T. A. (1987). Toward a psychology of dyadic organizing. In L. L. Cummings & B. Staw (Eds.), *Research in organizational behavior, 9,* 175–208.

Graen, G. B., & Uhl-Bien, M. (1995). Relationship-based approach to leadership: Development of leader–member exchange (LMX) theory of leadership over 25 years: Applying a multi-level multi-domain perspective. *Leadership Quarterly, 6,* 219–247.

Hancock, A. B., & Rubin, B. A. (2014). Influence of communication partner's gender on language. *Journal of Language and Social Psychology, 34*(1), 46–64.

Holmes, J. (1995). *Women, men, and politeness.* London, England: Longmann.

Jones, K., & King, E. (2016). Stop protecting women from challenging work. *Harvard Business Review*. Retrieved November 30, 2016, from https://hbr.org/2016/09/stop-protecting-women-from-challenging-work.

Kanter, R. M. (1977). Some effects of proportions on group life: Skewed sex rations and responses to token women. *American Journal of Sociology, 82*, 965–990.

Katz, E.T. (2014). Vocal fry, made famous by Kim Kardashian, is making young women 'less hirable.' *Huffington Post*. Retrieved from http://www.huffingtonpost.com/2014/10/31/vocal-fry_n_6082220.html

Koenig, A. M., Eagly, A. H., Mitchell, A. A., & Ristikari, T. (2011). Are leader stereotypes masculine? A meta-analysis of three research paradigms. *Psychological Bulletin, 137*(4), 616–642. doi:10.1037/a0023557

Landsbaum, C. (2016). Obama's female staffers came up with a genius strategy to make sure their voices were heard. *New York Magazine*. Retrieved November 30, 2016, from http://nymag.com/thecut/2016/09/heres-how-obamas-female-staffers-made-their-voices-heard.html.

Major, B., & O'Brien, L. T. (2005). The social psychology of stigma. *Annual Review of Psychology, 56*, 393–421.

Malholtra, A., Majchrzak, A., & Rosen, B. (2007). Leading virtual teams. *Academy of Management Perspectives, 21*, 60–70.

Martins, L. L., Gilson, L. L., & Maynard, M. T. (2004) Virtual teams: What do we know and where do we go from here? *Journal of Management, 30*(6), 805–835.

Maynard, M. T., & Gilson, L. L. (2014). The role of shared mental model development in understanding virtual team effectiveness. *Group & Organization Management, 39*(1), 3–32.

Milliken, F., & Martins, L. (1996). Searching for common threads: Understanding the multiple effects of diversity in organizational groups. *Academy of Management Review, 21*, 402–433.

Roberson, L., & Kulik, C. T. (2007). Stereotype threat at work. *Academy of Management Perspectives, 21*(2), 24–40.

Ruggieri, S. (2009). Leadership in virtual teams: A comparison of transformational and transactional leaders. *Social Behavior & Personality: An International Journal, 37*(8), 1017–1021.

Sabat, I., Goldberg, C., & King, E. (2016, April). *Pygmalion in the pipeline: How managers' perceptions influence minority turnover*. Presented at the Society for Industrial/Organizational Psychologists Conference, Anaheim, CA.

Scandura, T. A., & Lankau, M. J. (1996). Developing diverse leaders: A leader–member exchange approach. *The Leadership Quarterly, 72*, 243–263.

Shalley, C. E., & Gilson, L. L. (2004). What leaders need to know: A review of social and contextual factors that can foster or hinder creativity. *The Leadership Quarterly, 15*(1), 33–53.

Shaughnessy, B., Mislin, A., & Jones, A. (2015, August). *Skillful small talk: How the ability to chat and dyad gender composition affects the negotiation process*. Presented at Academy of Management (AOM) Conference, Vancouver, CA.

Stangor, C., Lynch, L., Duan, C., & Glass, B. (1992). Categorization of individuals on the basis of multiple social features. *Journal of Personality and Social Psychology, 62*, 207–218.

Steele, C. (1997). A threat in the air: How stereotypes shape intellectual identity and performance. *American Psychologist, 52,* 613–629.

Switzer, J. S. (2000). *Virtual teams: profiles of successful leaders* (Unpublished doctoral dissertation). Pepperdine University, Malibu, CA. ProQuest Dissertations 9983697

Tajfel, H., & Turner, J. C. (1986). The social identity theory of intergroup behavior. In S. Worchel & W. G. Austin (Eds.), *Psychology of intergroup relations* (2nd ed., pp. 7–24). Chicago, IL: Nelson-Hall.

Tannen, D. (1990). *You just don't understand: Women and men in conversation.* New York, NY: Morrow.

Tannen, D. (1995). The power of talk: Who gets heard and why. *Harvard Business Review, 73*(5), 138–148.

Tauriac, J. J., Kim, G., Sariñana, S. L., Tawa, J., & Kahn, V. D. (2013): Utilizing affinity groups to enhance intergroup dialogue workshops for racially and ethnically diverse students, *The Journal for Specialists in Group Work.* doi:10.1080/01933922.2013.800176

Tsui, A. S., Egan, T. D., & O'Reilly, C. (1992). Being different: Relational demography and organizational attachment. *Administrative Science Quarterly, 37,* 549–579.

U.S. Equal Employment Opportunity Commission. (n.d.). *African Americans in the workplace.* Retrieved November 30, 2016, from https://www.eeoc.gov/eeoc/statistics/reports/american_experiences/african_americans.cfm

Williams, K. Y., & O'Reilly, C. A. (1998). Demography and diversity in organizations: A review of 40 years of research. *Research in Organizational Behavior, 20,* 77–140.

Wojciske, B. (2005). Morality and competence in person- and self-perception. *European Review of Social Psychology, 16,* 155–188.

SECTION II
AGE AND GENERATIONS

CHAPTER 6

THE LEADER–MEMBER EXCHANGE (LMX) APPROACH TO AGE DIVERSITY

Jacqueline H. Stephenson
University of the West Indies

ABSTRACT

This chapter examines the age diversity (specifically as it relates to older workers) and the extent to which it can be impacted by the unique dyadic approach of leader–member exchange. One of the primary reasons older workers sometimes encounter difficulties in obtaining and retaining employment is the perpetuation of discrimination of older workers (via stereotypes). Invariably, this has led to older workers being considered as a homogeneous group, rather than individuals with varying levels of skills and competence, who are still able to contribute to the workplace. Organizational leaders have a key role in affecting this environment. Rather than focusing solely on the leader and their efficacy, LMX requires the active participation of both parties. According to the LMX, where there are higher levels of support from managers, there are likely to be higher levels of productivity, innovation, and job satisfaction. Thus, in order for the benefits of age diversity to be realized, leaders need to foster relationships with older employees that value contributions and in which they are respected. LMX theory acknowledges the heterogeneous nature of older workers and facilitates the development of an environment of trust, equitable treatment, and enhanced productivity. As it relates to age diversity and the aging population, there is a paucity of extant literature considering LMX as an effective leadership approach. This chapter offers a framework for academic discussion, as well as key considerations and guidance for human resource practitioners in relation to LMX practices they could adopt to realize the benefits of age diversity.

Diversity is one of the key issues that human resource practitioners face in today's contemporary organizations (Hertel, van der Heijden, de Lange, & Deller, 2013a), which has been attributed to globalization, increased levels of migration and technological advancements. Employees may be regarded as diverse because of differences in their sex, race/ethnicity, and age *(inter alia)*, which are ostensibly immutable characteristics. These are referred to as elements of *surface* level diversity (Phillips & Loyd, 2006) and are obvious and observable (Harrison, Price, & Bell, 1998). On the other hand, personal characteristics such as an employee's attitudes, beliefs, values, skills, education level, and social status are typically less visible and are categorized as *deep* level diversity traits (Phillips & Loyd, 2006). These traits are embedded in the employee and as such are typically conveyed to others through social encounters and interpretations of the employee's verbal and nonverbal behavior (Harrison, Price & Bell, 1998). This chapter examines the surface level trait of age diversity particularly as it relates to older workers. Age diversity has been defined as the extent to which age related characteristics are objectively different with employees within an organization (Harrison & Klein, 2007; Van Dick, Van Knippenberg, Hägele, Guillaume, & Brodbeck, 2008). In this chapter, older workers are defined as workers aged 50 and over, which is consistent with the classification used in previous research in this area (Kirton & Greene, 2006; Loretto & White, 2006; MacNicol, 2007; Whiting, 2005). This group should be an important consideration for organizations because the average age of employees is increasing as people remain employed for longer periods, and older workers comprise a larger proportion of the population. Organizations that are aware of the demographic shifts and are prepared to make the requisite changes to ensure continued high levels of productivity and positive employer/employee relationships are likely to enhance their relevance and their market presence.

This chapter explores older workers within organizations and the extent to which the consideration of an aging labor force, when contemplating human resource and leadership strategies, is likely to impact organizations. The leadership concept in focus is the leader–member exchange (LMX) with its unique focus on the nature and quality of the leader–member (supervisor-subordinate, employer-employee) dyad. The overarching concept of LMX is that within organizations employees are not homogeneous, consequently the most effective way to lead/manage them should reflect a heterogeneous approach. Arguably, where older workers present a management challenge, LMX may be useful in effectively managing employees in this age group. This group of employees may have some commonalities, but there will also be differences. In this chapter, the importance of examining the effective management of older workers is first examined. This will be followed by an examination of the extant literature as it relates to the challenges facing older workers in contemporary organizations. An overview of the concept of diversity will then be then examined, followed by an examination of the challenges of age diversity as well as its potential benefits. The contribution of the LMX approach to effectively managing employees will then be reviewed. The chapter ends with a review of the future directions for age diversity and LMX and key recommendations for supervisors and HR practitioners. It is important to examine the issues in this chapter because it broadens the research agenda for LMX and diversity, particularly as it relates to age where there is a paucity of research in the published literature. It also affords employers greater clarity in understanding their responsibilities for establishing diverse and nondiscriminatory workplace practices in relation to older workers. Furthermore, it offers employers insight into specific aspects of employment practice where age diversity and nondiscrimination of older workers could be facilitated.

CHALLENGES FACING OLDER WORKERS

It has been predicted that the labor pool of the future is likely to comprise a significant proportion of older workers (Duncan & Loretto, 2004; Encel, 2001, Posthuma & Campion, 2009). This is in part as a result of projected demographic and societal changes including declining birth rates, longer periods being spent in education by young adults, and an expected extended lifespan (Loretto & White, 2006; McNair, 2006; Warnes & John, 2005). Notwithstanding, older workers continue to face challenges in finding and retaining employment, and age discrimination is said to be one of the primary reasons for this (Loretto & White, 2006).

Stereotypes are rife about older workers, both positive and negative, though not all are supported by relevant evidence. It has been argued that stereotypes are used when managers are unable to apply more comprehensive and analytical methods (Chiu, Chan, Snape, & Redman, 2001; McGregor & Gray, 2002). Some negative stereotypes include the belief that older workers are slow to learn, resistant to change, prone to absenteeism (Chiu et al., 2001; Redman and Snape, 2002), less skilled and of less economic worth than employees of other ages (Finklestein & Burke, 1998), more costly to hire but less beneficial to the workplace (Kidwell,

2002; Steinberg, Walley, Tyman, & Donald, 1998), and less adaptable, less trainable and less willing to accept new technology (Lyon & Pollard, 1997). In the organizational context, willingness by managers to accept negative stereotypes can affect the ability of an older worker to find and retain gainful employment (Renskin, 2000). Conversely, positive stereotypes also exist suggesting that older workers are productive and hardworking, trustworthy, experienced, loyal, and have low turnover rates (McGregor, 2001; Taylor & Walker, 2003); are trainable (Bushko & Raynor, 1999; Salthouse & Maurer, 1996); possess greater problem solving skills and are more creative (Ranzijn, 2002); work better in teams, have good interpersonal skills, and are more conscientious (Lyon & Pollard, 1997).

It is important to note that despite positive qualities attributed to older workers, it appears that within organizations the negative stereotypes have a greater influence on employment practices (Arrowsmith & McGoldrick, 1996). Employers seem slow to acknowledge that older workers may be dissimilar (Claes & Heymans, 2008). However, as with any category older workers are a heterogeneous group, therefore generalized stereotypical views will not be applicable to all older workers, nor should they be relied upon to indicate competence or ability (McGoldrick & Arrowsmith, 1993) particularly in the absence of supporting evidence. In this respect, it has been argued that the physical and mental changes that accompany aging are rarely at a level that interfere with routine information processing, analysis, and retrieval (Patrickson, 2002), and as a consequence workplace performance does not always decline as age increases (McEvoy & Cascio, 1989). Indeed, older workers can still be productive within the workplace and capable of making a valid contribution to the workplace. On the other hand, it must be acknowledged that some older workers are affected by declines in cognition as they age. In fact, it has been contended that memory and speed of learning can decline with age (Kirasic, Allen, Dobson, & Binder 1996); however, these declines may be mediated by an employee's level of education and exposure to new learning situations (Warr, 1993; Williams & Klug, 1996). This suggests that rather than subscribing to discriminatory policies and practices based on assumptions about aging, organizations should treat older workers as distinct individuals who (like all others) should be assessed on merit rather than judged on the basis of preconceived ideas.

Nonetheless, this discussion should not be taken to mean that stereotypes are the only reason for the perpetuation of age discrimination against older workers. Indeed, there are additional reasons why older workers may be treated less favorably in the employment context, such as lack of knowledge by organizations as to how to effectively manage older workers or where managers' actions are based on fear of the unknown. It has been argued that employers generally do not have a good understanding of the issues surrounding older workers (Ranzijn, 2002), and perhaps as a consequence employment decisions may be made that could either directly or indirectly affect older workers. Additionally, where discrimination is institutionalized in a workplace (for example an established and accepted organizational practice of only hiring new employees who are under the age of 40), prejudicial patterns of employment practice may be followed without question as a result of expectations within the workplace (Renskin, 2000). Furthermore, the widespread existence of age discrimination in society (Levy & Banaji, 2002; McGregor, 2001) makes it more challenging for changes to be made to attitudes and practices within the workplace context.

In many developed and an increasing number of developing countries, antiage discrimination legislation has been enacted, and its utility is the extent to which it is effective in reducing or removing discriminatory barriers to employment for older workers or job seekers (Loretto, 2010). However, on its own legislation is unlikely to eliminate engrained accepted stereotypes and discriminatory practices as it relates to older workers. The perpetuation of discrimination of older workers within organizations has led to older workers being considered as a homogeneous group rather than individuals with varying levels of skills and competence who are still able to contribute to the workplace (Duncan, 2003). In turn, this has resulted in the perpetuation of age discrimination within organizations, which may be evidenced by lack of job prospects for older applicants and the failure of older employees to access training opportunities (Loretto & White, 2006; Metcalf & Meadows, 2006). Further, it has been suggested that continuous use of discriminatory practices could have a multiplier effect in many areas of the economy and thus the wider society. This effect could be manifested in an absence or deceleration of economic growth, reduced tax revenues and increases in public expenditures, for example in relation to increased income support required (McGuire & Robertson, 2007; Neumark, 2009). In the next section we examine the current state of older workers.

THE CURRENT STATE OF OLDER WORKERS

As indicated, older workers may experience discrimination in a variety of ways and in relation to different aspects of employment. There are three key areas as it relates to older workers in employment: recruitment and selection, training, and compulsory redundancy. Although other practices may also be important, these particular practices have arguably the most important impact on older workers in employment. Focusing on these three key practices in turn, what follows is a brief explanation of the challenges of the HR practice and relevant statistical data for the United Kingdom and the United States.

Recruitment

This is the stage of recruitment that older workers appear to have the greatest difficulty in securing employment because of the existence of age discrimination (Neumark, 1999; Stoney & Roberts, 2003; Wood, Harcourt, & Harcourt, 2004). Discrimination at this stage of the recruitment and selection process could be both direct and indirect and not easily identifiable as such. Moreover, because of the asymmetry of selection information (Dickens, 2007), it is not always possible to determine whether employment decisions are made according to legitimate criteria or whether age discrimination played a role in the final choices made.

In Tables 6.1 and 6.2, the employment and unemployment rates of British workers from 2004–2015 categorized according to age are shown. These tables give an indication of the employment levels of older workers as compared to workers of other ages within the United Kingdom.

Table 6.1 of older workers aged 50 to 64 indicates an incremental increase in the employment rate over the period 2004 to 2008 after which during 2009 and 2010 there is a marginal decline. There is a further decline (by 6%) in 2011 from the 2010 level. The period that followed (2011–2015) saw incremental increases in the employment rate for older workers.

Statistics for the United Kingdom in relation to the unemployment rate of workers categorized according to their age are shown in Table 6.2. This table of older workers aged 50 to 64 indicates the largest rate of

TABLE 6.1 Employment Rate of British Workers (% by age)

Year	All workers	Age			
		18–24	25–34	35–49	50–64
2004	60.0	66.9	79.7	82.2	70.0
2005	60.1	65.6	80.2	82.4	70.4
2006	60.1	65.4	80.2	82.3	71.2
2007	60.0	59.4	80.3	82.3	71.2
2008	60.0	63.9	80.4	82.4	71.9
2009	58.7	59.6	78.4	81.6	71.4
2010	58.3	58.3	78.3	81.0	71.2
2011	58.2	57.5	78.2	81.1	65.1
2012	58.3	57.1	78.1	81.5	65.5
2013	58.8	57.1	79.4	81.9	67.4
2014	59.4	60.1	80.4	83.3	68.7
2015	60.1	60.1	80.7	83.3	69.4

Source: U.K. Office for National Statistics–Labour Market Information (http://www.statistics.gov.uk/CCI/nscl.asp?ID=6584)

TABLE 6.2	Unemployment Rate of British Workers (% by age)				
	All	Age			
Year	workers	18–24	25–34	35–49	50–64
2004	4.8	10.2	4.5	3.2	2.9
2005	4.7	10.8	4.4	3.1	2.8
2006	5.5	12.5	5.1	3.7	3.2
2007	5.2	12.1	4.7	3.4	3.1
2008	5.4	13.1	4.9	3.7	3.3
2009	7.9	17.2	7.7	5.5	4.6
2010	7.9	17.8	7.9	5.6	4.8
2011	8.3	20.1	8.1	5.4	5.1
2012	8.1	19.1	7.8	5.5	4.9
2013	7.8	18.9	7.1	5.5	4.8
2014	6.1	16.1	5.9	4.3	4.2
2015	5.9	14.8	5.2	4.1	3.6

Source: U.K. Office for National Statistics–Labour Market Information (http://www.statistics.gov.uk/CCI/nscl.asp?ID=6584)

unemployment during 2011 and the lowest unemployment rate in 2008. During the overall period under consideration (2004–2015), there are incremental fluctuations in both directions by less than 1% for older workers.

Statistics for the United States of the employment rate of workers categorized according to their age are shown in Table 6.3. In relation to older workers (aged 45 to 54 and 55 to 64), these statistics indicate some incremental fluctuations. As relates to workers aged 45–54 from 2004 to 2007, the employment rate increases and then decreases in 2008 until 2010. There is a marginal increase in 2011, and these increases continue until 2015 although the rates do not achieve the 2004 level of employment. For those workers aged 55 to 64, there is an increase in the employment rate from 2004 to 2008 that then declines in 2009 until 2012, and where incremental increases continue until 2015 at which time it exceeds the 2004 employment levels.

Statistics for the United States in relation to the unemployment rate of workers categorized according to their age are shown in Table 6.4. In relation to older workers (aged 45–54 and 55–64), these statistics indicate some incremental fluctuations. Across the board (i.e., from 45 to 64 years), the lowest rate was shown to be in 2006 and the highest rate of unemployment was seen during 2010. As it relates to workers aged 45–54, from 2004 to 2006, the unemployment rate decreased, and then increased in 2007 until 2010. This is followed by a decreasing rate from 2011 through to 2015, at which time the unemployment rate was 0.1% lower than the rate in 2004.

TABLE 6.3 Employment Rate of U.S. Workers (% by age)

Year	All ages	Age					
		18–19	20–24	25–34	35–44	45–54	55–64
2004	62.3	48.6	67.9	79.0	80.0	78.7	59.9
2005	62.7	48.5	68.0	78.5	80.5	78.9	60.8
2006	63.1	49.0	68.5	79.2	80.9	79.4	61.8
2007	63.0	46.7	68.4	79.5	80.9	79.4	61.8
2008	62.2	45.1	66.8	78.5	80.2	78.5	62.1
2009	59.3	39.3	62.2	74.5	77.0	75.8	60.6
2010	58.5	37.2	60.3	73.9	76.5	74.9	60.3
2011	58.4	36.9	60.8	73.8	76.6	75.0	60.0
2012	58.6	37.2	61.5	74.9	77.1	75.2	60.6
2013	58.6	37.9	61.7	75.2	77.4	75.2	60.9
2014	59.0	38.8	62.9	75.9	78.3	76.0	61.4
2015	59.3	40.0	63.8	77.2	78.7	76.6	61.5

Source: U.S. Department of Labor–Bureau of Labor Statistics (http://www.bls.gov/bls/employment.htm)

TABLE 6.4 Unemployment Rate of U.S. Workers (% by age)

Year	All ages	Age					
		18–19	20–24	25–34	35–44	45–54	55–64
2004	5.5	15.0	9.4	4.6	4.4	3.8	3.8
2005	5.1	14.9	8.8	5.1	3.9	3.5	3.3
2006	4.6	14.1	8.2	4.7	3.6	3.1	3.0
2007	4.6	14.5	8.2	4.7	3.4	3.2	3.1
2008	5.8	16.8	10.2	5.8	4.6	4.1	3.7
2009	9.3	23.4	14.7	9.9	7.9	7.2	6.6
2010	9.6	24.2	15.5	10.1	8.1	7.7	7.1
2011	8.9	22.9	14.6	9.5	7.3	7.1	6.6
2012	8.1	22.3	13.3	8.3	6.6	6.2	5.9
2013	7.4	21.0	12.8	7.4	5.9	5.8	5.3
2014	6.2	18.5	11.2	6.5	4.7	4.4	4.3
2015	5.3	16.2	9.7	4.5	4.1	3.7	3.8

Source: U.S. Department of Labor–Bureau of Labor Statistics (http://www.bls.gov/bls/employment.htm)

For those workers aged 55 to 64, there was a decrease in the unemployment rate from 2004 to 2006, which is then followed by an increase from 2007 to 2010. During 2011 through to 2015, the unemployment rate declines and in 2015, the unemployment rate was equal to that of 2004.

Taken at face value, these statistics appear to be favorable in relation to employment opportunities available to older workers. However this does not necessarily indicate the existence of age diversity and inclusion or the absence of age discrimination. Indeed, as suggested by the literature, these employment rates could be indicative of the retention of older workers rather than an increase in the number of older recruits (Loretto & White, 2006; McNair, Flynn, Owen, Humphreys, & Woodfield, 2004; Warnes & John, 2005). The unavailability of specific recruitment statistics means that it is not possible to conclusively attribute any changes in the employment rate to the failure by organizations to hire older workers. Furthermore, over this period the economic climate was affected by recessionary pressures where there were widespread business contractions and closures. Such environmental factors would be likely to have an impact on the employment rates as well as the recruitment and selection of older employees (Elsby, Hobijn, & Sahin, 2010; Sahin, Song, & Hobijn, 2010). Therefore the possible influence of other factors makes it more challenging to determine the extent to which age discrimination plays a role in the employment of older workers.

Training

Training support may be offered by workplaces in various forms, but is typically offered with a view of enhancing the skills of workers and increasing their competence and efficiency in fulfilling their duties and by extension improving the productivity of the business (Barron, John, Berger, & Black, 1993). As it relates to off-the-job training, because of the investment required by organizations to support such training, there is a commensurate expectation of a good return on the investment made (Hirsch, 2000). Notwithstanding the potential benefits of training to an employer, research suggests that relative to younger workers, the older workers are given relatively less, limited, or no support within workplaces in relation to training (Farr, Tesluk, & Klein, 1998; Mirvis & Hall, 1996). This can occur for a variety of reasons including stereotypical misconceptions; for example, where workplaces accept the view that older workers have limited capacity to change and learn and are unlikely to benefit from training (Bennington & Wein, 2000; Chiu et al., 2001). This is not a universally applicable perspective; however, research suggests that highly skilled workers, who are arguably less likely to have difficulty seeking employment, are those more likely to receive job-related training (Martin, 1994; Urwin, 2006). It is important for employees to be trained in order to maintain and update their skills and to enhance their employability as well as the likelihood of being retained by an employer (Mitton & Hull, 2006; Smedley & Whitten, 2006). Where older workers are denied training or encounter age-related challenges when seeking access to training, this could result in a decline in job prospects and could negatively affect their longevity within the organization as productive employees.

Redundancies

As it relates to redundancies, older workers appear to be inequitably targeted for redundancies, indeed when compared to other age groups they appear more vulnerable to selection (Patrickson & Razijn, 2003). Such a decision could potentially signal the end of their participation in the labor force, since when displaced older workers are less likely to be re-employed (Redman & Snape, 2002; Taylor & Walker, 1997). Moreover, it has been found that the possibilities of becoming re-employed are inversely related to age, thus the length of time that older persons spend as unemployed is comparatively longer than a younger job seeker (Brewington & Nassar-McMillan, 2000; Heywood, Ho, & Wei, 1999). This unemployment will affect the worker personally, but could also have an extended effect on the society and economy where, for example, welfare payments and income support become necessary.

In the previous sections, context was provided for this chapter by outlining the projected increase in the number of older workers in the labor force and the challenges that they face. It is imperative that older workers are managed effectively so that they are motivated, engaged, and productive rather than feeling marginalized or discriminated against and demotivated. The leadership style that is adopted by organizational managers should be such that the individual, the team, and the organization benefit from their skills and experience. In the sections that follow, the LMX approach is discussed in relation to age diversity, specifically with respect to its impact on older workers within LMX dyads.

MANAGING AGE DIVERSITY IN ORGANIZATIONS

An alternative approach to homogeneity or equality of treatment is to find a way to value and utilize the differences among employees. This approach is referred to as managing diversity, where organizations are encouraged to strengthen their workforce and enhance their competitive advantage by employing people who are different from each other. This approach challenges the equal treatment model suggesting that people do not necessarily wish to be treated the same in every aspect of their working life, but by offering different working arrangements or benefits, managers facilitating the diversity approach may realize greater benefits within their organizations relative to those pursuing an equality approach (Liff & Wajcman, 1996). Managing diversity encourages a focus on inclusivity and the embracing of the skills and talents of all different types of employees (Thomas, 1990). This may involve changing workplace policies and practices such that there are no exclusions (intentional or unintentional) according to an employee's immutable characteristics (for example, age). Kandola and Fullerton (1998) suggest that successful diversity initiatives include retraining and re-education of staff, particularly the key organizational decision makers, but also the operational staff to ensuring transparency and fairness in the organization's decision-making processes, which will require eliminating age criteria from the selection process.

The business case motive for pursuing age diversity advances the view that business benefits are likely to result from inclusive and nondiscriminatory practices. The business case is the subject of much debate (Hayles & Mendez, 1997), and according to Taylor and Walker (1998, p. 69) "Concern about remaining competitive is the single most important factor influencing orientations towards older workers." It has been further asserted (Kirton & Greene, 2006) that the business case rationale is closely associated with managing diversity rather than the attainment of equality. Where workplaces engage with managing diversity policies, they may pursue employment practices that are inclusive irrespective of difference (for example age) as a means of achieving a competitive advantage. Within the context of anticipated demographic change where older workers are expected to comprise a greater proportion of the labor force, the effective use of a diverse workforce, including employees of diverse ages, could prove beneficial to organizations (Claes & Heymans, 2008; Duncan, 2003).

There are some workplaces that exemplify good practice in relation to older workers, which suggests it is possible for employers to engage in nondiscrimination practices on the basis of age while also having a workplace that is efficient and competitive. The best types of organizations for older workers are said to be within health care, education, and consultancy firms (Deems & Deems, 2009). Health-care employers appear to be proactive in recruiting workers over 50 and providing them with a range of health benefits that are useful to them. Educational institutions also appear to be good employers for older people and actively recruit older workers perhaps because of their experience. Similarly, financial institutions hire and employ older workers with a view of ensuring that their employees reflect the backgrounds of their client base. Finally, consulting companies also engage older workers in order to benefit from their experience and knowledge.

The American Association of Retired Persons (AARP) has developed an international award program that recognizes and awards employers across the globe for having the best policies for older workers. Several British organizations have been awarded including Centrica, Marks and Spencer Plc., and the Co-operative Group; some American-based awardees include, National Institutes of Health, YMCA (Greater Rochester), West Virginia University, and Michelin North America. International organizations have also been included such as Hana Bank (Korea), Welcia Kanto (Japan), Brammertz Carpentry (Germany) and West Pack Financial Group (Australia). The age diverse practices of these organizations include promoting age diversity; providing courses to employees, and educating them about age diversity and the benefits of hiring older workers; changing HR policies and practices to promote the recruitment and retention of older employees; and facilitating lifelong learning and training access. The experiences of these companies also indicate that the culture within organizations and the commitment to nondiscrimination by managers are also important determinants in whether older workers will successfully obtain and retain employment.

Consistent with extant research on organizational diversity, there is an absence of conclusive evidence of the definitive benefits that arise from diversity. Instead, the evidence seems to suggest that the organizational benefits may be context specific. Organizational age diversity offers a unique opportunity for businesses because they can harness the benefits of the insight of different generations and capitalize on the unique attributes each age group brings to the table (Kirton & Greene, 2006). Furthermore, age diversity could provide the workplace with resources that will enhance competitiveness both locally and globally (Schneider, 2000). The business case approach to age diversity does not necessarily equate to focusing solely on profit optimization, but could extend to preserving and extending the positive image of an employer; maintaining and extending the customer base; enhanced organizational performance; enhanced creativity and innovation; international awareness; better decision making and problem solving; flexibility; a better work environment; and employee satisfaction (Allard, 2002; Cornelius, Gooch, & Todd, 2001; Kulik & Roberson, 2008; Singh, Kumra, & Vinnicombe, 2002). Relatedly, diverse age groups also have different levels of knowledge and experience that they can contribute to the organization (Richard, 2000). In addition, employees can benefit from age diversity in the workplace, not only from mentors, but because interaction with different age groups can enhance the level of job satisfaction as well as the approach to workplace challenges where they arise (Hayles & Mendez, 1997). Such diversity in the workplace is also likely to contribute to increased adaptability and flexibility, which are essential skills to enhance organizational efficiency (see D'Netto & Sohal, 1999; Matthews, 1998). Indeed, the successful inclusion of workers of all ages is likely to reduce the potency of ageism and by extension the perpetuation of inaccurate stereotypes (Stoney & Roberts, 2003), which in turn contribute to improved employee retention, increased productivity, reduced absenteeism, better morale, an expanded marketplace, and improved services rendered to customers (Subelianai & Tsogas 2005; TUC, 2008).

Notwithstanding the possible advantages to organizations of engaging in diversity initiatives, the business case approach to diversity is not without its challenges. Key corporate decision makers will generally require quantifiable evidence before funds are disbursed or organizational practices are changed. Therefore, unless decision makers within the workplace can be convinced by quantitative data illustrating that it would be feasible to engage and retain older workers, they are unlikely to do so actively and purposefully (Noon, 2007). Competitive pressures to stay ahead may be considered a determinant in whether age diversity practices are pursued, particularly if the age of an employee is perceived negatively. Subelianai and Tsogas (2005) argue that heterogeneity within the workforce is desirable as it contributes to knowledge based innovation, while conceding that homogeneity may be preferred where the goal is to complete routine activities. Notwithstanding the primary goal of organizations, it is important for HR managers to recognize that "Labor cannot be treated in the same way as other commodities because skills and efforts cannot be separated from the needs of their embodied owners" (Weller, 2007, p. 420) and failure to realize this could result in organizational inefficiencies.

As we have seen, organizational diversity is somewhat challenging and there still remains some debate among diversity scholars about whether and the conditions under which organizations realize the benefits of diversity (Pitts & Wise, 2010). Notwithstanding, there is some evidence that diversity is beneficial to organizations, but these benefits may be moderated by time, task interdependence, task complexity, organizational culture, and climate (Roberge & van Dick, 2010). Specifically as it relates to the organization's diversity climate, this refers to perceptions that employees share about the organization's policies and practices on diversity; these perceptions in turn impact the employees' behavior and attitudes (McKay et al. 2007). These diversity climate perceptions are impacted by actions taken by organizations to promote diversity; whether and the extent to which efforts are made to increase the representation of diverse groups within the organization (e.g., older workers, if underrepresented); whether there is inclusion of diverse employees at all levels of the organization (including decision making); and the extent to which there is a culture of equity and a balance of power across all social groups represented within the organization (Kossek & Zonia, 1993). According to Gonzalez and Denisi (2009, p. 25), a diversity climate can influence the way in which employees "express and manage diversity-related tensions, and productivity is enhanced when people believe that cultural differences drive diverse knowledge and insight, but not when people assume that diversity is only valuable to gain niche markets or to avoid blatant discrimination or lawsuits." Thus, the affects of diversity are contingent on the organizational environment (Ferris, Frink, & Galang, 1993), and arguably one of these contextual elements or environmental factors include the leadership strategy that is adopted by organizations.

LEADER–MEMBER EXCHANGE (LMX) AND AGE DIVERSITY

The Role of LMX in Contemporary Organizations

Leader–member exchange is an emerging leadership concept that explores the relationship between leaders and members (managers/employees, supervisors/subordinates), also referred to as the dyad. Rather than simply focusing on the traits of effective leaders and the outcomes that their traits are likely to engender, the central theme of leader–member exchange theory is that different relationships exist among leaders and employees, and the quality of these relationships (including the extent to which they are reciprocal) will have an impact on the quality of the employee's and by extension organizational outcomes (Avolio, Walumbwa, & Weber, 2009; Brouer, Duke, Treadway, & Ferris, 2009; Dulebohn, Bommer, Liden, Brouer, & Ferris, 2012). Thus, according to the LMX strategy where there are higher levels of support for employees by managers there are likely to be higher levels of productivity, innovation, and job satisfaction (Stewart & Johnson, 2009). As aforementioned, older workers can be beneficial to organizations as they are loyal, have lower turnover rates, are more productive, and work better in teams (Lyon & Pollard, 1997; Taylor & Walker, 2003). However, simply employing workers of diverse ages or creating dyads with members of different ages without fostering a relationship with them where their contribution is valued and they are respected, may erode the realization of any potential benefits of diversity. The adoption of the LMX approach may be one means of circumventing this. LMX suggests that differentiation of treatment of high and low performing employees may be necessary for the benefits of LMX to be realized by the organization and its members (Stewart & Johnson, 2009). The theory acknowledges the heterogeneous nature of older workers and facilitates the development of an environment of trust, equitable treatment, and enhanced productivity (Stewart & Johnson, 2009).

In LMX, both the manager and the employee have an important role to play, and the application of the theory is ineffective without the active involvement of both participants. Further, within LMX the interaction must be ongoing and dynamic (Van Breukelen, Schyns & Le Blanc, 2006). The quality of the relationship is also an essential component particularly as it relates to communication. According to previous research in this area, while similarity in the members of the dyad seems to affect outcomes as it relates to deep level characteristics including attitudes and values (Hiller & Day, 2003), this has not been reflected in the assessment of surface level characteristics including age, education, and gender (Schriesheim, Castro, & Cogliser, 1999).

The LMX dyads that are regarded as most successful are those in which there is a reciprocal influence (Avolio et al., 2009); indeed, both parties to the dyad must contribute to the relationship in order to foster the development of a high quality relationship (van Breukelen et al., 2012). There are several factors that are used to assess the quality of an LMX dyad, these include loyalty, contributions, trust, respect, liking, attitude, ability, benevolence, integrity, communication, interaction, support, and rewards (Avolio et al., 2009; Brower et al., 2000; Graen & Uhl Bien, 1995; Schriesheim et al., 1999). Indeed, as the dyad is formed and the relationship between the supervisor and the subordinate develops, these characteristics are assessed by both the parties to the dyad (Brower et al., 2000). Where these attributes are present, the LMX relationship is said to be of high quality; however, where these attributes are absent or negligible, the LMX relationship is regarded as low quality. According to Van Breukelen et al. (2006), leaders may offer discretion, latitude, information, influence on decisions, support, attention, feedback, respect, recognition and rewards, attractive work assignments, and career opportunities. Whereas subordinates can offer some of these but they may also show loyalty, commitment, and greater levels of effort. High-quality relationships are those that offer the most benefits to the parties in the dyad, the work team, and the overall organization.

The outcomes of high-quality relationships include job satisfaction, organizational commitment, intention to stay, and organizational citizenship behaviors (Gerstner & Day, 1997; Graen & Uhl-Bien, 1995). Conversely, low-quality relationships are aligned with high rates of turnover, low job satisfaction, and poor organizational commitment (Uhl Bien, 1995). Accordingly, low quality LMX relationship are also associated with short time limits allowed for co-operative exchanges (i.e., the resulting outcomes are expected to be immediate/short term (Breukelen, Schyns, & Le Blanc, 2006). While these differential results may be regarded as attributable to discrimination, this is an essential component of LMX and arguably an important point of difference in the LMX theory of leadership. As traditional leadership strategies focus on leader traits where the role of the leader is assessed in relation to the extent to which it affects employees' behavior, team and organizational outcomes, the focus is on the equal value of the exchange in the leader–employee relationship ("high equivalence") and effort concentrated on self-centered goals ("high self-interest"; Uhl Bien & Maslyn, 2003). This suggests that any benefits that are derived from low-quality relationships are likely to be beneficial only to the supervisors/subordinates within that dyad. Conversely, with high-quality relationships, the scope of the exchange is much broader in focus and consequently there is a greater multiplier effect of benefits across the organization serving wider stakeholder interests. Along with its unique dyad consideration, the LMX approach to leadership is also valued for its exploration of the reciprocal nature of the dyad. Both members of the dyad influence the relationship and are mutually dependent on each other in their employment relationship. There is also continuous evaluation by both parties of their characteristics and likely behavior in different situations. Notwithstanding this, and perhaps as a consequence of the power asymmetry, dependence is greater for subordinates in the dyad than for the supervisors (cf. Dulebohn et al., 2012).

Rather than examining the antecedents and outcomes that are associated with effective leadership, LMX theorists consider the antecedents and outcomes for both the leaders and followers. Based on a meta-analysis of extant LMX research, Dulebohn et al. (2012) developed a framework of LMX antecedents and consequences (see Figure 6.1) in which they suggest that the characteristics of followers and leaders, along with the nature of their interpersonal relationship have an impact on the quality of the dyadic relationship as well as on the extent to which the consequences were realized. This model also suggests that there may be some moderating factors that impact

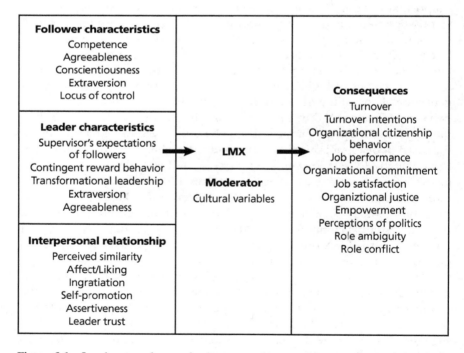

Figure 6.1 Leader–member exchange antecedents and consequences theoretical framework. (*Source:* Dulebohn et al., 2012)

the quality of the relationship and the outcomes achieved, which may include the cultural context. This is consistent with the concept of age diversity, which also considers that moderating factors may be influential on the extent to which organizations benefit from managing diversity in practice.

As indicated, managers develop different relationships with each of their employees (Colella & Varma, 2001). In earlier iterations of the LMX theory (Liden, Wayne, & Stillwell, 1993), employees were regarded as either being a part of the in-group or the out-group. Those members in the in-group experienced high-quality relationships (Colella & Varma, 2001). Current LMX theorists suggest that leaders should value all subordinates and make decisions that are objective, fair and free from bias, and make efforts to develop high-quality relationships (Van Breukelen et al., 2006). Notwithstanding, it must be noted that one characteristic of a high-quality LMX relationship is favorability/liking, this delineates the subjective nature and quality of the dyadic relationship.

From our analysis, we have identified several attributes of high- and low-quality relationships. There are some other key factors that are also taken into consideration in the LMX strategy. These include the level of performance by subordinates that would typically contribute to a good relationship between managers and employees; however, this is not without exception because employees who have already developed a high-quality relationship with supervisors based on other factors are still positively assessed even if their performance is not outstanding (i.e., not high performers). This is in contrast to that which obtains with employees with low quality relationships, whose performance is assessed according to their performance (Duarte, Goodson, & Klich, 1993).

Age Diversity and the Organizational Impact of LMX

The statistics presented in Tables 6.1 through 6.4 indicate the age composition of the labor force in the United Kingdom and the United States where the younger age groups (18 to 24 year olds) represent the lowest rates of employment and the highest rates of unemployment across the board (2004–2015) relative to all other age groups represented in the workplace. An age diverse labor force should also translate to age diverse workplaces. It has been argued that because of their different life stages (and perspectives), people of diverse ages may find it challenging to work together. According to Sullivan, Forret, Carraher, and Mainiero (2009), baby boomers (ages 52 to 70) "value extrinsic measures of success, are willing to work to get rewards, and value independent thinking"; Generation X workers (ages 33 to 51) are "accustomed to change, are highly mobile, are loyal to work groups and bosses, and believe rewards should be based on merit and dislike hierarchies"; and Generation Y workers (ages 14 to 32) are "technologically savvy, impatient and reliant on technology." Moreover, Baldwin and Strebler (2007) argue that notwithstanding one's age, the extent to which an employee is engaged within the context of work affects that person's attitude at work. They further suggest that while older people are motivated by the attainment of fair rewards and realization of organizational objectives, younger people pursue personal development and thrive on completing challenging tasks. Many of today's contemporary organizations have members of various generations working together, either as colleagues or in a manager/employee relationship (Bell & Narz, 2007) as organizations reflect the previously described demographic changes in society. Organizations must therefore ensure that their managers are sufficiently skilled or capable of effectively managing these employees so that they are actively engaged and performing optimally, and the LMX strategy provides a feasible alternative for doing so.

Similarities between the manager and the employee also appear to be important in determining the quality of the LMX relationship. Similarities as it relates to demography (age, sex, gender, education), and similar values, attitudes, and perceptions of similarities impact the quality of the dyadic relationship (Van Breukelen et al., 2012). Similarities (real or perceived) are likely to affect the extent to which managers and employees are likely to view other's contribution or their likelihood of adding value to the relationship, the team, or the organization, and the extent to which the contributions made are considered valuable (Van Breukelen et al., 2012; Brouer et al., 2009; Colella & Varma, 2001). Arguably, this suggests that subordinates who are demographically dissimilar from the supervisor (e.g., age, race) are more likely to face even greater challenges in developing a high-quality dyadic relationship (Brouer et al., 2009). As suggested by the "similarity attraction paradigm," similarity between individuals increases their liking for each other and affects interactions and behavior as a result (Colella & Varma, 2001).

Indeed, it has been found that the adoption of age diverse management policies results in negative organizational outcomes including poor communication and a challenging decision making process (Knight et al. 1999; Zenger & Lawrence, 1989). The negative outcomes of age diverse groups may be attributed to intergroup bias (Wegge, Roth, Neubach, & Schmidt, 2008) as managers and employees accept the negative stereotypes that exist about older employees, whether or not those stereotypes are relevant or applicable in the specific team or to the specific individual under consideration (Ellwart, Bundgens & Rack, 2013). To change people's perceptions and accepted stereotypes may be possible through training and re-education; however, this is not likely to result in immediate changes. Organizations will also need to follow this up with the adoption of fair and equitable policies and practices, which are visibly supported by all organizational members but particularly management staff and senior executives. Monitoring and training will also be beneficial to the extent that it is translated into everyday practice (Ellwart et al., 2013; Newton, 2006). This may include promoting "understanding the experiences and mindsets" of older workers (Baldwin & Strebler, 2007, p. 9). The business case argument in support of valuing older workers is related to how they can contribute to the organization, for example through their knowledge, experience, and skills.

In short, an increased number of older employees is likely to require some changes in management and leadership strategies and practices. Older workers have higher performance outcomes when there is congruence between their needs and the job requirements, they also value organizational citizenship behaviors (helping others in the workplace setting and sharing the benefit of their experiences; Hertel et al., 2013b). Managers therefore need to be aware of the conditions in which older workers thrive and perform at optimum levels and are motivated to continue doing so. This is consistent with the assertion by Hertel et al. (2013a, p. 730) that "Managers in organizations need to know more about age related differences in order to adapt their HRM strategies and leadership styles in an effective and sustainable way." Indeed, understanding the "comparative demographic characteristics of dyad or group members who interact regularly" might enable a better understanding of how differences in age diversity in work teams, or between a superior and a subordinate, might affect an employee's attitude and work behavior (Hertel et al., 2013a, p. 735).

Demographic dissimilarity has an adverse effect on LMX relationships (Turban & Jones, 1988). As it relates to age, accepted stereotypes may engender expectations of poor performance, and this may translate to low-quality relationships with older workers. Research (Scandura & Lankau, 1996) suggests that dyads will typically have an age differential with the projections of older workers comprising greater percentages of the workforce. Although culture has been proposed as a possible mediator (Dulebohn et al., 2012), this has not conclusively supported by extant research. Graen and Scandura (1987) propose a triad model of LMX development consisting of role-taking, role-making and role-routinization. This framework would be useful to managers and employees desirous of engaging in an LMX dyad. The initial role-taking phase is characterized by the supervisor assessing the competence and performance of the subordinate, while the subordinate simultaneously assesses the behavior of the supervisor. At this stage, mutual respect "for the other's ability and potential contribution" (Scandura & Lankau, 1996) is a key determinant of whether the relationship will be effective and progress toward a high-quality relationship. Where age dissimilarity is present in the dyad, one party may not respect the other as a result of the individual's age, and the relationship may be stymied by decisions made as a result of preconceived notions about the person's age and abilities. The next phase is that of role-making where there is mutual influence exerted on the other's attitudes and behavior. This occurs where there is mutual respect that leads to mutual trust and support by the supervisor for the subordinate's activities. According to Scandura and Lankau (1996, p. 247), "The role-making stage of LMX development is critical when the parties of the dyad are demographically different." In diverse dyads, it must be recognized that even one violation of trust may destroy the relationship since it may reinforce negative stereotypes and expectations of discriminatory practice; for example, if the supervisor fails to support a proposal made by the subordinate or if the subordinate is unproductive or inefficient in his role. The final stage is role-routinization; the LMX relationship matures during this stage and a sense of interdependence and "mutual obligation" develops based on the respect and trust fostered in the previous phases and the relationship becomes normalized. At this stage of the dyad relationship development, any diversity issues that may have arisen have been resolved and are not expected to have an adverse effect on the relationship.

Having considered the specific attributes that may contribute to the quality of the dyadic relationship including the supervisor's/subordinate's characteristics and personal traits, subordinates may use tactics such as self-promotion, ingratiation, and other political skills in order to develop high-quality relationships with their supervisor (Brouer et al., 2006; Dulebohn et al., 2012). Individuals who are likely to engage in such activity are socially aware of the organizational environment and a supervisor's character, and as such can better understand the behavior needed so as to develop a more effective dyadic relationship. This may require improving his or her efforts to enhance performance at work, recognizing those skills and attitudes that are valued by the supervisor and working toward developing those, and ensuring that from the perspective of the supervisor, the individual is an indispensable members of the staff. These tactics are beneficial to those who are demographically dissimilar to overcome the challenges that an age differential may present. As indicated by Brouer et al. (2009), "Political skill allows subordinates who are dissimilar to their supervisors to circumvent the negative consequences and relationship unfavorable" and develop high quality LMX relationships. Thus, as mentioned previously, in the LMX dyad there is reciprocal influence between the supervisor and the subordinate, thus engaging in ingratiation behavior could make the supervisor regard the employee in a more favorable light. This approach has been found to be more effective for demographically dissimilar subordinates in influencing the quality of LMX relationships (Colella & Varma, 2001), and arguably would be more necessary for them as they face the inevitable challenges.

CONCLUSION

Organizations are becoming more diverse, and in this chapter the focus has been on older workers who as a result of demographic changes are becoming more commonplace within contemporary organizations. As we have seen from the statistics presented, organizations will increasingly consist of mixed age dyads or older age dyads. While it might be convenient to assume that Generation Y workers have a greater propensity to discriminate against older workers or accept prevailing stereotypes against older workers, this has not been conclusively found to be accurate to the extent that older managers and older workers have also been found to discriminate against older workers and older managers as well. The examination of effectively managing age-diverse employees is timely for academics and practitioners to understand the nuances of the LMX relationship between managers and older workers and the implications for theory and practice. Within LMX, high-quality relationship are desired and characterized by loyalty, contributions, trust, respect, liking, attitude, ability, benevolence, integrity, communication, interaction, support, and rewards (Avolio et al., 2009; Brower et al., 2000). Understanding the dynamics of this interaction will invariably contribute to the understanding of how high-quality and effective dyads can be developed. Both leaders and employees should be aware of their biases and potential subjectivity when interacting with and developing relationships with employees. For older workers who have consistently experienced challenges with recruitment, training and development, and redundancy this emerging leadership model is a useful tool that may be used to examine and further understand the dynamics of the dyad and the factors that contribute to high-quality relationships. The impact of age is becoming increasingly important, and age is one of the more recently recognized grounds within legislation to be prohibited by antidiscrimination law. Within an organization, it is quite important not simply to treat employees fairly but to go beyond the equality required by law and embrace their differences and the potential benefits that diversity could add to the organization.

FURTHER RESEARCH

As an emerging area of research, further empirical studies are needed to conclusively identify the antecedents and outcomes of effective LMX. Specifically, as it relates to age diversity and the aging population (and workforce) there is a paucity of such literature. Therefore this chapter offers a framework for discussion as well as highlights key considerations and guidance for human resource practitioners as to the LMX practices that they could adopt, along with realizing the benefits of age diversity including improvements in team performance, culture, organizational environment, values, and accepted norms within the economic sector or industry of the organization. The number of contextual factors that directly and indirectly impact the response of age diverse dyads to the LMX style could also be an area that could be explored by further empirical research. The nature of these factors may impact the extent to which age diverse employees respond to different leadership styles, and may influence the relationship outcomes and the extent to which the efficiency and productivity of older workers are impacted. The dyadic interactions may be further examined along with the possible multiplier effects of LMX and age diversity on the organization. Finally, contemporary organizational leaders may not possess the requisite skills for the development of high-quality dyadic relationships, and as a consequence future research could examine the extent to which professional development programs could positively impact the development of desirable high quality LMX relationships.

PRACTICAL CONSIDERATIONS FOR ORGANIZATIONS

Developing high-quality relationships necessitates engagement and commitment by both parties to the dyad. Organizational leaders need to abandon any prevailing negative perceptions about limitations associated with older employees and consider the benefits that such workers could facilitate. Leadership can be a moderator for the extent to which organizations realize the benefits of age diversity in their organization, and adopting the LMX approach could be a catalyst for highly functioning employees and by extension productive organizations. In practical terms, Hertel et al. (2013a) has suggested some tips for the effective management of diverse groups (dyads) and these include avoid age discrimination; provide training and support for age diversity; consider having age diverse teams (dyads); and balance the needs and expectations of both supervisors and subordinates in age diverse dyads. As has been discussed, accepted stereotypes may cause subjective assumptions about the skills and abilities of older supervisors or subordinates, but the LMX leadership strategy provides an opportunity for both parties to the dyad to engage in a differentiated/heterogeneous approach when engaging in dyadic relationships with older dyadic partners (Riach, 2009). In addition to this, organizations must also give consideration to their environment and the development of an organizational culture where each employee's contribution is valued and there is mutual respect between organizational members. The dyadic nature of the leader–member exchange allows leaders and members to become familiar with each other instead of relying on stereotypes to determine the potential productivity or usefulness of employees or leaders. The dyadic approach also allows managers to become familiar with the strengths and limitations of their employees and the work environment and culture that would be more likely to promote high levels of motivation, engagement and commitment, and optimal employee efficiency.

REFERENCES

Allard, M. (2002). Theoretical underpinnings of diversity. In C. Harvey & M. Allard (Eds.), *Understanding and managing diversity*. Upper Saddle River, NJ: Prentice-Hall.

Arrowsmith, J., & McGoldrick, A. E. (1996). *Bridging the theory and practice divide through collaborative research: The case of ageism in employment* (Working paper). British Academy of Management Conference, Lancaster, England.

Avolio, B. J., Walumbwa, F. O., & Weber, T. J. (2009). Leadership: Current theories, research, and future directions. *Annual Review of Psychology, 60*, 421–449.

Baldwin, S., & Strebler, M. (2007). *Managing an age diverse workforce: Research and practice in the run-up to the employment equality (age) regulations*. Brighton, England: Institute for Employment Studies.

Barron, J. M., John, M., Berger, M.C., & Black, D. A. (1993). *Do workers pay for on the job training?* Working paper, No E-169-93 University of Kentucky, Lexington, KY.

Bell, N. S., & Narz, M. (2007). Meeting the challenges of age diversity in the workplace. *The CPA Journal, 77*(2), 56.

Bennington, L., & Wein, R. (2000). Anti-discrimination legislation in Australia: Fair, effective, efficient or irrelevant? *International Journal of Manpower, 21*(1), 21–33.

Brewington, J. O., & Nassar-McMillan, S. (2000). Older adults: Work-related issues and implications for counseling. *Career Development Quarterly, 49*(1), 2–15.

Brouer, R. L., Duke, A, Treadway, D. C., & Ferris, G. R. (2009). The moderating effect of political skill on the demographic dissimilarity: Leader–member exchange quality relationship. *The Leadership Quarterly, 20*(2), 61–69.

Bushko, D., & Raynor, M. (1999). More on the aging worker: Who are they and how can they stay vital? *Journal of Management Consulting, 10*(3), 68–69.

Chiu, W.C. K, Chan, W., Snape, E., & Redman, T. (2001). Age stereotypes and discriminatory attitudes towards older workers: An east-west comparison. *Human Relations, 54*(5), 629–661.

Claes, R., & Heymans, M. (2008). HR professionals' view on work motivation and retention of older workers: A focus group study. *Career Development International, 13*(2), 95–111.

Colella, A., & Varma, A. (2001). The impact of subordinate disability on leader–member exchange relationships. *Academy of Management Journal, 44*(2), 304–315.

Cornelius, N., Gooch, L., & Todd, S. (2001). Managing difference fairly: an integrated 'partnership' approach. In M. Noon & E. Ogbonna (Eds.), *Equality, diversity and disadvantage in employment*. Basingstoke, England: Palgrave.

Deems, R., & Deems, T. (2009). *Make job loss work for you: Get over it and get your career back on track.* Indianapolis, IN: Jist.

Dickens, L. (2007). The road is long: Thirty years of equality legislation in Britain. *British Journal of Industrial Relations, 45*(3), 463–494.

D'Netto, B., & Sohal, A. S. (1999). Human resources practices and workforce diversity: an empirical assessment. *International Journal of Manpower, 20*(8), 530–547.

Duarte, N. T., Goodson, J. R., & Klich, N. R. (1993). How do I like thee? Let me appraise the ways. *Journal of Organizational Behavior, 14*(3), 239–249.

Dulebohn, J. H., Bommer, W. H., Liden, R. C., Brouer, R. L., & Ferris, G. R. (2012). A meta-analysis of antecedents and consequences of leader–member exchange integrating the past with an eye toward the future. *Journal of Management, 38*(6), 1715–1759.

Duncan, C. (2003). Assessing anti-ageism routes to older worker re-engagement. *Work, Employment and Society, 17*(1), 101–120.

Duncan, C., & Loretto, W. (2004). Never the right age? Gender and age-based discrimination in employment. *Gender, Work and Organization, 11*(1), 95–115.

Ellwart, T., Bündgens, S., & Rack, O. (2013). Managing knowledge exchange and identification in age diverse teams. *Journal of Managerial Psychology, 28*(7/8), 950–972.

Elsby, M. W., Hobijn, B., & Sahin, A. (2010). *The labor market in the great recession.* Working Paper No. 15979. National Bureau of Economic Research.

Encel, S. (2001). Age discrimination in Australia: Law and practice. In Z. Hornstein, S. Encel, M. Gunderson, & D. Neumark (2001). *Outlawing age discrimination.* Bristol, England: Policy.

Farr, J. L., Tesluk, P. E., & Klein, S. R. (1998). Organizational structure of the workplace and the older worker. In K. W. Schaie & C. Schooler (Eds.), *Impact of work on older adults* (pp. 143–206). New York, NY: Springer.

Ferris, G. R., Frink, D. D., & Galang, M. C. (1993). Diversity in the workplace: The human resources management challenges. *Human Resource Planning, 16*(1), 41–51.

Finkelstein L. M., & Burke, M. J. (1998). Age stereotyping at work: The role of rater and contextual factors on evaluations of job applicants. *Journal of General Psychology, 125*(4), 317–345.

Gerstner, C. R., & Day, D. V. (1997). Meta-Analytic review of leader–member exchange theory: Correlates and construct issues. *Journal of Applied Psychology, 82*(6), 827–844.

Gonzalez, J. A., & Denisi, A. S. (2009). Cross-level effects of demography and diversity climate on organizational attachment and firm effectiveness. *Journal of Organizational Behavior, 30*(1), 21–40.

Graen, G. B., & Scandura, T. (1987). Toward a psychology of dyadic organizing. In L. Cummings & B. Staw (Eds.), *Research in organizational behavior* (Vol. 9, pp. 175–208). Greenwich, CT: JAI Press.

Graen, G. B., & Uhl-Bien, M. (1995). Relationship-based approach to leadership: Development of leader–member exchange (LMX) theory of leadership over 25 years: Applying a multi-level multi-domain perspective. *The Leadership Quarterly, 6*(2), 219–247.

Harrison, D. A., & Klein, K. J. (2007). What's the difference? Diversity constructs as separation, variety, or disparity in organizations. *Academy of Management Review, 32*(4), 1199–1228.

Harrison, D. A., Price, K. H., & Bell, M. P. (1998). Beyond relational demography: Time and the effects of surface-and deep-level diversity on work group cohesion. *Academy of Management Journal, 41*(1), 96–107.

Hayles, R., & Mendez, R.A. (1997). *The diversity directive.* New York, NY: McGraw Hill.

Hertel, G., van der Heijden, B., de Lange, A., & Deller, J. (2013a). Facilitating age diversity in organizations—Part I: Challenging popular misbeliefs. *Journal of Managerial Psychology, 28*(7/8), 729–740.

Hertel, G., van der Heijden, B., de Lange, A., & Deller, J. (2013b). Facilitating age diversity in organizations—Part II: Managing perceptions and interactions. *Journal of Managerial Psychology, 28*(7/8), 857–866.

Heywood, J. S., Ho, L. S., & Wei, X. (1999). The determinants of hiring older workers: Evidence from Hong Kong. *Industrial and Labor Relations Review, 52*(3), 444–459.

Hiller, N. J., & Day, D. V. (2003) LMX and teamwork: The challenges and opportunities of diversity. In G. B. Graen (Ed.), *Dealing with diversity* (pp. 29–57). Greenwich, CT: Information Age.

Hirsch, D. (2000). *Life after 50.* York, England: York Publishing Services.

Hornstein, Z., Encel, S., Gunderson, M., & Neumark, D. (2001). *Outlawing age discrimination foreign lessons:UK choices.* Bristol, England: Policy Press.

Kandola, R. S., & Fullerton, J. (1998). *Diversity in action: Managing the mosaic* (2nd ed.). Wimbledon, England: CIPD.

Kidwell, R. (2002). Helping older workers cope with continuous quality improvement. *Journal of Management Development, 22*(10), 190–205.

Kirasic, K. C., Allen, G. L., Dobson, S. H., & Binder, K. S. (1996). Aging, cognitive resources, and declarative learning. *Psychology Aging, 11,* 58–70.

Kirton, G., & Greene, A. (2006). *The dynamics of managing diversity* (2nd ed.). Oxford, England: Elsevier Butterworth Heinemann.

Knight, D., Pearce, C. L., Smith, K. G., Olian, J. D., Sims, H. P., Smith, K. A., & Flood, P. (1999). Top management team diversity, group process, and strategic consensus. *Strategic Management Journal,* 445–465.

Kossek, E. E., & Zonia, S. C. (1993). Assessing diversity climate: A field study of reactions to employer efforts to promote diversity. *Journal of Organizational Behavior, 14*(1), 61–81.

Kulik, C. T., & Roberson, L. (2008). Common goals and golden opportunities: Evaluations of diversity education in academic and organizational settings. *Academy of Management Learning and Education, 7,* 309–331.

Levy, B. R., & Banaji, M. R. (2002). Implicit ageism. In T. D. Nelson (Ed.) *Ageism: Stereotyping and prejudice against older persons* (pp. 49–75). Cambridge, MA: The MIT Press.

Liden, R. C., Wayne, S. J., & Stilwell, D. (1993). A longitudinal study on the early development of leader-member exchanges. *Journal of Applied Psychology, 78*(4), 662.

Liff, S., & Wajcman, J. (1996). Sameness and difference revisited: Which way forward for equal opportunity initiatives. *Journal of Management Studies, 33*(1), 79–94.

Loretto, W. (2010). Work and retirement in an ageing world: The case of older workers in the UK. *Contemporary Social Science: Journal of the Academy of Social Sciences, 5*(3), 279–294.

Loretto, W., & White, P. (2006). Employers' attitudes, practices and policies towards older workers. *Human Resource Management Journal, 16*(3), 313–330.

Lyon, P., & Pollard, D. (1997). Perceptions of the older employee: Is anything really changing? *Personnel Review, 26*(3), 245–257.

MacNicol, J. (2007). The American experience of age discrimination legislation. In W. Loretto, S. Vickerstaff, & P. White (Eds.), *The future for older workers: New perspectives* (pp. 27–41). Bristol, England: Policy Press.

Martin, S. (1994). Outsider within the station house: The impact of race and gender on black women police. *Social Problems, 41*, 383–400.

Mathews, A. (1998). Diversity: A principie of human resource management. *Public Personnel Management, 27*(2), 175–185.

McEvoy, G. M., & Cascio, W. F. (1989). Cumulative evidence of the relationship between employee age and job performance. *Journal of Applied Psychology, 74*, 11–17.

McGoldrick, A. E., & Arrowsmith, J. (1993). Recruitment advertising: Discrimination on the basis of age. *Employee Relations, 15*(5), 54–65.

McGregor, J. (2001). *Employment of the older worker.* Palmerston North, New Zealand: Massey University.

McGregor, J., & Gray, L. (2002). Stereotypes and older workers: The New Zealand experience. *Social Policy Journal of New Zealand, 18*, 163–177.

McGuire, S., & Roberson, M. (2007, June). *Assessing the potential impact of the introduction of age discrimination legislation in UK firms from an HRM and JKM perspective.* Proceedings of Organizational Learning, Knowledge and Capabilities Conference (OLKC), Learning Fusion. Ontario, Canada.

McKay, P. F., Avery, D. R., Tonidandel, S., Morris, M. A., Hernandez, M., & Hebl, M. R. (2007). Racial differences in employee retention: Are diversity climate perceptions the key? *Personnel Psychology, 60*(1), 35–62.

McNair, S. (2006). How different is the older labor market? Attitudes to work and retirement among older people in Britain. *Social Policy and Society, 5*(4), 485–494.

McNair, S., Flynn, M., Owen, L., Humphreys, C., & Woodfield, S. (2004). *Changing work in later life: A study of job transitions.* Guildford, England: University of Surrey.

Metcalf, H., & Meadows, P. (2006). *Survey of employers' policies, practices and preferences relating to age.* Research Report No. 325. DTI Employment Relations Research Series, No. 49. Leeds, England: Department for Work and Pensions.

Mirvis, P., & Hall, D. T. (1996). Psychological success and the boundaryless career. In M. B. Arthur & D. M. Rousseau (Eds.), *The boundaryless career* (pp. 237–255). New York, NY: Oxford University Press.

Mitton, L., & Hull, C. (2006). The information, advice and guidance needs of older workers. *Social Policy and Society, 5*(4), 541–550.

Neumark, D. (1999). *The employment effects of recent minimum wage increases: Evidence from a pre-specified research design.* Working Paper 7171. Cambridge, MA: National Bureau of Economic Research.

Neumark, D. (2009). The age discrimination in employment act and the challenge of population aging. *Research on Aging, 31*(1), 41–68.

Newton, B. (2006). Training an age-diverse workforce. *Industrial and Commercial Training, 38*(2), 93–97.

Noon, M. (2007). The fatal flaws of diversity and the business case for ethnic minorities. *Work Employment and Society, 21*(4), 773–784.

Patrickson, M. (2002, July). *Early retirement: Choosing whether to stay or go.* Paper presented to the IFSAM/ANZAM World Conference, Brisbane, Australia.

Patrickson, M., & Ranzijn, R. (2003). Employability of older workers. *Equal Opportunities International, 22*(5), 50–63.

Phillips, K. W., & Loyd, D. L. (2006). When surface and deep-level diversity collide: The effects on dissenting group members. *Organizational Behavior and Human Decision Processes, 99*(2), 143–160.

Pitts, D. W., & Wise, L. R. (2010). Workforce diversity in the new millennium: Prospects for research. *Review of Public Personnel Administration, 30*(1), 44–69.

Posthuma, R. A., & Campion, M. A. (2008). Age stereotypes in the workplace: Common stereotypes, moderators, and future research directions. *Journal of Management, 35*(1), 158–188.

Ranzijn, R. (2002). Towards a positive psychology of ageing: Potentials and barriers. *Australian Psychologist, 37*(2), 79–85.

Redman, T., & Snape, E. (2002). Ageism in teaching: Stereotypical beliefs and discriminatory attitudes: Towards the over-50s. *Work, Employment and Society, 16*(2), 355–371.

Renskin, B. F. (2000). The proximate causes of employment discrimination. *Contemporary Sociology, 29*, 319–328.

Riach, K. (2009). Managing "difference": Understanding age diversity in practice. *Human Resource Management Journal, 19*(3), 319–335.

Richard, O. C. (2000). Racial diversity, business strategy, and firm performance: A resource-based view. *Academy of Management Journal, 43*(2), 164–177.

Roberge, M. É., & van Dick, R. (2010). Recognizing the benefits of diversity: When and how does diversity increase group performance? *Human Resource Management Review, 20*(4), 295–308.

Sahin, A., Song, J., & Hobijn, B. (2010). The unemployment gender gap during the 2007 recession. *Current Issues in Economics and Finance, 16*(2), 1–7.

Salthouse, T. M., & Maurer, T. J. (1996). Aging, job performance, and career development. In J. E. Birren & K. W. Schaie (Eds.), *The handbook of aging* (pp. 353–364). San Diego, CA: Academic Press.

Scandura, T. A., & Lankau, M. J. (1996). Developing diverse leaders: A leader–member exchange approach. *The Leadership Quarterly, 7*(2), 243–263.

Schneider, B. (2000). The psychological life of organizations. In N. M. Ashkanasy, C. P. M. Wilderon & M. F. Petersom (Eds.), *Handbook of organizational culture and climate.* Thousand Oaks, CA: SAGE.

Schriesheim, C. A., Castro, S. L., & Cogliser, C. C. (1999). Leader–member exchange (LMX) research: A comprehensive review of theory, measurement, and data-analytic practices. *The Leadership Quarterly, 10*(1), 63–113.

Singh, V., Kumra, S., & Vinnicombe, S. (2002). Gender and impression management: Playing the promotion game, *Journal of Business Ethics, 37*(1), 77–89.

Smedley, K., & Whitten, H. (2006). *Age matters: Employing, motivating and managing older employees.* Hampshire, England: Gower.

Steinberg, M., Walley, L., Tyman, R., & Donald, K. (1998). Too old to work? In M. Patrickson, & L. Hartmann (Eds.), *Managing an ageing workforce* (pp. 53–68). Warriewood, Australia: Woodslane.

Stewart, M. M., & Johnson, O. E. (2009). Leader–member exchange as a moderator of the relationship between work group diversity and team performance. *Group & Organization Management, 34*(5), 507–535.

Stoney, C., & Roberts, M. (2003). *The case of older workers at Tesco: An examination of attitudes, assumptions and attributes.* Working Paper No. 53. Carleton University School of Public Policy and Administration, Ontario, Canada.

Subeliani, D., & Tsogas. G. (2005). Managing diversity in the Netherlands: A case study of Rabobank. *International Journal of Human Resource Management, 16*(5), 831–851.

Sullivan, S. E., Forret, M. L., Carraher, S. M., & Mainiero, L. A. (2009). Using the kaleidoscope career model to examine generational differences in work attitudes. *Career Development International, 14*(3), 284–302.

Taylor, P., & Walker, A. (1998). Policies and practices towards older workers: A framework for comparative research. *Human Resource Management Journal, 8*(3), 61–76.

Taylor, P., & Walker, A. (2003). Age discrimination in the labor market and policy responses: The situation in the United Kingdom. *The Geneva Papers on Risk and Insurance, 28,* 612–624.

Thomas, R. R. (1990). From affirmative action to affirming diversity. *Harvard Business Review, 68*(2), 107–117.

Trade Union Congress. (2008). *Talent not tokenism: The business benefits of workforce diversity.* London, England: Author.

Uhl-Bien, M., & Maslyn, J. M. (2003). Reciprocity in manager–subordinate relationships: Components, configurations, and outcomes. *Journal of Management, 29*(4), 511–532.

Urwin, P. (2006). Age discrimination: Legislation and human capital accumulation. *Employee Relations, 28*(1), 87–97.

Van Breukelen, W., Schyns, B., & Le Blanc, P. (2006). Leader–member exchange theory and research: Accomplishments and future challenges. *Leadership, 2*(3), 295–316.

Van Dick, R., Van Knippenberg, D., Hägele, S., Guillaume, Y. R., & Brodbeck, F. C. (2008). Group diversity and group identification: The moderating role of diversity beliefs. *Human Relations, 61*(10), 1463–1492.

Warnes, T., & John, A. (2005). *Facts and misconceptions about demography and the workforce.* Retrieved May 25, 2015, from https://www.researchgate.net/publication/238746964_Facts_and_Misunderstandings_about_Demography_and_the_Workforce

Warr, P. (1993). In what circumstances does job performance vary with age. *European Work and Organizational Psychologist, 3*(3), 237–249.

Wegge, J., Roth, C., Neubach, B., Schmidt, K. H., & Kanfer, R. (2008). Age and gender diversity as determinants of performance and health in a public organization: The role of task complexity and group size. *Journal of Applied Psychology, 93*(6), 1301–1313.

Weller, S. A. (2007). Discrimination, labor markets and the labor market prospects of older workers: What can a legal case teach us? *Work, Employment and Society, 21*(3), 417–437.

Whiting, E.c(2005). The labor market participation of older people. *Labour Market Trends, 113*(7), 285–296.

Williams, J. D., & Klug, M. G. (1996, July/September). Aging and cognition: Methodological differences in outcome. *Experimental Aging Research,* 219–244.

Wood, G., Harcourt, M., & Harcourt, S. (2004). The effects of age discrimination legislation on workplace practice: A New Zealand case study. *Industrial Relations Journal, 35*(4), 359–371.

Zenger, T. R., & Lawrence, B. S. (1989). Organizational demography: The differential effects of age and tenure distributions on technical communication. *Academy of Management Journal, 32*(2), 353–376.

CHAPTER 7

LEADER–MEMBER RELATIONS IN AN AGING WORKFORCE

Barbara A. Fritzsche and Ghada Baz
University of Central Florida

ABSTRACT

While researchers and practitioners increasingly recognize the importance of creating and maintaining high quality leader–member exchange (LMX) in supporting organizational performance and workers' well-being, a new challenge emerges with the aging of the global workforce. This chapter aims to examine challenges brought by the aging workforce while focusing on the role of leader, both young and old, in developing high quality interaction with older subordinates. First, we will examine current literature in leadership behaviors and outcomes as a function of age; second, we will present research that has examined the LMX relationship as a function of age, with a focus on research that examines LMX when the supervisor is younger than the subordinate; third, we will provide an overview of research on age-related stereotypes, workplace ageism, and the job performance, turnover, and job attitudes of older workers to inform leaders about the challenges and opportunities associated with an aging workforce; and finally, we will present research-based ideas for building high-quality, leader–member relationships with older subordinates.

Older workers are the fastest growing segment of the U.S. workforce (Benz, Sedensky, Tompson, & Agiesta, 2013). Currently there are more than 44 million people aged 50 plus in the U.S. workforce. By 2020, 38% of the workforce is expected to be 55 years old or more with fully 22% of the workforce aged 65 or older (AARP, 2013). This demographic shift is not limited to the U.S. workforce but reflects a trend in many nations around the world (Chand & Tung, 2014). For example, in 2014 the old-age dependency ratio (the extent to which a country relies on older workers) was already 42% in Japan and 34% in Italy (The World Bank Group, 2016). As birth rates decline and people live longer, healthier lives, people want and need to work longer. Moreover, organizations are finding that they must find ways to retain older workers as valuable contributors to their success. In fact, 72% of human resource professionals polled stated that the loss of older workers is "a problem" or "a potential problem" for their organizations, citing a loss from both "basic" (writing, grammar, and spelling skills) and "applied" (professionalism and work ethic) skills gaps between younger and older workers. Despite widespread knowledge of the aging workforce and the potential problems associated with losing valuable older workers, many organizations report that they have not taken systematic steps to proactively address the problem (Minton-Eversole, 2012).

The extent to which leaders develop strong LMX relations appears to be central to solving this problem because LMX provides the social and emotional context in which employees feel valued and inspired to perform. In a recent study (Gottfredson & Aguinis, 2016) of 3,327 primary studies that were previously examined in 35 meta analyses, LMX was found to be the most central mediator of the relationship between several leadership behaviors and subordinate performance. Specifically, the relationship between the use of rewards for performance (i.e., contingent rewards) and subordinate behavior could be explained by the quality of LMX relationships. The relationship between transformational leadership (how leaders inspire subordinates to perform above and beyond previous levels) and subordinate performance could be explained by LMX. Moreover, LMX mediated the relation between the Ohio State leadership behaviors (initiating structure and consideration) with subordinate performance. Specifically, a strong LMX relationship provides subordinates with the social and emotional context in which they can succeed. The authors reasoned that by showing concern and respect for subordinates the leaders communicate to their subordinates that they are valued, which strengthens the LMX relationship. When leaders provide an initiating structure through organizing work and roles, subordinates perceive that their leaders want them to be successful, which strengthens LMX. Gottfredson and Aguinis (2016) concluded:

If leaders want to serve as catalysts for high levels of follower performance, our results suggest that they need to focus on one particular follower perception: LMX, or the improve follower performance, namely: their followers' perception of their relationship with them. In short, our results simplify what leaders need to focus on in an effort to improve follower performance, namely the followers' perceptions of their relationship with their leader.

This chapter focuses on the challenges brought by an increasingly older workforce with an emphasis on what leaders both young and old need to know in order to develop strong relationships with older subordinates. First, we will discuss what we know about leadership behaviors and outcomes as a function of age. In other words, as our workforce ages more leaders will be older and supervising both younger and older subordinates. What can we expect from an older leader as compared to a younger leader? Second, we will present research that has examined the leader–member exchange (LMX) relationship as a function of age. Until recently, most leaders were older than their subordinates. In fact, commonly accepted age norms suggest that older people are expected to hold jobs higher on the organizational chart than younger workers (Shore & Goldberg, 2005). Thus, the vast majority of LMX studies conducted describe the leader–member exchange relationship between an older supervisor paired with younger subordinates. In recent times, an unprecedented number of older workers are being supervised by younger leaders due to reorganizations and mergers and the sheer number of older people in the workforce. The focus of this section will be on research that examines LMX when the supervisor is younger than the subordinate. Third, because the literature is surprisingly sparse linking LMX to age, we will discuss what is known about age-related stereotypes as they relate to workplace ageism and the empirical literature on the job performance, turnover, and job attitudes of older workers. This literature will bring to light the challenges and opportunities that leaders face in developing good leader–member relationships in an increasingly aging workplace. This will bring us to our fourth section where suggestions will be presented for building high-quality leader–member relationships with older subordinates.

WHAT DO WE KNOW ABOUT OLDER LEADERS?

As the workforce ages, more older people will become leaders supervising both younger and older workers (Sonnenfeld, 1991). Yet, despite this reality age has been the focus of only a few empirical studies on leadership in general (Walter & Scheibe, 2013) and LMX theory in particular (e.g., Epitropaki & Martin, 1999; Smith & Harrington, 1994; Vecchio, 1993). To help guide empirical research and make sense out of conflicting findings on the

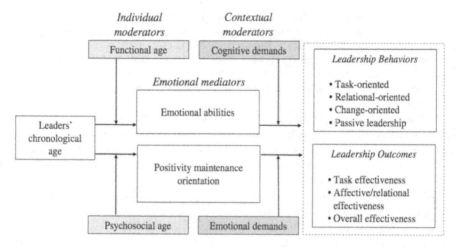

Figure 7.1 Walter and Scheibe's (2013) conceptual model.

links between leaders' chronological age and leadership behaviors and outcomes, Walter and Scheibe (2013) have offered a conceptual model (Figure 7.1) that draws upon research on the emotional basis for leadership.

According to Walter and Scheibe (2013), well-documented emotional changes occur with age and mediate the relationship between age and leadership. Three emotional abilities relevant to leadership performance include emotion recognition, understanding, and regulation (Joseph & Newman, 2010). Emotion recognition is the ability to accurately identify the emotions of others, whereas emotion understanding is the comprehension of the signs of emotions, their causes, and how to regulate them. These two abilities help leaders identify subordinates' problems and meet their emotional needs through how they give direction, support, and feedback. Emotion regulation is the ability to control one's emotional experience and the expression of emotion, which has been linked to high-quality LMX relations with subordinates.

Lifespan development research on aging suggests that aging tends to bring declines in emotion recognition but heightened emotion understanding and regulation, suggesting that age can have positive and negative effects on leader outcomes. In addition to age-related changes in emotional abilities, aging has also been associated with greater positivity maintenance and positivity bias (the motivation to experience positive and avoid negative feelings). Whereas positivity bias is not always beneficial to leadership, research suggests (e.g., Newcombe & Ashkanasy, 2002) that positive leaders generally have better LMX relationships.

To help explain when older leaders will likely have better leadership outcomes, Walter and Scheibe (2013) suggest that functional age, psychosocial age, cognitive demands, and emotional demands moderate the relationship. Specifically, leaders' emotional abilities are negatively impacted when they have fewer physical and cognitive resources (a lower functional age), and their positivity maintenance is negatively impacted when they feel or are perceived as older (a higher psychosocial age). In other words, higher functional and lower psychosocial age can provide a buffer to the effects of chronological age on leader outcomes. Likewise, highly cognitively demanding situations (requiring high fluid intelligence) and highly emotionally demanding situations (requiring an accurate assessment of highly negative information) will likely result in poorer outcomes for older leaders. Yet, older leaders are likely to outperform younger leaders in low cognitively and emotionally demanding situations where their superior crystallized intelligence and positivity maintenance will benefit them.

Walter and Scheibe (2013) provide a much needed link between the lifespan development literature on how emotional functioning changes with age and its potential effect on leadership behavior and outcomes. Their model addresses the direct effect of age by suggesting that older and younger people are expected to have different leadership styles and strengths. Beyond the direct effects of age, it is also important to understand the effects of the relative age of a leader to the subordinate on their LMX relationship. In other words, what can be expected in terms of the quality of the relationship between a supervisor and a subordinate when there are large age differences between them, particularly when a younger leader is paired with an older subordinate? The next section summarizes that literature.

WHAT DO WE KNOW ABOUT LMX AND AGE?

Tsui and colleagues (e.g., Tsui, Egan, & O'Reilly, 1992; Tsui & O'Reilly, 1989) argued that demographic differences between supervisors and subordinates affect work outcomes beyond the direct effects of demographic characteristics. Termed *relational demography*, demographic differences (age or other demographic differences such as sex or ethnic background) in dyadic relationships is predicted to lead supervisors to perceive lower effectiveness and attraction to subordinates, which results in lower quality exchange relationships and categorizations in the outgroup. At the same time, subordinates also categorize supervisors, which further influences the exchange relationship. According to relational demography theory, problems emerge when those who are in supervisory roles have different demographic characteristics than their subordinates. Thus, poor LMX relationships among age-different supervisor-subordinate dyads are expected. Research has shown a host of negative outcomes such as increased employee turnover and lower job performance, job satisfaction, commitment, and attachment attributed to lower quality LMX relationships in age-different dyads. The negative outcomes have been linked to poorer communication, greater misunderstandings between supervisor and subordinates, and more social distance between them. For example, poorer task-oriented communication results in more role ambiguity leading to poorer performance (Green, Anderson, & Shivers, 1996).

Whereas the relational demography perspective is commonly cited, other ideas have been proposed to explain how age differences can affect LMX. Vecchio (1993) argued that age differences could be positively, negatively, or curvilinearly related to work outcomes depending on the impact of status congruence, similarity attraction, social competition, and loyalty and commitment. Some of these ideas are consistent with the relational demography perspective but others are not.

From a status congruence perspective, positive outcomes occur when all variables related to higher status in an organization are aligned (or congruent) with each other. Thus congruence exists when those who have the higher positions in the workplace are also those who have the most experience, expertise, pay, tenure, and age. When younger people supervise older subordinates, older subordinates view this as violating implicit career timetables (Lawrence, 1987, 1988). Career timetables theory suggests that occupations have age-related norms and older people should occupy higher positions in organizations. Those who are promoted with their age group are considered on time; those who are promoted ahead of schedule are considered to be on the "fast track"; and those who are promoted later than others are considered "dead wood." This suggests that younger supervisors may evaluate older subordinates negatively and prefer to hire and supervise younger subordinates. Older subordinates may feel as though they are entitled to greater input into decisions due to their age seniority. As a result, younger supervisors may experience difficulties supervising older subordinates. Thus, from this perspective the most positive outcomes are expected when there are age-related differences between supervisors and subordinates under the condition when the supervisor is older.

The similarity attraction hypothesis suggests that supervisor-subordinate dyads will have the best outcomes when there are little to no age differences between them. This idea is consistent with the work of Tsui and suggests that similarity breeds attraction and perceptions of effectiveness as values, generational experiences, and attitudes are likely to be more similar among demographically similar individuals. According to self-categorization theory, the need to think positively of ourselves leads us to prefer and have positive evaluations of similar others. This idea comes from the work of Byrne (1971) and was originally applied to similarity in attitudes, but now has been applied to similarity in demographics (Riordan, 2000).

In contrast, the social competition approach suggests the opposite of the similarity attraction hypothesis. Specifically, social competition is expected to be greatest between similarly aged supervisors and subordinates, leading to lower evaluations of each other. Finally, because higher age is associated with greater loyalty and commitment, this last perspective would argue that older subordinates would be most valued by younger supervisors.

Given the competing ideas about the nature of the effects of age-diverse LMX relationships, it is no surprise that the empirical tests of these relationships find inconsistent results. In an early study of relational demography and LMX, for example, Epitropaki and Martin (1999) found that when there was a large age difference between a supervisor and subordinate and poor LMX, the subordinate reported poor well-being. Yet, when LMX was high a large age difference between the supervisor and subordinate did not result in poor outcomes. These results suggest that a large age difference between the supervisor and subordinate does not necessarily lead to a poor LMX relationship, which is good news for a rapidly demographically changing workforce.

Several studies have shown support for a relational demography perspective that age differences in either direction matter. For example, Shore, Cleveland, and Goldberg (2003) found that when there was greater age similarity between the supervisor and subordinate the subordinate felt as though he or she had the best career future. Older subordinates experienced negative outcomes when their supervisors were either older or younger than they were. Specifically, younger supervisors offered fewer developmental opportunities to them and older supervisors gave them low performance evaluations.

Also finding support for the relational demography perspective, Malangwasira (2013) focused his efforts on examining the mediating effect of LMX on the relationship between various demographic characteristics (including age) and job satisfaction. Job satisfaction (the affective state underlying job attitudes) was expected to be linked to LMX as leader–member relations are among the most salient relationships at work. If trust, liking, and respect are low between the leader and the follower, this can have a large impact on experienced satisfaction at work. Malangwasira found that as age differences between supervisor-subordinate dyads increased LMX decreased, which then negatively impacted job satisfaction in a sample of manufacturing employees.

The bulk of the work on LMX and demographic variables has been conducted in Western cultures, yet LMX relationships may differ by culture. In a study of demographically diverse dyads in Malaysia, Bakar, Jian, Fairhurst, and Connaughton (2011) examined the relationship between LMX and performance outcomes. According to the Global Leadership and Organizational Behavior Effectiveness study (GLOBE; Kennedy, 2002), Malaysian employees tend to prefer to work as a group and highly value interpersonal communication and relationships. They found that higher quality LMX relationships were related to both in-role and extra-role measures of job performance when there was greater demographic similarity (including age) between the supervisor and subordinate. Interestingly, the effects for age differences specifically were found for measures of extra-role performance, but not for measures of in-role performance.

In an initial attempt to understand the cultural links between age and the quality of LMX relationships, Gellert and Schalk (2012) studied respect, cooperation, and autonomy as linked to the quality of age-diverse LMX relationships. They defined respect as "a social exchange of positive attitudes between employees of different ages... related to the mutual respect of 'others competencies.'" (p. 46). Cooperation was conceptualized as an emotional aspect of respect and autonomy "includes freedom, independence, and discretion in the individual task" (p. 47). They argued that age leads to better perceptions of LMX relationships when age is culturally linked to respect, cooperation, and autonomy. In other words, when cultures automatically ascribe respect to older individuals and where age stereotypes of incompetence are lower, one would expect LMX relationships among age diverse dyads to be more positive. They found that older workers were more satisfied with their jobs when they had higher autonomy and better quality LMX relationships with their supervisors. Thus across several studies evidence has been found that age differences lead to poor LMX relations, which can lead to poor in-role and extra-role job performance and job satisfaction.

Looking for ways to combat age differences in the technology sector, Van der Heijden et al. (2010) examined the role of LMX and age-related supervisory practices such as providing training to update skills. They reasoned that to help increase employability, supervisors can promote growth and prevent obsolescence of older workers by encouraging training and development programs and helping with career plans, mentoring, and social networking. Yet, they found that subordinate expertise was high when LMX was high regardless of the age-related supervisory practices. In other words, having a good quality LMX relationship was all that was needed suggesting the critical importance of LMX for older subordinates.

Providing some context to the relational demography findings, Haeger and Lingham (2013) qualitatively examined interviews from 12 supervisors under the age of 36 and 13 subordinates who were at least 20 years older than their supervisors. Their major finding was that young supervisors reported task-oriented supervision, but older subordinates *expected* relationship-oriented supervision. Haeger and Lingham called the perceptual collisions that they found, *generational normative collisions* that lead to strained interactions within the age-diverse dyads. The generational normative collisions centered on (a) leader style, (b) types of tasks, and (c) relationships. Specifically, older subordinates expected leaders who focused on coaching, development, and close, personal relationships. Older subordinates expected leaders to listen, give them voice in decisions, and offer support with personal matters. Yet, younger supervisors reported being very task centered, valued obedience, and did not see a value in getting involved in conflict in the workplace unless it was directly impeding task performance. Older subordinates valued quality over quantity of work completed and resented some uses of technology, whereas younger supervisors valued quantity of work completed (multitasking) over quality and resented older subordinates for not embracing technology. This study gives organizations some clues as to what issues they may need to address to improve the quality of LMX relationships in age-different dyads. These issues may represent generational differences that may change over time (and may not be generalizable, given the small sample size) suggesting that the key contribution of this study is the idea that an open dialog with older subordinates and younger supervisors can reveal leadership patterns that may be leading to poor LMX relations that require change.

Haeger and Lingham's (2013) study suggests that subordinates' evaluation of the supervisor is critical to understanding the quality of LMX relationships. Yet, most research on LMX and age has focused on downward evaluations of older subordinates. In contrast, Collins, Hair, and Rocco (2009) focused on studying upward expectancy effects (also known as reverse Pygmalion effects) by examining subordinates' perceptions of their supervisors' leadership behaviors and how that influenced leader behavior. Due to violations in workplace status norms, older subordinates may believe that younger supervisors are less effective leaders. They may perceive that younger supervisors have less wisdom and experience, have less upward influence, provide less support, and are less cooperative. Low expectations of leadership performance can elicit poorer supervisory performance and poorer LMX relationships with subordinates. Collins et al. studied employees who were in one of four different categories: a younger (age 39 or younger) subordinate with an older supervisor (age 50 and older), an older subordinate with a younger supervisor, or where the individuals in the dyad were in the same age group. They found that older workers with younger supervisors expected less effective leadership behaviors and reported poorer leadership from their supervisors than did workers from any other age pairing, thereby confirming the idea that lower expectations elicit less effective leadership performance.

Looking beyond the dyad, Nishii and Mayer (2009) focused on LMX at the group level, examining it as a moderator between diversity and turnover. Their idea was that group performance can be improved if leaders establish high-quality relationships with subordinates of various demographic backgrounds. Uniformly high-quality LMX relationships help establish norms of equality, and inclusion thereby encourages group members to share power and establish high-quality relationships with each other. In other words, leaders who demonstrate acceptance of diversity through high LMX relationships with diverse subordinates will encourage acceptance and high-quality relationships among coworkers, which is expected to result in better group functioning and, ultimately less turnover. They argue that high-quality LMX relationships offer power to subordinates, which affects them and their status in the group. Using a large sample of supermarket employees, Nishii and Mayer (2009) averaged age, race, and gender diversity to create an overall measure of diversity rather than looking at age separately from the other demographic variables. Thus, their results cannot be interpreted as indicative of age differences alone, but their findings included age diversity and were strong. The three-way interaction between diversity, LMX mean (average level of LMX within a group), and LMX differentiation (level of dispersion in the quality of LMX within the group) suggested that groups were harmed the most when the leader established high-quality LMX relationships with most but not all subordinates. Their study generally establishes the importance of leadership that is inclusive of people of various demographic characteristics, including older workers.

In summary, surprisingly few studies have been done that directly examine LMX and age. Yet, from the studies that have been done the data suggest that (a) age differences between supervisor and subordinate matter, (b) high-quality LMX relationships are linked to better in- and extra-role performance outcomes and positive job attitudes of older subordinates, (c) there is a reciprocal relationship in which high-quality LMX relationships are linked to better leadership performance, and (d) having uniformly high LMX relationships with diverse subordinates is important for creating a climate of inclusion. The larger literature on LMX and this smaller literature on age and LMX clearly informs leaders of the importance of building strong relationships with subordinates that communicate trust, respect, and inclusion. Yet, what is lacking in this literature is how to create such relationships. In other words, what special challenges do older workers face that leaders should be cognizant of to help develop good quality LMX relationships?

WHAT DO LEADERS NEED TO KNOW ABOUT AGING AND AGEISM?

A comprehensive review of the literature on aging at work and workplace ageism is beyond the scope of this chapter. However, this section will provide the reader with an overview of common stereotypes about the older worker focusing on myths and realities of working with older subordinates with the hope that awareness will be a good start toward improving LMX relationships between age-diverse supervisor-subordinate dyads.

Before addressing the stereotypes of older workers, it is important to discuss how stereotyping fits into LMX relationships. LMX is posited to emerge from a series of social exchanges between supervisors and subordinates. According to the role episode model (Graen & Scandura, 1987), LMX develops through three stages: role-taking, role-making, and role-routinization. Success in role-taking, when supervisors and subordinates first interact and determine whether each person is going to contribute meaningfully to the relationship is critical to the establishment of high-quality LMX relations. It is in this first stage where surface demographic characteristics (such as age) matter the most as individuals do not have much information about each other as they begin their relationship. Over time as people learn more about each other, surface-level characteristics become less important in determining the quality of relationships than do deep-level characteristics (such as attitudes; Harrison, Price, & Bell, 1998). Yet, the initial interactions often based on surface-level characteristics and influenced by stereotypes determine the quality of role-taking that ultimately impacts role-making and role-routinization. Thus stereotypes can have a significant impact on the quality of LMX.

According to the stereotype content model (Fiske, Cuddy, Glick, & Xu, 2002; Fiske, Cuddy, & Glick, 2007), there are two primary dimensions of stereotype content: competence and warmth. These content dimensions combine to form three basic forms of prejudice: paternalistic (when one is viewed as low on competence but high on warmth), envious (when one is viewed as high on competence but low on warmth), and contemptuous (when one is viewed as low on competence and warmth); high competence and warmth is typically reserved for one's in-groups (Cuddy & Fiske, 2002).

Across many studies, older workers have been viewed as warm but incompetent (Kroon, Van Selm, ter Hoeven, & Vliegenthart, 2016; Ng & Feldman, 2012) thereby commonly experiencing paternalistic forms of prejudice (Krings, Sczesny, & Kluge, 2011). The negative stereotypes associated with age mean that older workers are perceived as less flexible, less interested in technology, less trainable, less active, less willing to change, and less motivated (e.g., Ng & Feldman, 2012; Perry et al., 2017). There are also positive stereotypes associated with older adults that impact how they are treated in the workplace. Specifically, older adults are positively stereotyped as friendly, warm, and dependable (Gordon & Arvey, 2004). The combination of the negative and positive stereotypes of older adults suggests that they are paternalistically thought of as "doddering but dear" (Cuddy & Fiske, 2002).

Whether age stereotypes matter often depends on whether older workers are in an age-salient situation (Marcus & Fritzsche, 2015). This idea has its roots in social identity theory in that we have "situational selves": our category membership changes depending on which of the many social categories we belong to is made salient (Fiske, 1998; Pettigrew, 1981). When age is made salient, people are characterized as "old" or "young" and other social group characteristics are ignored (Kruse & Schmitt, 2006). As expected, when age-based stereotypes are negative, older workers in age salient situations are likely to be discriminated against. Age can be made more salient by asking people to compare older and younger workers (e.g., Cleveland, Festa, & Montgomery, 1988) or by varying the age diversity of the workplace (where age is more salient when there are fewer older workers). Recently, Reeves, Fritzsche, Dhanani, and Marcus (2015) showed that older workers perceived more age discrimination when they occupied jobs dominated by younger workers and when they had younger supervisors. Older workers reported that having colleagues who were typically much younger made them feel "behind schedule." Casper, Rothermund, and Wentura (2011) found that when age-relevant stereotypes were emphasized, age became more salient. Diekman and Hirnisey (2007) found that older adults received the lowest hireability evaluations relative to younger adults when applying for jobs in dynamic as opposed to stable companies, suggesting that age was made salient by activating the "inadaptability" stereotype. Thus, age becomes salient when a context is created in which older workers are a numerical minority in a particular job or by comparing older workers to jobs that require characteristics stereotypically associated with younger workers (Perry & Finkelstein, 1999). And when the context makes negative stereotypes regarding old age (incompetence, inadaptability) salient, older workers are most likely to be impacted.

As suggested, older worker stereotypes can have harmful effects. As Desmette and Gaillard (2008) point out, a large literature shows that "from the moment they are categorized as 'older workers,' individuals become potential targets for prejudice and discrimination related to aging" (p. 169). Older workers are often denied job opportunities, training and development opportunities, the opportunity to advance, and even voice in decision making. It is true that age is related to a decline in physical and mental abilities (e.g., Schieber & Kline, 1982; Laux, 1995; Salthouse, 1992), but the decline is gradual and greatly overestimated by stereotypes. Moreover, older workers have been shown to be capable of compensating for their diminished capacities with a greater level of experience (Avolio, Waldman, McDaniel, 1990). They engage in more organizational citizenship behaviors, have better attendance at work, and are less likely to engage in counterproductive behavior than younger workers (Ng & Feldman, 2008) thus making them valuable contributors to the workplace. In other words, systematic stereotyping and prejudice (i.e., ageism) can often explain why older workers are seen as less competent, trainable, and motivated. The result is that once people are labeled as older workers they become members of a stigmatized group. Social identity theory suggests that if older workers feel devalued by this social identity they are likely to cope with that by withdrawing from the workforce (Tajfel & Turner, 1979). In addition to being subject to age stereotyping from others, older workers themselves may self-identify as an older worker, which can also have detrimental effects. Again, the most likely consequence of self-identifying as an older worker is withdrawal from work or the workplace as a way to avoid age-related stigmatization (Desmette & Gaillard, 2008).

To improve their self-image, social identity theory suggests that individuals use cognitive or behavioral strategies to move themselves out of the stigmatized group or change the image of the entire group so that the group itself is no longer a stigmatized group. Retiring is one way that older workers move themselves out of the stigmatized group. Alternatively, older workers can withdraw by psychologically disengaging at work. More positive coping mechanisms include reigniting commitment to work in order to refute age stereotypes, redefining aging to be more positive, or competing with younger workers to try to change the image of older workers.

A key variable in which strategy is chosen is whether younger workers are open to the idea of valuing older workers regardless of age (termed intergroup permeability). In their study of 352 private sector workers aged 50-59, Desmette and Gaillard (2008) found that intergroup impermeability and cognitive identification with the older worker group predicted early retirement intentions, psychological disengagement from work, and intergenerational competition. In other words, separatism led to negative work-related attitudes and intentions. The key implication for leaders interested in retaining engaged older workers is to create a common group identity through the relationships that they develop with their subordinates and those that they foster between their subordinates. Workers of various age groups need to identify as part of a larger group with superordinate goals and have a common organizational identity rather than an age-based identity.

It can be challenging for leaders to create a common organizational identity that discourages age-based categorization processes that lead to negative age-discrimination climates. Yet negative age-discrimination climates can lead to poorer company performance. Kunze, Boehm, and Bruch (2013) suggest a relatively simple solution; use diversity-friendly HR policies and create top leaders who do not have negative age stereotypes. Specifically, as Kunze et al. describe, social exchange theory (Blau, 1964) suggests that organizational success depends on employees perceiving a fair and mutual exchange relationship. Using data from 147 companies, they found that organizational age diversity led to a negative age discrimination climate, which led to poorer company performance. They reasoned that as people in organizations perceive the emergence of age-based subgroups and age-based practices, a climate of age discrimination emerges through socialization and contagion, which leads workers to feel as though they are treated unfairly and makes them less engaged and committed to the success of the organization. Thus they found that poorer age climates were associated with poorer organization performance. Importantly, however, this relationship was moderated by leaders' personal age stereotypes and diversity-friendly HR practices. When top leaders did not have high negative age stereotypes and when organizations had diversity-friendly HR practices, the relation between age diversity and company performance was not significant. Once again this research highlights the important role of leaders in creating an age-friendly work environment. However this study was conducted at the organization level rather than the individual level, so details about how leaders interact with their subordinates to effect change were not included.

From a different line of research focused on what older workers do to successfully age at work more specific strategies can be offered to leaders interested in developing strong LMX relationships with their older subordinates. There are large individual differences in the rate of cognitive and physical declines associated with age (Hansson, DeKoekkoek, Neece, & Patterson, 1997), and when cognitive and physical declines impact job performance there are often relatively simple adjustments to the work environment that leaders can make to accommodate older workers. For example, leaders can provide equal access to training throughout the work life of all employees while paying attention to the specific needs of older employees such as more time to complete training. This may include the creation of training programs to update existing skills or acquire new skills as well as the adaptation of a variety of instructional methods to meet age-diverse trainees' needs. While training leads to improved productivity and performance of employees in general, it also serves as a form of acknowledgement that has a motivational effect, especially for older workers (Boehm, Schröder, & Kunze, 2013). Older workers themselves compensate for losses, as described by the theory of selective optimization with compensation (SOC; Baltes & Baltes, 1990). SOC is a life span developmental model that has been linked to successful aging (e.g., Freund & Baltes, 1998). According to SOC, people are aware of age-related declines and attempt to conserve their waning abilities through selection, optimization, or compensation (Freund & Baltes, 2002). Selection is when older individuals make decisions that allow them to minimize resource losses. For example, aging might require a person to search for new goals or reconstruct their goal hierarchy in the face of failure. Compensation means that older workers reduce the effects of age-related losses through reliance on resources that they have in abundance; for example, by relying on technology or their wealth of job-related experience. Optimization is the process of garnering resource gains through personal development; for example, by returning to school or seeking training. Overall, using SOC strategies has been related to subjective indicators of aging well such as satisfaction with aging, lack of agitation, absence of emotional and social loneliness, with compensation and optimization found to be the most important predictors of successful aging (Freund & Baltes, 1998; 1999). Freund and Baltes (2002) also found that middle-aged individuals used the most SOC strategies compared with individuals in both young adulthood and late adulthood, which suggests that middle-aged people have less need to explore many different pathways in their lives and careers than younger people and age-related declines in physical and cognitive resources affect the expression of SOC strategies into old age.

More recent work has focused on how SOC strategies apply specifically at work and to workplace outcomes (e.g., Yeung & Fung, 2009). Zacher and Frese (2011), for example, examined the relation between use of SOC strategies and occupational future time perspective, the perception of how much time one has left at work and beliefs about how many new goals and opportunities one has left. Not surprisingly, as people age both aspects of occupational future time perspective decrease. More interestingly when work is more complex (requiring high-level skills and is mentally demanding) and offers high control over decisions at work, older workers are able to maintain a focus on opportunities. Zacher and Frese found that use of SOC strategies were particularly helpful for older workers who were in less complex, low control jobs where the SOC strategies helped refocus workers on future opportunities at work when the jobs themselves were not designed to provide many opportunities to grow and learn. Zacher and Frese argue that "Employees who use SOC strategies adapt more successfully to various changes in personal resources and work-related demands, and engage more often in autonomous goal setting, goal adaptation to external circumstances, and goal pursuit" (p. 307). This enhances workers perception of future opportunities at work, which they found to be important for successful aging at work. These findings are consistent with those of Yeung and Fung (2009) who examined the use of SOC strategies in a sample of salespeople. They found that the use of SOC strategies was not especially helpful for younger workers nor were they especially helpful for older workers when their job tasks were perceived to be highly difficult. However, use of SOC strategies was associated with better sales performance for older workers when the task was perceived as low or moderate in difficulty. Like Zacher and Frese's (2011) findings, this study suggests that SOC strategies can be especially useful for successful aging at work when the job itself is not enriched.

Perhaps using SOC strategies helps older workers maintain or increase physical or cognitive resources. The idea of increasing physical and cognitive resources as we age runs counter to the idea that the aging process is characterized only by loss (Lerner & Gignac, 1992) and that the series of cognitive, physical, and social losses results in increasing levels of stress (Labouvie-Vief, 1985). This research demonstrates that older workers can remain active and productive within the workplace and actively engage in cognitive and physical resource management and coping behaviors (Hobfoll, 1988). Leaders can support older employees in their pursuit of better fitting work by providing equal opportunities to progress within the organization regardless of age and by relocating employees as a response to performance constraints to maintain proper job fit through lateral career moves. The expected benefits of such practices include increased performance, intrinsic job motivation, and prevention of health issues resulting from unfitness for work, and assuring employment until retirement age (Boehm, Schröder, & Kunze, 2013).

In addition to the SOC model, another important contribution from life-span development theory that can impact leaders' perceptions of subordinates is socioemotional selectivity theory (Carstensen, 1995). According to socioemotional selectivity theory, people select goals depending on their perceptions of time. Older individuals are more likely to adopt a shorter time frame for goals due to seeing time as more limited (a "time till death" perspective) than do younger people. From a goal orientation perspective, older individuals are therefore more likely to take a mastery-avoidance goal orientation in which they focus on not losing their skills, not performing worse than before, and not stagnating. In fact, one study (de Lange, Van Yperen, Van der Heijden, & Bal, 2010) found that the prototypical goal orientation of older workers in their study of 450 employees over age 65 was a mastery-avoidance goal orientation. Understanding goal orientation is important, as mastery-approach more than mastery-avoidance goals have been linked to work engagement (the extent to which one experiences vigor, dedication, and absorption) and the meaning of work, which are both strongly linked to positive well-being and performance at work. In de Lange et al.'s study, as expected older workers with more of a mastery-approach (with a focus on intrapersonal standards of competence) scored highest on measures of work engagement and the social and personal meaning of work. Whereas those with more of a mastery-avoidance goal orientation scored lower on work engagement and social and personal meaning of work. Luckily, a good deal of research on goal orientation suggests that goal orientation is heavily influenced by situational factors (Payne, Youngcourt, & Beaubie, 2007). Thus de Lange et al. suggest that leaders can help older workers stay focused on mastery-approach goals through emphasizing progress and improvement and accepting errors as part of the learning process. Leaders can also lengthen the time horizons that they discuss with their older subordinates by investing in their training and development to develop new skills that can be applied to future work.

Another important aspect to older workers' motivation is how age itself is perceived (Kooij, de Lange, Jansen, & Dikkers, 2008). There are different ways to conceptualize age and the different ways that people view age have different consequences for work motivation. Aging occurs in biological, social, and psychological functioning over time, and people with the same chronological age experience different rates of aging regarding health and job performance. Aging generally has a negative impact on motivation to work, but the nature of the impact varies according to how aging is conceptualized. For example, as people age functionally their self-efficacy tends to decrease, which leads people to want to avoid new and demanding tasks. Subjective age refers to how an individual acts, feels, and looks. As people age subjectively, others tend to stereotype them and therefore they are provided fewer developmental opportunities. Fewer developmental opportunities creates a self-fulfilling prophecy by leading older workers to actually have outdated skills.

The personal beliefs that older workers hold regarding how others perceive their age group impacts their ability to interact successfully with other age groups. Recent research suggests very different implications for successful aging of thinking of older adults as envied seniors with high social status versus pitied seniors with low social status. When older people believe that their age group has lower social status and others view them in age-stereotypical ways, they are more likely to suffer from anxiety, tension, and miscommunication and to believe they are targets of age discrimination (Vauclair, Lima, Abrams, Swift, & Bratt, 2016). Vauclair et al. also found that social norms that encourage people to be unprejudiced toward older people are associated with less perceived age discrimination. Thus even if personal attitudes are negative, institutions and societies can inhibit age prejudice through creating a social climate where age prejudice is discouraged. Clearly leaders' relations with individual subordinates can go a long way toward promoting a positive age climate at work.

It is hoped that this section helps leaders understand the stereotypes of older workers and the realities of working with older workers. As people age, their work experience and job attitudes tends to improve while they experience gradual losses in some cognitive and physical abilities. Research shows that stereotypes tend to exaggerate the cognitive and physical declines associated with aging, and thus older workers tend to be impacted negatively by the stigma associated with being identified as an "older worker." Moreover, life-span theories suggest that aging brings with it changes in strategies in how work is approached, goal orientation, and motivation. If understood, leaders can use this information to develop strong LMX relationships through creating superordinate goals, providing support for use of SOC strategies, and providing opportunities that are more likely to lead older subordinates to adopt a mastery-approach achievement motivation.

CONNECTING WITH OLDER WORKERS

While older workers typically have higher job satisfaction than younger workers (Ghazzawi, 2011), it is important to note the risks associated with age differences between leaders and members on LMX and job satisfaction (Malangwasira, 2013). Recall that he found that as the age difference between the leader and the follower increased LMX quality decreased, which negatively affected job satisfaction. Job satisfaction is important as it has been linked to prosocial behavior at work, less counterproductive behavior, and other withdrawal behaviors (Bateman & Organ, 1983). Moreover, research suggests that once older workers self-identify as "older," their job attitudes decline leading to thoughts about withdrawal and retirement. What appears to combat this issue is to create an organizational climate that does not use age to distinguish between employees thereby supporting positive attitudes toward work (Desmette & Gaillard, 2008).

It is important to note that creating high-quality LMX relationships with all subordinates should be a priority for leaders. If leaders have different LMX relationships with followers and the reason for that is ambiguous or potentially attributable to demographic (or other non-work-related) characteristics such as age, this can create feelings of exclusion and powerlessness. If differentiation in LMX quality within a group is due to differences in subordinate needs or the leader is focused on developing the strongest relationships with top performers, it may not be as harmful to the success of demographically-different others or the overall group performance (Nishii & Mayer, 2009). Moreover, the well-being of the leaders themselves can be negatively affected by differentiation of LMX quality within their groups (Bernerth & Hirschfeld, 2016). To avoid unfair distribution of LMX among subordinates, leaders should be encouraged by senior leadership (and given the tools and support) to get to know everyone with whom they work on a personal level, remove barriers for all employees, and refrain from using language that excludes some employees.

Changing demographic trends have reshaped workforce norms. Employees of all ages can now be found in all career stages and as a result younger supervisors with relatively older subordinates are becoming increasingly common (Burlacu, 2013). As today's workplace adjusts with this new norm, it is not uncommon for older subordinates to have lower expectations of their younger supervisors, which can negatively impact subordinates' rating of their supervisors' performance and also lead to poorer leadership behavior from their supervisors (Collins, Hair, Rocco, 2009). One the bright side, Collins, Hair, and Rocco suggest that developing high-quality LMX relationships with older subordinates helps mitigate the impact of erroneous age-related expectations. Perhaps the first step for younger leaders is educating them on this research to prepare them for possible hurdles and equip them with solutions. Likewise, older employees should be trained on reverse Pygmalion effects, which is if they have lower expectations of their younger supervisors this can lead to poorer leadership behavior from their supervisors. Clearly, research suggests that older employees can support positive LMX relationships through their own behaviors and expectations of younger supervisors.

To complement leaders' efforts to develop high-quality LMX relationships in an aging workforce, organizations should consider how to more broadly support successful aging at work. These efforts will provide individual leaders with tools and ideas for supporting their older subordinates. Moreover, older workers may trust and respect their leaders' LMX efforts if the larger organization climate is supportive of an age-diverse workforce. Workforce age management (Boehm, Schröder, & Kunze, 2013; Boehm, Kunze, & Bruch, 2014) has been shown empirically to increase organizational performance. It is a set of measures taken to mitigate the consequences of aging and allow workers to stay productive in spite of age-related declines (Ciutiene & Railaite, 2015). Boehm, Schröder, and Kunze (2013) suggest strategies such as focusing on recruiting, training and lifelong learning, career management and redeployment, flexible working times and alternative work arrangements, health management and workplace accommodations, performance measurement and remuneration, and transition to retirement activities.

A practical model for age management is the Balanced Scorecard developed by Voelpel and Streb (2010). In this model, the researchers identified five organizational action fields to manage the aging workforce. Those action fields included a managerial mindset toward older workers through which their capabilities are fostered and trusted, new knowledge management processes to harness the knowledge of older workers while taking their physical capabilities into consideration, health management practices to address safety and ergonomics, adaptation of inclusive human resource management practices, and work environment and physical tools. Similarly, Boehm, Schröder, and Kunze (2013) encourage leaders to foster employees' long-term health and work ability by paying close attention to safe working conditions, health promotion programs, workplace accommodations and ergonomics, psychological health programs, and a health oriented culture within the organization. Health management and workplace accommodation practices can lessen performance differences between younger and older employees and reduce early retirement decisions as employees maintain productivity and the ability to work. Improved health can also reduce absenteeism and shorten recovery times.

Organizations can train and encourage SOC (selective optimization with compensation) strategies for life management (Freund & Baltes, 1998). Recall that the SOC model includes selecting domains to pursue, the optimization and allocation of internal and external resources to achieve goals, and the development of processes to compensate for possible loss of goal-related resources in order to maintain functionality in targeted domains. Aging people who reported using life management strategies consistent with the SOC model also reported indicators of successful aging such as satisfaction with one's own aging, positive emotions, and the absence of loneliness (Freund & Baltes, 1998). Organizations can encourage employees to pursue SOC related life management strategies through employee training programs that explain the different applications of the model at work and in the employee's personal life.

As employees age their work-life balance needs and expectations may change. Major, Fletcher, Davis, and Germano (2008) found significant direct effects of LMX and coworker support on work interference with family and indirect effects of work–family culture on work interference with family. These findings shed light on the importance of LMX in creating a climate where employees feel supported in pursuing a healthy work-life balance. This becomes increasingly important as older workers often have elder care and childcare responsibilities ("the sandwich" generation; Hammer & Neal, 2008). The caregiving role especially impacts older working women. Flexible work hours is a common request of older workers that leaders may have the option to accommodate (Remery, Henkens, Schippers, & Ekamper, 2003). Allowing older employees flexible work schedules compliant with their changing needs and preferences as they age includes offering part-time employment, flexible starting times, working from home, job sharing, and sabbatical systems. Boehm, Schröder, and Kunze (2013) suggest that companies using such practices stand to benefit from increased employee motivation and performance, better utilization of labor resources, and improved work-life balance and employee health. In all cases communication is clearly key as the needs of employees change over time. Once leadership confirms that ideal conditions are made possible for older employees, an important practice to overcome age-related biases is to implement fair methods of performance evaluation and remuneration. Leaders can achieve fair and nondiscriminatory assessment and rewarding of employees through defining or redefining performance standards and using standardized evaluation systems that reduce age bias. Seeking information from a variety of sources through 360 degree evaluation for instance can also lessen the negative impact of age bias if present, and a pay-for-performance philosophy allows leaders to effectively reward performance gains (Boehm, Schröder, & Kunze, 2013).

Nilsson (2016) relates social aging to social inclusion, expectations, and a sense of identity and belonging within different positions and groups through the different phases of life. As such, older employees' social aging experience can play a major role in their decision of whether to extend their working life or to retire. Nilsson found that the attitude of managers and organizations toward older employees along with family, leisure, and surrounding society to be influencing factors in an employee's social aging experience. Doyle, McKee, and Sherriff (2012) also encouraged social engagement and emphasized the importance of social activity along with physical activity as factors supporting successful aging. The workplace can be isolating to older workers or enriching to their social lives. As part of these efforts, leaders can encourage their employees to volunteer in their areas of interest and ensure their work assignments allow the time for engaging in volunteer activities. Leaders may also encourage their employees to participate in causes sponsored by the organization through corporate social responsibility initiatives. It has been shown that older employees can protect their psychological well-being and slow down the rate of mental health decline by engaging in low-level volunteering along with their full-time work (Hao, 2008).

There is a variety of nontraditional ways in which older workers can contribute to organizations given they have the appropriate experience. With their knowledge of the organization or the industry, they may be able to offer consulting and mentoring roles to younger workers. Boehm, Schröder, and Kunze (2013) suggest recruiting older candidates for job openings to benefit from customer orientation through fit with age of a company's older customer groups. They also propose regular career talks and workshops for employees to ensure clear communication and understanding of management expectations and employee career goals. For employees who have no ambition or possibility for promotion, companies may offer alternative career models. For instance, in addition to lateral career moves, companies can also offer project work assignments and downshifting to less stressful but more fulfilling career roles such as coaching and mentoring that allow older employees to continue contributing to a company's success through sharing their experience with less seasoned employees.

While recruiting for vacant positions, leaders can avoid potential age-based discrimination by providing equal or special access to jobs for older employees and eliminate direct or indirect discrimination based on the age of applicants. This can be accomplished through creating age-neutral job advertisements and descriptions, avoiding negative age-related stereotypes among HR personnel and hiring managers, and focusing on experience in interviews. Beyond the obvious benefits of enlarging the hiring pool, these recruitment practices lead to a diverse workforce, which in turn prevents groupthink and enhances problem solving (Boehm, Schröder, & Kunze, 2013).

Numerous studies (as summarized by Podsakoff, MacKenzie, Paine, & Bachrack, 2000) have found that in order for organizations to thrive, they must have employees who engage in organizational citizenship behaviors supporting the social and contextual milieu of work. Older workers make great candidates for furthering the organization's social support and organizational citizenship climate since they have the experience and the willingness to give back, as suggested by Erikson's stages of psychosocial development particularly the stage of generativity versus stagnation during which old adults aim to contribute to society and guide the next generation (Erikson, 1980), which makes such roles a great opportunity for both the organization and older workers (Paullin & Whetzel, 2012). Based on the contingency theories of leadership that focus on situationally contingent traits and behaviors (Jago, 1982), organizations also stand to benefit from placing older workers in leadership positions. This possibility opens the door for a variety of opportunities for older workers to engage in task forces or lead projects that can benefit from their strong ability to regulate emotions and maintain positivity.

Most importantly, engaging an older workforce requires a personalized approach between leaders and their subordinates. Leaders can tailor workplace retention strategies by understanding the worker's ability to physically and cognitively complete the work that needs to be done, the individual's personal financial situation after retirement, the individual's family situation, the individual's and family member's health, and the individual's feelings about being valued at work. As previously mentioned in this chapter, older workers themselves question their value so a really simple retention strategy is for leaders to make it very clear to older workers that they are personally valued by asking them to stay and giving them recognition and rewards (Paullin & Whetzel, 2012).

Finally, when the time comes for older employees to retire, a smooth transition to retirement can be attained through providing employees with different forms of gradual transition such as partial or phased retirement, trial retirements, or retirement with call-back arrangements. Companies may also make retirement workshops and counseling activities available to their employees to prepare them for retirement as they age. Such gradual retirement prevents sudden loss of knowledge within the company and allows ample time for knowledge transfer to job successors. Keeping contact with retiring employees also allows companies to turn to them when special projects that require their skills arise (Boehm, Schröder, & Kunze, 2013).

CONCLUSION

The purpose of this chapter has been to summarize the literature on LMX in an aging workforce. As noted, there are surprisingly few studies that directly examine LMX and age. Yet there is a large and growing literature on successful aging at work and on workplace ageism from which implications for LMX relations can be drawn. In conclusion, we present a few ideas for future research that may help answer some lingering questions about age and LMX.

Globally the workplace is aging but not every older worker is the same. Older workers come with diverse experience, capabilities, and social and personal needs. Moreover, older workers are diverse in terms of other demographic characteristics. An older, White, male worker will likely have different experiences than an older, Black, female worker. Intersectionality poses an important challenge when researchers attempt to answer questions regarding LMX-age relationships, because age cannot be studied in isolation from other intersecting demographic characteristics (Marcus & Fritzsche, 2015, 2016).

The relational norm of age (Van der Heijden et al., 2010) clearly also needs to be examined. What is "old" depends on context. Age-typing of jobs (Reeves, Fritzsche, Dhanani, & Marcus, 2015) suggests that a young supervisor is normal in certain jobs thereby possibly eliminating the potential negative effects of age differences in supervisor-subordinate LMX relationships. Furthermore, as people move in and out of careers and organizations, it is important to understand the impact on LMX relations by a young, external leader versus a young leader promoted from within the organization. And, we need to better understand the extent that generational differences in attitudes and experiences impact LMX relations in age-diverse dyads, as only one qualitative study was found on this topic.

Regarding work on age stereotyping as it applies directly to LMX relations, research suggests that age stereotypes are likely to impact the role-taking phase of LMX relations (as described in the role episode model; Graen & Scandura, 1987). Yet, little work has been done to understand how initial age stereotyping then impacts the subsequent role-making and role-routinization stages of LMX relations when leaders and members know more deep level characteristics of each other. Does the initial age stereotyping set the tone of the LMX relationship or are age stereotypes easily overcome as leaders and subordinates develop deeper relationships?

Truxillo and Burlacu (2016) offer several additional questions worth pursuing about the relation between LMX and age. For example, they recommend that research examine whether age-related personality changes prepare people for their roles as leaders and followers, what the expectations are from different age groups as they assume leadership roles, and if the ability of older individuals to regulate their emotions prepares them for leadership. As workers age, they experience changes in their motivation, goals, and career aspirations. Truxillo and Burlacu suggest that future research explore whether such changes in motivation impact the quality of

LMX over time; how the aspirations of younger leaders impact their followers, and the LMX quality; and whether differences in career goals between leaders and members impact leader–member relationships.

All in all, the aging workforce in the United States and around the globe is bringing about exciting opportunities for researchers and organizational leaders alike. Worldwide, governments are dependent on workers staying in the workforce beyond traditional retirement ages. Organizations are experiencing shortfalls in available new entrants to the workforce and due to living longer lives, individuals often want and need to work beyond traditional retirement ages (Hannon, 2013), yet organizations are finding it difficult to retain valuable older workers (Paullin & Whetzel, 2012). Because LMX provides the social and emotional context in which employees feel valued and inspired to perform, the extent to which leaders develop strong LMX relations appears to be central to solving this problem (Gottfredson & Aguinis, 2016). Both leaders and members can benefit from understanding the challenges older workers face in the workplace and the solutions offered by current literature to mitigate the negative impact of those challenges. Building high-quality LMX relations certainly has the potential to help people successfully age at work thereby improving workplace outcomes for individuals, organizations, and ultimately societies as a whole.

REFERENCES

AARP (2013), *AARP workforce profiles: Selected characteristics of us workers and non-workers aged 40+*. Washington, DC: Author.

Abu Bakar, H., Jian, G., Fairhurst, G., & Connaughton, S. L. (2011, May). *The interactive effect of leader–member exchange agreement and relational demography on performance ratings.* Paper presented at the annual meeting of the International Communication Association, Boston, MA.

Avolio, B. J., Waldman, D. A., & McDaniel, M. A. (1990). Age and work performance in nonmanagerial jobs: The effects of experience and occupational type. *Academy of Management Journal, 33*(2), 407–422.

Bakar, H. A., Jian, G., Fairhurst, G. T., & Connaughton, S. L. (2011). The interactive effect of leader–member exchange agreement and relational demography on performance ratings. *Conference Papers: International Communication Association, 1*, 1–44.

Baltes, P. B., & Baltes, M. M. (1990). Psychological perspectives on successful aging: The model of selective optimization with compensation. *Successful Aging: Perspectives From the Behavioral Sciences, 1*(1), 1–34.

Bateman, T. S., & Organ, D. W. (1983). Job satisfaction and the good soldier: The relationship between affect and employee "citizenship." *Academy of Management Journal, 26*(4), 587–595.

Benz, J. K., Sedensky, M., Tompson, T. N., & Agiesta, J. (2013). *Working longer: Older Americans' attitudes on work and retirement.* Chicago, IL: The Associated

Press–NORC Center for Public Affairs Research. Retrieved from http://www.apnorc.org/projects/Pages/working-longer-older-americans-attitudes-on-work-and-retirement.aspx

Bernerth, J. B., & Hirschfeld, R. R. (2016). The subjective well-being of group leaders as explained by the quality of leader–member exchange. *The Leadership Quarterly, 27*(4), 697–710. doi:10.1016/j.leaqua.2016.04.003

Blau, P. M. (1964). *Exchange and power in social life.* Piscataway, NJ: Transaction.

Boehm, S. A., Kunze, F., & Bruch, H. (2014). Spotlight on age-diversity climate: The impact of age-inclusive HR practices on firm-level outcomes. *Personnel Psychology, 67*(3), 667–704.

Böehm, S. A., Schröder, H. S., & Kunze, F. (2013). Comparative age management: Theoretical perspective and practical implications. In J. Field, R. J. Burke, & C. L. Cooper (Eds.), *The SAGE handbook on work, aging, and society* (pp. 211–237). Thousand Oakes, CA: SAGE.

Burlacu, G. (2013). Supervisor–subordinate directional age differences and employee reactions to formal performance feedback: Examining mediating and moderating mechanisms in a Chinese sample. (Dissertations and Theses, Portland State University, 2013).

Byrne, D. E. (1971). *The attraction paradigm* (Vol. 2). San Diego, CA: Academic Press.

Carstensen, L. L. (1995). Evidence for a life-span theory of socioemotional selectivity. *Current Directions in Psychological Science, 4*(5), 151–156.

Casper, C., Rothermund, K., & Wentura, D. (2011). The activation of specific facets of age stereotypes depends on individuating information. *Social Cognition, 29*(4), 393.

Chand, M., & Tung, R. L. (2014). The aging of the world's population and its effects on global business. *The Academy of Management Perspectives, 28*(4), 409–429.

Ciutiene, R., & Railaite, R. (2015). Challenges of managing an aging workforce. *Engineering Economics, 26*(4), 391–397.

Cleveland, J. N., Festa, R. M., & Montgomery, L. (1988). Applicant pool composition and job perceptions: Impact on decisions regarding an older applicant. *Journal of Vocational Behavior, 32*(1), 112–125.

Collins, M., Hair, J., & Rocco, T. (2009). The older-worker-younger-supervisor dyad: A test of the reverse pygmalion effect. *Human Resource Development Quarterly, 20*(1), 21–41.

Cuddy, A. J., & Fiske, S. T. (2002). Doddering, but dear: Process, content, and function in stereotyping of elderly people. In T. D. Nelson (Ed.), *Ageism* (pp. 3–26). Cambridge, MA: MIT Press.

de Lange, A. H., Van Yperen, N. W., Van der Heijden, B. I., & Bal, P. M. (2010). Dominant achievement goals of older workers and their relationship with motivation-related outcomes. *Journal of Vocational Behavior, 77*(1), 118–125.

Desmette, D., & Gaillard, M. (2008). When a "worker" becomes an "older worker": The effects of age-related social identity on attitudes towards retirement and work. *Career Development International, 13*(2), 168–185.

Diekman, A. B., & Hirnisey, L. (2007). The effect of context on the silver ceiling: A role congruity perspective on prejudiced responses. *Personality and Social Psychology Bulletin. 33*, 1353–1366.

Doyle, Y., McKee, M., & Sherriff, M. (2012). A model of successful aging in British populations. *European Journal of Public Health, 22*(1), 71–76.

Epitropaki, O., & Martin, R. (1999). The impact of relational demography on the quality of leader–member exchanges and employees' work attitudes and well-being. *Journal of Occupational & Organizational Psychology, 72*(2), 237–240.

Erikson, E. H. (1980). On the generational cycle: An address. *The International Journal of Psychoanalysis, 61*(2), 213–224.

Fiske, S. T. (1998). Stereotyping, prejudice, and discrimination. In D. T. Gilbert, S. T. Fiske, & G. Lindzey (Eds.), *The handbook of social psychology* (Vol. 2, pp. 357–411). New York, NY: McGraw-Hill.

Fiske, S. T., Cuddy, A. J., Glick, P., & Xu, J. (2002). A model of (often mixed) stereotype content: competence and warmth respectively follow from perceived status and competition. *Journal of Personality and Social Psychology, 82*(6), 878.

Fiske, S. T., Cuddy, A. J., & Glick, P. (2007). Universal dimensions of social cognition: Warmth and competence. *Trends in Cognitive Sciences, 11*(2), 77–83.

Freund, A. M., & Baltes, P. B. (1998). Selection, optimization, and compensation as strategies of life management: correlations with subjective indicators of successful aging. *Psychology and Aging, 13*(4), 531.

Freund, A. M., & Baltes, P. B. (2002). Life-management strategies of selection, optimization and compensation: Measurement by self-report and construct validity. *Journal of Personality and Social Psychology, 82*(4), 642.

Freund, A. M., Li, K. Z. H., & Baltes, P. B. (1999). Successful development and aging: The role of selection, optimization, and compensation. In J. Brandtstädter & R. M. Lerner (Eds.), *Action & self-development: Theory and research through the life span* (pp. 401–434). Thousand Oaks, CA: Sage.

Gellert, F. J., & Schalk, R. (2011). The influence of age on perceptions of relationship quality and performance in care service work teams. *Employee Relations, 34*(1), 44–60.

Gellert, F. J., & Schalk, R. (2012). Age-related attitudes: the influence on relationships and performance at work. *Journal of Health Organization and Management, 26*(1), 98–117.

Ghazzawi, I. (2011). Does age matter in job satisfaction? The case of U.S. information technology professionals. *Journal of Organizational Culture, Communications and Conflict, 15*(1), 25.

Gordon, R. A., & Arvey, R. D. (2004). Age bias in laboratory and field settings: A meta-analytic investigation. *Journal of Applied Social Psychology, 34*(3), 468–492.

Gottfredson, R. K., & Aguinis, H. (2016). Leadership behaviors and follower performance: Deductive and inductive examination of theoretical rationales and underlying mechanisms. *Journal of Organizational Behavior.* doi:10.1002/job.2152.

Graen, G. B., & Scandura, T. A. (1987). Toward and psychology of dyadic organizing. In L. L. Cummings & B. M. Staw (Eds.), *Research in organizational behavior* (Vol. 9, pp. 175–208). Greenwich, CT: JAI Press.

Green, S. G., Anderson, S. E., & Shivers, S. L. (1996). Demographic and organizational influences on leader–member exchange and related work attitudes. *Organizational Behavior and Human Decision Processes, 66*(2), 203–214.

Haeger, D. L., & Lingham, T. (2013). Intergenerational collisions and leadership in the 21st century. *Journal of Intergenerational Relationships, 11*(3), 286–303.

Hammer, L. B., & Neal, M. B. (2008). Working sandwiched-generation caregivers: Prevalence, characteristics, and outcomes. *The Psychologist-Manager Journal, 11*(1), 93–112.

Hannon, K. (2013, January 25). Why older workers can't be ignored. *Forbes*. Retrieved from https://www.forbes.com/sites/kerryhannon/2013/01/25/why-older-workers-cant-be-ignored/#3975afcf8b7b

Hansson, R. O., DeKoekkoek, P. D., Neece, W. M., & Patterson, D. W. (1997). Successful aging at work: Annual review, 1992–1996: The older worker and transitions to retirement. *Journal of Vocational Behavior, 51*(2), 202–233.

Hao, Y. (2008). Productive activities and psychological well-being among older adults. *The Journals of Gerontology: Series B: Psychological Sciences and Social Sciences, 63*(2), S64–S72. doi:10.1093/geronb/63.2.S64

Harrison, D. A., Price, K. H., & Bell, M. P. (1998). Beyond relational demography: Time and the effects of surface–and deep-level diversity on work group cohesion. *Academy of Management Journal, 41*(1), 96–107.

Hobfoll, S. E. (1988). *The ecology of stress*. Boca Raton, FL: Taylor & Francis.

Jago, A. G. (1982). Leadership: Perspectives in theory and research. *Management Science, 28*(3), 315–336.

Joseph, D. L., & Newman, D. A. (2010). Emotional intelligence: An integrative meta-analysis and cascading model. *Journal of Applied Psychology, 95*(1), 54.

Kennedy, J. C. (2002). Leadership in Malaysia: Traditional values, international outlook. *The Academy of Management Executive, 16*(3), 15–26.

Knottnerus, J. D. (1997). The theory of structural ritualization. *Advances in Group Processes, 14*, 257–279.

Kooij, D., de Lange, A., Jansen, P., & Dikkers, J. (2008). Older workers' motivation to continue to work: Five meanings of age: A conceptual review. *Journal of Managerial Psychology, 23*(4), 364–394.

Krings, F., Sczesny, S., & Kluge, A. (2011). Stereotypical inferences as mediators of age discrimination: The role of competence and warmth. *British Journal of Management, 22*(2), 187–201.

Kroon, A. C., van Selm, M., ter Hoeven, C., & Vliegenthart, R. (2016). Dealing with an aging workforce: Locating threats and opportunities in corporate media. *Educational Gerontology, 42*(12), 818–834.

Kruse, A., & Schmitt, E. (2006). A multidimensional scale for the measurement of agreement with age stereotypes and the salience of age in social interaction. *Ageing and Society, 26*(03), 393–411.

Kunze, F., Boehm, S., & Bruch, H. (2013). Organizational performance consequences of age diversity: Inspecting the role of diversity-friendly HR policies and top managers' negative age stereotypes. *Journal of Management Studies*, (3), 413–442.

Labouvie-Vief, G. (1985). Intelligence and cognition. In J. E. Birren & K. W. Schaie (Eds.), *Handbook of the psychology of aging* (Vol. 2, pp. 500–530). New York, NY: Van Nostrand Reinhold.

Laux, L. (1995). *Aging techniques: Research techniques in human engineering*. Englewood Cliffs, NJ: Prentice Hall.

Lawrence, B. S. (1987). An organizational theory of age effects. *Research in the Sociology of Organizations, 5*, 37–71.

Lawrence, B. S. (1988). New wrinkles in the theory of age: Demography, norms, and performance ratings. *Academy Of Management Journal, 31*(2), 309–337. doi:10.2307/256550

Lerner, M. J., & Gignac, M. A. (1992). Is it coping or is it growth? A cognitive-affective model of contentment in the elderly. In L. Montada, S. Filipp, & M. J. Lerner (Eds.), *Life crises and experience of loss in adulthood* (pp. 321–337). Hillsdale, NJ: Erlbaum.

Major, D. A., Fletcher, T. D., Davis, D. D., & Germano, L. M. (2008). The influence of work–family culture and workplace relationships on work interference with family: A multilevel model. *Journal of Organizational Behavior, 29*(7), 881–897.

Malangwasira, T. E. (2013). Demographic differences between a leader and followers tend to inhibit leader-follower exchange levels and job satisfaction. *Journal of Organizational Culture, Communication and Conflict, 17*(2), 63.

Marcus, J., & Fritzsche, B. A. (2015). One size doesn't fit all: Toward a theory on the intersectional salience of ageism at work. *Organizational Psychology Review, 5*(2), 168–188.

Marcus, J., & Fritzsche, B. A. (2016). The cultural anchors of age discrimination in the workplace: A multilevel framework. *Work, Aging and Retirement, 2*(2), 217–229.

Minton-Eversole, T. (2012, April 9). *Concerns grow over workforce retirements and skills gaps*. Retrieved from https://www.shrm.org/ResourcesAndTools/hr-topics/talent-acquisition/Pages/WorkforceRetirementandSkillGaps.aspx

Newcombe, M. J., & Ashkanasy, N. M. (2002). The role of affect and affective congruence in perceptions of leaders: An experimental study. *The Leadership Quarterly, 13*(5), 601–614.

Ng, T. W., & Feldman, D. C. (2008). Can you get a better deal elsewhere? The effects of psychological contract replicability on organizational commitment over time. *Journal of Vocational Behavior, 73*(2), 268–277.

Ng, T. W., & Feldman, D. C. (2012). Evaluating six common stereotypes about older workers with meta-analytical data. *Personnel Psychology, 65*(4), 821–858.

Nilsson, K. (2016). Conceptualization of aging in relation to factors of importance for extending working life: A review. *Scandinavian Journal of Public Health, 44*(5), 490–505. doi:10.1177/1403494816636265

Nishii, L. H., & Mayer, D. M. (2009). Do inclusive leaders help to reduce turnover in diverse groups? The moderating role of leader–member exchange in the diversity to turnover relationship. *Journal of Applied Psychology, 94*(6), 1412.

Paullin, C., & Whetzel, D. L. (2012). Retention strategies and older workers. In W. C. Borman & J. W. Hedge (Eds.), *The Oxford handbook of work and aging* (pp. 392–418). Oxford, England: Oxford University Press.

Payne, S. C., Youngcourt, S. S., & Beaubien, J. M. (2007). A meta-analytic examination of the goal orientation nomological net. *Journal of Applied Psychology, 92*(1), 128–150.

Perry, E. L., & Finkelstein, L. M. (1999). Toward a broader view of age discrimination in employment-related decisions: A joint consideration of organizational

factors and cognitive processes. *Human Resource Management Review, 9*(1), 21–49.
Perry, E. L., Golom, F. D., Catenacci, L., Ingraham, M. E., Covais, E. M., & Molina, J. J. (2016). Talkin' 'bout your generation: The impact of applicant age and generation on hiring-related perceptions and outcomes. *Work, Aging and Retirement, 3*(2), 186–199.
Pettigrew, T. F. (1981). Extending the stereotype concept. In D. L. Hamilton (Ed.), *Cognitive processes in stereotyping and intergroup behavior* (pp. 303–332). Hillsdale, NJ: Erlbaum.
Podsakoff, P. M., MacKenzie, S. B., Paine, J. B., & Bachrach, D. G. (2000). Organizational citizenship behaviors: A critical review of the theoretical and empirical literature and suggestions for future research. *Journal of Management, 26*(3), 513–563.
Reeves, M., Fritzsche, B., Dhanani, L., & Marcus, J. (2015, April). *A survivor's guide to age discrimination*. Paper presented at the annual meeting of the Society for Industrial and Organizational Psychology, Philadelphia, PA.
Remery, C., Henkens, K., Schippers, J., & Ekamper, P. (2003). Managing an aging workforce and a tight labor market: Views held by Dutch employers. *Population Research and Policy Review, 22*(1), 21–40.
Riordan, C. M. (2000). Relational demography within groups: Past developments, contradictions, and new directions. In *Research in personnel and human resources management* (pp. 131–173). Bingley, England: Emerald Group.
Salthouse, T. A. (1992). Why do adult age differences increase with task complexity? *Developmental Psychology, 28*(5), 90.
Schieber, F., & Kline, D. W. (1982). Age and the discrimination of visual successiveness. *Experimental Aging Research, 8*(3), 159–161.
Shore, L. M., Cleveland, J. N., & Goldberg, C. B. (2003). Work attitudes and decisions as a function of manager age and employee age. *Journal of Applied Psychology, 88*(3), 529.
Shore, L. M., & Goldberg, C. B. (2005). Age discrimination in the workplace. In R. L. Dipboye & A. Colella (Eds.), *Discrimination at work: The psychological and organizational bases* (pp. 203–225). Mahwah, NJ: Erlbaum
Smith, W. J., & Harrington, K. V. (1994). Younger supervisor-older subordinate dyads: A relationship of cooperation or resistance? (Part 1). *Psychological Reports, 74*(3), 803–812. doi:10.2466/pr0.1994.74.3.803
Sonnenfeld, J. A. (1991). *The hero's farewell: What happens when CEOs retire*. New York, NY: Oxford University Press.
Tajfel, H., & Turner, J. C. (1979). An integrative theory of intergroup conflict. *The Social Psychology of Intergroup Relations, 33*(47), 74.
The World Bank Group. (n.d.). *Age dependency ratio (% of working–age population)*. Retrieved November 07, 2016, from http://data.worldbank.org/indicator/SP.POP.DPND
Truxillo, D. M., & Burlacu, G. (2016). Does age matter to LMX and its outcomes? A review and future research directions. In T. N. Bauer, B. Erdogan, T. N. Bauer, B. Erdogan (Eds.), *The Oxford handbook of leader–member exchange* (pp. 397–411). New York, NY: Oxford University Press.

Tsui, A. S., Egan, T. D., & O'Reilly, C. A., III. (1992). Being different: Relational demography and organizational attachment. *Administrative Science Quarterly, 37,* 549–579.

Tsui, A. S., & O'Reilly, C. A. (1989). Beyond simple demographic effects: The importance of relational demography in superior-subordinate dyads. *Academy of Management Journal, 32*(2), 402–423.

Van der Heijden, B. I., Scholarios, D., Van Der Schoot, E., Jedrzejowicz, P., Bozionelos, N., Epitropaki, O.,..., Indic@ tor Study Group. (2010). Supervisor-subordinate age dissimilarity and performance ratings: The buffering effects of supervisory relationship and practice. *The International Journal of Aging and Human Development, 71*(3), 231–258.

Vauclair, C. M., Lima, M. L., Abrams, D., Swift, H. J., & Bratt, C. (2016). What do older people think that others think of them, and does it matter? The role of meta-perceptions and social norms in the prediction of perceived age discrimination. *Psychology and Aging, 31*(7), 699.

Vecchio, R. P. (1993). The impact of differences in subordinate and supervisor age on attitudes and performance. *Psychology and Aging, 8*(1), 112–119. doi:10.1037/0882-7974.8.1.112

Voelpel, S. C., & Streb, C. K. (2010). A balanced scorecard for managing the aging workforce. *Organizational Dynamics, 39*(1), 84–90.

Walter, F., & Scheibe, S. (2013). A literature review and emotion-based model of age and leadership: New directions for the trait approach. *The Leadership Quarterly, 24*(6), 882–901.

Yeung, D. Y., & Fung, H. H. (2009). Aging and work: How do SOC strategies contribute to job performance across adulthood? *Psychology and Aging, 24*(4), 927.

Zacher, H., & Frese, M. (2011). Maintaining a focus on opportunities at work: The interplay between age, job complexity, and the use of selection, optimization, and compensation strategies. *Journal of Organizational Behavior, 32*(2), 291–318.

CHAPTER 8

SOME OF MY BEST FRIENDS AT WORK ARE MILLENNIALS

Leader–Member Exchange in the Face of Evolving Generational Diversity in the Workplace

Daniel P. Gullifor, Lori L. Tribble, and Claudia C. Cogliser
Texas Tech University

ABSTRACT

The purpose of this study is to explore leader–member exchange across baby boomer, Generation X, and Millennial generations. A total of 132 U.S. employees were interviewed with 22 leaders and 22 followers of each generation. These interviews were coded for patterns of action and interaction. Our analyses produced seven themes. We found that Gen X workers believe work is less important than both baby boomers and Millennials. Differences between generations were found in perceptions regarding leader–member exchange (LMX) and its four dimensions: affect, loyalty, contribution, and professional respect. Gen Xers were intent upon their followers following directions and simply doing what they are told. Baby boomers and Millennials exhibited more interest in a follower's exhibition of independence and the individual's ability to give and receive feedback. Our data showed little evidence from the Millennial transcripts that supports entitled/narcissistic tendencies. We found little evidence of ill will toward Millennials from the baby boomers, but some evidence from the Gen Xers. Baby boomers were more willing to work with Millennials than Gen Xers were, stating excitement for the opportunity to learn from those who are young and eager to have more experiences. Many baby boomers also preferred to have younger leaders. We believe this is the first study of LMX across multiple generations, and we offer that understanding the characteristics of the Millennial generation and how they lead and wish to be led is a critical step in managing the way business is conducted in today's fast-paced and digital environment such that all generations may thrive at work.

> *What we've seen is that every single generation enters the workforce and feels like they're a unique generation, and the generation that's one or two ahead of them looks back and says, "Who are these weird, strange kids coming into the workforce with their attitudes of entitlement and not wanting to fit in?" ... It's a cycle that's been repeated every 10 to 15 years for the last 50 years.*
>
> —Laszlo Bock
> Head of human resources at Google (quoted in Manjoo, 2016)

Recently, the Millennial generation has moved ahead of the baby boomers as the nation's largest living generation, and this generation's population is expected to peak in 2036 at 82.1 million (Fry, 2016; Pew Research Center, 2010). This expansion of the Millennial generation and its impact on the world is demonstrated by the fact that by the year 2025, Millennials will comprise 75% of the U.S. workforce. Echoing the public's fascination with the meteoric rises of prominent c-suite Millennials such as Mark Zuckerberg of Facebook, Ben Silbermann and Evan Sharp of Pinterest, Kevin Systrom and Mike Krieger of Instagram, and Drew Houston and Arash Ferdowsi of Dropbox, most employees born after 1980 will begin their careers with bosses who are Millennials just like themselves (Watkins & Neal, 2015).

While much has been reported in the popular media regarding Millennials and their sense of entitlement and narcissistic tendencies (Manjoo, 2016), little scholarly work explores this growing generation's attitudes and behaviors about leadership and leader-follower dynamics. The purpose of our qualitative study is to explore Millennials and leader-follower relations from a diversity perspective. Specifically, our focus is on how Millennials may differ from the generations who entered the workforce before them in their understanding of leader-follower relations as well as an exploration of perceptions that previous generations may hold about Millennials as either leaders or followers.

The leader–member exchange (LMX) model of leadership (Graen & Scandura, 1987; Graen & Uhl-Bien, 1995) is particularly fruitful for exploring generational diversity in the workplace because of its explicit focus on leader–follower relationships and the quality of the relationship that develops through the dyadic role-taking, role-making, and role-routinization processes (Graen & Scandura, 1987). LMX theory proposes that social exchanges not only form the basis for leader-follower relationships to develop (e.g., Cropanzano & Mitchell, 2005), but also acknowledges that these perceptions are not always shared (e.g., Sin, Nahrgang, & Morgeson, 2009).

Research regarding the similarity of leaders and followers within the dyad and its impact on relationship quality has been equivocal. Some studies (e.g., Turban & Jones, 1988) have found that similarity is related to higher LMX, while others have found no effects despite similar ratings of LMX (e.g., Matkin & Barbuto, 2012). To our knowledge, there is no study that explores LMX and its processes explicitly across multiple generations with a specific emphasis on Millennials.

We ground our research on LMX and generational differences in social identity theory (Ashforth & Mael, 1989), which posits that individuals will engage in behaviors that are congruent with salient aspects of their identities, and with higher levels of organizational identification they will behave in ways that benefit the organization and its members (e.g., Ashford & Barton, 2007). Unlike other generations Millennials are "digital natives," a term coined by Mark Prensky (2001) to refer to the first generation to grow up surrounded by and immersed in the tools and toys of digital technology. Although the Gen Xers and baby boomers who were not born into the language of computers, video games, and the Internet may adopt the technology of the digital world (therefore making them "digital immigrants"), their feet may still be rooted in aspects of their own generation. For example, digital immigrant behavior would be calling a colleague into your office to view something interesting outside of your window, rather than just Snapchatting a video of this through your mobile device.

There are a number of intended contributions of our research. First, we seek to establish whether perceptions of the dimensions of LMX (e.g., affect, loyalty, contribution, and professional respect) (Liden & Maslyn, 1998) remain consistent across generations. By taking this parsimonious approach we attempt to not only ascertain if generational differences in perceptions regarding LMX relationships exist, but to also explore what some of these specific distinctions might be. These insights could have extensive theoretical and practical implications. Should the dimensions of LMX take on different meanings across generations, the theory's ability to make explanations and understand complex phenomena would be altered. We would also see shifts such as differing needs for loyalty from the dyadic partner in the leader-follower dynamic, which would lead to alternative attitudes and behaviors in the workplace.

Second, we explore the relationships of generational differences with the LMX dimensions and revisit existing boundary conditions of LMX. Bacharach (1989) discusses the importance of the articulation of the assumptions made by theory (e.g., time, value, space) so as to avoid, among other outcomes, overgeneralization and misapplication of the theory. While work has been done to reveal the boundaries of LMX (Dulebohn, Bommer, Liden, Brouer, & Ferris, 2012), these boundary conditions have not been approached with regard to the potentially differing dimensions produced by generational differences. These differences may influence the boundaries of LMX and thus its applicability across generations.

Finally, as more Millennials enter the workforce most do so by assuming managerial positions (Watkins & Neal, 2015). As such, there is a need to examine the cross-generational differences and their impact on leader-follower interactions (Lyons & Kuron, 2014). Understanding both the development and the outcomes of the LMX relationship that is composed of individuals from differing generations will provide insights into the theoretical underpinnings of LMX that will guide its continued development.

RESEARCH QUESTIONS

Drawing from the specific management literature on LMX and the broader sociology, psychology, government, and management research streams on generations, we propose the following research questions to direct our exploration. Due to space limitations, we have not fully outlined the literature and theory from which these questions derived but have included citations to specific work that has help guide our development of these questions. Specifically, we ask:

- Will the four dimensions of LMX be consistent across different generations? Do the values of Millennials play a role in how they view the LMX dimensions? (Chou, 2012; Graen & Grace, 2015; Harrison & Klein, 2007; Twenge, Campbell, Hoffman, & Lance, 2010; Twenge, Konrath, Foster, Campbell, & Bushman, 2008)
- Does technology play a differential role in LMX development for Millennials than for other generations? Does LMX development rely on face-to-face communication with Millennials in a similar fashion as it does with Generation X and Baby Boomer leaders and followers or is it less relevant? (Balda & Mora, 2011)
- Do narcissism and entitlement play a role in LMX development with a Millennial leader or follower? Are narcissism and entitlement truly

part of the Millennial's interpretation of leadership, or are those factors more of an urban myth? (Galvin, Lange, & Ashforth, 2015; Horvath & Morf, 2009; Kernis & Sun, 1994; Westerman, Bergman, Bergman, & Daly, 2012).
- Do cross-generational LMX relationships develop differently than within-generational LMX relationships? If so, how (e.g., time, quality, etc.)? Can managers develop LMX across generations and not alienate other generational groups? (Graen & Schiemann, 2012; Randolph-Seng et al., in press; Sin, Nahrgang, & Morgeson, 2009).
- Does LMX need to develop at a more rapid pace in the organization for Millennials to be content? (Campione, 2015; Twenge et al., 2010).

METHOD AND PARTICIPANTS

The present study was guided by descriptive phenomenology (Porter, 1998) to capture the "essence" of an individual's experience relevant to a particular phenomenon. By this process, it is thought that the researcher would be able to capture a participant's consciousness of the phenomenon of interest (e.g., phenomena of being a Millennial follower who is supervised by a baby boomer). The methodological guidelines and analysis techniques of descriptive phenomenology developed by Porter (1998) produce two distinct aspects of the phenomena of interest, (a) lived experience and (b) life world context, which is the focus of the present study. Lived experience data reflect what the participant thinks about and "does" (intentions) with the experience. Life world context refers to data reflecting participants' perceptions of their social environment including both micro and macro levels. For example, family members, friends, leadership, followers, and co-workers' comments, reactions, and behaviors as well as broader messages/assumptions in culture (e.g., media, holidays) about leader-follower relations are all considered life world context data. Following Gioia, Corley, and Hamilton (2013), we wanted to explore "concepts" of leader-follower relationships across generations—"a more general, less well-specified notion capturing qualities that describe or explain a phenomenon of theoretical interest" (Gioia et al., 2013, p. 16).

The study included 132 individuals; the sample was 48.24% male. Demographic characteristics of the informants across leader/follower and generation are identified in Table 8.1. Participants were recruited through snowball sampling (Miles & Huberman, 1994) by graduate business students in a large southwestern university as part of a class assignment.

TABLE 8.1 Participants and Demographics		
Generation	Employee (Nonsupervisory)	Leader (Supervises > 3 people)
Baby Boomer (born between 1946 and 1964) $n = 44$ Males = 52.27% Mean age = 57.64 years	Boomer Employee $n = 22$ Males = 45.45% Mean age = 57.64 years	Boomer Leader $n = 22$ Males = 59.09% Mean age = 57.63 years
Generation X (born between 1965 and 1979) $n = 44$ Males = 42.45% Mean age = 42.95 years	Generation X Employee $n = 22$ Males = 38.10% Mean age = 42.77 years	Generation X Leader $n = 22$ Males = 52.38% Mean age = 43.14 years
Millennial (born after 1980) $n = 44$ Males = 50.00% Mean age = 26.09 years	Millennial Employee $n = 22$ Males = 42.86% Mean age = 24.41 years	Millennial Leader $n = 22$ Males = 57.14% Mean age = 27.77 years

Note: $N = 132$, Males = 48.24%, Mean age = 42.06 years

PROCEDURE

Twenty-two MBA students in a summer term graduate organizational behavior class each conducted structured interviews of six currently working participants over a two-week period for a team class project on organizational behavior across generations. Each student completed six, 27-question interviews of both a leader (who supervised at least three people) and a follower from the Millennial generation (born during or after 1980), Generation X (born between 1965 and 1979), and the baby boomer generation (born between 1946 and 1964) as part of the course project. The six interviews were transcribed by each student and compiled with the transcriptions of their three to five person teams. A paper was completed by each team that compared and contrasted the interview results of the Millennial, Generation X, and baby boomer leaders and followers.

The interview protocol used for the assignment was originally crafted by the author team before the class and is provided in Table 8.2.

DATA ANALYSES

Upon completion of the class and submission of grades, these 132 narratives were then read and analyzed by the first and second author separately for patterns of action and interaction (Strauss & Corbin, 1994). To facilitate the data analysis process, the authors employed the R-based qualitative data

TABLE 8.2 Interview Questions

1. In what type of industry are you employed?
2. What is your dream job (that is feasible)? Is this it? What are some responsibilities you have in your current job?
3. Tell me about a time you were particularly motivated at work? What motivated you specifically in this particular instance? Were you more or less successful in this instance?
4. Tell me about a time when you felt overwhelmed at work. How did you handle this scenario? What would you change about how you handled it?
5. Tell me about a time when you felt bored at work. How did you handle this scenario? What would you change about how you handled it?
6. On a scale of 1–10, how important is work to you when asked to define who you are as a person. What other spheres of life rank ahead of work? What other spheres rank behind work?
7. Tell me about your worst leader or boss with whom you were involved. What didn't you like about this leader? How did this leader make you feel about both yourself and your work? How soon did you know you didn't like this leader?
8. Tell me about your best leader or boss. What did you like about this leader? How did this leader make you feel about both yourself and your work? How soon did you know you liked this leader?
9. Have you ever taken a job or left a job based on your relationship with a leader or boss?
10. How has the development and advancement of technology and social media affected your relationships at work or school, especially with your leader or boss, both during work and non-work times?
11. If you could choose your leader or boss, would you select a leader that is younger than you, the same age as you, or older than you? Why would you make this selection?
12. If you could select the people who work for you, would you select people that are younger than you, the same age as you, or older than you? Why would you make this selection?
13. Describe the ideal leader.
14. Describe the ideal follower.
15. Do you think a leader should suppress their emotions and moods to be effective? Why or why not?
16. What do you think is the biggest challenge in leading a diverse workforce? What can leaders do to address this challenge?
17. What do you think satisfies people on the job the most?
18. Why do people quit jobs most often?
19. If you make a bad first impression in an interview, what would you try to do to change it?
20. Do you think that impression management is important at work? Would employees react positively, negatively, or neutral to impression management by their boss? [Impression management is a set of behaviors that people use to protect their self-image or change the way they are seen by others (or both)]
21. Do you think it is important for employees to participate in setting their own goals? Why or why not?

(continued)

TABLE 8.2 Interview Questions (continued)
22. Is punishment an effective way to encourage learning at work? Why or why not?
23. Do you think that paying someone to do something reduces their intrinsic motivation? [Intrinsic motivation is when someone works on a task because they find it interesting and gain satisfaction from the task itself.]
24. Is it a good idea for a boss to seek feedback from their employees? Why or why not?
25. How can you keep a team from procrastinating on the start of a project?
26. What year were you born?
27. What is your gender?

analysis (RQDA; Huang, 2012). Consistent with descriptive phenomenology, the interview guide contained enough questions so that the participant had the opportunity to more fully share his or her experiences thus minimizing the researcher "imposing" preconceived ideas/parameters on participants. Additionally, following this same line of thinking, the first and second authors "bracketed" (i.e., set aside knowledge and experiences with the phenomena of interest; Porter, 1995).

Despite the considerable attention garnered by generational differences, the support for differences observed between generations is indistinct. Accordingly, we adopted an inductive approach that would allow for the emergence of themes within the data. Previous studies that had adopted an inductive approach have often received criticism, particularly for their perceived lack of rigor. In an attempt to ameliorate this concern, we elected to adopt the guidelines presented by Gioia, Corley, and Hamilton (2013) to ensure our analysis was exposed to an appropriate level of rigor.

Initial coding was completed independently by two of the authors. This initial coding, or 1st order coding (Gioia et al., 2013), was completed in a manner that did not attempt to categorize or abstract to theoretical explanation. Rather, this first order coding, which as noted by Gioia and colleagues (2013) was a similar process to Strauss and Corbin's (1994) "open-coding," allowed for the emergence of terms, concepts, and codes that would serve as the foundation on which the data structure would be built. The rhetoric used in the development of codes emerged from those used by the respondents of the interviewees. This ensured a level of purity in regards to the data set, which is necessary given that the first order codes provide the basis for the subsequent analysis. In order to achieve consistency and agreement regarding these first order codes, meetings between the two coders were held on a weekly basis to reconcile any discrepancies in the produced codes. In the case of any competing beliefs regarding the codes produced, discussion was held until a consensus was reached.

This first order coding process resulted in hundreds of initial codes. This large number is not unusual given the study's inductive nature. As Gioia and colleagues (2013) note, Gioia is fond of stating "You gotta get lost before you can get found" (Gioia, 2004). Once these first order codes had been created and agreed upon, the two independent coders came together to share notes and codes to achieve somewhat more abstract categorizations or second order codes. These second order codes were the first step up a ladder of abstraction to gain a more complete understanding of the role generational differences played in leader-follower dynamics. The authors began to make sense of the large number of first order codes by showing both similarities and differences in responses as well as initial attempts at translating from respondent terminology to researcher terminology.

Once these second order codes were in place, all three authors came together to complete the abstraction process to facilitate the discussion of the theoretical implications of the findings. This was done by reviewing the data structure of both first order and second order codes to identify themes and how they related to and were explained by our phenomena of—LMX. While this study produced various findings, it is the findings of the greatest consequence to LMX and its closely related topics to which we turn our attention. The final set of seven themes that emerged from our analyses include the following: work as identity, loyalty, respect and merit, leader emotions, follower relations, technology, and cross-generational relations.

FINDINGS AND DISCUSSION

Our findings reveal both similarities and differences across the seven themes we identified, some of which contradict those of previous research. This section provides our discussion of the themes we discovered as we compared and contrasted these across generations and in relation to extant research. We have summarized the key findings in Table 8.3.

It has been suggested that work in itself may not be as important to Millennials as it has been to older generations (Campione, 2015; Twenge, Campbell, Hoffman, & Lance, 2010). However, our analysis revealed that of the three generations, it is actually Generation X that rated work the lowest in terms of defining themselves. To reach this conclusion, all three generations were asked, "On a scale of 1 to 10, how important is work to you when asked to define who you are as a person? What other spheres of life rank ahead of work? What other spheres rank behind work?" Baby boomers generally ranked work as either first or second in its importance in defining themselves. Millennials mostly ranked work as third or fourth highest in importance. However, Generation X bosses on average rated work as fifth highest in importance, while Generation X employees mostly rated work as one of the least important aspects of their lives in defining themselves. It would seem that Gen Xers generally identify less with work than both baby

TABLE 8.3 Summary of Key Findings

		Baby-Boomer	Generation X	Millennials
Leader		Loyalty important	Loyalty important	Loyalty not required
		Prefer receptive followers	Prefer cooperative followers	Prefer receptive followers
		Technology burden to work–family domain divide	Technology burden to work–family domain divide	Technology indifferent to work–family domain divide
		Merit and respect	Merit and respect	Merit and respect
		Rated work highest in importance of defining themselves	Rated work 5th highest in importance of defining themselves	Rated work 4th highest in importance of defining themselves
		Leaders should suppress emotions at work	Undecided on suppression of emotion at work	Leaders should suppress emotions at work
		No follower age preference	No follower age preference	No follower age preference
		No leader age preference	Older leader age preference	Strong older leader age preference
Follower		Loyalty important	Loyalty not required	Loyalty not required
		Prefer receptive followers	Prefer receptive followers	Prefer receptive followers
		Technology burden to work–family domain divide	Technology burden to work–family domain divide	Technology indifferent to work–family domain divide
		Merit and respect	Merit and respect	Merit and respect
		Rated work 2nd highest in importance of defining themselves	Rated work lowest in importance of defining themselves	Rated work 3rd highest in importance of defining themselves
		Leaders should suppress emotions at work	Undecided on suppression of emotions at work	Leaders should suppress emotions at work
		No follower age preference	No follower age preference	No follower age preference
		No leader age preference	Older leader age preference	Strong older leader age preference

* Trust served as a proxy for loyalty

boomers and Millennials. These results seem to challenge previous studies' suggestions (e.g., Twenge et al., 2010; Wey Smola & Sutton, 2002) that Millennials are not as invested in their work as preceding generations.

This particular difference between the generations may be more related to age than to generational culture, however. For example, baby boomers are older and may have different components of their life that contribute to their identity than they did earlier in their life. Baby boomers are more likely to have mostly grown children and be characterized as "empty nesters," such that their time commitment and identity are no longer derived so powerfully from their family. Whereas, Millennials are younger and may not have children at all, so their career plays a more prominent role in their identification process. These described lifestyles of baby boomers and Millennials contrast sharply to many Gen Xers who are at a stage in life where family duties (i.e., raising children and teenagers) are more demanding and may be a more integral part of their life. Therefore, they do not identify themselves in terms of what they do at work.

These differences between generations continue to show themselves, especially when we consider LMX and its four dimensions: loyalty (mutual obligation and loyalty), professional respect (respecting each other's capabilities), contribution (going above and beyond the job description), and affect (friendship and liking) (Liden & Maslyn, 1998). Our findings suggest that some of these LMX dimensions may not be as important to one generation as they are to others.

The loyalty dimension seems to hold true for the baby boomers in our sample. When describing their best leader experience, baby boomers often spoke of the trust that existed in their relationships. For example, one baby boomer leader said his/her best leader or direct supervisor "trusted my judgment and allowed me to make decisions." While one baby boomer follower said, "My best boss was one that left me alone and trusted me to do my job correctly." The importance of loyalty and trust partially transcended into the Generation Xers as well. For example, one Generation X leader was quoted as saying, "My best leader has been someone who has trusted and respected my knowledge and background." Interestingly, however, trust and loyalty were not nearly as prominent in the interviews of both Generation X followers and Millennial leaders and followers. This would suggest that perhaps the loyalty dimension of LMX is not as critical for younger generations and thus may not serve as a prerequisite to the establishment of a high quality LMX relationship across all generations, particularly those involving Millennials.

The professional respect dimension seemed to hold true for all generations. All participants seemed to understand the importance of experience and the merit of a leader. When asked to describe their ideal leader, many participants across all generations mentioned experience and/or some type of merit. For example, one baby boomer leader said he/she wanted "someone who is skilled and experienced in the field"; while a baby boomer follower said, "The ideal leader is someone who knows their job and their responsibilities." Gen Xers were similar in their responses with one boss reporting that he/she desires "someone who is intelligent"; while an employee noted, "My ideal leader is knowledgeable and hardworking." Finally the Millennials were similar with a leader and follower agreeing that their ideal leader is "knowledgeable" and "experienced." According to our findings, the LMX dimension of professional respect transcends all generations and is still important even with younger generations.

The affect dimension and the contribution it makes to the LMX relationship was found to vary across generations. When asked if leaders should suppress their emotions, most baby boomers and Millennials agreed that leaders needed to suppress emotions in the workplace. However, Gen Xers were not in agreement and fairly split on this issue. Therefore, the role affect would play in LMX would appear to vary across generations and influence the leader-follower dynamics in the workplace. As noted previously, this divergence seen in Gen Xers could be attributed to age and life stage rather than generational values. Borrowing from the work-family literature, spillover theory (Edwards & Rothbard, 2000) could explain part of this variance. Hill, Ferris, and Martinson (2003) relate spillover theory to ecology such that work and family are their own separates ecosystems situated next to each other in a larger mesosystem. Accordingly, due to increasing demands in each ecosystem, the boundaries become progressively permeable where emotions and their presence becomes expected in each domain. Indeed, the increased spillover at certain life stages may be affecting the LMX development of Gen Xers in different ways than it does baby boomers and Millennials.

Another area of dissent between the three generations that emerged was regarding feedback and the amount of control exhibited over followers by leaders. In particular, Gen Xers were intent upon their followers following directions and simply doing what they are told. Whereas, baby boomers and Millennials exhibited more interest in a follower's exhibition of independence and their ability to give and receive feedback. For example, when asked about the ideal follower, Generation Xers said the ideal follower follows directions; listens to instructions, reads the complete email, and understands their responsibilities; and follows commands. The baby boomers and Millennials seemed to be more in agreement with each other on this element. Several baby boomers reported that the ideal follower is capable of working independently; is one who obeys their leader, but also if there is a concern can go to the leader and discuss it; and it is also someone who listens first and is not afraid to speak up and ask questions on what the leader says. Millennials were similar thematically and described the ideal follower as someone who can follow, but is also not afraid to put forth suggestions, questions, or comments; someone who respectfully challenges their superiors, are vocal with questions and concerns; and is a smart, constructive thinker not a blind follower. The ideal follower is clearly different for the generations, and these different conceptualizations have an effect on how LMX is developed between a leader and a follower and how social exchange may develop after the initial transaction relationship is established.

LMX development relies on face-to-face communication and communicating through technology may hinder LMX development (Balda & Mora, 2011). This may be true for older generations due to the greater adjustments they need to make in the wake of technological advancement and adjustment. However Millennials are "digital natives." They have grown up in a world where texting in order to communicate is a normal and even preferred method of communication. Our findings suggest that technology is so integrated into Millennials' lives that they either see technology and social media as helpful in the workplace, or as not affecting work at all. They do not view texting after hours or having a social media presence as blurring the boundaries between work and home at all. For example, one Millennial boss said,

> I keep my social media presence very professional, so if I am added by a coworker or boss, and consider them a friend, I generally accept. Because I manage the company Facebook and website, I am required to be on the [web]sites during work hours. At first, I found it strange as being on social media during work hours is generally discouraged, but I was able to adjust. Technological advancements have allowed for communication at all hours—it has become normal to receive a work-related text at 11:00 P.M. or a work call at 6:00 A.M. (especially with clients spanning different time zones).

While one Millennial employee stated, "I don't know that my work relationships have been greatly affected by technology or social media, other than that it is easier to keep in touch and get (and give) immediate feedback on issues in the workplace."

However for Gen Xers and baby boomers, technology and social media seemed to be more problematic. More specifically, both credited the advancements in technology for excessively increasing accessibility to the point of blurring the boundaries between work and home life. Gen Xers commented that, "You never get down time. Text and calls are a requirement to work at our company to stay in touch with our transferees and company 24/7." Another complained that he "cannot seem to get away from email/work." While yet another Gen Xer explained, "I don't like the intrusion of privacy—I don't want my coworkers to be my friends on social media, but they friend me anyway and then I have to choose, which is uncomfortable." Baby boomers generally shared the same sentiment as Gen Xers with one stating, "I am not friends with anyone I work with and especially my boss on social media." Another said, "Technology has changed my work a lot and relationship with my boss; it is hard to maintain boundaries between work and leisure. Given when I am outside work, because of technology it follows me whenever I go." Perhaps this baby boomer explained the feelings of these generations the best, stating,

> Communication can be perceived as more but it's less effective. Texting and email are diluting the art of conversation, and verbal communication is less. Nonverbal communication causes misunderstanding and creates issues that aren't there. It also means you are never in a position to switch off out of work, as its connectivity 24/7. I spend less face to face time with my boss now than I ever have.

Previous researchers that have stressed the importance of face-to-face communication in the development of LMX were correct. However, this new generation of workers demonstrate a preference to work autonomously. Furthermore, they view social media as an appropriate and often preferred medium for contact with direct reports and team members (Espinosa, Ukleja, & Rusch, 2010). While that has been less relevant for previous generations, all workers today are facing an increasing need to be "digitally literate" and to stay up to date with emerging technologies (Palfrey & Gasser, 2008). Some of the Millennials' need for immediate and constant feedback may be provided by the "constantly on" aspect of social media (Sujansky & Ferri-Reed, 2009) substituting for the relationship building that occurred face-to-face previously. Accordingly we suggest that while we do not question the importance of communication universally, the method of communication may best be decided on a more individual basis to achieve optimal results.

Previous research has suggested that Millennials are entitled and narcissistic (Bergman, Westerman, Daly, 2010; Campione, 2015; Twenge et al. 2010). Additionally, as indicated by the introductory quote by Laszlo Bock, older generations harbor a certain level of disdain for younger generations due to a sense of entitlement. However, in the interviews we collected we found very little evidence from the Millennial transcripts that supports their supposed entitled/narcissistic tendencies. Regarding the ill-feelings toward Millennials, the results were mixed. We found little indication of this irritation with the Millennials from the baby boomer transcripts. However, we did find some evidence from the Generation X transcripts. A few Gen Xers did suggest that Millennials are more entitled than previous generations. One said, "The younger group has a strong sense of entitlement and acts as if everything is owed to them. They don't seem to be willing to work for their success. They seem to think it just magically appears." Another Gen Xer stated, "The younger leaders want to be a VP within 6 months and not work for it. They expect things in life to be given to them and do not appreciate anything."

This displeasure with the Millennials from the Generation Xers could be the result of any number of circumstances. However, we posit that this may be what came to be known in the discussion among authors as "middle child syndrome." While little work has been done in the management field to explore this phenomenon, it has been discussed in tangential fields. For example, Sulloway (2001) adopts a Darwinian approach to show how the middle child is often neglected due to parental motivations for supplying the eldest with resources due to their tendency to reproduce earlier and the youngest due to their vulnerability to threats of disease, predators, and the like. This leaves the middle child neglected and more inclined to harbor resentment toward the older and younger siblings for receiving attention and advantages that they did not. Sulloway also notes the work of Hertwig, Davis, & Sulloway (2002) and the further support they provide by highlighting that the oldest and youngest experience at least some period of time where they are the only child. Whereas, the middle child is always sharing and may never truly attain the resource advantage that the oldest and youngest are assured to enjoy.

It is this analogy of the middle child that we think may explain some of the Gen Xers disdain for Millennials and not so publicly due to hierarchical repercussions, baby boomers. For the longest time, baby boomers received the attention and resources of society. How would the world handle the influx of the largest, potentially most successful, generation ever? This type of attention was paid to the baby boomer generation just long enough until the Millennial generation became the fixture of the public's eye. Today, the Millennial generation and the challenges of engaging with the Millennial generation are ubiquitously dispersed throughout the popular media. Additionally, the middle child Gen Xers have yet to receive the "hand-me-downs" from the baby boomers due to their elongated stay in the workforce and unforeseen economic conditions. This leaves Generation X indefinitely stuck sharing resources and attention with both an older and a younger generation.

Despite Generation X's contempt for Millennials, baby boomers seem to be very willing to work with Millennials. In fact, baby boomers seem excited for the opportunity to learn from people who are young and eager to have more experiences. When asked what age leader they would choose, many baby boomers stated that they would choose younger leaders. For example, this baby boomer boss said, "I would choose a boss that is younger than me because they are so engaged in the new technology they keep pushing me to go beyond what I would normally consider my limits." While another said, "Younger leaders are more open to suggestions and seem to be more positive." The baby boomer employees felt similarly stating, "I work with a whole office that is younger than me. This has been the most positive work experience in my life." Another one chose a younger leader and stated, "I say this because my current boss that I love is younger and he has allowed me to run with my creative ideas and is constantly pushing me to new levels. This doesn't seem to happen much later in a teacher's career."

LIMITATIONS AND DIRECTIONS FOR FUTURE RESEARCH

While our study makes important contributions to the literature, is it not without limitations that need to be addressed. First, we note that our study is cross-sectional in nature. Thus we cannot determine whether the differences or similarities in perspectives are due to our respondents' ages, stage in their career, or their generation, and causal inferences cannot be made. If we were able to track our respondents across time, we could understand more fully the elements that contribute to generational preferences without the potential confound of age, career stage, or generation.

Second, our sample was drawn from employees in the southwestern United States. Future research should employ samples that represent additional regions of the United States as well as studies that explore national culture to determine if the differences and similarities we found hold more broadly. A broader, more inclusive sample would provide additional insights to the generalizability of generational differences and the influence they have on LMX.

Research on generational differences, specifically with an emphasis on Millennials, is still in its nascent stage and the research questions in this study are exploratory in nature. We encourage future work to be more directive and build on the themes that we explore to understand causes, consequences, and mediating or moderating conditions that demonstrate generational differences.

The number of generation-specific results in our study indicate that research on LMX should take generational differences into account, particularly when exploring dyads that cross generations (e.g., Millennial leader and Generation X follower). Longitudinal research of LMX dyads would allow causal conclusions to be made and to see whether patterns across generations are a result of age, career stage, or generation.

Generation Z (also known as post-Millennials, the iGeneration, or the Homeland Generation) is the demographic cohort that immediately follows the Millennials. This generation is just beginning its entry into the workplace and is thus ripe for emerging research in this domain. While there is still some debate about when the first babies of Generation Z actually arrived, consensus among demographers places this generation's emergence around the mid-1990s to the mid-2000s yielding the oldest of this cohort just now beginning life in their 20s (Williams, 2015). What may distinguish Generation Z from the Millennials is not just technology—clearly Millennials are tech savvy. But Generation Z members have come of age in a multicultural world where smartphones and communicating with 140 characters and videos that disappear after viewing are the norm. The addition of Generation Z to leader–member dyads provides an additional layer of research on leader-follower relationships in this millennium.

PRACTICAL IMPLICATIONS

As the workforce steadily ages and younger generations continue to flood the job market, the workplace is going to continue to become increasingly diverse. Not only are baby boomers extending their stay, but Millennials and even Gen Zers are not only entering the workforce, but moving into more influential roles at an increasing pace. As such, the workplace and the relationships within it are becoming more intertwined. These multigenerational relationships foster not only challenges, but also opportunities. Here, we address how some of these challenges and opportunities may present themselves in the workplace. While it is not our intention to present a comprehensive discussion of every finding, we want to provide an overview of some of the more prominent implications likely to be encountered and discuss them in the context of various themes we identified.

Among the observed differences across generations is the desire for loyalty and commitment from the organization and individuals within it. Baby boomers expressed a specific desire for loyalty and reciprocity from the organization that did not seem as paramount for Gen Xers or Millennials. This can become a challenge if the environment becomes increasingly volatile. In this case, significant changes would need to be made that may alter both the explicit and implicit agreements between individuals and their organization. To mitigate the potential harm from a perceived breach of loyalty, organizations and individuals should be prepared to honor commitments made to everyone, but particularly to baby boomers.

The expressed desire for loyalty made by baby boomers at least partially stems from the importance work plays in their ability to answer the question, Who am I? Work and their relationship to it has endured for years and their investment continues to grow, particularly as retirement approaches and they begin to look at their accomplishments and the impact they have made. For other generations work, while still important, is not as critical to how they define themselves. Both Millennials and Gen Xers have alternative contributories to who they are such as social lives and family lives, respectively. Rather than demanding these individuals reprioritize the various aspects of their lives, we suggest fostering a sense of empathy for these individuals in the form of more flexible work hours or personalization of work spaces, which may cultivate appreciation and enhanced commitment.

Previous research has shown face-to-face communication to be necessary for the development of high quality leader-follower relationships. However, our findings suggest this may not be universally true. While we agree the need for communication is present across all generations, we question its need to be face-to-face particularly for Millennials. Due to their familiarity with technology and its constant presence, communicating through various technologically based alternatives (i.e., Facebook, Twitter, Snapchat, etc.) is actually preferred. Communication in this form allows Millennials to feel connected. Feeling disconnected is an uncomfortable feeling for an individual who for most of their life has been connected to critical information at all times. Technology facilitates this connectedness and keeps Millennials in the know while maintaining their independence by not having a physical person standing over their shoulders all the time.

Contrary to the comfort and desire for communication felt by Millennials, constant communications through technology can be a major source of anxiety and stress, especially for baby boomers and Gen Xers. While Millennials have an implicit desire for connectedness, baby boomers and Gen Xers have a desire to disconnect, particularly outside of working hours. Because communication outside of work hours is more feasible due to technology, Millennials generally have no problem communicating outside of normal working hours. However, many Gen Xers and baby boomers felt overwhelmed and stressed when work impeded on their nonwork hours. As such, this can cause problems for intergenerational dyads with one person feeling overwhelmed with work communication or the other person feeling anxious due to not receiving enough communication and feeling disconnected. While we do not advocate for either increasing or decreasing communication outside of work, we do advocate for the explicit discussion of expectations concerning the degree of communication. This should address expectations regarding the use of technology as a communication tool and communication outside of normal working hours. This facilitates a better understanding of the nature of the communication within the dyad and its impact on both recipients.

In addition to setting expectations regarding communication, leaders and followers must communicate regarding their general expectations for each other. More specifically, the role of the follower within an LMX dyad must be addressed. Baby boomers and Millennials had similar conceptions of the role of followers and agreed they should be involved and participative. However, Gen Xers believed followers should be more obedient and not challenge the status quo particularly when that status quo is set by the leader. This divergence in follower expectations among the generations can have harmful repercussions in cross-generational leader-follower relationships. With the proliferation of intergenerational dyads, it seems to be of utmost importance that the structure and expectations of each party be made explicit. Clear expectations allow for both parties to agree upon a relationship structure that may facilitate a better fit and the ability to perform in their respective roles.

While this study revealed many differences across generations, a constant and ubiquitously essential theme across all three generations was the presence of respect and the importance placed on merit within the LMX relationship. Both leaders and followers' ability and respect for each other professionally are critical for the achievement of a high quality relationship. The positive outcomes discussed previously in a relationship that is not characterized by professional respect is one that is set up to fail regardless of whether its parties come from the same or different generations. Mutual respect is the necessary characterization of beneficial relationships in any generation.

CONCLUSION

Millennials may be misunderstood. But as the largest generation in the workforce, they have a significant influence. It's only a matter of time before they begin redefining leadership and other workplace trends.
—Morgan, 2015

As an author team of one boomer and two Millennials, we agree that the leadership field can advance only when those who study it are willing to accept its dynamic nature. Understanding the unique characteristics of the Millennial generation and how they lead and wish to be led is a critical step in managing not only the way business is conducted in today's fast-paced and digital environment, but also how all generations may thrive at work as they impact the global economy.

REFERENCES

Ashford, S. J., & Barton, M. A. (2007). Identity-based issue selling. In C. A. Bartel, S. Blader, & A. Wrzesniewski (Eds.), *Identity and the modern organization* (pp. 223–244). Mahwah, NJ: Erlbaum

Ashforth, B. E., & Mael, F. (1989). Social identity and the organization. *Academy of Management Review, 14*, 20–39.

Bacharach, S. B. (1989). Organizational theories: Some criteria for evaluation. *Academy of Management Review, 14*(4), 496–515.

Balda, J. B., & Mora, F. (2011). The networked, millennial generation. *Journal of Leadership Studies, 5*(3), 13–24.

Bergman, J. Z., Westerman, J. W., & Daly, J. P. (2010). Narcissism in management education. *Academy of Management Learning & Education, 9*(1), 119–131.

Campione, W. A. (2015). Corporate offerings: Why aren't millennials staying? *The Journal of Applied Business and Economics, 17*(4), 60–75.

Chou, S. Y. (2012). Millennials in the workplace: A conceptual analysis of millennials' leadership and followership styles. *International Journal of Human Resource Studies, 2*(2), 72–83.

Cropanzano, R., & Mitchell, M.S. (2005). Social exchange theory: An interdisciplinary review. *Journal of Management, 31*(6), 874–900.

Dulebohn, J. H., Bommer, W. H., Liden, R. C., Brouer, R. L., & Ferris, G. R. (2012). A meta-analysis of antecedents and consequences of leader–member exchange integrating the past with an eye toward the future. *Journal of Management, 38*(6), 1715–1759.

Edwards, J. R., & Rothbard, N. P. (2000). Mechanisms linking work and family: Clarifying the relationship between work and family constructs. *Academy of Management Review, 25*(1), 178–199.

Espinoza, C., Ukleja, M., & Rusch, C. (2010). *Managing millennials: Discover the core competencies for managing today's workforce.* Hoboken, NJ: Wiley.

Fry, R. (2016). Millennials overtake baby boomers as America's largest generation. *Pew Research Center.* Retrieved from http://www.pewresearch.org/fact-tank/2016/04/25/Millennials-overtake-baby-boomers/

Galvin, B. M., Lange, D., & Ashforth, B. E. (2015). Narcissistic organizational identification: Seeing oneself as central to the organization's identity. *Academy of Management Review, 40*(2), 163–181.

Gioia, D. A. (2004). A renaissance self: Prompting personal and professional revitalization. In P. J. Frost & R. E. Stablein (Eds.), *Renewing research practice: scholars' journeys* (pp. 97–114). Stanford, CA: Stanford University Press.

Gioia, D. A., Corley, K. G., & Hamilton, A. L. (2013). Seeking qualitative rigor in inductive research: Notes on the Gioia methodology. *Organizational Research Methods, 16*(1) 15–31.

Graen, G., & Grace, M. (2015). Positive industrial and organizational psychology: Designing for tech-savvy, optimistic, and purposeful millennial professionals' company cultures. *Industrial and Organizational Psychology, 8*(3), 395–408.

Graen, G. B., & Scandura, T. A. (1987). Toward a psychology of dyadic organizing. *Research in Organizational Behavior, 9*, 175–208.

Graen, G. B., & Schiemann, W. A. (2012). Leadership-motivated excellence theory: An extension of LMX. *Journal of Managerial Psychology, 28*(5), 452–469.

Graen, G. B., & Uhl-Bien, M. (1995). Relationship-based approach to leadership: Development of leader–member exchange (LMX) theory of leadership over 25 years: Applying a multilevel multidomain perspective. *The Leadership Quarterly, 6*(2), 219–247.

Harrison, D. A., & Klein, K. J. (2007). What's the difference? Diversity constructs as separation, variety, or disparity in organizations. *Academy of Management Review, 32*(4), 1199–1228.

Hertwig, R., Davis, J. N., & Sulloway, F. J. (2002). Parental investment: how an equity motive can produce inequality. *Psychological Bulletin, 128*(5), 728–745.

Hill, E. J., Ferris, M., & Märtinson, V. (2003). Does it matter where you work? A comparison of how three work venues (traditional office, virtual office, and home office) influence aspects of work and personal/family life. *Journal of Vocational Behavior, 63*(2), 220–241.

Horvath, S., & Morf, C.C. (2009). Narcissistic defensiveness: Hypervigilance and avoidance of worthlessness. *Journal of Experimental Social Psychology, 45*, 1252–1258.

Huang, R. (2012). *RQDA: R-based qualitative data analysis.* R package version 0.2-3. Available at http://rqda.r-forge.r-project.org/

Kernis, M. H., & Sun, C. (1994). Narcissism and reactions to interpersonal feedback. *Journal of Research in Personality, 28,* 4–13.

Liden, R. C., & Maslyn, J. M. (1998). Multidimensionafity of leader–member exchange: An empirical assessment through scale development. *Journal of Management, 24*(1), 43–72.

Lyons, S., & Kuron, L. (2014). Generational differences in the workplace: A review of the evidence and directions for future research. *Journal of Organizational Behavior, 35*(S1), S139–S157.

Manjoo, F. (2016, May 15). Corporate America chases the mythical millennial. *The New York Times.* Retrieved from https://www.nytimes.com/2016/05/26/technology/corporate-america-chases-the-mythical-millennial.html

Matkin, G. S., & Barbuto, J. E. 2012. Demographic similarity/difference, intercultural sensitivity, and leader–member exchange: A multilevel analysis. *Journal of Leadership & Organizational Studies, 19*(3), 294–302.

Miles, M. B., & Huberman, A. (1994). *Qualitative data analysis, 2.* Thousand Oaks, CA: SAGE.

Morgan, H. (2015, June 22). What kind of leaders are millennials? *U.S. News & World Report.* Retrieved from http://money.usnews.com/money/blogs/outside-voices-careers/2015/07/22/what-kind-of-leaders-are-Millennials

Palfrey, J., & Gasser, U. (2008). *Born digital: Understanding the first generation of digital natives.* New York, NY: Basic Books.

Pew Research Center. (2010). *Millennials: Confident. Connected. Open to change.* Retrieved from http://www.pewsocialtrends.org/2010/02/24/Millennials-confident-connected-open-to-change/.

Porter, E. J. (1995). The life-world context of older widows: The context of lived experience. *Journal of Women & Aging, 7,* 31–46.

Porter, E. J. (1998). On being inspired by Husserl's phenomenology: Reflections on Omery's exposition of phenomenology as a method of nursing research. *Advances in Nursing Science, 21,* 16–28.

Prensky, M. (2001). Digital natives, digital immigrants. *On The Horizon, 9*(5), 1–6.

Randolph-Seng, B., Cogliser, C. C., Randolph, A. F., Scandura, T. A., Miller, C. D., & Smith-Genthôs, R. (in press). Diversity in leadership: Race in leader–member exchanges. *Leadership & Organizational Development Journal.*

Sin, H., Nahrgang, J. D., & Morgeson, F. P. (2009). Understanding why they don't see eye to eye: An examination of leader–member exchange (LMX) agreement. *Journal of Applied Psychology, 94*(4), 1048–1057.

Strauss, A., & Corbin, J. (1994). Grounded theory methodology: An overview. In Denzin & Lincoln (Eds.), *Handbook of qualitative research.* Thousand Oaks, CA: SAGE.

Sujansky, J. G., & Ferri-Reed, J. (2009). *Don't be so touchy! The secrets for giving feedback to millennials.* Retrieved from http://ehstoday.com/safety/management/touchy-feedback-millennials-1009

Sulloway, F. J. (2001). Birth order, sibling competition, and human behavior. In *Conceptual challenges in evolutionary psychology* (pp. 39–83). Dordrecht, the Netherlands: Springer.

Turban, D. B., & Jones, A. P. (1988). Supervisor-subordinate similarity: Types, effects, and mechanisms. *Journal of Applied Psychology, 73*(2), 228–234.

Twenge, J. M., Campbell, S.M., Hoffman, B.J., Lance, C.E. (2010). Generational differences in work values: Leisure and extrinsic values increasing, social and intrinsic values decreasing. *Journal of Management, 36*(5), 1117–1142.

Twenge, J. M., Konrath, S., Foster, J. D., Campbell, W. K., & Bushman, B. J. (2008). Egos inflating over time: A cross-temporal meta–analysis of the narcissistic personality inventory. *Journal of Personality, 76*(4), 875-901.

Watkins, M., & Neal, P. J. (2015). Millennial in training. *Workforce, 94*(1), 36–48.

Westerman, J., Bergman, J., Bergman, S., & Daly, J. (2012). How narcissistic are business students? An empirical examination of narcissism in millennial students and its implications. *Journal of Management Education, 36*(1), 5–32.

Wey Smola, K., & Sutton, C. D. (2002). Generational differences: Revisiting generational work values for the new millennium. *Journal of Organizational Behavior, 23*(4), 363–382.

Williams, A. (2015). *Move over millennials, here comes generation Z.* Retrieved from https://www.nytimes.com/2015/09/20/fashion/move-over-millennials-here-comes-generation-z.html

CHAPTER 9

MYTHS AND MISCONCEPTIONS ABOUT LEADING GENERATIONS

Setting the Record Straight

Cort W. Rudolph
Saint Louis University

Hannes Zacher
*University of Leipzig
and Queensland University of Technology*

ABSTRACT

In this chapter, we argue that the most common myths regarding generations and generational differences at work are both incorrect and indeed potentially dangerous when blindly accepted as doctrine. To address this concern and with an eye toward the role of age in various leadership processes, we offer an alternative life span perspective on leadership that better addresses age-related changes in work attitudes, motivations, and behaviors. This framework serves to shape evidence-based practical recommendations regarding leading older workers and age-diverse work groups. Our hope here is to redirect attention away from generations as a unit of understanding age-related changes at work and toward demonstrable, actionable, and relevant issues regarding aging as a continuous and lifelong process.

The idea of generational differences in work attitudes, motivations, and behaviors has recently become a "hot topic" in the popular management and leadership press (e.g., Baldonado, 2008; Eisner, 2005; Kapoor & Solomon, 2011) and among organizational researchers (e.g., Costanza & Finkelstein, 2015; Rudolph & Zacher, 2016). While the term generation can be used in multiple ways (e.g., to describe genealogical lineage or single birth cohorts, see Baltes & Reinert, 1969), sociological conceptualizations of generations as facilitators for social change ascribe additional meaning to this concept. From this perspective, generations are considered an important mechanism by which such broadly defined changes are transmitted and codified. For example, from a classically social-constructivist standpoint Mannheim (1952) suggested that generations comprises groups of individuals of similar ages who share common experiences (see Rudolph & Zacher, 2016, for a review of similar definitions). Thus as most typically understood, generation defines a group of similarly aged people who have experienced common social or historical events by virtue of birth-year proximity. The notion of "generational differences" as understood in the popular management and leadership press suggests that there are demonstrable disparities between members of such generations who are tied to such common experiences; it is argued that such experiences have a commensurate influence on work attitudes, motivations, and behaviors (Rudolph & Zacher, 2016).

A great deal of attention has been paid to the notion that generational differences exist and must be actively managed in the workplace. Moreover, considering collections of recommended leadership practices, it is relatively easy to find references to the need to treat employees of different ages in line with the idea that generational differences exist and serve as important drivers of work processes and outcomes. As such, leadership best practices recommendations have suggested that generational differences at work must be proactively addressed by leaders (e.g., Anderson, Buchko, & Buchko, 2016; Caraher, 2014; Espinoza & Ukleja, 2016; Gilbert, 2011; Kauppinen, 2016; Tulgan, 2016).

Consistent with past scholarship, we use the term leadership to refer to various processes that are applied to achieve shared goals by structuring tasks and influencing group processes. Thus, leadership may refer to a variety of ways in which a leader influences follower behavior to focus on specific goals or outcomes (Bass, 1990; Yukl, 1998). Among the numerous models of leadership, we take a leader–member exchange perspective (LMX, Graen & Uhl-Bien, 1995) that considers how social exchanges between leaders and followers emerge and develop over time. LMX theorists have posited that the quality of such exchange relationships is in part dictated by the way in which formal roles are defined and negotiated. Given that much of our understanding of generational differences at work is based upon (incorrect) assumptions regarding how members of various generational groups approach their work roles, LMX provides a good framework for understanding and rectifying phenomena associated with leadership and generations.

Despite all of the attention and effort toward establishing practical recommendations for leading members of different generations at work, there is little to no empirical evidence suggesting that such generational differences actually exist or that they meaningfully influence work outcomes (see Costanza, Badger, Fraser, Severt, & Gade, 2012 for a quantitative meta-analytic review and Stassen, Anseel, & Levecque, 2016 for a systematic qualitative review). The scant evidence that does exist is based upon research that has employed inappropriate methods for drawing valid conclusions about generational differences (e.g., Davis, Pawlowski, & Houston, 2006; Dilworth & Kingsbury, 2005; Hess & Jepsen, 2009). This leaves us with a problem: organizational practitioners are realizing that there are differences between employees from different age groups that can have an influence on the effectiveness of a wide variety of human resources management processes (e.g., Kooij et al., 2012). However, best practices regarding the management of such processes are often based upon untenable notions regarding generational differences (i.e., the incorrect assumption that they exist) and a misguided belief in the need for differentiated approaches to leading generations (e.g., the dubious suggestion that members of various generations must be led differently, Crampton & Hodge, 2006).

Considering this problem, the goals of this chapter are threefold. First, we outline and debunk several common myths and misconceptions about generations at work. The purpose of this discussion is to "set the record straight" regarding the idea of generational differences at work. Second, we introduce the life span developmental perspective (Baltes, 1987) and discuss a life span approach to leadership that specifically addresses the process of leading workers of different ages. In doing so, we argue that this approach is more suitable for managing and leading an increasingly aging and age-diverse workforce than the model of generational differences. Finally, we argue that leadership best practice recommendations should be based on this life span perspective and a notable body of literature that more appropriately considers the role of age and aging in work processes. To this end, we integrate several ideas into a set of updated leadership best-practice guidelines for applying this life span approach to leading members of an aging and age-diverse workforce.

TABLE 9.1 Summary of Generational Myths and Reality

Generational Myth	Reality
Myth 1: Generational differences affect work attitudes, motivations, and behaviors.	**Reality:** Generations and generational differences have no tangible impact on such workplace outcomes.
Myth 2: Generational group membership matters more than age-related changes or contemporaneous contextual influences for predicting work attitudes, motivations, and behaviors.	**Reality:** Aging (i.e., ontogenesis) and context (i.e., sociogenesis) will always matter more than generational group membership for explaining individual behavior.
Myth 3: Actively managing generational differences (i.e., applying differentiated strategies for leading members of generational groups) can alleviate differences in work attitudes, motivations, and behaviors.	**Reality:** Because generational differences do not exist, efforts towards their management are both futile and dangerous.

COMMON MYTHS AND MISCONCEPTIONS REGARDING GENERATIONS AT WORK

The first goal of this chapter is to outline the prevailing "folklore" regarding generations at work. In considering this literature, three core myths emerge (summarized in Table 9.1), including:

- **Myth 1:** Generational differences affect work attitudes, motivations, and behaviors.
- **Myth 2:** Generational group membership matters more than age-related changes or contemporaneous contextual influences for predicting work attitudes, motivations, and behaviors.
- **Myth 3:** Actively managing generational differences (i.e., applying differentiated strategies for leading members of generational groups) can alleviate differences in work attitudes, motivations, and behaviors.

In the following, we will directly address each of these myths, outline evidence for their origins, and in turn dispel misconceptions regarding how generations operate (or more precisely, do not operate) in work contexts. This section serves to "set the stage" for a discussion of a differentiated life span approach to leadership.

GENERATIONAL MYTH 1

The first myth regarding generations at work is that there is "real" (i.e., valid and empirically demonstrable) variability between members of different generational groups that is manifested in differences in work attitudes (e.g., job satisfaction, work commitment), motivations (e.g., work engagement), and behaviors (e.g., task performance). The origins of this myth are complex, however the more general notion of generational differences can be traced throughout time (see Reeve, 2013, for a historical review). Recent empirical evidence suggests that there may be relatively enduring and longstanding negative perceptions of emerging adults in general (e.g., Trzesniewski & Donnellan, 2014), which may explain the pervasiveness of this phenomenon. Comparative reviews of the historical rhetoric characterizing various generations (e.g., Wesner & Miller, 2008) reach similar conclusions.

Generational thinking as a general, sociologically grounded mode for understanding social order and change is persistent and cyclical. If it were a public health concern, considering references to generational differences at large would lead one to conclude that we have been suffering nothing short of a chronic and persistent epidemic for much of recorded history. Indeed, as early as 700 BC Homer's *Iliad* cautioned against the recklessness of youth, suggesting, "Thou dost know the faults to which the young are ever prone; the will is quick to act, the judgment weak" (Bryant, 1870, p. 368). These sentiments are reflected in far more contemporary works as well. For example, referencing social change that accompanied the postwar baby boom, Wolfe (1976) cautioned against the rise of the "me generation," while Lasch (1979) warned of the rise of a "culture of narcissism." Nearly identical sentiments characterizing the members of contemporaneous younger generational cohorts are offered by Twenge (2014).

Given this broader focus on generations and generational differences in general attitudes, motivations, and behaviors, it is perhaps not surprising that at some point this idea became manifest in the literature on work and organizational psychology, and management and organizational behavior. While it is difficult to exactly pinpoint the source of the emergence of these ideas in this literature, some early accounts can be found in *Administrative Science Quarterly* (e.g., Diamant, 1960, describes generational differences with respect to political leadership; Wallace, 1967 describes generational differences in the context of educational achievement). Similarly, Paul and Schooler (1970) and DeSalvia and Gemmil (1971) report on "generation gaps" in values that influence management outcomes in the *Academy of Management Journal*. A more recent work by Smola and Sutton (2002) likewise has been influential in shaping the study of generational differences via cross-temporal methodologies.

While it is clear that there have been (relatively) longstanding arguments made for the influence of generational differences on work attitudes, motivations, and behaviors, what evidence do we have to support such conclusions? The short answer to this question is almost none. Expanding upon this, a recent meta-analysis of generational differences in work attitudes by Costanza and colleagues (2012, p. 375) concluded that "meaningful differences among generations probably do not exist...differences that appear to exist are likely attributable to factors other than generational membership." There are two considerations that contribute to the conclusion that meaningful generational differences are unlikely to exist. First, in general the methods for studying generational differences are insufficient to unequivocally conclude whether or not such differences exist (Rudolph, 2015). Second, existing research has often ignored other far more tenable explanations for age-related differences in work outcomes (i.e., ontogenesis, See Rudolph & Zacher, 2016; Zacher, 2015).

Insufficient Methods

As a means to better understand these methodological shortcomings, it is perhaps helpful to consider what a prototypical design for a generational differences study in the work and organizational psychology and management and organizational behavior domains looks like. This design typically possesses three rather undesirable qualities. First, studies on generational differences at work most often adopt cross-sectional designs (e.g., Jurkiewicz, 2000; Lyons, Duxbury, & Higgins, 2007). That is to say, data are collected from a sample of respondents at one point in time. For example, a sample of workers of different chronological ages (and, hence, memberships in different generational groups) could be administered a survey designed to assess work attitudes such as organizational commitment or job satisfaction.

Second, some data bifurcation procedure is applied to split respondents into generational groups that define broader groupings of birth cohorts (e.g., 1946 to 1964 for baby boomers, 1965 to 1980 for Generation X, etc.). Of note, even within Western cultures, there is no single agreed upon scheme for grouping individuals into such artificial birth cohort clusters (see Figure 9.1 of Costanza et al., 2012 for a visual representation of such discrepant operationalizations). Even if there were agreement here, this approach would still be plagued by additional statistical and methodological concerns that bear further consideration as well.

Finally, group-based comparisons are made on the basis of these artificial birth cohort clusters that now represent generational groupings, and conclusions are drawn regarding generational differences to the extent that mean differences among such groupings are observed (e.g., cohort group X is found to have statistically significantly higher/lower work attitudes as compared to cohort group Y). Let us now consider a critique of these three particularly concerning methodological features in more detail.

Recognize Differences in Age-Related Abilities	Acknowledge Dynamics in Personality and Differences in Age-Related Needs and Motivations
• Recognize changes in physical and cognitive capacities associated with aging. • Account for such changes when assigning work tasks to maintain the motivation and performance of younger and older workers.	• Understand how changes and reorganizations in personality over time have implications for a variety of work processes. • Recognize differences in age-related needs and motivations.
Leading Aging Workers and an Age-Diverse Workforce *Lifespan-Based Best Practices*	
Understand Age-Related Differences in Various Life Situations	**Design Work Systems to Optimally Integrate Age-Related Dynamics**
• Offer formal support for the positive integration of work and non-work roles for workers of all ages. • Enact policies that afford the latitude to self-manage where and when work tasks are completed.	• Champion the design of work systems to optimally integrate age-related dynamics. • Promote complete task designs that promote work performance and well-being across the work lifespan.

Figure 9.1 Summary of life span-based best practices for leading aging workers and an age-diverse workforce

Age, Period, and Cohort Dependence in Cross-Sectional Designs

The first methodological concern to consider is the common use of cross-sectional designs for studying generations. Because data are collected at only one time point in such designs, there are necessary conflations of three conceptually important variables: age, period, and cohort. Age refers to one's chronological age (e.g., 32 years old), period refers to contemporaneous time (e.g., 2016), and cohort refers to one's birth year (e.g., 1984). In any single time point design, these three factors are linearly dependent and perfectly confounded with one another, as knowing two of the three values determines the third. For example, for data collected in 2016 from cohorts of people born in 1984, 1994, and 2004 we know that their ages (respectively) are 32, 22, and 12. This example underscores a simple mathematical law (see Glenn, 2005):

$$i_{age} = j_{period} - k_{cohort}$$

What this implies is that cross-sectional designs cannot separate age, period, and cohort effects in statistically appropriate ways. Because one cannot unequivocally separate these effects in cross-sectional designs, drawing any conclusions regarding the influence of one effect in isolation is perfectly confounded by the influence of the other two. While other methodologies can be applied to study generational effects (e.g., cohort-sequential designs, see Baltes, Reese, & Nesselroade, 1977), no single methodology, and hence no single study—no matter how sophisticated—can neatly (i.e., independently) estimate parameters for all three effects. Moreover, while more recent cross-temporal methodologies have been proposed to better understand cohort effects (e.g., Gentile, Wood, Twenge, Hoffman, & Campbell, 2015), such approaches still unreasonably conflate cohort and period effects (see Rudolph & Zacher, 2016, for a more thorough review of these methodologies and a critique of various approaches that have addressed this age-period-cohort problem).

Artificial Bifurcation of Data

The second methodological concern has to do with the operationalization of generations as broader groupings of birth cohorts (i.e., single birth years). Even if we could assume that there was some validity to the practice of broadly grouping individuals into generational groups (again, there is no agreed upon generational typology to be found in the literature, see Costanza et al., 2012), this practice would still suffer on statistical grounds. Specifically, this operationalization of generations in the prototypical design necessitates the bifurcation and re-aggregation of a continuous birth cohort variable (i.e., birth year) into broader generational categories. The composition (cf. Chan, 1998) of such generational groupings has never been adequately addressed theoretically or statistically. More pragmatically, there is a great deal of information lost when artificially splitting and recombining data in this way (e.g., MacCallum, Zhang, Preacher, & Rucker, 2002). Unfortunately, the consequence is a loss of statistical power (i.e., the ability to detect the presence of an age effect, typically). What this means is that it becomes more difficult to demonstrate statistically meaningful effects of age-related variables in such analyses; a recent Monte Carlo simulation study concerning the biasing effect of this phenomena estimated that as much as 36.80% of statistically significant age effects may be "missed" (i.e., incorrectly rejected) if one were to bifurcate age into generational groupings (Rudolph, 2015).

Fallacious From Grouped Data

The final methodological concern has to do with problems inherent in the conclusions that one may draw from grouped data, such as those one would have in the prototypical operationalization of generations. These problems can be broadly defined in terms of either atomistic or ecological fallacies (Klein & Kozlowski, 2000). Most generally, these faults derive from a failure to recognize that variables defined or measured at one level (e.g., group or individual) may tap into different constructs than a corresponding construct construed at another level of analysis. The atomistic fallacy occurs when one draws inferences regarding variability across groups based on individual level data (Klein & Kozlowski, 2000). More generally, it refers to the error of drawing conclusions regarding variability across units (e.g., generational groups) defined at a higher level of analysis based on data collected from units that exist at a lower level of analysis (e.g., chronological age). This is a problematic issue for the study of generations under the prototypical methodology, because it is well known that associations between variables at the individual level may differ from associations between similar variables measured at the group level (e.g., Ostroff, 1993).

The second potential fault in the conclusions one may draw from this prototypical conceptualization of generations, the ecological fallacy, occurs when one draws inferences regarding phenomena at the individual level (i.e., regarding relationship between individual-level variables) on the basis of group level data (Klein & Kozlowski, 2000). Ecological fallacies are likewise concerning to the study of generations, because relations between variables at the group level are likely to differ from relationships between similar variables at the individual level of analysis. Ecological fallacies occur whenever data from units at a higher level of analysis are used to draw inferences regarding variability among units at a lower level of analysis. This happens when individuals are characterized on the basis of conclusions drawn from their group membership. Considering criticisms of generational thinking, the operation of this fallacy in thinking about generations has been characterized as "cohort determinism" (e.g., Walker, 1993) and is particularly insidious when considering how dubious conclusions drawn from this literature are applied to craft policies and practices within organizations and beyond (e.g., Hershatter & Epstein, 2010; Twenge, 2013).

Ignoring More Tenable Explanations

With respect to the second factor that has contributed to the conclusion that meaningful generational differences are unlikely to exist, existing research has often ignored other far more tenable explanations for age-related differences (e.g., bio-psycho-social development processes) in favor of generation based explanations (Myth 2). In addition to ignoring obviously developmental influences, it is very important to realize that the common understanding and operationalization of generations is achieved by collapsing across all individual differences (e.g., race, culture, gender, personality, and really, all other sources of between-person variation including age), suggesting that such artificially created generational groups matter "most." This phenomenon is a manifestation of what sociologists have deemed the "cohort trap" (Walker, 1993). The idea of cohort traps describes the observation that people place an unwarranted amount of weight upon the role that generations play in various psychosocial manifestations of attitudes, motivations, and behaviors. This overemphasis can be further explained by cognitive perspectives of social judgment and decision making (e.g., Bargh & Chartrand, 1999; Macrae, Milne, & Bodenhausen, 1994). From an information processing and sense-making perspective it is far easier (i.e., more cognitively efficient) to group individuals by generational cohort and to ascribe differences to groups of individuals on the basis of cohort membership, than to consider continuous age as a factor influencing others' work attitudes, motivations, and behaviors (e.g., Oakes & Turner, 1990). That is to say, from a cognitive perspective ecological fallacies in thinking about generations are to be expected, as this mode of thinking about and constructing our understanding of age is simplified and thus far more resource-efficient. Criticism of this reductionist view is echoed by Thomas, Hardy, Cutcher, and Ainsworth (2014, p. 1576):

> The reduction of individual differences to generational categories posits the idea that regardless of, for example, gender, ethnicity, race, sexuality and place of birth, people born within 20 years of each other all demonstrate the same attitudes, values, and preferences. Clearly, this is a highly spurious assertion and it is far more likely that within-group differences would outweigh any definitive differences between generations. As such, it is too simplistic—and insensitive—to attribute a fixed set of assumptions to an extremely diverse set of individuals. The reductive nature of generational difference, which suggests little variation among particular age cohorts while ignoring the importance of other forms of social identity that intersect with age as well as the significance of sociocultural and historical settings, does not seem a viable basis for either the study or the management of contemporary organizations.

Beyond skewed judgments and overgeneralizations, this process has the potential to drive unintended effects at the dyadic level of abstraction (e.g., self-fulfilling prophecies, see Merton, 1948; Snyder, Tanke, & Berscheid, 1977), which has distinct implications for leadership practice and in particular leader–member exchanges. For example, research concerning Pygmalion effects has shown that there are complex reciprocal dyadic relationships between leader and subordinate expectations that manifest over time and predict the quality of leader–member exchanges (e.g., Liden, Wayne, & Stilwell, 1993). In this context, Pygmalion effects may manifest when, for example, a leader develops certain expectations about a subordinate on the basis of assumed qualities that are defined by their generational group membership. Such expectations influence the leader's actions toward their subordinate to be in line with these expectations. The leader's actions are subsequently interpreted by the subordinate, who over time internalizes these expectations and translates them into their own behavior.

In summary, the first myth regarding generations—that they exist and affect work attitudes, motivations, and behaviors—is easily dispelled by considering various lines of evidence that speak to the contrary. Indeed, the evidence that does exist is generally based on studies that have adopted insufficient and flawed methodologies, meaning that conclusions regarding generational differences are equivocal at best. Moreover, the myth of generational differences is propagated, in part, because it is simply easier to reduce complicated processes (i.e., aging) into easier to understand and define units (i.e., generations). This reductionist view of age may drive deleterious and unintended consequences if applied by leaders in organizational contexts.

GENERATIONAL MYTH 2

The second myth regarding generations at work is that generational group membership matters more than age-related changes or contemporaneous contextual influences for predicting work attitudes, motivations, and behaviors. To understand the basis of this myth, it is helpful to better understand the foundational research that has contributed to the idea that there are cohort differences in other meaningful life outcomes. Sociological research concerning contextual influences on human development across the life course has demonstrated evidence for reciprocal relationships between individual developmental processes and intergenerational stability. For example, Elder's (1994) work suggests that human development is mutually influenced by both biological factors (e.g., losses in physical strength) as well as sociocultural factors (e.g., intergenerational relationships, distributions of resources at a societal level).

Likewise, research on psychological life span development has also offered some evidence for birth cohort-based influences on psychologically relevant outcomes (however, without grouping birth cohorts into synthetic generational categories). For example, cohort effects have been demonstrated for certain developmental outcomes, such as cognitive abilities (Baltes, 1968; Riley, Johnson, & Foner, 1972; Schaie, 1965). Indeed, Schaie's (1994, 1996, 2013) research concerning patterns of adult cognitive development demonstrates that fluid cognitive abilities (e.g., working memory, processing speed), typically decrease with age; however, there are notable improvements in such abilities across consecutive birth cohorts

(Gerstorf, Ram, Hoppmann, Willis, & Schaie, 2011; Schaie, 2013). More contemporary cross-temporal evidence likewise supports this conclusion (e.g., Pietschnig & Voracek, 2015).

While evidence from these works suggests that there may be cohort effects (i.e., effects of successive birth years, *not* effects of groups containing artificially clustered birth years) for certain developmental processes (e.g., cognitive development), emerging evidence suggests that for many claims made regarding generational differences, the effect of aging (i.e., the long term, unfolding bio-psycho-social process of development) overrides that of any generational effect. For example, despite strong evidence to the contrary (e.g., Arnett, 2013; Bianchi, 2014; Trzesniewski, Donnellan, & Robins, 2008), the "rise of narcissism" is a commonly cited generational difference (e.g., Twenge, Konrath, Foster, Campbell, & Bushman, 2008). However, more recent works have suggested that age is a better predictor of one's level of narcissism than generational membership. Indeed, at the person level narcissism tends to decline with age sometime after the transition from adolescence to young adulthood (see Roberts, Edmonds, & Grijvala, 2010). This underscores an important point: While cohort effects on development have been noted in the literature for certain outcomes, their influence on any given individual is by no means determined by their presence or absence among other members of any given cohort. Any conclusion that speaks contrary to this (i.e., ascribing characteristics that define a cohort to an individual member thereof) is representative of an ecological fallacy. In terms of absolute magnitude of effect size, the influence of aging (i.e., time) on an individual's developmental trajectory will outweigh that of cohort influences.

In summary, the myth that generational differences matter more than the influence of the aging processes can be redressed on numerous grounds, including a great deal of research concerning human development that speaks to the relative influence of aging effects versus the influence of cohort effects. While theoretically interesting, the presence of cohort effects by no means determines the trajectory of any individual's developmental course. Thus, the broader ascription of assumed characteristics of a cohort to any individual member of that cohort represents an ecological fallacy or a "cohort trap."

GENERATIONAL MYTH 3

The third myth regarding generations at work suggests that actively managing generational differences (i.e., applying differentiated strategies for leading members of different generational groups) can alleviate differences in work attitudes, motivations, and behaviors. This myth is especially manifest in the management and leadership best-practices literature on generations at work, and prescribes that there is something intrinsically different about members of such groups that necessitates a differentiated approach to leadership. What is particularly troubling about this myth and its manifestations in such best-practices literature is the recommendation to actively treat members of generational groups differently at work and even to afford different resources (e.g., flexible work options, Eversole, Venneberg, & Crowder, 2012; tailored performance feedback, Meister & Willyerd, 2010) on the basis of assumed differences in needs between generational groups. As such groups are typically construed around age brackets (i.e., groupings of birth cohorts), this advice tacitly suggests that people should be treated differently on the basis their age. Of note, if such advice were offered for any other protected group (e.g., race or sex) in the workplace, one might assume *prima facie* evidence for discrimination on the basis of many best practices for managing and leading generations. This idea has led to the conclusion that in some ways the propagation of generational myths is little more than a thinly veiled guise for overt ageism (e.g., Rudolph & Zacher, 2016).

Of course, this third myth is also a corollary to the other two myths presented here, in that it assumes that generational differences do exist and are manifest as differences in work attitudes, motivations, and behaviors. To recapitulate our previous point, generational differences do not have an appreciable influence on such work processes and outcome variables. While this assertion largely negates the premise of Myth 3, what still bears consideration herein is the perception that such differences matter. Indeed, as suggested by Fineman (2014, p. 1720):

> The trouble with generational typologies is that the odd grain of truth is developed into an undisputed fact about essentially heterogeneous population groups, but stereotyped by their birth date. And once a generational typology takes hold (reinforced by the popular media, marketing, and quasi-scientific usage) then it is hard to dislodge; it is taken as an undisputed fact. Granted that offspring represent a new generation in a family's lineage, and each generation is exposed to certain, possibly unique, societal events and technological happenings. But thereafter the imprint of the times is blurred within and across generational cohorts. Generation oversimplifies organizational dynamics, and more so as non-traditional careers thrive and workforces become more ethnically, racially and gender diverse. The evidence that conflict at work can be boiled down to generational difference is shaky, to say the least.

Regardless of empirical evidence to the contrary, the idea that generational differences matter is still prevalent and understood to be true by many. That said, what are the implications of this mythology to leadership practice and the dynamics and quality of leader–member exchanges? We will consider two important psychologically relevant consequences associated with this here: reinforcing identification and stereotyping processes, and fortifying in-group/out-group distinctions.

Reinforcing Identification and Stereotyping Processes

As discussed earlier, self-fulfilling prophecies such as Pygmalion effects may manifest from the application of generational thinking and particularly so in leader–member dyads. Additionally, subordinates' knowledge that their leader endorses generational thinking may be a catalyst for and signal to employees to "behave as you ought" (Skinner, 1974) in line with these expectations. This general idea can be couched among stereotype threat phenomena (e.g., Steele & Aronson, 1995). Most generally, stereotype threat refers to a situation in which one is made to feel at risk of conforming to stereotypes that define their social group. Research has cautioned that generational thinking may lead to the emergence of such stereotype threats (e.g., Cadiz, Truxillo, & Fraccaroli, 2015; Perry, Golom, & McCarthy, 2015). More directly, research concerning age-based stereotype threats demonstrates that cognitive task performance diminishes among older adults who face evaluative comparisons with younger adults; however, engaging in high-quality, positive intergenerational exchanges mitigates this effect to some extent (Abrams, Eller, & Bryant, 2006). Moreover, hinting at the possibility for intervention, this protective effect of positive intergenerational contact against diminished performance may be experienced via merely thinking about such positive interactions rather than directly engaging in them (e.g., Abrams et al., 2008). Additionally, research by von Hippel, Kalokerinos, and Henry (2013) has suggested that experiencing age-related stereotype threats among older workers is related to more negative job attitudes and poorer well-being as well as increased intentions to resign and retire.

A related line of research that bears consideration here can be found in the literature on age metastereotyping: employees' beliefs regarding the stereotypes that outgroup members hold about their own group (see Finkelstein, King, & Voyles, 2015 for a review). To the extent that stereotypes that define one's generational group are perceived to be held by one's leader (e.g., if the leader construes ingroup/outgroup distinctions along the lines of such overgeneralizations), the influence of age metastereotyping may be particularly pronounced. Using a stigma consciousness framework, recent work by Ryan, King, and Finkelstein (2015) suggests that the chronic awareness of age metastereotypes in the workplace may drive negative affective, attitudinal, and behavioral outcomes. In general, given that these stereotyping processes are likely to be derived from dyadic interactions and supported by leaders' generational thinking, these ideas have direct implications for understanding the quality of leader–member exchanges.

Fortifying In-Group/Out-Group Distinctions

A focal premise of leader–member exchange perspectives is that unique exchange relationships develop between leaders and their subordinates, and that over time an in-group/out-group continuum emerges that corresponds to and indexes the quality of these exchange relationships. As suggested, adopting generational thinking may drive in-group/out-group dictions that fall along generational lines (see Tonks, Dickenson, & Nelson, 2009) and precipitate interage and intergenerational conflicts (e.g., resource conflicts, see Rudolph & Zacher, 2015). Recent work by North and Fiske (2013) has suggested that resource-based dilemmas are an important indicator of interage stereotyping processes.

Beyond these psychological implications at the individual level, for organizations the myth of generations has implications for liabilities and bottom-line productivity. First, buying into the myth of generations opens up the possibility of covert ageism (Rudolph & Zacher, 2015). Indeed, recent thinking on this issue posits strong links between ageism and intergenerational conflicts (e.g., North & Fiske, 2012). Second, given that there is no evidence to support generational differences at work, any efforts guided toward managing and leading generations are little more than a waste of time and resources. While some strategic management scholarship has (wrongly) suggested that recognizing and actively managing generations represents a competitive advantage (e.g., Elliot, 2011; Glass, 2007), the irony is that the collected evidence (or, perhaps more accurately, the lack of evidence) suggests that such efforts are actually a disadvantage in terms of lost time and effort and the potential for degradations in the quality of leader–member relationships.

In summary, the evidence and arguments offered to resolve the first two myths presented here beg the premise of the third. Given that available evidence does not strongly support the presence of generational differences in work attitudes, motivations, and behaviors, consequent efforts to manage generations are at best a futile waste of time and resources and at worst a potential liability to organizations that adopt such practices.

A LIFE SPAN APPROACH TO LEADERSHIP

To reiterate a core argument offered here, little evidence supports the presence of generational differences in work attitudes, motivations, and behaviors. That said, research is increasingly recognizing that there are age-related influences in various leadership processes (e.g., Day, 2011; Riggio & Mumford, 2011; Rosing & Jungman, 2016; Rudolph & Zacher, 2015; Walter & Scheibe, 2013; Zacher, Clark, Anderson, & Ayoko, 2015) that should be recognized. Where does this leave us? If the generationally based model is not a valid representation of reality, and if the further propagation of generational myths has a potentially negative impact of work processes, is there a more valid, nuanced perspective for understanding the role of age in leadership processes?

To address these questions, we next introduce the life span developmental perspective (Baltes, 1987) and outline its advantages compared to the model of generations (see also Rudolph & Zacher, 2016) for understanding age-related differences at work. Our focus here is on how leaders can best address these age-related differences among their followers by adopting a life span (i.e., rather than a generational) approach to leadership (Zacher et al., 2015). Generally, this life span approach recognizes that followers' work attitudes, motivations, and behaviors can either remain stable or change continuously with age (and, in the latter case, manifest as age-related differences at any given point in time), but do not differ based on their generational group membership.

We begin by outlining the fundamental propositions of the life span developmental perspective, including the notions of historical and sociocultural embeddedness as well as normative age-graded, normative history-graded, and idiosyncratic influences on development. We then summarize empirical findings based on the life span developmental perspective from research on work and aging that are relevant to the leadership context (e.g., Hertel & Zacher, in press; Rudolph, 2016). Based on this review, we suggest leadership behaviors and best practices that may be most appropriate when leading followers of different ages. We will also discuss the increasingly important issue of leading age-diverse work teams. Finally, we describe various lines of research that inform our understanding of how age differences between leaders and followers may influence leadership behaviors and success.

The Life Span Developmental Perspective

Developmental researchers proposed the life span perspective in the 1970s and 1980s to overcome problems of life-stage models of human development, which similar to the generational approach, inappropriately separate an individual's life span into multiple discrete phases at more or less arbitrary (and historically influenced) cut-off ages (e.g., the "midlife" stage between 40 and 60 years). In contrast, the life span developmental perspective examines intraindividual stability, continuous changes, and plasticity (i.e., intraindividual modifiability) in individuals' experiences and behavior across the entire life span, as well as interindividual differences in these intraindividual trajectories (Baltes, 1987; Baltes, Reese, & Lipsitt, 1980; Baltes, Reuter-Lorenz, & Rosler, 2006).

Baltes (1987) outlined seven theoretical propositions that characterize the life span developmental perspective. First, individual development is conceived as a lifelong process (from conception until death) that involves phases of stability, continuous changes, and idiosyncratic elements that emerge at certain time points. Second, development is multidirectional, meaning that characteristics can increase or decrease, remain stable, or follow nonlinear patterns with age. Third, development entails experiences of gains and losses at all ages, but losses are thought to increasingly outweigh gains with increasing age. Fourth, an individual's development is modifiable by individual and contextual influences, and this plasticity can occur at any point in the life span. Fifth, development is influenced by historical, evolutionary, and sociocultural factors. Sixth, development is the result of the interplay of normative age-graded influences, normative history-graded influences, and nonnormative idiosyncratic influences. Finally, Baltes (1987) explicitly characterized the field of life span development as multidisciplinary.

Propositions five (historical and sociocultural embeddedness) and six (multiple influences on development) are particularly important for our discussion of generations. With proposition five, the life span perspective acknowledges that individual development is not only influenced by biological factors, but also by historical and sociocultural conditions such as certain historical time periods, structural factors (e.g., economic conditions, access to high-quality education and medical care) and interactions among these biological and contextual factors. For instance, as noted earlier, early research found evidence for successive birth cohort effects on cognitive abilities and personality characteristics (Elder, 1974; Elder & Liker, 1982; Nesselroade & Baltes, 1974; Schaie, 1994, 2013), which may be explained by improvements in education, health and medical care, and increasing complexity in work and home environments over time (Baltes, 1987). With proposition six, the life span perspective similarly acknowledges the existence of multiple influences on development. Specifically, normative age-graded influences include biological and environmental influences that most people encounter as they age (e.g., maturation, age of school entry). History-graded influences include factors that impact most people living during a certain historical period (e.g., the Great Depression). Finally, nonnormative influences include factors that are unique to each individual (e.g., job loss, severe illness).

While life span researchers accept that at the individual level, historical and sociocultural contexts can influence development (and thus typically include individuals' birth years in their models), they do not make assumptions about broader categories of individuals based on a range of artificially clustered birth years (i.e., as generations are commonly defined and operationalized) or shared generational effects. That is to say, even though the life span perspective suggests that history-graded effects are "normative," life span theorists do not make assumptions about group-level effects on collective experiences and behaviors.

The life span perspective has several additional advantages when compared to other theoretical models of human development. First, the explicit recognition of intra and interindividual change processes means that the life span perspective is inherently multilevel. The life span perspective is thus particularly well suited for understanding other inherently multilevel phenomena, such as leadership (see Zacher et al., 2015). Likewise, the life span perspective is inherently multidisciplinary, recognizing that no one particular field of study or school of thought can fully understand or explain the totality of human development. Finally, the life span perspective is inherently contextualized—and particularly so in more recent conceptualizations (e.g., Charles, 2010; Ford & Lerner, 1992; Salmela-Aro, 2009). That is to say, the life span perspective recognizes that development co-occurs along with various constraints and facilitators that are imposed by one's environment and via person-environment interactions. These complex networks of constraining and facilitating factors have been well elaborated, both theoretically and empirically, via what Bronfenbrenner referred to as "ecological developmental systems" (e.g., Bronfenbrenner, 1979). Of particular note to leadership and the LMX perspective, Salmela-Aro (2009) emphasizes that people regulate their development via exercises in "co-agency" (i.e., relational agency), which suggests that other people play important roles in defining one's goal-setting context and also channeling people's personal goals.

Empirical Findings Relevant for Leadership Processes

The life span developmental perspective has stimulated a large body of empirical work both inside and outside the work context (for reviews, see Baltes, Rudolph, & Bal, 2012; Baltes et al., 2006; Hertel & Zacher, in press; Rudolph, 2016; Truxillo, Cadiz, & Hammer, 2015). In the following, we summarize empirical evidence that is particularly relevant for our discussion of the role of age in leadership and leader–member exchange processes.

First, with regard to abilities research has shown that physical strength and fluid cognitive abilities (e.g., fast information processing, working memory, and abstract reasoning) tend to decline with age (i.e., these changes represent age-related losses). In contrast, crystallized cognitive abilities (e.g., general and domain-specific knowledge, vocabulary, and experiential judgment) remain stable or even increase with age (i.e., age-related gains; Baltes, Staudinger, & Lindenberger, 1999; Salthouse, 2012). These patterns of gains and losses have been noted as important determinants of a variety of work outcomes, including motivation and performance (see Kanfer & Ackerman, 2004). Second, personality characteristics undergo a reorganization with age, which can be explained by biophysiological processes and socialization influences (e.g., career entry; Roberts & Jackson, 2008; Roberts & Wood, 2006). Specifically, conscientiousness, agreeableness, and social dominance (a facet of extraversion) on average tend to increase with age, whereas neuroticism and openness to experience slightly decrease with age (Roberts & Mroczek, 2008; Roberts, Walton, & Viechtbauer, 2006). Meta-analytic evidence offered by Roberts and DelVecchio (2000) concluded that while personality is reasonably stable across adulthood, there is evidence to suggest certain dynamic qualities in personality particularly may surround life course transitions (e.g., from school to work; work to retirement).

Third, individuals' goal priorities tend to change with age with young people focusing more strongly on gains and growth-related goals and older people focusing more strongly on maintenance and loss-prevention goals (Ebner, Freund, & Baltes, 2006). Likewise, goal content tends to change across time. For example, Carstensen (1995) notes shifts in goal content priorities from knowledge acquisition to emotion regulation with advancing age. Similar conclusions are reached by Brandtstädter and Renner (1990) with respect to coping strategies applied in service of goal pursuit.

Fourth, with regard to socioemotional experience, young people, presumably due to their open-ended future time perspective, prioritize instrumental goals that help maximize future outcomes such as knowledge acquisition (which may involve the experience of negative emotions). In contrast, older people, presumably due to their more constrained future time perspective, prioritize goals that maximize more immediate positive emotional experiences and experiences of momentary meaningfulness such as emotion regulation and helping others (Carstensen, Isaacowitz, & Charles, 1999). There is evidence that certain emotional competencies such as emotion regulation skills, show improvements with age (Charles & Carstensen, 2010; Doerwald, Scheibe, Zacher, & Van Yperen, 2016). Moreover, research suggests that older people have stronger generativity motives. Generativity refers to a set of motives that include the concern for establishing and guiding future generations and for leaving a lasting legacy (e.g., by influencing others and society, see McAdams & de St Aubin, 1992).

Finally, while internal resources, demands, and barriers change with age, the life contexts in which individuals act change as well. For instance, older people are more likely to have caregiving responsibilities for aging parents, grandchildren, or even adult children still living at home (Parkinson, 2002; Zacher, Rudolph, & Reinicke, in press). Szinovacz, DeViney, and Davey (2001) report that older workers with dependent care responsibilities are less likely to retire and withdraw from the labor force than those without. Likewise, as many as 20% of older workers who expect to engage in post-retirement bridge employment anticipate doing so in order to help support dependents as caregivers (EBRI, 2004).

While this discussion has focused on age-related changes (i.e., general developmental patterns) in person characteristics (i.e., abilities, personality, motivations, affect), there are also notable age-related correlates with work outcomes that likewise bear some consideration in this discussion. For example, research has suggested that older workers are typically healthier than individuals of the same age in the general population (i.e., the so-called "healthy worker effect," Monson, 1986). Similarly, there is some evidence for positive relationships between age and job attitudes (e.g., job satisfaction, Ng & Feldman, 2010). Finally, age and objective work performance (i.e., task performance) are positively correlated (Waldman & Avolio, 1986), suggesting that accrued experience, wisdom, and the compilation of job knowledge over time transfer into improved productivity (e.g., Beier & Ackerman, 2005). Moreover, meta-analyses suggest that older workers on average tend to engage in more organizational citizenship (e.g., helping others and the organization) and less counterproductive work behaviors than young workers (Ng & Feldman, 2008). Of note, each of these findings underscores an antithetical argument to common stereotypes of older workers (e.g., that they are unhealthy, dissatisfied, and poor performing relative to younger workers, see Posthuma & Campion, 2009 for a review).

Leading Followers of Different Ages and Age-Diverse Teams

Our life span approach to leadership suggests that leadership processes are more likely to be successful if leaders adapt their behavior to their followers' age-related abilities and needs, including both strengths and weaknesses in these factors. In other words, our approach adopts a leader-follower fit perspective to the role of age in the work context (Perry, Dokko, & Golom, 2012). With regard to age-related changes in physical and cognitive abilities as well as personality characteristics, leaders should assign appropriate tasks to their followers and provide support in the form of workplace accommodations. Moreover, the previous review suggests that younger workers may benefit more from task-oriented leadership behaviors such as initiating structure and mentoring, which help them achieve their instrumental career goals (e.g., Ayree, Wyatt, & Stone, 1996). In contrast, older workers are more likely to flourish if leaders engage in relationship-oriented behavior such as individualized consideration (e.g., Vecchio & Boatright, 2002) to meet their maintenance and loss-prevention needs and to enhance their experience of positive effect. Moreover, to meet older workers' needs for meaningful work, leaders should afford older workers autonomy to use their knowledge and skills for the benefit of others and the organization (Kooij, De Lange, Jansen, Kanfer, & Dikkers, 2011; Kooij, Tims, & Kanfer, 2015). Indeed, recent scholarship concerning age-conscious job design has adopted such a life span perspective (e.g., Truxillo, Cadiz, Rineer, Zaniboni, & Fraccaroli, 2012). Finally, leaders need to take their followers' life contexts, including responsibilities at home, into account (Kossek, Pichler, Bodner, & Hammer, 2011).

In the context of demographic changes, the issue of leading age-diverse teams is becoming an increasingly important concern for organizations. With regard to individuals working in age-diverse teams, it is important that leaders show individualized consideration for followers of different ages to support their workability and occupational well-being (Rosing & Jungmann, 2016). Moreover, it is important that leaders are neither prejudiced against younger nor older workers and encourage participation of workers of all ages. Finally, research has shown that a transformational leadership style (e.g., communicating a vision, being an inspiring role model) is most effective when leading age diverse teams as this style facilitates the constructive exchange of different perspectives and reduces emotional conflict by focusing all followers on the same higher-order goals (Kearney & Gebert, 2009). Likewise, research concerning team age diversity and productivity suggests that transformational leadership may positively augment the effects of team-level age diversity on productive energy (i.e., teams' collective experience of positive affective arousal, shared cognitive activation in pursuit of team goals, and collective efforts to achieve such goals; Kunze & Bruch, 2010).

Age Differences Between Leaders and Followers

Researchers in the field of work and aging have suggested that it is important to take age differences between leaders and followers into account (Perry et al., 2012; Zacher et al., 2015). Both leaders' and followers' abilities and motives change with age, and may impact their motivation to lead, follow, and cooperate. For instance, as leaders get older their goal priorities also shift from more instrumental, future-oriented motivations (e.g., task achievement, own career development) to more socioemotional, present-oriented motivations (e.g., consideration for others, mentoring). Thus, leadership success may depend on the fit between age-related differences (or similarities) between the characteristics of leaders and followers.

For example, invoking the idea of contextual status cues that dictate age-appropriate leadership behaviors, Buengeler, Homan, and Voelpel (2016) demonstrate that younger leaders are more effective at using contingent reward versus participative leadership styles for reducing follower turnover.

Moreover, research suggests that followers compare leaders to idealized, prototypical mental representations of younger and older leaders. Leadership categorization theory suggests that leaders who—based on their personal characteristics or behaviors—fulfill implicit assumptions held by their followers about effective leaders are perceived and rated as more effective, whereas leaders whose characteristics and behaviors do not meet expectations are perceived and rated as less effective (Lord, Foti, & DeVader, 1984). Followers' implicit assumptions may differ based on their leaders' age and their own age-related stereotypes and expectations. For instance, experimental research shows that followers perceive older leaders as more effective in times of war and conflict, and more generally, in situations when stability is more important than change (Spisak, 2012; Spisak, Grabo, Arvey, & van Vugt, 2014). Moreover, research based on leadership categorization and implicit leadership theories has shown that only those older leaders with high (compared to low) levels of generativity motives and legacy beliefs are rated as effective leaders by their followers, whereas these motivations did not impact follower ratings of young leaders (Zacher, Rosing, Henning, & Frese, 2011).

Another theoretical perspective, the relational demography approach, suggests that age differences between leaders and followers may influence leadership success because followers evaluate leaders based on implicit organizational age norms and career timetables (e.g., Lawrence, 1984, 1988, 1996). Specifically, age norms are defined by expectations, beliefs, and generalized observations regarding "when," in terms of an age-appropriateness principle, one should assume certain roles within an organization. With respect to leadership roles, most normative expectations suggest a vertical age arrangement such that leaders are chronologically older than their subordinates. In more traditional organizations and industries, leaders are expected to be older and more experienced than their followers, as they have worked their way through an established career timetable with increasingly higher levels of responsibility and authority (e.g., Tsui, Xin, & Egan, 1995). This arrangement is said to encompass *status congruence* with respect to organizational age norms. Relatively younger leaders do not meet these implicit expectations (i.e., reflecting *status incongruence*) and their older followers may react negatively to such authority arrangements (e.g., Perry, Kulik, & Zhou, 1999; Shore, Cleveland, & Goldberg, 2003). Moreover, based on social comparison processes relatively older followers may also be less satisfied and perform poorly on the job because they feel "behind time" with respect to such age norms and are disappointed about not having been promoted into a leadership role themselves (Lawrence, 1988). In contrast, leaders who meet shared expectations and norms are generally evaluated and treated more positively by their followers (Lawrence, 1988). Beyond the effect of status incongruence, age similarity between leaders and their subordinates may also signal feelings that one is "behind" time. For example, Pelled and Xin (2000) demonstrated that age similarity between leaders and their followers had negative effects on leader–member exchange quality and follower trust in their leader.

RECOMMENDATIONS FOR LEADING AGING WORKERS AND AN AGE-DIVERSE WORKFORCE

With these ideas in mind, how do we apply the life span model of leadership to actual leadership practice? Let us next consider several updated best-practice recommendations for leading aging workers and an age-diverse workforce. These best practices are organized around common themes that can be derived directly from our life span approach to leadership and are supported by empirical research evidence (see Figure 9.1 for a graphical summary).

Recognize Differences in Age-Related Abilities

Leaders must recognize differences in age-related abilities (e.g., changes in physical and cognitive capacities) and take these into account when assigning tasks to maintain motivation and performance of younger and older workers (cf. Kanfer & Ackerman, 2004). To this end, work tasks may be designed to optimally engage workers' abilities at specific points across their life span. In particular, collaborative work tasks can be designed to take advantage of older workers' accrued experience, relevant domain specific knowledge, and emotional competencies. For example, accrued experiences of older workers are associated with increased capacities to recognize and react to irregularities in work procedures, and some have argued that the identification of such exceptions is a function of both intuition and tacit (i.e., experientially derived) knowledge that comes from long-term work experience (e.g., Torff & Sternberg, 1998). As younger workers may rely more on learned knowledge that is taught during educational and/or job-training activities, pairing older and younger employees may represent an optimal "mix" of tacit and more explicit formal knowledge in collaborative work environments. This notion has distinct implications for the design of team work and leadership in age-diverse workgroups.

Acknowledge Dynamics in Personality and Differences in Age-Related Needs and Motivations

Leadership practices must acknowledge that changes and reorganizations in personality over time have implications for a variety of work processes, including the design of work systems (e.g., Rudolph, Toomey, & Baltes, in press). Leadership must likewise acknowledge differences in age-related needs and motivations (e.g., generativity; Zacher et al., 2011). One way of accomplishing this would be to engage generativity needs among older leaders via provision of mentoring to (younger) followers. Research has suggested that optimizing generativity motives among older workers may be especially important for easing transitions from work and career roles to retirement and leisure roles (e.g., Calo, 2005; Lindbo & Schultz, 1998). Such practices have direct positive benefits for knowledge transfer and retention processes within organizations (e.g., Harvey, 2012). Likewise, such practices may benefit younger workers by fulfilling specific growth needs (e.g., Rudolph, Baltes, & Zabel, 2013; Thrasher, Zabel, Wynne, & Baltes, 2016).

Understand Age-Related Differences in Various Life Situations

Leadership must understand age-related differences in life/career-stage/work situations (e.g., caregiving, approaching retirement, etc.). One directly actionable way in which this principle can be leveraged is through formal provisions that directly support positive integrations of work and nonwork roles (e.g., work and family roles). Recent research suggests that workers of all ages benefit from flexible HR policies that afford individuals the latitude to self-manage where and when they complete assigned work tasks (e.g., Rudolph & Baltes, 2016). This is important to note as different age-relevant patterns of work and nonwork conflict have been noted in the literature (e.g., Allen & Finkelstein, 2014).

Design Work Systems to Optimally Integrate Age-Related Dynamics

Finally, leadership must champion the design of work systems to optimally integrate age-related dynamics (e.g., Zacher, Hacker, & Frese, 2016). With respect to traditional job design elements, Truxillo and colleagues (2012) have outlined several principles for ideally designing jobs to promote job satisfaction, engagement, and performance across the work life span. Considering more elemental aspects of job design, Zacher et al.

(2016) outline a life span-based action regulation framework that emphasizes optimal complete task designs that are in line with core principles of action regulation theory and promote work performance and well-being. Finally, emerging evidence suggests that affording individuals autonomy to self-initiate changes to their jobs via either collaboratively negotiated arrangements with their leader (idiosyncratic deals, see Bal & Jansen, 2015) or through more general provisions for job crafting (e.g., Kooij et al., 2015) may be particularly beneficial to older workers.

CONCLUSIONS

Considered against the arguments and evidence offered and reviewed here, it is clear that the most common myths regarding generations are both incorrect and indeed potentially dangerous when blindly accepted as doctrine. Generational differences do not affect work attitudes, motivations, and behaviors. Generational group membership does not matter more than age-related changes or contemporaneous contextual influences for predicting work attitudes, motivations, and behaviors. Finally, actively managing generational differences (i.e., applying differentiated strategies for leading members of generational groups) does nothing to alleviate differences in work attitudes, motivations, and behaviors. As we have suggested, leadership best practices must be refocused and aligned with the life span recommendations offered here.

Overall, this chapter contributes to an emerging literature that acknowledges the limited utility of generational thinking for understanding work attitudes, motivations, and behaviors. Additionally, this work contributes to emerging scholarship concerning the role of age in various leadership processes, including exchanges between leaders and followers. In addition to our review and critique of various generational myths, we offer an alternative life span perspective on leadership that better addresses age-related changes in work attitudes, motivations, and behaviors. This framework serves to shape evidence-based practical recommendations regarding leading older workers and age-diverse work groups. Our hope is this chapter will help redirect attention away from generations as a unit of understanding age-related changes at work and toward demonstrable, actionable, and relevant issues regarding aging as a continuous and lifelong process.

REFERENCES

Abrams, D., Crisp, R. J., Marques, S., Fagg, E., Bedford, L., & Provias, D. (2008). Threat inoculation: Experienced and imagined intergenerational contact prevents stereotype threat effects on older people's math performance. *Psychology and Aging, 23*, 934–939. doi:10.1037/a0014293

Abrams, D., Eller, A., & Bryant, J. (2006). An age apart: The effects of intergenerational contact and stereotype threat on performance and intergroup bias. *Psychology and Aging, 21*, 691–702. doi:10.1037/0882-7974.21.4.691

Allen, T. D., & Finkelstein, L. M. (2014). Work-family conflict among members of full-time dual-earner couples: An examination of family life stage, gender, and age. *Journal of Occupational Health Psychology, 19*, 376–384. doi:10.1037/a0036941

Anderson, E., Buchko, A. A., & Buchko, K. J. (2016). Giving negative feedback to millennials: How can managers criticize the "most praised" generation. *Management Research Review, 39*, 692–705. doi:10.1108/MRR-05-2015-0118

Arnett, J. J. (2013). The evidence for generation we and against generation me. *Emerging Adulthood, 1*, 5–10. doi:10.1177/2167696812466842

Aryee, S., Wyatt, T., & Stone, R. (1996). Early career outcomes of graduate employees: The effect of mentoring and ingratiation. *Journal of Management Studies, 33*, 95–118. doi: 10.1111/j.1467-6486.1996.tb00800.x

Bal, P. M., & Jansen, P. G. (2015). Idiosyncratic deals for older workers: Increased heterogeneity among older workers enhance the need for I-deals. In P. M. Bal, D. T. Kooi, & D. Rousseau (Eds.), *Aging workers and the employee-employer relationship* (pp. 129–144). New York, NY: Springer. doi:10.1007/978-3-319-08007-9_8

Baldonado, A. M. (2008). *25 ways to motivate generation Y: A pocket-book guide.* New York, NY: iUniverse.

Baltes, B. B., Rudolph, C. W., & Bal, A. C. (2012). A review of aging theories and modern work perspectives. In J. W. Hedge & W. C. Borman (Eds.), *The Oxford handbook of work and aging* (pp. 117–136). New York, NY: Oxford University Press. doi:10.1093/oxfordhb/9780195385052.013.0069

Baltes, P. B. (1968). Longitudinal and cross-sectional sequences in the study of age and generation effects. *Human Development, 11*, 145–171. doi:10.1159/000270604

Baltes, P. B. (1987). Theoretical propositions of life-span developmental psychology: On the dynamics between growth and decline. *Developmental Psychology, 23*, 611–626. doi: 10.1037/0012-1649.23.5.611

Baltes, P. B., Reese, H. W., & Lipsitt, L. P. (1980). Life-span developmental psychology. *Annual Review of Psychology, 31*, 65–110. doi:10.1146/annurev.ps.31.020180.000433

Baltes, P. B., Reese, H. W., & Nesselroade, J. R. (1977). *Life-span developmental psychology: Introduction to research methods.* Monterey, CA: Brooks/Cole. doi:10.4324/9781315799704

Baltes, P. B., & Reinert, G. (1969). Cohort effects in cognitive development of children as revealed by cross-sectional sequences. *Developmental Psychology, 1*, 169–177. doi:10.1037/h0026997

Baltes, P. B., Reuter-Lorenz, P. A., & Rösler, F. (Eds.). (2006). *Life span development and the brain: The perspective of biocultural co-constructivism.* Cambridge, England: Cambridge University Press. doi:10.1017/cbo9780511499722

Baltes, P. B., Staudinger, U. M., & Lindenberger, U. (1999). Life span psychology: Theory and application to intellectual functioning. *Annual Review of Psychology, 50*, 471–507. doi:10.1146/annurev.psych.50.1.471

Bargh, J. A., & Chartrand, T. L. (1999). The unbearable automaticity of being. *American Psychologist, 54,* 462–479. doi:10.1037/0003-066X.54.7.462

Bass, B. M. (1990). *Bass and Stogdill's handbook of leadership: Theory, research, and managerial applications.* New York, NY: Free Press.

Beier, M. E., & Ackerman, P. L. (2005). Age, ability, and the role of prior knowledge on the acquisition of new domain knowledge: Promising results in a real-world learning environment. *Psychology and Aging, 20,* 341–355. doi:10.1037/0882-7974.20.2.341

Bianchi, E. C. (2014). Entering adulthood in a recession tempers later narcissism. *Psychological Science, 25,* 1429–1437. doi:10.1177/0956797614532818

Brandtstädter, J., & Renner, G. (1990). Tenacious goal pursuit and flexible goal adjustment: Explication and age-related analysis of assimilative and accommodative strategies of coping. *Psychology and Aging, 5,* 58–67. doi:10.1037/0882-7974.5.1.58

Bronfenbrenner, U. (1979). *The ecology of human development: Experiments by nature and design.* Cambridge, MA: Harvard University Press.

Bryant, W. C. (1870). *The Iliad of Homer: Translated into English blank verse* (Vol. 2). Houghton, Mifflin.

Buengeler, C., Homan, A. C., & Voelpel, S. C. (2016). The challenge of being a young manager: The effects of contingent reward and participative leadership on team-level turnover depend on leader age. *Journal of Organizational Behavior.* doi:10.10 02/job.2101

Cadiz, D. M., Truxillo, D. M., & Fraccaroli, F. (2015). What are the benefits of focusing on generation-based differences and at what cost? *Industrial and Organizational Psychology, 8,* 356–362. doi:10.1017/iop.2015.49

Calo, T. J. (2005). The generativity track: A transitional approach to retirement. *Public Personnel Management, 34,* 301–312. doi:10.1177/009102600503400402

Caraher, L. (2014). *Millennials & management: The essential guide to making it work at work.* Brookline, MA: Bibliomotion.

Carstensen, L. L. (1995). Evidence for a life-span theory of socioemotional selectivity. *Current Directions in Psychological Science, 4,* 151–156. doi:10.1111/1467-8721.ep11512261

Carstensen, L. L., Isaacowitz, D., & Charles, S. T. (1999). Taking time seriously: A theory of socioemotional selectivity. *American Psychologist, 54,* 165–181. doi:10.1037/0003-066x.54.3.165

Chan, D. (1998). Functional relations among constructs in the same content domain at different levels of analysis: A typology of composition models. *Journal of Applied Psychology, 83,* 234–246. doi:10.1037/0021-9010.83.2.234

Charles, S. T. (2010). Strength and vulnerability integration: A model of emotional well-being across adulthood. *Psychological Bulletin, 136,* 1068–1091. doi:10.1037/a0021232

Charles, S. T., & Carstensen, L. L. (2010). Social and emotional aging. *Annual Review of Psychology, 61,* 383–409. doi:10.1146/annurev.psych.093008.100448

Costanza, D. P., Badger, J. M., Fraser, R. L., Severt, J. B., & Gade, P. A. (2012). Generational differences in work-related attitudes: A meta-analysis. *Journal of Business and Psychology, 27,* 375–394. doi:10.1007/s10869-012-9259-4

Costanza, D. P., & Finkelstein, L. M. (2015). Generationally based differences in the workplace: Is there a there there? *Industrial and Organizational Psychology, 8*, 308–323. doi:10.1017/iop.2015.15

Crampton, S. M., & Hodge, J. W. (2006). The supervisor and generational differences. *Allied Academies International Conference: Academy of Organizational Culture, Communications, and Conflict Proceedings, 11*(2), 19–22.

Davis, J. B., Pawlowski, S. D., & Houston, A. (2006). Work commitments of baby boomers and gen-Xers in the IT profession: Generational differences or myth? *E-Journal of Computer Information Systems, 46*, 43–49. doi:10.1080/08874417.2006.11645897

Day, D. V. (2011). Integrative perspectives on longitudinal investigations of leader development: From childhood through adulthood. *Leadership Quarterly, 22*, 561–571. doi:10.1016/j.leaqua.2011.04.012

DeSalvia, D. N., & Gemmill, G. R. (1971). An exploratory study of the personal value systems of college students and managers. *Academy of Management Journal, 14*, 227–238. doi:10.2307/255309

Diamant, A. (1960). The relevance of comparative politics to the study of comparative administration. *Administrative Science Quarterly, 5*, 87–112. doi:10.2307/2390826

Dilworth, J. E. L., & Kingsbury, N. (2005). Home-to-job spillover for generation X, boomers, and matures: A comparison. *Journal of Family and Economic Issues, 26*, 267–281. doi:10.1007/s10834-005-3525-9

Doerwald, F., Scheibe, S., Zacher, H., & Van Yperen, N. W. (2016). Emotional competencies across adulthood: State of knowledge and implications for the work context. *Work, Aging and Retirement, 2*(2), 159–216. doi:10.1093/workar/waw013

Ebner, N. C., Freund, A. M., & Baltes, P. B. (2006). Developmental changes in personal goal orientation from young to late adulthood: From striving for gains to maintenance and prevention of losses. *Psychology and Aging, 21*, 664–678. doi:10.1037/0882-7974.21.4.664

Eisner, S. P. (2005). Managing generation Y. *SAM Advanced Management Journal, 70*, 4–15. doi:10.1109/emr.2011.5876168

Elder, G. H., Jr. (1974). *Children of the great depression: Social change in life experience.* Chicago, IL: University of Chicago Press.

Elder, G. H., Jr. (1994). Time, human agency, and social change: Perspectives on the life course. *Social Psychology Quarterly, 57*, 4–15. doi:10.2307/2786971

Elder, G. H., Jr., & Liker, J. K. (1982). Hard times in women's lives: Historical influences across 40 years. *Journal of Sociology, 88*, 241–269. doi:10.1086/227670

Elliott, S. (2011). *Ties to tattoos: Turning generational differences into a competitive advantage.* Dallas, TX: Brown Books.

Employee Benefits Research Institute (EBRI). (2004, April). *Will Americans ever become savers? The 14th retirement confidence survey.* EBRI Issue Brief No. 268. Washington, DC. Retrieved from https://www.ebri.org/publications/ib/index.cfm?fa=ibDisp&content_id=496

Espinoza, C., & Ukleja, M. (2016). *Managing the millennials: Discover the core competencies for managing today's workforce.* Hoboken, NJ: Wiley.

Eversole, B. A., Venneberg, D. L., & Crowder, C. L. (2012). Creating a flexible organizational culture to attract and retain talented workers across generations. *Advances in Developing Human Resources, 14,* 607–625. doi:0.1177/1523422312455612

Fineman, S. (2014). Age matters. *Organization Studies, 35,* 1719–1723. doi:10.1177/0170840614553771

Finkelstein, L. M., King, E. B., & Voyles, E. C. (2015). Age metastereotyping and cross-age workplace interactions: A meta view of age stereotypes at work. *Work, Aging and Retirement, 1,* 26–40. doi:10.1093/workar/wau002

Ford, D. H., & Lerner, R. M. (1992). *Developmental systems theory: An integrative approach.* Thousand Oaks, CA: SAGE.

Gentile, B., Wood, L. A., Twenge, J. M., Hoffman, B. J., & Campbell, W. K. (2015). The problem of generational change: Why cross-sectional designs are inadequate for investigating generational differences. In C. E. Lance & R. J. Vandenberg (Eds.), *More statistical myths and methodological urban legends.* New York, NY: Routledge.

Gerstorf, D., Ram, N., Hoppmann, C., Willis, S. L., & Schaie, K. W. (2011). Cohort differences in cognitive aging and terminal decline in the Seattle longitudinal study. *Developmental Psychology, 47,* 1026–1041. doi:10.1037/a0023426

Gilbert, J. (2011). The millennials: A new generation of employees, a new set of engagement policies. *Ivey Business Journal, 75*(5), 26–28. Retrieved from http://iveybusinessjournal.com/publication/the-millennials-a-new-generation-of-employees-a-new-set-of-engagement-policies/

Glass, A. (2007). Understanding generational differences for competitive success. *Industrial and Commercial Training, 39,* 98–103. doi:10.1108/00197850710732424

Glenn, N. D. (2005). *Cohort analysis* (2nd ed.). Thousand Oaks, CA: SAGE.

Graen, G. B., & Uhl-Bien, M. (1995). Relationship-based approach to leadership: Development of leader–member exchange (LMX) theory of leadership over 25 years: Applying a multi-level multi-domain perspective. *Leadership Quarterly, 6,* 219–247. doi:10.1016/1048-9843(95)90036-5

Harvey, J. F. (2012). Managing organizational memory with intergenerational knowledge transfer. *Journal of Knowledge Management, 16,* 400–417. doi:10.1108/13673271211238733

Hershatter, A., & Epstein, M. (2010). Millennials and the world of work: An organization and management perspective. *Journal of Business and Psychology, 25,* 211–223. doi:10.1007/s10869-010-9160-y

Hertel, G., & Zacher, H. (in press). Managing the aging workforce. In C. Viswesvaran, N. Anderson, D. S. Ones, & H. K. Sinangil (Eds.), *The SAGE handbook of industrial, work, & organizational psychology* (2nd ed., Vol. 3). New York, NY: SAGE.

Hess, J., & Jepsen, D. M. (2009). Career stage and generational differences in psychological contracts. *Career Development International, 14,* 261–283. doi:10.1108/13620430910966433

Jurkiewicz, C. (2000). Generation X and the public employee. *Public Personnel Management, 29,* 55–74. doi:10.1177/009102600002900105

Kanfer, R., & Ackerman, P. L. (2004). Aging, adult development, and work motivation. *Academy of Management Review, 29,* 440–458. doi:10.5465/AMR.2004.13670969

Kapoor, C., & Solomon, N. (2011). Understanding and managing generational differences in the workplace. *Worldwide Hospitality and Tourism Themes, 3*, 308–318. doi:10.1108/17554211111162435

Kauppinen, M. (2016, May). Leading millennials: What every manager needs to know. *Training*. Retrieved from https://trainingmag.com/leading-millennials-what-every-manager-needs-know

Kearney, E., & Gebert, D. (2009). Managing diversity and enhancing team outcomes: The promise of transformational leadership. *Journal of Applied Psychology, 94*, 77–89. doi:10.1037/a0013077

Klein, K. J., & Kozlowski, S. J. (2000). From micro to meso: Critical steps in conceptualizing and conducting multilevel research. *Organizational Research Methods, 3*, 211–236. doi:10.1177/109442810033001

Kooij, D. T. A. M., De Lange, A. H., Jansen, P. G. W., Kanfer, R., & Dikkers, J. S. E. (2011). Age and work-related motives: Results of a meta-analysis. *Journal of Organizational Behavior, 32*, 197–225. doi:10.1002/job.665

Kooij, D. T. A. M., Guest, D. E., Clinton, M., Knight, T., Jansen, P. G., & Dikkers, J. S. (2012). How the impact of HR practices on employee wellbeing and performance changes with age. *Human Resources Management Journal, 23*, 18–35. doi:10.1111/1748-8583.12000

Kooij, D. T. A. M., Tims, M., & Kanfer, R. (2015). Successful aging at work: The role of job crafting. In P. M. Bal, D. T. A. M. Kooij, & D. M. Rousseau (Eds.), *Aging workers and the employee–employer relationship* (pp. 145–161). New York, NY: Springer. doi:10.1007/978-3-319-08007-9_9

Kossek, E. E., Pichler, S., Bodner, T., & Hammer, L. B. (2011). Workplace social support and work–family conflict: A meta-analysis clarifying the influence of general and work–family-specific supervisor and organizational support. *Personnel Psychology, 64*, 289–313. doi:10.1111/j.1744-6570.2011.01211.x

Kunze, F., & Bruch, H. (2010). Age-based faultlines and perceived productive energy: The moderation of transformational leadership. *Small Group Research, 41*, 593–620. doi:10.1177/1046496410366307

Lasch, C. (1979). *The culture of narcissism: American life in an age of diminishing expectations*. New York, NY: Warner Books.

Lawrence, B. S. (1984). Age grading: The implicit organizational timetable. *Journal of Organizational Behavior, 5*, 23–35. doi:10.1002/job.4030050104

Lawrence, B. S. (1988). New wrinkles in the theory of age: Demography, norms, and performance ratings. *Academy of Management Journal, 31*, 309–337. doi:10.2307/256550

Lawrence, B. S. (1996). Organizational age norms: Why is it so hard to know one when you see one? *The Gerontologist, 36*, 209–220. doi:10.1093/geront/36.2.209

Liden, R. C., Wayne, S. J., & Stilwell, D. (1993). A longitudinal study on the early development of leader–member exchanges. *Journal of Applied Psychology, 78*, 662–674. doi:10.1037//0021-9010.78.4.662

Lindbo, T. L., & Shultz, K. S. (1998). The role of organizational culture and mentoring in mature worker socialization toward retirement. *Public Productivity & Management Review, 22*, 49–59. doi:10.2307/3380589

Lord, R. G., Foti, R. J., & DeVader, C. L. (1984). A test of leadership categorization theory: Internal structure, information processing, and leadership perceptions. *Organizational Behavior and Human Performance, 34*, 343–378. doi:10.1016/0030-5073(84)90043-6

Lyons, S., Duxbury, L., & Higgins, C. (2007). An empirical assessment of generational differences in basic human values. *Psychological Reports, 101*, 39–352. doi:10.2466/pr0.101.2.339-352

MacCallum, R. C., Zhang, S., Preacher, K. J., & Rucker, D. D. (2002). On the practice of dichotomization of quantitative variables. *Psychological Methods, 7*, 19–40. doi:10.1037/1082-989X.7.1.19

Macrae, C. N., Milne, A. B., & Bodenhausen, G. V. (1994). Stereotypes as energy-saving devices: A peek inside the cognitive toolbox. *Journal of Personality and Social Psychology, 66*, 37–47. doi:10.1037/0022-3514.66.1.37

Mannheim, K. (1952). The problem of generations. In K. Mannheim (Ed.), *Essays on the sociology of knowledge* (pp. 276–322). London, England: Routledge.

McAdams, D. P., & de St Aubin, E. D. (1992). A theory of generativity and its assessment through self-report, behavioral acts, and narrative themes in autobiography. *Journal of Personality and Social Psychology, 62*, 1003–1015. doi:10.1037/0022-3514.62.6.1003

Meister, J. C., & Willyerd, K. (2010). Mentoring millennials. *Harvard Business Review, 88*(5), 68–72. Retrieved from https://hbr.org/

Merton, R. K. (1948). The self-fulfilling prophecy. *Antioch Review, 8*, 193–210. doi:10.2307/4609267

Monson, R. R. (1986). Observations on the healthy worker effect. *Journal of Occupational Medicine, 28*, 425–433. doi:10.1097/00043764-198606000-00009

Nesselroade, J. R., & Baltes, P. B. (1974). Adolescent personality development and historical change: 1970-72. *Monographs of the Society for Research in Child Development, 39*(1), 1–80. doi:10.2307/1165824

Ng, T. W., & Feldman, D. C. (2008). The relationship of age to ten dimensions of job performance. *Journal of Applied Psychology, 93*, 329–423. doi:10.1037/0021-9010.93.2.392

Ng, T. W., & Feldman, D. C. (2010). The relationships of age with job attitudes: A meta-analysis. *Personnel Psychology, 63*, 677–718. doi:10.1111/j.1744-6570.2010.01184.x

North, M. S., & Fiske, S. T. (2012). An inconvenienced youth? Ageism and its potential intergenerational roots. *Psychological Bulletin, 138*, 982–997. doi:10.1037/a0027843

North, M. S., & Fiske, S. T. (2013). A prescriptive intergenerational-tension ageism scale: Succession, identity, and consumption (SIC). *Psychological Assessment, 25*, 706–713. doi:10.1037/a0032367

Oakes, P. J., & Turner, J. C. (1990). Is limited information processing capacity the cause of social stereotyping? *European Review of Social Psychology, 1*, 111–135. doi:10.1080/14792779108401859

Ostroff, C. (1993). Comparing correlations based on individual level and aggregate data. *Journal of Applied Psychology, 78*, 569–582. doi:10.1037/0021-9010.78.4.569

Parkinson, D. (2002). *Voices of experience: Mature workers in the future workforce*. New York, NY: The Conference Board.

Paul, R. J., & Schooler, R. D. (1970). An analysis of performance standards and generation conflict in academia. *Academy of Management Journal, 13*, 212–216. doi:10.2307/255109

Pelled, L. H., & Xin, K. R. (2000). Relational demography and relationship quality in two cultures. *Organization Studies, 21*, 1077–1094. doi:10.1177/0170840600216003

Perry, E. L., Dokko, G., & Golom, F. (2012). The aging worker and person-environment fit. In J. W. Hedge & W. C. Borman (Eds.), *Oxford handbook of work and aging* (pp. 187–212). Oxford, England: Oxford University Press. doi:10.1093/oxfordhb/9780195385052.013.0084

Perry, E. L., Golom, F. D., & McCarthy, J. A. (2015). Generational differences: Let's not throw the baby boomer out with the bathwater. *Industrial and Organizational Psychology, 8*, 376–382. doi:10.1017/iop.2015.53

Perry, E. L., Kulik, C. T., & Zhou, J. (1999). A closer look at the effects of subordinate–supervisor age differences. *Journal of Organizational Behavior, 20*, 341–357. doi:10.1002/(SICI)1099-1379(199905)20:3<341::AID-JOB915>3.0.CO;2-D

Pietschnig, J., & Voracek, M. (2015). One century of global IQ gains: A formal meta-analysis of the Flynn effect (1909–2013). *Perspectives on Psychological Science, 10*, 282–306. doi:10.1177/1745691615577701

Posthuma, R. A., & Campion, M. A. (2009). Age stereotypes in the workplace: Common stereotypes, moderators, and future research directions. *Journal of Management, 35*, 158–188. doi:10.1177/0149206308318617

Reeve, E. (2013, May). Every every every generation has been the me me me generation. *Atlantic Wire*. Retrieved from http://www.thewire.com

Riggio, R. E., & Mumford, M. D. (2011). Introduction to the special issue: Longitudinal studies of leadership development. *The Leadership Quarterly, 22*, 453–456. doi:10.1016/j.leaqua.2011.04.002

Riley, M. W., Johnson, M. E., & Foner, A. (1972). *Aging and society* (Vol. 3): *A sociology of age stratification*. New York, NY: Russell Sage.

Roberts, B. W., & DelVecchio, W. F. (2000). The rank-order consistency of personality traits from childhood to old age: A quantitative review of longitudinal studies. *Psychological Bulletin, 126*, 3–25. doi:10.1037/0033-2909.126.1.3

Roberts, B. W., Edmonds, G., & Grijalva, E. (2010). It is developmental me, not generation me: Developmental changes are more important than generational changes in narcissism: Commentary on Trzesniewski & Donnellan (2010). *Perspectives on Psychological Science, 5*, 97–102. doi:10.1177/1745691609357019

Roberts, B. W., & Jackson, J. J. (2008). Sociogenomic personality psychology. *Journal of Personality, 76*, 1523–1544. doi:10.1111/j.1467-6494.2008.00530.x

Roberts, B. W., & Mroczek, D. (2008). Personality trait change in adulthood. *Current Directions in Psychological Science, 17*, 31–35. doi:10.1111/j.1467-8721.2008.00543.x

Roberts, B. W., Walton, K. E., & Viechtbauer, W. (2006). Patterns of mean-level change in personality traits across the life course: A meta-analysis of longitudinal studies. *Psychological Bulletin, 132*, 1–25. doi:10.1037/0033-2909.132.1.1

Roberts, B. W., & Wood, D. (2006). Personality development in the context of the neo-socioanalytic model of personality. In D. K. Mroczek & T. D. Little (Eds.), *Handbook of personality development* (pp. 11–39). Mahwah, NJ: Erlbaum. doi:10.4324/9781315805610.ch2

Rosing, K., & Jungmann, F. (2016). Leadership and aging. In N. Pachana (Ed.), *Encyclopedia of geropsychology* (pp. 1–8). New York, NY: Springer. doi:10.1007/ 978-981-287-080-3_23-1

Rudolph, C. W. (2015). A note on the folly of cross-sectional operationalizations of generations. *Industrial and Organizational Psychology, 8,* 362–366. doi:10.1017/ iop.2015.50

Rudolph, C. W. (2016). Life span developmental perspectives on working: A literature review of motivational theories. *Work, Aging and Retirement, 2,* 130–158. doi:10.1093/workar/waw012

Rudolph, C. W., & Baltes, B. B. (2016). Age and health jointly moderate the influence of flexible work arrangements on work engagement: Evidence from two empirical studies. *Journal of Occupational Health Psychology, 22,* 40–58.

Rudolph, C. W., Baltes, B. B., & Zabel, K. L. (2013). Age and work motives. In R. Burke, C. L. Cooper & J. Field (Eds.), *SAGE handbook on aging, work, and society* (pp. 118–139). London, England: SAGE. doi:10.4135/9781446269916.n7

Rudolph, C. W., Toomey, E., & Baltes, B. B. (2017). Considering age diversity in recruitment and selection: An expanded work life span view of age management. In J. McCarthy & E. Parry (Eds.), *Handbook of age diversity and work* (pp. 607–638). London, England: Palgrave-Macmillan.

Rudolph, C. W., & Zacher, H. (2015). Intergenerational perceptions and conflicts in multi-age and multigenerational work environments. In L. M. Finkelstein, D. M. Truxillo, F. Fraccaroli, & R. Kanfer (Eds.), *Facing the challenges of a multiage workforce: A use-inspired approach* (pp. 253–282). New York, NY: Routledge. doi:10.4324/9780203776322

Rudolph, C. W., & Zacher, H. (2016). Considering generations from a life span development perspective. *Work, Aging and Retirement, 0,* 1–17. doi:10.1093/ workar/waw019

Ryan, K. M., King, E. B., & Finkelstein, L. M. (2015). Younger workers' metastereotypes, workplace mood, attitudes, and behaviors. *Journal of Managerial Psychology, 30,* 54–70. doi:10.1108/JMP-07-2014-0215

Salmela-Aro, K. (2009). Personal goals and well-being during critical life transitions: The four C's—Channelling, choice, co-agency and compensation. *Advances in Life Course Research, 14,* 63–73. doi:10.1016/j.alcr.2009.03.003

Salthouse, T. A. (2012). Consequences of age-related cognitive declines. *Annual Review of Psychology, 63,* 201–226. doi:10.1146/annurev-psych-120710-100328

Schaie, K. W. (1965). A general model for the study of developmental problems. *Psychological Bulletin, 64,* 92–107. doi:10.1037/ h0022371

Schaie, K. W. (1994). The course of adult intellectual development. *American Psychologist, 49,* 304–313. doi:10.1037/0003-066X.49.4.304

Schaie, K. W. (1996). *Intellectual development in adulthood.* Cambridge, England: Cambridge University Press.

Schaie, K. W. (2013). *Developmental influences on adult intelligence: The Seattle longitudinal study* (2nd ed.). New York, NY: Oxford University Press.

Shore, L. M., Cleveland, J. N., & Goldberg, C. B. (2003). Work attitudes and decisions as a function of manager age and employee age. *Journal of Applied Psychology, 88,* 529–537. doi:10.1037/0021-9010.88.3.529

Skinner, B. F. (1974). *Walden two.* Indianapolis, IN: Hackett.

Smola, K., & Sutton, C. D. (2002). Generational differences: Revisiting generational work values for the new millennium. *Journal of Organizational Behavior, 23*, 363–382. doi:10.1002/job.147

Snyder, M., Tanke, E. D., & Berscheid, E. (1977). Social perception and interpersonal behavior: On the self-fulfilling nature of social stereotypes. *Journal of Personality and Social Psychology, 35*, 656–666. doi:10.1037/0022-3514.35.9.656

Spisak, B. R. (2012). The general age of leadership: Older-looking presidential candidates win elections during war. *PLoS ONE, 7*, e36945. doi:10.1371/journal.pone.0036945

Spisak, B. R., Grabo, A. E., Arvey, R. D., & van Vugt, M. (2014). The age of exploration and exploitation: Younger-looking leaders endorsed for change and older-looking leaders endorsed for stability. *The Leadership Quarterly, 25*, 805–816. doi:10.1016/j.leaqua.2014.06.001

Stassen, L., Anseel, F., & Levecque, K. (2016). Generational differences in the workplace: A systematic analysis of a myth. *Gedrag & Organisatie, 29*, 44–46.

Steele, C. M., & Aronson, J. (1995). Stereotype threat and the intellectual test performance of African Americans. *Journal of Personality and Social Psychology, 69*, 797–811. doi:10.1037/0022-3514.69.5.797

Szinovacz, M., DeViney, S., and Davey, A. (2001). Influences of family obligations and relationships on retirement: Variations by gender, race, and marital status. *Journal of Gerontology: Social Sciences, 56*, s20–s27. doi:10.1093/geronb/56.1.s20

Thrasher, G. R., Zabel, K., Wynne, K., & Baltes, B. B. (2016). The importance of workplace motives in understanding work-family issues for older workers. *Work, Aging and Retirement, 2*, 1–11. doi:10.1093/workar/wav021

Thomas, R., Hardy, C., Cutcher, L., & Ainsworth, S. (2014). What's age got to do with it? On the critical analysis of age and organizations. *Organization Studies, 35*, 1569–1584. doi:10.1177/0170840614554363

Tonks, G., Dickenson, K., & Nelson, L. (2009). Misconceptions and realities: The working relationships of older workers and younger managers. *Research and Practice in Human Resource Management, 17*(2), 36–54.

Torff, B., & Sternberg, R.J. (1998). Changing mind, changing world: Practical intelligence and tacit knowledge in adult learning. In M. C. Smith & T. Pourchot (Eds.), *Adult learning and development: Perspectives from educational psychology* (pp. 109–126). Mahwah, NJ: Erlbaum.

Truxillo, D. M., Cadiz, D. M., & Hammer, L. B. (2015). Supporting the aging workforce: A review and recommendations for workplace intervention research. *Annual Review of Organizational Psychology and Organizational Behavior, 2*, 351–381. doi:10.1146/annurev-orgpsych-032414-111435

Truxillo, D. M., Cadiz, D. M., Rineer, J. R., Zaniboni, S., & Fraccaroli, F. (2012). A life span perspective on job design: Fitting the job and the worker to promote job satisfaction, engagement, and performance. *Organizational Psychology Review, 2*, 340–360. doi:10.1177/2041386612454043

Trzesniewski, K. H., & Donnellan, M. B. (2014). "Young people these days...": Evidence for negative perceptions of emerging adults. *Emerging Adulthood, 2*, 211–226. doi:10.1177/2167696814522620

Trzesniewski, K. H., Donnellan, M. B., & Robins, R. W. (2008). Do today's young people really think they are so extraordinary? An examination of secular trends in narcissism and self-enhancement. *Psychological Science, 19*, 181–188. doi:10.1111/j.1467-9280.2008.02065.x

Tsui, A. S., Xin, K. R., & Egan, T. D. (1995). Relational demography: The missing link in vertical dyad linkage. In S. E. Jackson & M. N. Ruderman (Eds.), *Diversity in work teams: Research paradigms for a changing workplace* (pp. 97–129). Washington, DC: American Psychological Association. doi:10.1037/10189-004

Tulgan, B. (2016). *Not everyone gets a trophy: How to manage the millennials* (2nd ed.). Hoboken, N.J.: John Wiley. doi:10.1002/9781119215073

Twenge, J. M. (2013). Teaching generation me. *Teaching of Psychology, 40*, 66–69. doi:10.1177/0098628312465870

Twenge, J. M. (2014). *Generation me, revised and updated: Why today's young Americans are more confident, assertive, entitled—and more miserable than ever before*. New York, NY: Simon & Schuster.

Twenge, J. M., Konrath, S., Foster, J. D., Campbell, W. K., & Bushman, B. J. (2008). Egos inflating over time: A cross-temporal meta-analysis of the narcissistic personality inventory. *Journal of Personality, 76*, 875–902. doi:10.1111/j.1467-6494.2008.00507.x

Vecchio, R. P., & Boatwright, K. J. (2002). Preferences for idealized styles of supervision. *The Leadership Quarterly, 13*, 327–342. doi:10.1016/S1048-9843(02)00118-2

von Hippel, C., Kalokerinos, E. K., & Henry, J. D. (2013). Stereotype threat among older employees: Relationship with job attitudes and turnover intentions. *Psychology and Aging, 28*, 17–27. doi:10.1037/a0029825

Waldman, D. A., & Avolio, B. J. (1986). A meta-analysis of age differences in job performance. *Journal of Applied Psychology, 71*, 33–38. doi:10.1037/0021-9010.71.1.33

Walker, A. (1993). Intergenerational relations and welfare restructuring: The social construction of an intergenerational problem. In V. L. Bengtson & W.A. Achenbaum (Eds.), *The changing contract across generations* (pp. 141–165). New York, NY: Aldine de Gruyter.

Wallace, W. L. (1967). Faculty and fraternities: Organizational influences on student achievement. *Administrative Science Quarterly, 40*, 228–255. doi:10.2307/2391080

Walter, F., & Scheibe, S. (2013). A literature review and emotion-based model of age and leadership: New directions for the trait approach. *Leadership Quarterly, 24*, 882–901. doi:10.1016/j.leaqua.2013.10.003

Wesner, M. S., & Miller, T. (2008). Boomers and millennials have much in common. *Leadership and Organization Development Journal, 26*, 89–96.

Wolfe, T. (1976, August). The me decade and the third great awakening. *New York Magazine, 23*, 26–40. Retrieved from http://nymag.com/news/features/45938/

Yukl, G. (1998). *Leadership in organizations*. Upper Saddle River, NJ: Prentice Hall.

Zacher, H. (2015). Using life span developmental theory and methods as a viable alternative to the study of generational differences at work. *Industrial and Organizational Psychology, 8*(03), 342–346.

Zacher, H., Clark, M., Anderson, E. C., & Ayoko, O. B. (2015). A life span perspective on leadership. In P. M. Bal, D. T. Kooij, & D. M. Rousseau (Eds.), *Aging workers and the employee-employer relationship* (pp. 87–104). New York, NY: Springer. doi:10.1007/978-3-319-08007-9_6

Zacher, H., Hacker, W., & Frese, M. (2016). Action regulation across the adult life span (ARAL): A metatheory of work and aging. *Work, Aging and Retirement, 2,* 286–306. doi:10.1093/workar/waw015

Zacher, H., Rosing, K., Henning, T., & Frese, M. (2011). Establishing the next generation at work: Leader generativity as a moderator of the relationships between leader age, leader–member exchange, and leadership success. *Psychology and Aging, 26,* 241–252. doi:10.1037/a0021429

Zacher, H., Rudolph, C. W., & Reinicke, C. (in press). Caregiving and organizational support. In L. Calvano & R. Burke (Eds.), *The sandwich generation: Caring for oneself and others at home and work.* Northhampton, MA: Edward Elger.

SECTION III
EMERGING TRENDS

CHAPTER 10

LMX AND AUTISM

Effective Working Relationships

Amy E. Hurley-Hanson and Cristina M. Giannantonio
Chapman University

ABSTRACT

It is predicted that over the next decade close to half a million people with autism spectrum disorder (ASD) will reach adulthood (Centers for Disease Control and Prevention, 2015). Relatively little is known about the work and career experiences of individuals with ASD including how ASD may impact the development of effective working relationships between leaders and employees with ASD. Leader member exchange theory (LMX) with its focus on leader–member relationships (Scandura, 2015) may contribute greatly to creating effective working relationships between leaders and their employees with ASD.

One of the most challenging issues confronting organizations in the 21st century is how diversity may impact the development of effective working relationships. Having a diverse workforce was predicted to be one of the top workplace trends organizations focused on in 2016, according to a survey by the Society of Industrial and Organizational Psychologists (SIOP). SIOP is working with businesses to develop strategies that will result in a more diverse workforce and reward individuals who are able to develop effective working relationships with diverse teams (Brooks, 2016).

It is predicted that over the next decade, close to half a million people with autism spectrum disorder (ASD) will reach adulthood (CDC, 2015). Relatively little is known about the work and career experiences of individuals with ASD including how ASD may impact the development of effective working relationships. It is imperative to research the issues associated with the transition of individuals with ASD into the world of work (Taylor, & Seltzer, 2011) and to gain a better understanding of their career and work experiences (Griffiths, Giannantonio, Hurley-Hanson & Cardinal, 2016). Adults with disabilities may have career experiences that differ from the mainstream populations who have been commonly studied in the management literature (Heslin, Bell & Fletcher, 2012; Zikic & Hall, 2009). Similarly, it is important to understand the work experiences of individuals with disabilities and the relationships between leaders and employees with ASD. Leader member exchange theory (LMX) with its focus on leader–member relationships (Scandura, 2015) may contribute greatly to creating effective working relationships between leaders and employees with ASD. Examining the relationships between leaders and employees with ASD has the potential to contribute to research on LMX and to improve workplace diversity and inclusion initiatives.

AUTISM AND EMPLOYMENT

According to Autism Speaks (2016), autism spectrum disorder and autism are both general terms for a group of complex disorders of brain development. These disorders are characterized, in varying degrees, by difficulties in social interaction, verbal and nonverbal communication, and repetitive behaviors. The World Health Organization (2013) refers to ASD as "neurodevelopmental impairments in communication and social interaction and unusual ways of perceiving and processing information" (2013, p. 7). Individuals with ASD often have difficulty understanding the thoughts, intentions, and emotions of others (Bruggink, Goei, & Koot, 2016) and they often have difficulty regulating their own emotions (Samson, Huber, & Gross, 2012).

Autism statistics from the CDC (2015) are startling and the statistics have implications for organizations and the changing workforce. It is estimated that 1 in 68 children are on the autism spectrum, with autism four to five times more common in boys (1 in 42) than in girls (1 in 189). The number of people affected by ASD is estimated to be in the tens of millions worldwide with 3.5 million in the United States (Autism Speaks, 2016). There are few reliable statistics on the number of individuals with ASD who are currently working or planning to enter the workforce. Given that occupational choices are one way in which individuals define themselves, finding and maintaining employment is critical for adults with ASD to become engaged and active citizens who experience a positive quality of life and feelings of dignity and self-worth. The experience of working and developing a work identity—the process of defining who one is in relation to work—is a psychological process that is a key part of the experience of adulthood (Dutton, Roberts, & Bednar, 2010; Gini, 1998; Kira & Balkin, 2014; Saayman & Crafford, 2011; Sveningsson & Alvesson, 2003). Working should ideally provide adults with an environment where they can have a sense of accomplishment and connection with other people (Krieger, Kinebanian, Prodinger, & Heigl, 2012; Saayman & Crafford, 2011; Scott, Falkmer, Girdler, & Falkmer, 2015).

There is anecdotal evidence that individuals with autism can be fully integrated and engaged in work organizations. Recently, several high-profile companies have announced efforts to hire individuals with autism as part of their diversity initiatives. SAP and Specialisterne are two well-known firms developing programs to hire people with ASD (Holland, 2016). However, research has found that many employers are concerned that prospective employees with ASD are not qualified for jobs at their firms and that the costs of hiring and training them may reduce profitability (Bruyère, 2000; Dixon, Kruse, & Van Horn, 2003, Domzal, Houtenville, & Sharma, 2008). Although not specific to ASD, research has also found that negative stereotypes of employees with disabilities affect corporate hiring and promotion decisions (Ren, Paetzold, & Colella, 2008; Stone & Colella, 1996).

It is important that research on autism in the workplace is included in diversity and inclusion research (Shore et al., 2011). However, following high school many people with ASD struggle to find employment, to complete academic courses, and to live independently. Finding meaningful employment is particularly difficult for these young adults. For example, the U.S. Department of Labor reports that the unemployment rate for people with disabilities is more than 40% higher than that of the general population.

Organizations that act responsibly by providing meaningful employment for individuals with ASD can contribute to the greater good of society. Research showing the value that individuals with ASD can contribute to an organization will help to create employment opportunities for this underemployed yet growing segment of the labor market. Employers are increasingly including disability in their definitions of diversity (Shore et al., 2009) and some employers pride themselves on their inclusion of adults with disabilities in their workforce (Boekhorst, 2015; Donnelly, 2015; Brite, Nunes & Souza, 2015; Dwertmann & Boehm, 2016; Gerber & Price, 2003). It has been found that larger companies have better track records for ADA accommodations than smaller firms (Gerber & Price, 2003). Identifying companies with strong inclusion and accommodation practices may help adults with ASD to self-select into these potential workplaces.

The leaders of Winston Capital Management believe the highly developed analytical skills of some people with autism can give their organization a valuable competitive advantage. Similarly, Goldman Sachs has been actively recruiting individuals with ASD for internships since 2003, which has resulted in permanent employment contracts for some (Tickle, 2009). In 2015, Microsoft created a pilot program to focus on hiring individuals with autism. According to Mary Ellen Smith, vice president of worldwide operations,

> People with autism bring strengths that we need at Microsoft, each individual is different, some have an amazing ability to retain information, think at a level of detail and depth, or excel in math or code. It's a talent pool that we want to continue to bring to Microsoft! (Autism Speaks, 2016)

Similarly, Walgreens has championed autistic employees exemplified by their South Carolina distribution center that employs several employees with disabilities such as autism (Autism Speaks, 2016).

THE COSTS OF AUTISM

Research suggests that the work and life outcomes for young adults with ASD are poor when compared with the general population. For example, research suggests that 70% of these young adults will be unable to live independently. In fact 85% of young adults with ASD still live with their parents, siblings, or other relatives (Buescher, Cidav, Knapp, & Mandell, 2014). If they are not able to be employed and live independently, the services they will require will place a financial toll on society. Supporting an individual with ASD may exceed $2 million over the course of their lifetime (Buescher et al., 2014). The cost of autism support services in the United States exceeds $236 billion dollars annually (Buescher et al., 2014). This number is expected to rise to $1 trillion by 2025 (Leigh & Du, 2015). There are additional costs that are difficult to measure, such as lost income for both the individual with autism and their parents and caregivers. The unemployment rate for individuals with autism is estimated at 85% (National Autistic Society, 2016). Previous research suggests that 35% of young adults with autism have never held a job, been members of the labor force, nor attended educational programs after high school (Cidav, Marcus & Mandell, 2012; Shattuck, Narendorf, Cooper, Sterzing, Wagner, & Taylor, 2012). Even among those individuals who have secured employment, their career path may involve multiple movements in and out of the labor market. The cost of these adults not working contributes to the financial toll on their families as well as society.

There is relatively little research on the work experiences of young adults with ASD. It is very difficult to track individuals with ASD once they leave high school. There is little coordination among the agencies providing transition services to assist young adults and their families with career planning, job search, and placement activities (Pellicano, Dinsmore, & Charman, 2014). For young adults with ASD, the transition period from high school to the world of work with myriad new tasks and experiences can be particularly difficult. Over the next decade about half a million people with ASD will reach adulthood. Many of these young adults will be exiting their school districts and losing the services they have been provided in the past. While some young adults with ASD will enroll in postsecondary education programs, others will be searching for jobs and looking to enter the workforce. Most will continue to need some type of support to reach their educational and occupational goals (Griffiths, Giannantonio, Hurley-Hanson, & Cardinal, 2016).

LEADERSHIP AND AUTISM

There is little research that has examined the challenges and opportunities of leading, managing, and working with individuals with ASD. Since individuals with ASD may display highly variable levels of intellectual abilities and emotional capabilities, the types of jobs that they will be able to obtain over their careers will be influenced by their skill levels and need for support (Nicholas, Attridge, Zwaigenbaum, & Clark, 2014). Moreover, these varying levels of intellectual and emotional skills would seem to be important variables that will have profound influences on the types of relationships individuals with ASD will form with their managers, supervisors, and coworkers.

There are some unique challenges that employees with ASD may present at work. Organizations will need to be proactive and prepared to deal with these challenges in order to benefit from the contributions employees with ASD can make in the workplace. Employers should be aware that some of the obstacles employees with ASD may face at work include difficulties in communication, balancing multiple demands, adapting to change, and heightened sensitivity to sensory stimuli (Baldwin, Costley, & Warren, 2014; Higgins, Koch, Boughfman, & Vierstra, 2008; Hendricks, 2010; Hurlbutt & Chalmers, 2004; Mynatt, Gibbons, & Hughes, 2014).

As organizations prepare for the wave of people with ASD who are about to enter the workforce, researchers must ask whether current theories of leadership are broad enough to be applicable to the work experiences of individuals with ASD. It is hypothesized that managers will not be able to develop relationships with subordinates with ASD in the same way that they form relationships with their employees without ASD. Impairments in social interactions and communications may require managers to develop even more individualized ways of communicating and forming relationships with employees with ASD. Given the social nature of most jobs, many of the difficulties with career attainment and success for adults with ASD are related to social concerns, rather than to actual job performance (Higgins et al., 2008; Scott, Falkmer, Girdler, & Falkmer, 2015).

Some of these challenges may be reduced with workplace accommodations, but access to accommodations depends on whether the individual discloses their condition (Santuzzi, Waltz, Rupp, & Finkelstein, 2014). ASD has been called an "invisible disability" because in some cases it cannot be readily observed by others (Richards, 2012). Adults with invisible disabilities have the option to reveal or to conceal their disability from others (Clair, Beatty, & MacLean, 2005). There are both positive and negative consequences with revealing invisible disabilities in the workplace (Chaudoir & Fisher, 2010; DeJordy, 2008; Ragins, 2008). Disclosure has the potential to help with acceptance at work and may make it easier for supervisors and peers to separate the work from the person (Davidson & Henderson, 2010; Gerber & Price, 2003; Meister, Jehn, & Thatcher, 2014). Disclosure may also pave the way for training supervisors and peers about the needs of employees with ASD (Wilczynski, Trammell, & Clarke, 2013). Adults with ASD need to weigh the potential pitfalls of disclosing their diagnosis against the potential gains. High functioning adults with ASD may not be perceived as having a disability by their coworkers. Atypical behaviors may be incorrectly attributed to personality quirks rather than to neurological differences (Patton, 2009).

Certain aspects of the workplace have been cited repeatedly for fostering positive reception of disclosure. A supportive organization that enforces strong antidiscrimination policies can encourage disclosure (Chaudoir & Fischer, 2010; Clair et al., 2005; Ragins, 2008). A company culture that actively promotes diversity may also be important (Gerber & Price, 2003). Having a positive, trusting relationship with a manager or having a manager that is known to have the same disorder could also impact an employee's decision to disclose (Chaudoir & Fischer, 2010; Clair et al., 2005; Ragins, 2008). The presence of coworkers who are known to have ASD and who have been accepted could also signal that a workplace is safe for disclosure (Clair et al., 2005; Ragins, 2008).

There have been a limited number of empirical studies on the most effective ways of managing and building relationships with individuals with ASD in the workplace. In part, this may be explained by the fact that individuals with ASD may need highly variable levels of support in order to succeed in the workplace. Several leadership theories may offer insights into managing and building effective relationships between a leader/manager and his or her subordinates with ASD. Building on Parr and Hunter's (2014) examination of three leadership theories to investigate which leadership behaviors would produce the best outcomes for employees with ASD, this chapter will examine five leadership theories to investigate which leadership behaviors would result in developing effective working relationships with employees with ASD.

TWO-FACTOR THEORY

The two-factor theory of leadership may be beneficial for managing employees with ASD as it calls for leaders to coach, provide encouragement, set goals for tasks, and coordinate work activities for their employees (Judge, Piccolo, & Ilies, 2004; Tracy, 1987). Leaders who exhibit high levels of consideration and initiating structure behaviors may provide followers with ASD the type of support needed to be successful in the workplace. Leaders high in consideration behaviors are likely to both support employees who are faced with difficult tasks and will attempt to lower the employees' anxiety. They would be expected to also mentor and coach their employees toward goal completion. Leaders high in initiating structure are likely to set goals and clarify the work activities of their followers. Employees with ASD may need leaders high in both factors. These employees will need the support and mentoring of their leaders to help them with anxiety regarding difficult tasks. These employees will also need a leader to be clear about the employee's goals and job duties. Research suggests that for employees with ASD it is important for leaders to clearly describe performance expectations and job duties, to provide clear instructions, and to maintain consistency in the workplace (Hagner & Cooney, 2005; Hurlbutt & Chalmers, 2004). Thus, both consideration and initiating structure seem to be appropriate for effectively leading employees with ASD, and it is expected that leaders displaying these behaviors would elicit positive outcomes from this population.

PATH-GOAL THEORY

Path-goal theory (House, 1971) describes leadership that motivates followers by showing them the path toward completing their goals and by removing obstacles in the way of goal completion and barriers to performance. This is particularly important when managing employees with ASD who might face an increased number of obstacles and barriers to performance. Path-goal theory also emphasizes the importance of rewarding goal completion. Path-goal theory calls for leaders to provide direct communication and clear instructions to their employees that may be beneficial to employees with ASD because this reduces ambiguity and uncertainty related to expectations regarding job performance. It will be important for managers to identify the obstacles that might obstruct the performance of employees with ASD, especially if the individual with ASD is not aware of the obstacles and barriers hindering performance.

Path-goal theory identifies four leadership behaviors: directive, achievement oriented, participative, and supportive. When choosing which leadership behavior to utilize with their followers, leaders should consider which behaviors might be more effective with their employees with ASD. For example, directive behavior might be well suited for managing employees with ASD as the leader tells followers what is expected of them and how to perform their job, especially when the job is ambiguous. Achievement oriented behavior with its emphasis on setting challenging goals and high performance expectations might be appropriate with individuals who are very high functioning, but less appropriate with individuals who require significant levels of support. Supportive behavior would be expected to be effective with employees with ASD especially when those employees experience distressing situations in the workplace. Research is needed to determine if and when participative behavior would be appropriate with employees with ASD.

TRANSFORMATIONAL LEADERSHIP

Transformational leadership occurs when a leader uses emotional value based messages in an attempt to motivate employees to go above and beyond what they think they can accomplish. Value-based messages are often ambiguous and employees with ASD who view concepts in concrete terms may not respond well to ambiguous appeals (Hurlbutt & Chalmers, 2004). People with ASD often have difficulty understanding abstract concepts related to their jobs (Hillier et al., 2007). Transformational leaders often call for employees to extend or expand their work productivity to help transform the organization. These demands may lead to sensory overload and increased levels of stress and anxiety for employees with ASD (Parr & Hunter, 2014; Parr, Hunter, & Ligon, 2013).

Transformational leadership suggests that leaders utilize inspirational motivation, idealized influence, intellectual stimulation, and individualized consideration to motivate employees (Bass & Avolio, 1993). Thus, transformational leaders may attempt to inspire and motivate followers, serve as an ideal role model, challenge followers to be innovative and creative, and demonstrate concern for the needs and feelings of their followers. When utilizing these strategies with their followers, leaders should consider which strategies might be more effective with their employees with ASD. For example, employees with ASD might respond favorably to intellectual stimulation because they admire the leader's intellect and having the opportunity to be recognized for using their own intellectual abilities to solve problems. Individualized consideration, with its emphasis on demonstrating concern for the needs and feelings of the follower, might also be effective with employees with ASD as the leader would be attuned to employees' feelings of anxiety, being overwhelmed, and uncomfortable with change and ambiguity (Kirby, Paradise, & King, 1992). Inspirational motivation and idealized influence with their emphasis on emotional appeals and visionary goals may be less effective for motivating employees with ASD given challenges with recognizing and responding to social cues and adapting to change (Parr, Hunter, & Ligon, 2013; Simic, 1998). Leaders may need to be specific in identifying the behaviors they want their followers to exhibit and the goals they should achieve. Leaders might also consider using rational means of persuasion instead of emotional persuasion (e.g., explaining why the change is necessary) as meaningfulness appears to clarify ambiguity (Kirby, Paradise & King, 1992). It should be recognized that change in general, and specifically these four strategies, have the potential to create ambiguity for followers with ASD and the resulting anxiety it evokes may interfere with effective working relationships (Parr, Hunter, & Ligon, 2013).

Ambiguity is one of the most common outcomes when transformations are occurring in organizations. Mindfulness has been researched as a tool to help employees handle ambiguity in the workplace (Gärtner 2013; Gondo, Patterson, & Palacios, 2013). A recent study found that mindfulness was positively related to transformational leadership. The study of transformational leaders found that they felt the concept of mindfulness was very important to the success of their transformation effort. The leaders found their own mindfulness made their followers accept them more and allowed the leaders to be more aware and cognizant of the concerns of their employees. The leaders also found that mindfulness helped the firm's employees to deal with the ambiguity resulting from the ongoing transformation (Wylson & Chesley, 2016). Additionally, mindfulness may also be useful in helping employees with ASD handle ambiguity even if they are not in the midst of a transformation.

AUTHENTIC LEADERSHIP THEORY

Authentic leadership theory may offer managers guidance in building relationships with employees with ASD. Authentic leadership calls for leaders to have high moral standards, demonstrate honesty, consider the views of all involved, and show concern for their followers. Parr and Hunter (2014) hypothesized that authentic leadership would lead to more positive outcomes for employees with ASD than transformational or two-factor leadership. It may be important for managers of employees with ASD to display high levels of honesty as these employees often interpret things literally. Parr and Hunter's (2014) study supported the notion that leadership behaviors had a large effect on employees with ASD, and that individuals, including those on the spectrum, have different needs and preferences for their leaders.

INDIVIDUALIZED LEADERSHIP

Individualized leadership calls for leaders and their followers to create individualized relationships with each other independent of others in the workplace (Dansereau, Yammarino, & Markham, 1995). Leaders' expectations of their followers are based on the person's unique characteristics and needs rather than comparing them to other employees (Dansereau et al., 1995). This theory may be appropriate for employees with ASD as the leader would be able to identify the strengths and needs of their followers on an individualized basis and create a unique relationship with each of their followers. Individualized leadership recognizes the importance of leader–member relations, a concept expanded on in the leader–member exchange theory.

LMX AND AUTISM

Leader–member exchange theory (LMX) may be one of the most useful leadership theories for understanding the individualized relationships that leaders create with their subordinates. It has long been recognized that leaders do not treat all employees equally (Dansereau, Graen & Haga, 1975). LMX theory explicitly examines the relationships that develop between leaders and their followers. LMX theory posits that leaders have different exchanges with their followers and that they form relationships characterized by trust and respect with some, but not all, members of a team. Research on LMX has shown that leader–member relationships can be seen as a continuum from low to high quality relationships between leaders and their employees (Graen, & Uhl-Bien, 1995; Loi, Mao, & Ngo, 2009). High quality LMX relationships involve mutual trust and respect based on employees performing additional tasks assigned by their supervisors. In contrast, in low-quality LMX relationships employees perform only the work they are required to do (Loi, Chan & Lam, 2014). Over time, employees in high quality LMX relationships become members of the in-group, while employees in low quality relationships become members of the out-group. Since not all employees will be part of the in-group with high level LMX relationships (Gran & Uhl-Bien, 1995), it is important to understand how LMX relationships develop and the implications for employees with ASD. There are three steps in LMX relationship development (Graen & Scandura, 1987). These steps are role-taking, role-making, and role-routinization. While LMX shows great potential for managing employees with ASD, it is important to examine how employees with ASD may respond in each step of the LMX relationship development model.

In the first step, role-taking, leaders offer their employees extra work as a way to assess their commitment to the leader. Employees need to interpret the offer of extra work as a test and positively indicate their willingness to take on the extra work, thus being assessed favorably by the leader. Leaders will evaluate a worker's commitment based on their responses to extra assignments (Loi, Chan & Lam, 2014). The number of tests given by the leader will vary. Research has found that the more testing episodes that occur the more likely it is that supervisors and subordinates will share the same evaluation of their relationship quality (Loi, Chan & Lam, 2014).

Employees with ASD may not perceive the offer of extra work as a "test" nor understand the implications of saying no to taking on extra tasks. While this may be true for employees in general, especially newer, naive employees, this step may be particularly challenging for employees with ASD as this step requires them to pick up subtle cues and hidden messages from their bosses and managers. Leaders may need diversity and inclusion training to help them understand that employees with ASD may have trouble understanding the importance of the offer of extra work and the implications of turning down such a request. Additionally, employees with ASD, who may prefer clear and unambiguous work directions, may become stressed and anxious if their work routine is changed through the addition of tasks outside the scope of their job description.

Moreover, because the leader's test leads to the important decision of who is part of the in-group and who is part of the out-group, employees with ASD may be unfairly classified into the out-group if they do not go beyond their job descriptions and take on extra work. Over time, this may contribute to the leader's decision to keep them in the out-group and not allow them to move into the in-group, which has been shown to increase productivity and satisfaction. In this step of LMX relationship development, it becomes important for leaders to explain that they are offering the employee the opportunity to learn new skills that will help them in the future or that taking on this assignment may lead to future career success.

In the second step, role-making, leaders and subordinates achieve mutual expectations of each other's roles. The follower role becomes more transparent. Employees will expect and trust that they will be rewarded for the tasks they are completing (Sin, Nahrgang, & Morgeson, 2009). This second step of LMX theory may work effectively with employees with ASD. Employees will see that the duties requested by their supervisor are part of their job requirements. Once the reciprocal relationship is achieved, employees with ASD are expected to appreciate the stability of knowing what to expect from their leader if they perform the requested duties. However, any changes from the expectations by the leader may cause an employee with ASD to lose trust in the leader and the LMX relationship will fail to motivate the employee.

The third step in LMX role development is role routinization. In this step, the roles of the leader and the member become stable (Graen & Scandura, 1987). The two parties develop patterns of behavior that are now routine and the parties know what to expect from the relationship. This is an important step in LMX for employees with ASD as they need to feel that their leader understands their needs. In this final step, leaders will have achieved the goal of employees bypassing their own self-interests and becoming committed to the mission of the organization (Graen & Uhl-Bien, 1991). This may be a step toward transformational leadership.

Employees with ASD could have high level relationships with their leaders if the leaders understand how the three steps of the LMX process may need to be modified to accommodate employees with ASD. It may be important to educate employees with ASD about the three steps of relationship development in LMX. Employees should be concerned with managing the relationship by demonstrating that they are dependable. Leaders should be concerned with managing the relationship by demonstrating their trustworthiness.

Research on the quality of LMX relationships has found that leaders and members often do not view the quality of the relationship equally (Graen & Schiemann, 1978). Agreement has been shown to be higher the longer the relationship exists (Sin, Nahrgang, & Morgeson, 2009). Essentially, when the role-taking step is longer, leaders and followers tend to agree more on the quality of their relationship. This may be problematic for employees with ASD as the consistent testing of their commitment by additional assignments may lead some employees with ASD to view the relationship poorly and to experience anxiety. For LMX to work with autism it is important that leaders consistently obtain feedback about their followers' perceptions of the relationship. Leaders may need to be trained on how to create high quality relationships with employees with ASD since LMX may lead to some of the most important outcomes for employees with ASD. For example, employees with high LMX relationships have been found to have improved career development within their organizations (Tangirala, Green, & Ramanuja, 2007). Little research has focused on understanding how a more diverse workforce may affect the development of leader–member exchanges and associated outcomes (Mourino-Ruiz, 2010). This could be an important component of diversity and inclusion training for organizations that are committed to creating positive work relationships for their employees.

CONSIDERATIONS AND RECOMMENDATIONS FOR ORGANIZATIONS AND LEADERS

One of the most challenging issues confronting organizations in the 21st century is how diversity may impact the development of effective working relationships. Organizations and leaders who are committed to developing effective working relationships with their employees with ASD are encouraged to consider the following recommendations. These include developing diversity and inclusion training for coworkers, managers, and supervisors; understanding the costs of accommodating employees with ASD, as well as the benefits; encouraging leaders to develop empathy; developing mentoring programs for employees with ASD; and examining all of the company's human resource programs and policies. A 2014 study of firms hiring employees with disabilities found nine practices that were implemented by a majority of the firms (Erikson, von Schrader, Bruyere & Von Looy, 2014). These nine practices were (a) requiring subcontractors to adhere to disability nondiscrimination requirements, (b) providing training on disability awareness and nondiscrimination, (c) including people with disabilities in the diversity and inclusion plan, (d) allowing extended leave as an accommodation, (e) having relationships with community organizations, (f) having a return to work/disability management program, (g) designating a specific person or office for accommodations, (h) establishing a grievance procedure for reasonable accommodations, and (i) offering flexible work arrangements. The study also found three practices that received very high ratings of effectiveness but which were only implemented by a few organizations. These three practices were formalizing the decision-making process for the case-by-case provision of accommodations, establishing a disability-focused network (employee resource/affinity group), and creating a fund for accommodations.

One of the key issues that organizations will need to consider if they wish to hire and retain employees with ASD is the need to develop diversity and inclusion training for coworkers, managers, and supervisors. Accommodation efforts should include training for all members of the organization to encourage more awareness and sensitivity around issues of disability in the workplace (Neely & Hunter, 2014). These efforts should include an emphasis on understanding the specific needs of employees with ASD such as the need for more frequent and more explicit feedback than managers are used to providing their subordinates. In general, adults with ASD tend to prefer work environments where the instructions and expectations are clearly defined (Lorenz, Frischling, Caudros, & Heinitz., 2016; Wilczynski et al., 2013). Putting performance expectations, work assignments, and deadlines in writing may be helpful. The freedom to focus on one task at a time rather than multitasking may also be helpful for employees with ASD (Lorenz et al., 2016). Being placed in a job that is a good fit and in a structured environment contributes to job satisfaction and positive outcomes at work for adults with ASD (Scott et al., 2015; Wilczynski et al., 2013).

Additionally, organizations that wish to initiate or expand programs to hire more individuals with ASD will need to have a realistic understanding of both the costs and the benefits of accommodating individuals with ASD. Research suggests that adults with ASD may be highly skilled at visual and technical tasks (Baldwin, Costley, & Warren, 2014) and have positive qualities like "honesty, efficiency, precision, consistency, low absenteeism, and a disinterest in 'office politics'" (Baldwin et al., 2014, p. 2440; Richards, 2012). Companies must balance these benefits with the costs of accommodation.

Leaders who wish to develop effective relationships with their followers will also need to become more empathetic. Empathetic leaders may be able to develop more effective individualized relationships with their employees with ASD. Traditional leadership research has often included the need for leaders to empathize with their employees. Empathy is defined as a person's "ability to comprehend another's feelings" (Salovey & Mayer, 1990, p. 194). Wolff, Pescosolido, and Druskat (2002) found that higher levels of empathy predicted better performance for leaders. For those managing employees with ASD, empathy would seem to be an important component of effective leadership, allowing leaders to understand and see problems from the perspective of an employee with ASD. In a recent study, 66% of respondents with ASD said that they would like to have more support in the workplace, including more understanding and respect (Baldwin et al., 2014).

Many organizations that have successfully employed those with ASD stress the importance of providing a mentor, champion, or job coach for that employee (Autism Speaks, 2016). A mentor could provide both career support and psychosocial support (Kram, 1988). Adults with ASD may find mentors inside the workplace through formal mentoring programs or develop informal mentoring relationships with a supervisor or coworker. Mentors and job coaches may be available through autism-specific support agencies and organizations. At SAP, individuals with ASD are given mentors and team buddies. Team buddies are current SAP employees who are willing to team up with a new hire with ASD. SAP also takes advantage of outside agencies that can provide job and/or life skill coaches for the individual (Holland, 2016).

Finally, it is recommended that organizations examine all of their company's human resource programs and policies. For example, in order to attract, select, and retain qualified applicants with ASD, companies must examine their recruitment and selection processes, policies, and practices. It is important to be precise in writing job descriptions because applicants with ASD likely will interpret words and phrases literally. In addition, organizations must question the emphasis that is put on communication skills to determine the required level of competency for various jobs. During the interview, managers must be aware that individuals with ASD may not demonstrate the types of nonverbal behaviors (e.g., eye contact and body language) that are traditionally recommended to job candidates to create a positive impression in the interview. Employees with ASD may struggle with the informal, "small talk" portion of an interview and interviewers may need training to recognize differences in candidates' verbal response patterns. SAP, a company well-known for hiring people with ASD, has an innovative interview process for applicants with ASD. They have the applicants come to their office and work on LEGO Mindstorm projects that increase in difficulty as the day progresses. The second half of the day they participate in team projects. Once hired, employees participate in a five-week training program. The training program was developed by Specialisterne, one of the premiere organizations that hires individuals with ASD (Holland, 2016).

Once hired, managers must be very clear about job tasks, expected performance standards, and the deadlines for completing them. This has implications for the performance appraisal and management process. Performance feedback is important for all employees. With employees with ASD, how the performance feedback is delivered becomes important. It has been found that immediate feedback was important and effective for individuals with disabilities (Barbetta, Heward, Bradley, & Miller, 1994). An interesting stream of research has begun examining the effectiveness of delivering feedback to individuals with ASD covertly through earbud speakers. This way of delivering feedback is called covert audio coaching. A study by Bennett, Brady, Scott, Dukes, and Frain (2010) found that covert audio coaching produced improvements in the participant's job skills and that the skills were maintained over time. Covert audio coaching has many similarities to side-by-side job coaching but may offer long term advantages. One difficulty with side-by-side job coaching is how and when to reduce the presence of the coach from the workplace. Covert audio coaching has an advantage in that as an employee performs better there are less verbal prompts from the coach. It may also be advantageous to have a process where employees with ASD start out with a side-by-side coach and eventually move to a covert audio coaching situation. One limitation of covert audio coaching is that it is only possible with individuals who have excellent attention and receptive language skills (Bennett, Ramasamy, & Honsberger, 2013).

In addition, training and development may help employees with ASD understand their current job and what is required for advancement in the organization. Managers also should be willing to make minor adjustments for qualified employees who may be over-sensitive to workplace stimuli (e.g., bright lights, background noise, etc.). Finally, managers should not force employees with ASD into unnecessary teamwork or social gatherings without their consent (Tickle, 2009). In addition, coworkers of employees with ASD should receive training. At SAP, there is a large effort to train current employees on the benefits of working with individuals with ASD and how they can help make the program a success (Holland, 2016).

CONCLUSION

Considering the fact that that over the next decade, close to half a million people with autism spectrum disorder (ASD) will reach adulthood (Centers for Disease Control and Prevention, 2015), organizations can expect a large increase in the number of potential employees with ASD. In the future, organizations may choose to include individuals with ASD in their workforce for a number of reasons. Some of these may be altruistic reasons. They will also have to respond to legal pressures such as nondiscrimination laws and community pressure from ASD support agencies. However, organizations have to also recognize the benefits that may accrue to them from hiring people with ASD. There is research showing that employees with disabilities have lower absentee rates and lower turnover rates than employees without disabilities. Some individuals with autism enjoy repetitive tasks and look forward to jobs where they can do the same task over and over. This may help reduce the need for job enrichment and job enlargement efforts necessary for organizations to motivate employees in routine jobs. There are also federal tax breaks and various state tax breaks for organizations that hire individuals with ASD. Finally, there are positive reputational effects that may occur for organizations that hire employees with ASD. Organizations that act responsibly by providing meaningful employment for individuals with ASD can contribute to the greater good of society.

While this chapter focused on leaders and managers building relationships with their subordinates with ASD, it should also be recognized that very little is known about the leadership behaviors of managers with ASD. This relationship would call for training for both employees and leaders. Leaders with ASD would need to become aware of how their behaviors may affect their followers. Employees would need to be trained on understanding why the leader acts or speaks in a certain manner. In this situation, the power differential may be reversed with employees having to learn how to manage the relationship with a leader with ASD. LMX with its focus on leader–member relationships (Scandura, 2015) may contribute greatly to understanding the benefits and challenges of leader–member relationships when both individuals have ASD.

REFERENCES

Autism Speaks. (2016). *What is autism?* Retrieved April 2016 from https://www.autismspeaks.org

Baldwin, S., Costley, D., & Warren, A. (2014). Employment activities and experiences of adults with high-functioning autism and asperger's disorder. *Journal of Autism and Developmental Disorders, 44,* 2440–2449.

Barbetta, P. M., Heward, W. L., Bradley, D. M., & Miller, A. D. (1994). Effects of immediate and delayed error correction on the acquisition and maintenance of sight words by students with developmental disabilities. *Journal of Applied Behavior Analysis, 27,* 177–178. doi:10.1901/jaba.1994.27-177.

Bass, B. M., & Avolio, B. J. (1993). Transformational leadership: A response to critiques. In M. M. Chemers, & R. Ayman (Eds.), *Leadership theory and research: Perspectives and directions* (pp. 49–80). San Diego, CA: Academic Press.

Bennett, K., Brady, M. P., Scott, J., Dukes, C., & Frain, M. (2010). The effects of covert audio coaching on the job performance of supported employees. *Focus on Autism and Other Developmental Disabilities, 25*(3) 173–185. doi:10.1177/1088357610371636

Bennett, K. D., Ramasamy, R., & Honsberger, T. (2013). The effects of covert audio coaching on teaching clerical skills to adolescents with autism spectrum disorder. *Journal of Autism and Developmental Disorders, 43,* 585–593. doi:10.1007/s10803-012-1597-6

Boekhorst, J. A. (2015). The role of authentic leadership in fostering workplace inclusión: A social information processing perspective. *Human Resource Management. 54*(2), 241–264.

Brite, R., Nunes, F., & Souza, D. (2015). Labor inclusion of individuals with disabilities: Managers' conceptions as a contributing factor. *Work, 50*(4), 553–561.

Brooks, C. (2016, February 29). 10 workplace trends you'll see in 2016. *Business News Daily.* Retrieved from http://www.businessnewsdaily.com/7616-top-workplace-trends.html

Bruggink, M., Goei, S. L., & Koot, H. M. (2016). Teachers' capacities to meet students' additional support needs in mainstream primary education. *Teachers and Teaching: Theory and Practice, 22*(4), 448–460.

Bruyère, S. (2000). *Disability employment policies and practices in private and federal sector organizations.* Ithaca, NY: Cornell University Extension Division.

Buescher, A. V. S., Cidav, Z., Knapp, M., & Mandell, D. S. (2014). Costs of autism spectrum disorders in the United Kingdom and the United States. *JAMA Pediatric, 8*(168), 721–728.

Centers for Disease Control and Prevention. (2015). *Autism spectrum disorder: Data and statistics.* Retrieved March 2016 from www.cdc.gov/ncbddd/autism/data.html

Chaudoir, S. R., & Fisher, J. D. (2010). The disclosure processes model: Understanding disclosure decision-making and post-disclosure outcomes among people living with a concealable stigmatized identity. *Psychological Bulletin, 136*(2), 236–256.

Cidav, Z., Marcus, S. C., & Mandell, D. S. (2012). Implications of childhood autism for parental employment and earnings. *Pediatrics, 129,* 617–623.

Clair, J. A., Beatty, J. E., & Maclean, T. L. (2005). Out of sight but not out of mind: Managing invisible social identities in the workplace. *The Academy of Management Review, 30*(1), 78–95.

Dansereau, F., Graen, G. B., & Haga, W. (1975). A vertical dyad linkage approach to leadership in formal organizations. *Organizational Behavior and Human Performance, 13,* 46–78.

Dansereau, F., Yammarino, F. J., & Markham, S. E. (1995). Leadership: The multi-level approaches. *Leadership Quarterly, 6,* 251–263.

Davidson, J., & Henderson, V. L. (2010). Travel in parallel with us for a while: Sensory geographies of autism. *The Canadian Geographer, 54*(4), 462–475.

DeJordy, R. (2008). Just passing through stigma, passing, and identity decoupling in the work place. *Group & Organization Management, 33*(5), 504–531.

Dixon, K. A., Kruse, D., & Van Horn, C. E. (2003). *Restricted access: A survey of employers about people with disabilities and lowering barriers to work.* New Brunswick, NJ: Heldrich Center for Workforce Development, Rutgers University.

Domzal, C., Houtenville, A., & Sharma, R. (2008). *Survey of employer perspectives on the employment of people with disabilities: Technical report.* McLean, VA: CESSI.

Donnelly, R. (2015) Tensions and challenges in the management of diversity and inclusion in IT services multinationals in India. *Human Resource Management, 54*(2), 199–215. doi: 10.1002/hrm.21654.

Dutton, J. E., Roberts, L. M., & Bednar, J. (2010). Pathways for positive identity construction at work: Four types of positive identity and the building of social resources. *Academy of Management Review, 35*(2), 265–293.

Dwertmann, D. J. G., & Boehm, S. A. (2016). Status matters: The asymmetric effects of supervisor-subordinate disability incongruence and climate for inclusion. *Academy of Management Journal, 59*(1), 44–64. Retrieved from http://dx.doi.org/10.5465/amj.2014.0093

Erickson, W. A., von Schrader, S., Bruyère, S. M., & Van Looy, S. A. (2014). The employment environment: Employer perspectives, policies, and practices regarding the employment of persons with disabilities. *Rehabilitation Counseling Bulletin, 57*(4), 195–208.

Gärtner, C. (2013). Enhancing readiness for change by enhancing mindfulness. *Journal of Change Management, 13*(1), 52–68.

Gerber, P. J., & Price, L. A. (2003). Persons with learning disabilities in the workplace: What we know so far in the Americans with Disabilities Act era. *Learning Disabilities Research & Practice, 18*(2), 132–136.

Gini, A. (1998). Work, identity and self: How we are formed by the work we do. *Journal of Business Ethics, 17*(7), 707–714.

Goleman, D. (2006). *Emotional intelligence* (10th ed.). New York, NY: Bantam Dell.

Gondo, M., Patterson, K. D. W., & Palacios, S. T. (2013). Mindfulness and the development of a readiness for change. *Journal of Change Management, 13*(1), 36–51.

Graen G. B., & Scandura T. A. (1987). Toward a psychology of dyadic organizing. *Research in Organizational Behavior, 9,* 175–208.

Graen, G. B., & Schiemann, W. (1978). Leader–member agreement: A vertical dyad linkage approach. *Journal of Applied Psychology, 63*(2), 206–212.

Graen, G. B., & Uhl-Bien, M. (1991). The transformation of professionals into self-managing and partially self-designing contributors: Toward a theory of leadership-making. *Management Department Faculty Publications.* Retrieved from http://digitalcommons.unl.edu/managementfacpub/16

Graen G. B, & Uhl-Bien, M. (1995) Relationship-based approach to leadership: Development of leader–member exchange (LMX) theory of leadership over 25 years: Applying a multi-level multi-domain perspective. *Leadership Quarterly, 6*(2), 219–247.

Griffiths, A. J., Giannantonio, C. M., Hurley-Hanson, A. E., & Cardinal, D. (2016). Autism in the workplace: Assessing the transition needs of young adults with autism spectrum disorder *Journal of Business and Management, 22*(1), 5–22.

Hagner, D., & Cooney, B. F. (2005). "I do that for everybody": Supervising employees with autism. *Focus on Autism & Other Developmental Disabilities, 20*(2), 91–97.

Hendricks, D. (2010). Employment and adults with autism spectrum disorders: Challenges and strategies for success. *Journal of Vocational Rehabilitation, 32,* 125–134.

Heslin, P. A., Bell, M. P., & Fletcher, P. O. (2012). The devil without and within: A conceptual model of social cognitive processes whereby discrimination leads stigmatized minorities to become discouraged workers. *Journal of Organizational Behavior, 33*(6), 840–862.

Higgins, K. K., Koch, L. C., Boughfman, E. M., & Vierstra, C. (2008). School-to-work transition and asperger syndrome. *Work, 31*(3), 291–298.

Hillier, A., Campbell, H., Mastriani, K., Izzo, M. V., Kool-Tucker, A., Cherry, L., & Beversdorf, D. Q. (2007). Two-year evaluation of a vocational support program for adults on the autism spectrum. *Career Development for Exceptional Individuals, 30,* 35–47.

Holland, R. (2016, July 11). *The benefits of recruiting employees with cognitive disabilities.* Retrieved from http://www.forbes.com/sites/hbsworkingknowledge/2016/07/11/the-benefits-of-recruiting-employees-with-autism-spectrum-disorder/#728781502f7f

House, R. J. (1971). A path goal theory of leader effectiveness, *Administrative Science Quarterly, 16*(3), 321–339.

Hurlbutt, K., & Chalmers, L. (2004). Employment and adults with asperger syndrome. *Focus on Autism and Other Developmental Disabilities, 19*(4), 215–222.

Judge, T. A., Piccolo, R. F., & Ilies, R. (2004). The forgotten ones? The validity of consideration and initiating structure in leadership research. *Journal of Applied Psychology, 89*(1), 36–51.

Kira, M., & Balkin, D. B. (2014). Interactions between work and identities: Thriving, withering, or redefining the self? *Human Resource Management Review, 24*(2), 131–14.

Kirby, P. C., Paradise, L. V., & King, M. I. (1992). Extraordinary leaders in education: Understanding transformational leadership. *Journal of Educational Research, 85*(5), 303–311.

Kram, K. E. (1988). *Mentoring at work. Developmental relationships in organizational life.* Lanham, MD: University Press of America.

Krieger, B., Kinebanian, A., Prodinger, B., & Heigl, F. (2012). Becoming a member of the workforce: Perceptions of adults with Asperger syndrome. *Work, 43*(2), 141–157.

Leigh, J. P., & Du, J. J. (2015). Brief report: Forecasting the economic burden of autism in 2015 and 2025 in the United States. *Journal of Autism and Developmental Disorders, 45*(12), 4135–4139.

Loi, R., Chan, K. W., & Lam, L. W. (2014), Leader–member exchange, organizational identification, and job satisfaction: A social identity perspective. *Journal of Occupational and Organizational Psychology, 87,* 42–61. doi:10.1111/joop.12028

Loi, R., Mao, Y., & Ngo, H. (2009), Linking leader–member exchange and employee work outcomes: The mediating role of organizational social and economic exchange. *Management and Organization Review, 5,* 401–422. doi:10.1111/j.1740-8784.2009.00149.x

Lorenz, T., Frischling, C., Cuadros, R., & Heinitz, K. (2016). *Autism and overcoming job barriers: Comparing job-related barriers and possible solutions in and outside of autism-specific employment.* Retrieved from http://journals.plos.org/plosone/article?id=10.1371/journal.pone.0147040

Meister, A., Jehn, K. A., & Thatcher, S. M. (2014). Feeling misidentified: The consequences of internal identity asymmetries for individuals at work. *Academy of Management Review, 39*(4), 488–512.

Mouriño-Ruiz, E. L. (2010). Leader–member exchange (LMX): The impact of leader-employee relationships in the 21st century workplace: Implications for research on Latinos in the workforce. *The Business Journal of Hispanic Research, 4*(1), 35–42.

Mynatt, B. S., Gibbons, M. M., & Hughes, A. (2014). Career development for college students with asperger's syndrome. *Journal of Career Development, 41,* 185–198.

National Autistic Society. (2016). *Facts and statistics.* Retrieved April 2016 from www.autism.org.uk

Neely, B. H., & Hunter, S. T. (2014). In a discussion on invisible disabilities, let us not lose sight of employees on the autism spectrum. *Industrial and Organizational Psychology, 7*(2), 274–277.

Nicholas, D. B., Attridge, M., Zwaigenbaum, L., & Clark, M. (2014). Vocational support approaches in autism spectrum disorder: A synthesis review of the literature. *Autism, 19*(2), 235–245.

Parr, A. D., & Hunter, S. T. (2014). Enhancing work outcomes of employees with autism spectrum disorder through leadership: Leadership for employees with autism spectrum disorder. *Autism, 18*(5), 545–554.

Parr, A. D., Hunter, S. T., & Ligon, G. S. (2013). Questioning universal applicability of transformational leadership: Examining employees with autism spectrum disorder. *Leadership Quarterly, 24*(4), 608–622.

Patton, E. (2009). When diagnosis does not always mean disability: The challenge of employees with attention deficit hyperactivity disorder (ADHD). *Journal of Workplace and Behavioral Health, 24*, 326–343.

Pellicano, E., Dinsmore, A., & Charman, T. (2014). What should autism research focus upon? Community views and priorities from the United Kingdom. *Autism, 18*, 756–770.

Ragins, B. R. (2008). Disclosure disconnects: Antecedents and consequences of disclosing invisible stigmas across life domains. *The Academy of Management Review, 33*(1), 194–215.

Ren, L. R., Paetzold, R. L., & Colella, A. (2008). A meta-analysis of experimental studies on the effects of disability on human resource judgments. *Human Resource Management Review, 18*, 191–203.

Richards, J. (2012). Examining the exclusion of employees with asperger syndrome from the workplace, *Personnel Review, 41*(5), 630–646.

Saayman, T., & Crafford, A. (2011). Negotiating work identity. *SA Journal of Industrial Psychology, 37*(1), 1–12. Retrieved from http://dx.doi.org/10.4102/sajip.v37i1.963

Salovey, P., & Mayer, J. D. (1990). Emotional intelligence. *Imagination, Cognition and Personality, 9*(3), 185–211.

Samson, A. C., Huber, O., & Gross, J. J. (2012). Emotion regulation in asperger's syndrome and high-functioning autism. *Emotion, 12*(4), 659–665.

Santuzzi, A. M., Waltz, P. R., Rupp, D., & Finkelstein, L. M. (2014). Invisible disabilities: Unique challenges for employees and organizations. *Journal of Industrial and Organizational Psychology: Perspectives on Science and Practice, 7*(2), 204–219.

Scandura, T. A. (2015). *Essentials of organizational behavior: An evidence-based approach.* Thousand Oaks, CA: SAGE.

Scott, M., Falkmer, M., Girdler, S., & Falkmer, T. (2015). *Viewpoints on factors for successful employment for adults with autism spectrum disorder.* Retrieved from http://journals.plos.org/plosone/article?id=10.1371/journal.pone.0139281

Shattuck, P. T., Narendorf, S. C., Cooper, B., Sterzing, P. R., Wagner, M., & Taylor, J. L. (2012). Postsecondary education and employment among youth with an autism spectrum disorder. *Pediatrics, 129*(6), 1042–9.

Shore, L. M., Chung-Herrera, B. G., Dean, M. A., Ehrhart, K. H., Jung, D. I., Randel, A. E., & Singh, G. (2009). Diversity in organizations: Where are we now and where are we going? *Human Resource Management Review, 19*, 117–133.

Shore, L. M., Randel, A. E., Chung, B. G., Dean, M. A., Ehrhart, K. H., & Singh, G. (2011). Inclusion and diversity in work groups: A review and model for future research. *Journal of Management, 37*(4), 1262–1289. 0149206310385943.

Simic, I. (1998). Transformational leadership–the key to successful management of transformational organizational changes. *Facta Universitas, 1*(6), 49–55.

Sin, H. P., Nahrgang, J.D., & Morgeson, F. P. (2009). Understanding why they don't see eye to eye: An examination of leader–member exchange (LMX) agreement. *Journal of Applied Psychology, 94*(4), 1048–1057.

Sveningsson, S., & Alvesson, M. (2003). Managing managerial identities: Organizational fragmentation, discourse and identity. *Human Relations, 56*(10). doi:10.1177/0018726703561000.1

Stone, D., & Collla, A. (1996). A model of factors affecting the treatment of disabled individuals in organizations. *Academy of Management Review, 21*(2), 352–401.

Tangirala, S., Green, S. G., & Ramanujam, R. (2007). In the shadow of the boss's boss: Effects of supervisors' upward exchange relationships on employees. *Journal of Applied Psychology, 92*(2), 309–320.

Taylor, J. L., & Seltzer, M. M. (2011). Employment and post-secondary educational activities for young adults with autism spectrum disorders during the transition to adulthood. *Journal of Autism and Developmental Disorders, 41*(5), 566–74. doi:10.1007/s10803-010-1070-3

Tickle, L. (2009). Employing adults with autism: Don't write them off. *The Guardian*. Retrieved from www.theguardian.com/money/2009/oct/17/employing-adults-with-autism

Tracy, L. (1987). Consideration and initiating structure: Are they basic dimensions of leader behavior? *Social Behavior and Personality, 15*(1), 21–33.

Wilczynski, S. M., Trammell, B., & Clarke, L. S. (2013). Improving employment outcomes among adolescents and adults on the autism spectrum. *Psychology in the Schools, 50*(9), 876–887.

Wolff, S. B., Pescosolido, A. T., & Druskat, V. U. (2002). Emotional intelligence as the basis of leadership emergence in self-managing work teams. *Leadership Quarterly, 13*, 505–522.

World Health Organization. (2013). *Autism spectrum disorders and other developmental disorders: From raising awareness to building capacity*. Geneva, Switzerland: Author.

Wylson, A., & Chesley, J. A. (2016). The benefits of mindfulness in leading transformational change: Managing ambiguity. *Graziadio Business Review, 19*(1).

Zikic, J., & Hall, D. T. (2009). Toward a more complex view of career exploration. *The Career Development Quarterly, 58*(2), 181–191.

CHAPTER 11

TRANS FORMATIONAL

LMX, Cisgenderism, and Building Inclusive Workplaces

Manuel J. Tejeda
Barry University and Alliance for GLBTQ Youth

ABSTRACT

Conversations about gender identity and expression have become complex, thought-provoking, and prevalent dialogues in contemporary organizational dialogues. Partly responses to legal challenges and partly policy change to improve inclusivity, gender nonconformity have become a central issue in dialogues about and responses regarding corporate diversity. While there should be no doubt that transgender individuals experience the fiercest brunt from violations of cisnormativity, other individuals whose sexual anatomy or gender expression transgress the binary essentialist paradigm experience marginalization as well. The purpose of this chapter is to explore the ways in which the workplace—as both a social and physical environment—is designed to maintain gender essentialism, reinforcing stereotypical representations that restrain gender identity and expression. The chapter first reviews some of the terminology around gender identity and expression focusing predominantly on transgender issues in the workplace. The chapter next describes how the organizational environment aligns to favor cisnormativity and marginalizes those with nonbinary gender or expression by reviewing the current state of empirical and theoretical work on the topic. The chapter then explores the role of leader–member relationships as both a reinforcement of and ultimately a mechanism for dismantling the coded privilege within the workplace and thus promoting inclusivity. Finally, the chapter concludes with recommendations and considerations for organizations and leaders to address workplace cisnormativity.

While contemporary public discourse has increased attention to transgender issues in modern society, acceptance of transgender individuals remains a challenge. Gender identity and expression have become prevalent and thought-provoking topics in organizations today. As gender scholars have noted, organizations are not only imbued within a gender binary social structure, but they are also active agents in securing that sexual duality is consistently reinforced. The interpersonal and interactional aspects of organizations actively reward cisnormativity, the presumption that individuals' performative gender expression is aligned with their sexual assignment. Indeed, organizations are coded social systems designed to promote the privilege of the historically powerful and masculine archetype of the straight White cisgender male. Social interactions—from the interpersonal to the procedural—that comprise the rational and goal-oriented activities of an organization are often complicit in promoting a power hierarchy that maintains that straight White cisgender male archetype as the paragon of the desirable manager to the exclusion or disfavoring of other groups.

Unlike other forms of inequality based on gender and sexuality where overt or even violent expressions of discrimination have become rarified, transgender persons remain targets of interpersonal and institutional discrimination. Current estimates suggest that there are at least some 700,000 trans-identified individuals in the United States (Gates, 2011). And these individuals experience significant challenges in society generally, and the workplace specifically, if not the fiercest of modern discrimination.

In the 2016 U.S. Trans Survey, 6,400 participants exposed some staggering inequities against transgender individuals (National Center for Transgender Equality, 2016). Transgender youth in grades K–12, for example, reported significant experiences with verbal harassment, physical assault, and sexual violence. Adults experienced household incomes below $10,000 per year at rates four times greater than the national average and equally alarming rates of homelessness, housing insecurity, and violent experiences accessing public accommodations. Nearly half of respondents reported attempting suicide.

Data on transgender individuals in the workplace expose some equally serious issues. A stunning 90% of the 2016 U.S. Trans Survey sample reported workplace discrimination with overt mistreatment. Burns and Krehely (2011) also report that 26% of their sample reported losing their employment as a result of being transgender or gender nonconforming. Furthermore, in their aggregation of samples they found between 8% and 17% of sample participants reported being not only overlooked for a promotion, but also overtly informed that they received negative job evaluations because of gender nonconformity. Up to 41% percent experienced verbal violence in their workplaces or had their workstations vandalized. Unable to continue in their work environments, almost 20% sought employment in the underground economy involving illicit drug sales or sex work. Even still, nearly three-quarters of individuals who underwent gender transition reported feeling more comfortable at work despite continued mistreatment, underscoring the dramatic normative forces in play.

Grant et al. (2011) note that transgender individuals represent one of the most vulnerable segments of the current adult population. Moreover, gender role violations are among the most likely of transgressive behaviors to experience significant and severe backlash (Rudman & Fairchild, 2004). The presentation of counternormative behavior attracts immediate attention from workplace colleagues that range from gossip to more overt actions of disapproval, and culminates in the most serious of dangers including interpersonal violence. This is particularly true for men who fail to present with normative role expectations, but impacts all persons who violate binary normativity. Gender conformity is a performative stance that signals to surrounding actors an individual's compliance with a binary gender classification; that is, that individuals are participating in a social schema with a compulsory gender binary. Violations of that performance, as Burns and Krehely (2011) reported, are often immediate and severe.

The workplace climate remains an important area of research regarding gender and gender nonconformity (Ruggs et al., 2013). Yet, there remains significant shortfalls in our understanding of workplace challenges faced by individuals who fail to conform to a gender structure that meets the binary expectations of most organizational leaders and other authorities (Grant et al., 2011).

Indeed, conforming to normative binary gender roles promotes a social safety and offers some refuge from a stigmatized status (Becker, 1963). This is, of course, advantageous in the relatively conservative work environment. Individuals who avoid any ostracism on the basis of their gender nonconformity succeed also in avoiding a host of other adverse outcomes including physical abuse and dehumanization (Crocker, Major, & Steele, 1998)

TRANSGENDER IN THE WORKPLACE

Reflecting on workplace issues related to transgender discrimination is a current managerial imperative for several reasons. First and foremost, discrimination against individuals who are gender nonconforming or transgender (hereafter *transgenders*) is not only malignant but has proven to be metastatic. Substantive research evidence has accumulated attesting to the negative experiences of transgenders in workplace settings and—as like in the general population—ranges from avoidance to bullying and overt harassment to denial of promotion and termination (Levitt & Ippolito, 2014; Dispenza, Watson, Chung, & Brack, 2012; Budge, Tebbe & Howard, 2010). Some experiences shockingly included verbal and organizationally sanctioned challenges to the authenticity of an individual's gender identity (Schilt & Connell, 2007). These experiences materialized from a variety of sources surrounding transgenders including clients, supervisors, and coworkers. The consequences were severe.

Second, all forms of workplace discrimination have interpersonal as well as dynamic, systemic effects. The impact of minute aggressions promotes cultures of exclusion that become increasingly intolerant of diversity and ultimately lead to distilling homogenous workplace (Shore, Randel, Chung, Ehrhart, & Singh, 2011). While such systemic discrimination is illegal in the most Western societies, legal action is typically a last step toward remedy by transgenders. Meanwhile, the normative effects of culture, not only through interpersonal behavior but also through the construction of policy and expectations, can inculcate a recalcitrant system of bigotry whether in the forms of racism, misogyny, heterosexism, transphobia, or any other form of discrimination.

Third, transgenders are a vulnerable population. Not only do all gender nonconforming individuals face unrestrained—even socially sanctioned—discrimination, but such individuals have few legal protections. In the United States, recent rulings by the Equal Employment Opportunity Commission such as *Macy versus Holder* (2012), found on appeal that "discrimination based on gender identity, change of sex, and/or transgender status is cognizable under Title VII" and is a form of sex discrimination. This offers some protection at the federal level in the United States, but narrowly applies to mainly government employees. Broader protections are not available, though there has been legislation proposed such as the Employment Non-Discrimination Act (ENDA) that at this time is still pending passage in the U.S. House of Representatives.

At state and local levels, legal protections against employment discrimination toward transgenders is a patchwork. The states of California, Colorado, Connecticut, Delaware, Hawaii, Illinois, Iowa, Maine, Maryland, Massachusetts, Minnesota, Nevada, New Jersey, New Mexico, Oregon, Rhode Island, Vermont, Washington, and the District of Columbia all have codified protections, but these protections vary. Maine's covers access to credit and education; while Nevada's bans discrimination in employment as well as housing, hospitals, state services and places of business. Finally, many municipalities have responded to offer legal protections where state laws do not exist or do not offer comprehensive protections. The lack of legal recourse also promotes a permissive climate toward discriminatory behavior.

THEORETICAL OVERVIEW

Our models from gender theory and queer theory provide context—and even predict—discrimination against transgenders. Essentialists conceptions of gender have noted that the emergence of gender-based form of oppression emerge from challenges to the socially constructed normative sexual behavior. Scholars have noted that gender goes beyond the classification of sex roles into areas such as milieu stability power differentials (Hawkesworth, 2006). Table 11.1 provides an overview of terminology employed in this article that also has entered use in many organizations.

TABLE 11.1 Transgender Terminology and Definitions for This Chapter

Term	Definition
Binarism/Binarist	The systemic or interpersonal ideology that insists on stable opposites to construct special reality. Binarist refers to an individual espousing this approach.
Bigender	Bigender refers to individuals who experience exactly two gender identities, which while typically male and female may also include nonbinary identities.
Cis	*Cis* is a Latin prefix meaning "one the same side of." This term is sometimes written in prefix form as cis- or as a single word without the dash as an adjective.
Cisgender	Cisgender is an umbrella term to describe persons whose birth-assigned bodies and gender identity are congruent.
Cis-male/cisman	Cis-male or Cis man refers to a male whose birth-assigned body is congruent with his gender identity and expresses culturally normative masculinity.
Cis-woman/cisfemale	Cis-woman or cisfemale refers to a female whose birth-assigned body is congruent with her gender identity and expresses culturally normative femininity.
Cissexism	This terms refers to a systemic or interpersonal ideology that disparages individuals whose gender identities do not confirm to normative expectations of the gender binary.
Cisgenderism	This is a more expansive term than cissexism describing systemic or personal ideology that denigrates the feminine as well persons whose identities challenge normative expectations of gender.

(continued)

TABLE 11.1 Transgender Terminology and Definitions for This Chapter (continued)

Term	Definition
Gender Binary	This term refers to the classification of sex and gender into the distinct, disconnected and opposite forms of masculine and feminine.
Gender Identity	A person's internal sense of one's gender.
Gender Expression	The culturally-fluid, external manifestations of gender that can include appearance, dress, mannerisms and body characteristics.
Gender Fluid	This refers to gender identity where an individual may identify across a gender spectrum over time including being genderless.
Gender Non-Conforming	Individuals whose expression of their gender violates the socially normative and binary expectations of gender.
Genderqueer	This is often a catchall category for all nonbinary gender identities that are not exclusively feminine or masculine. An alternative term for genderqueer is gender-expansive.
Sexual Orientation	An individual's enduring affectional, physical, and romantic attraction to another gender.
Trans	Trans is a Latin prefix meaning "on the opposite side of."
Transgender	This is another umbrella term for persons whose gender identity and/or expression differs from the normative expressions derived from their birth-assigned gender. Note this term is sometimes written as trans*, with the asterisk denoting a wild card for all variations. Leaders in the transgender community have criticized the presence of the asterisk noting that it is redundant, unnecessary and unwelcome, commenting that the asterisk has other uses inconsistent with the wildcard.
Transition	The process of altering one's birth-sex. It is not a "sex change." The process includes social, medical, legal as well as personal steps toward an individual's authentic gender.
Transphobia	The term refers to the dislike, prejudice and aversion to transgender persons. Although commonly used in society, the term cissexism more accurately describes this bias.
Trans man	A gender identity that may be held by an individual who rejects a birth-assigned female gender and identifies/expresses as male.
Trans woman	A gender identity that may be held by an individual who rejects a birth-assigned male gender and identifies/expresses as female.

Special note: Trans and gender fluid terminology is constantly progressing and evolving. This is not an exhaustive list: its purpose is only to offer readers unfamiliar with the area of gender and sexuality some vocabulary related to this chapter. The terminology here is sourced from a variety of experts and journals.

Gender Theory

Gender is a critical component toward organizing relationships, offering rules of normative behavior as well as promoting meaning and context to interpersonal interactions (Harding, 1986). Other theorists have extended that thinking and suggested that gender is an epistemology for understanding how culture defines not only identities but also socially constructs a narrative of belongingness (Hausman, 2001). Social structures are built and reinforced to empower an essentialist social system that attributes personal and interpersonal characteristics to sexual anatomy. As noted by Stryker (1994),

> Bodies are rendered meaningful only through some culturally and historically specific mode of grasping their physicality that transforms the flesh into a useful artifact. ... Gendering is the initial step in this transformation, inseparable from the process of forming an identity by means of which we're fitted to a system of exchange in a heterosexual economy. (p. 249)

The gendering of our world is cemented into our social systems by assertions that binary gendering is an outcome of nature (Garfinkel, 1967). As a result, failure to conform to gender expectations destabilizes relationships whether between a person and a peer or a person and an organization. As Scott (1986) comments,

> Gender is a constitutive element of social relationships based on perceived differences between the sexes, and, gender is a primary way of signifying relationships of power.... Changes in the organization of social relationships always correspond to changes m representations of power. (p. 1067)

Indeed, she adds that this element of gender becomes a powerful organizing force through social institutions (religious, educational, legal, political and even scientific) such that challenging gender binary assertion will result in unequivocal opposition.

Individuals with essentialist views of gender in the workplace, particularly those in positions of power such as supervisors, will be inclined to resist or pathologize attempts to recognize gender nonconformity because it violates the binary interpretation of their social reality (Foucault, 1994). The workplace contains not only the cultural tools of conformity but even the physical devices to support the conformity. While these devices include bathrooms, they include the social behaviors such as recognizing gender using "sir" or "madam," the use of gendered pronouns, and persistently categorizing by gender (Maccoby, 1988). Sadjadi (2013), for example, notes how medical providers subtly advocate for gender conformity and even police interventions that might lead to nonbinary ambiguities during body modification. The process is not overt. It is embedded within the technologies employed by the medical practitioner, and the outcomes are deemed successful if clear sexuality is assigned to trans or intersex individuals.

Indeed, as Weingberg and Cleveland (2017) describe elsewhere in this volume, the process of gendered communication is deeply embedded in organizations and across all person-organization interactions. They identify gender as a deep-level construct firmly entrenched within organizations and enacted in all social situations. These behavioral and communication codes serve to legitimize gendered role interactions and maintain a rigid separation of the masculine and feminine. While they further serve to buttress the male-centered power structure, they equally serve to establish binary-centered role expectations.

Gender theory offers further insights into additional consequences faced by transgenders should they also choose to medically transition. The power structure of the workplace inherently privileges the masculine. As such, gender theory would generally propose (a) that there will be benefits to achieving perceived gender conformity, and (b) that individuals who experience a male-to-female transition would encounter greater adversity or consequences than individuals who experience female-to-male transitions. Indeed, Schilt and Connell (2007) colleagues of the same posttransition gender were more likely to mentor transgenders post transition. In other words, once individuals aligned their bodies medically to a gender binary, they were more likely to receive the benefits of mentoring from other employees of the same sex. As to the second consequence, Schilt (2006) found that female-to-male transgender individuals received higher performance ratings after transition. Moreover, Schilt and Wiswall (2008) reported that male-to-female transgender employees reported a decrease in pay after transition.

Queer Theory

Like gender theory, queer theory explores the architecture of social privilege and power as it is based in heteronormative gender identity and binary-normative compliance (Gamson & Moon, 2004; Herek, 2004; Seidman, 1996). Queer theory represents a direct challenge to an essentialist construction about gender roles and sexual orientation bound to biologically-centered gender-binary heteronormative schema (Kimmel, 1996). It is an attempt to expose the cultural demands of identity (particularly sexual identity) as social constructions that serve to promote oppression (Jagose, 1996). However, it is important to note carefully that transgenders are not necessarily violating heteronormativity, nor does disregarding the gender binary imply a violation of identity, especially as one to resist oppression. Rather, it is the social contraption that enforces identity, and it is that contraption that is opposed by any type of sexual nonconformity.

Discrimination based on sex is a well-understood and elaborated concept in the research literature that penalizes all genders (Uhlmann & Cohen, 2005; Cialdini & Trost, 1998). As Schein (2001) noted, the attributions assigned to women, for example, are divergent from the role qualities society assigns to managerial success such as assertiveness, leadership, and dominance. As an example, Carli (2001) found that women expressing a dominant and assertive communication style—a stereotypically gender inconsistent behavior—were viewed as less influential by males than women who tempered their communication styles with displays of warmth, a stereotypically gender-consistent behavior.

Butler (1999), for example, suggests that identity can be understood as "tenuously constituted in time" through a "stylized repetition of acts" that seek to "approximate the ideal of a substantial ground of identity," which moves various dimensions off the ground of a "substantial model of identity" toward a "constituted social temporality" (p. 179). That is, identity is a performative act learned by individuals and sanctioned by culture. It is an act of performance that validates the socially expected roles dictated by society as well as organizations. And as Landström (2007) notes, through this lens we are able to question the binary exclusivity of such labels as "masculine" and "feminine" regardless of where that binary emerges, whether it be the society or the workplace.

Indeed, as a partial verification of both the social enforcement of role expectations and the impact of performativity, Schilt (2010) found that some transmen gain the social privilege of male sexuality. While transwomen gained the marginalization associated with female gender expression, some transmen gained acceptance and with it the dominance, influence and privilege of the male gender.

Longstanding social forces rooted in essentialist culture are both ubiquitous and unrelenting. Through its effect, heterosexuality continues to be the undisputed norm. And the anticipation of heterosexuality reinforces the social requirement of the gender binary. The expectation of heterosexual behavior buttresses the social need for fixed identities like man/woman and husband/wife and the performances of these roles in a manner that appeases society. Violations of these categories are stigmatized (Becker, 1963) because they violate a form of social trust between individuals. Or differently said, anticipated categories like the performance of husband/wife are betrayed.

The workplace—as it is gender coded—is also heteronormatively coded. Photos of spouses are presumed to be opposite gendered; families are presumed to be biologically-based or matrimonially bound; honeymoon stories and pictures, binary pronouns (whether in speech, policy, or advertising), all bolster normative conformity. Transgressive performances (such as two male partners kissing on their honeymoon) are socially sanctioned oftentimes with a policy restricting any such performances including heterosexual ones (Gedro & Mizzi, 2014; Seidmen, 1996; Tejeda, 2004, 2006).

Queer theory would suggest that transgenders perform in ways that challenge not only the overarching binary role expectations of society, but also challenge the systemic structure that craves individuals who belong to clear and distinct categories whether they are biological, social or otherwise. The response to such transgressions will be swift, protean, and multipronged. As Bornstein (1994) described, transgenders are "gender outlaws" and their "mere presence is often enough to make people sick" (p. 72). And indeed, in a sample of 139 transgender employees, Brewster, Velez, DeBlaere, and Moradi (2012) employed a grounded theory framework to determine the scope of hostilities toward transgenders. The findings suggest a uniform and universal constellation of hostile sources impacting the workplace experience. As expected by theory, hostilities emerged at the interpersonal level with similar reports of experienced bigotry by other researchers. However, this research also exposed the systemic level hostilities (such as bathroom use policies), while others were related to gendered expectations of dress and personal appearance (Herman, 2013).

CISGENDERISM

The term *cisgender* refers to individuals whose assigned sex (that is birth sex) aligns with their gender identity (Schilt & Westbrook, 2009). And there are derivative terms such as *cismale* to describe one whose birth sex is male and whose gender identity is also male. Walls and Costello (2010) extended the use to identify a social privilege that is gained by experiencing the alignment of birth sex and gender identity. As they noted, cisgender privilege is the "set of unearned advantages that individuals who identify as the gender they were assigned at birth accrue solely due to having a cisgender identity" (p. 83). These advantages range from the social to the political to the economic. Most prominently perhaps is that "cisgender individuals don't live with the fear of being targeted for violence, humiliation, and exclusion based on gender identity, nor do they face interrogation about what their bodies look like" (p.83). These privileges both go unnoticed and facilitate daily interactions.

Like heterosexism, cisgenderism refers to the aggregation of these privileges in a manner that denigrates and pathologizes any individual who is gender nonconforming. As Lennon and Mistler (2014) note, this aggregation results in a rigid hierarchy of gender conforming behaviors that has the intent of subordinating violators and enforcing coded gender norms. It extends the term *transphobia* by focusing on oppression as well as aversion.

Understanding trans inclusivity in the workplace requires an understanding of how the workplace is cisgender coded. And promoting inclusivity through mechanisms such as leadership, as will be addressed later in this chapter, requires an understanding of cisgender privilege.

The Cisgender Workplace

As with gender and heterosexism, the workplace is intimately and stubbornly coded to support cisgender privilege. The workplace is neither a neutral nor barrier free environment to transgenders, and their experience has already been documented in the research, as noted earlier in this chapter. However, the nature of privilege is poorly documented in the research literature though clearly scholarship has begun to address it (Lennon & Mistler, 2014; Yarovsky, 2016). Moreover, Schilt (2010) documents how transgender (particularly trans men) can conditionally attain cisgender privileges usually held by birth-assigned males. Nevertheless, while privilege acquisition may be partially socially fluid, its presence can be observed.

Table 11.2 identifies some examples of cisgender privilege in the workplace. Perhaps the most notable of these cisgender privileges, or at least the most commonly discussed, is access to bathrooms without the potential for fear and ridicule. Cisgender individuals rarely if ever question the dangers around using a public bathroom. Yet, by no means the only form. An example of how language frames these observations is an offensive term like "she was born a man"; people are actually born as babies, not adults.

TABLE 11.2 Some Workplace Examples of Cisgender Privilege

1. The use of workplace restroom without fear, intimidation or, in some cases, arrest.
2. The use changing room facilities for jobs requiring uniform or clothes rotations during the day (cf. operating room nurse).
3. Freedom from being asked about genitalia or gender confirmation surgery, privately or publicly.
4. Freedom for being required to have your authentic gender externally validated as a function of how well you "pass."
5. Your identity is not questioned in the context of a pathology.
6. Your identity is not confounded with your suitability to do a job.
7. You have no concerns self-identifying your gender on job applications or on hiring documents.
8. You can readily identify potential role models and mentors.
9. You do not experience justifications about colleagues' behaviors as a context of your gender identity (you are not told that you made a colleague panic).
10. Your name and/or use of pronouns is not questioned.
11. You are able to present legal identification without concern.
12. Gender exclusive spaces and events are accessible without question (for example professional women's networking groups or men's corporate team sport).

LEADERSHIP AND INCLUSIVITY

Management research on diversity has almost focused exclusively on mitigating risks. Shore et al. (2009) note that the research on diversity is dominated by addressing the problems that must be allayed, such as discrimination, tokenism, and bias. Nevertheless, as the research on diversity has developed more attention has centered on addressing organizational mechanisms that promote valuing diversity instead of simple managing it, (Gonzalez & DeNisi, 2009) and the concept of inclusion has been consistently overlooked in the research. Yet, as Riordan (2014) alludes, diversity is irrelevant without inclusivity.

Inclusivity has entered other social sciences such as psychology (cf. Brewer, 1991) and social work (Mor Barak, 2000), but only recently in the organizational literature. Pelled, Ledford, and Mohrman (1999) offered a definition of inclusion as "the degree to which an employee is accepted and treated as an insider by others in a work system" (p. 1014), whereas Miller (1998) defined inclusion as the degree to which diverse individuals "are allowed to participate and are enabled to contribute fully" (p. 151). More recently, though, in an attempt to build a measurement instrument for inclusivity, Roberson (2006) argued that inclusion refers to "the removal of obstacles to the full participation and contribution of employees in organizations" (p. 217). Roberson eventually defined inclusion as

> the way an organization configures its systems and structures to value and leverage the potential, and to limit the disadvantages, of differences. Accordingly, inclusion in organizations would be characterized by different perspectives and by structures, policies, and practices to recognize and use these perspectives, (p. 221)

But the terminology addressing the removal of obstacles, and leveraging potential and configuring systems, inherently suggests leadership as a vehicle for promoting inclusivity.

Recently, Shore and colleagues (2011) drew attention to the lack of research on inclusivity in the organizational literature. They noted that the concept of inclusivity can not only advance our understanding of diversity, but also advances our management practices by offering a more supportive paradigm that supports embracing diversity as a managerial objective. Like Acquavita, Pittman, Gibbons, and Castellanos-Brown (2009) suggest, perceptions of inclusivity can lead to positive workplace outcomes like job satisfaction. Moreover, other work outcomes such as loyalty, cooperation, and trustworthiness among group members enhance the security of individual members (Brewer, 2007). These set of outcomes are important also in the context of leadership as well as how interpersonal roles in organizations are developed.

The diversity literature has been enriched by a significant amount of attention to the role of identification in creating in-groups and out-groups (Ashforth & Mael, 1989). Whereas these represent symbolic categories of attachment to specific groups (ie, Roccas & Brewer, 2002), they are also part of social identities reflecting belongingness. As Shore and her colleagues (2011) note, "Belongingness and uniqueness is an underlying theme in the inclusion literature as well as in some of the diversity literature that is focused on the individual within the group" (p. 1264). These are also important elements of trust and the treatment of individuals as insiders to the work groups, and the local power structure represents interpersonal elements that leaders can address in their interactions with subordinates.

As mentioned, Shore et al. (2011) proposed a framework describing the psychological consequences of promoting inclusivity. The framework is particularly illustrative in understanding both the research on diversity as well as how it is addressed in organization. The model identifies two principle axes: value in uniqueness and value in belongingness (Figure 11.1). When organizations fail to value both uniqueness and belongingness, individuals are not integrated into the social fabric of the organization; individuals are treated as outsiders and they feel excluded. When organizations place low value in uniqueness but high value in belonging ness, individuals experience pressures to assimilate. The organizational culture expresses role expectations, specifically the expectation of conformity. When organizations place high value on uniqueness but low value in belongingness, individual exceptionality is seen as valuable to the organizational culture, but these individuals are not treated as insiders. This quadrant—called differentiation—is particularly relevant to marginalized populations. In this organizational circumstance, minorities are valued but never included.

	Belongingness	
	Low	High
Value in Uniqueness — Low	**Exclusion** Individual is not treated as an insider; but there are no insiders.	**Assimilation** Individual is treated as insiders but they must conform to social norms downplaying their uniqueness.
Value in Uniqueness — High	**Differentiation** Individuals is not treated as an insider but their uniqueness in perceived as valuable to success.	**Inclusion** Individual is treated as an insider and uniqueness is valued/encouraged.

Figure 11.1 Inclusion framework. (*Source:* Shore et al., 2011)

Marginalized populations would feel isolated. Finally, when organizations place high value on both uniqueness and belongingness, they create cultures of inclusivity where individuals feel treated as insiders of a group, and their uniqueness is not just respected but perhaps celebrated. More importantly, though, their uniqueness is not an obstacle for fully participating in their workplace or establishing relationships that promote high opportunity such as the leader–member exchange (LMX) construct.

Indeed, Shore and colleagues (2011) noted that one of the outcomes of inclusive leadership and inclusive practices would be high-quality relations with group members and supervisors in addition to other benefits such as job satisfaction, organizational citizenship, organizational commitment, and career opportunities. However, it seems that these hypothesized relationships could be promoted as effectively through the LMX construct. In fact, the LMX construct has already accumulated the evidence that these same outcomes are the consequence of high-quality relationships.

LMX AND INCLUSIVITY

Leader–member exchange is a prominent leadership theory that understands leader effectiveness through the quality of the exchange relationship between leader and follower. Over the last four decades, research on LMX has been positively related to an significant set of employee outcomes including organizational commitment, organizational citizenship behavior, performance ratings, productivity, job satisfaction, procedural and distributive justice, and perhaps most importantly autonomy, emotional support, and trust (Dansereau, Graen & Haga, 1975; Dunegan, Duchon, & Uhl-Bien, 1992; Graen & Cashman, 1975; Liden & Graen, 1980; Scandura, Graen, & Novak, 1986; Scandura & Pellegrini, 2008; Schreisheim, Neider & Scandura, 1998; Schyns & Day, 2010).

The history of LMX research exposes how the construct has become increasingly relevant and more sophisticated in understanding its role in diversity (Scandura & Lankau, 1996). Early research and theoretical development of the LMX construct focused on the development of trusted assistants who gained (termed in-group) distinct advantages in their working relationship to the leader when compared to the out-group (Graen & Uhl-Bien, 1995). Subsequent research by Graen and Uhl-Bien (1995) exposed a "leader-making" process where key subordinates received an investiture from their leader in the form of affective support that furthered their own ambitions of leadership.

LMX is unique among the leadership theories because it co-occurs with trust and is rooted in social exchange. LMX is not only embedded in the dyadic relationship, but is itself a mechanism for affecting change within and among subordinates, particularly those that belong to the set of trusted followers. Indeed, Scandura and Pellegrini (2008) reported positive associations between LMX and identification-based trust. This type of trust is particularly interesting in that the concept aligns with affective trust (see Lewicki, Wiethoff & Tomlinson, 2005); that is, this type of trust promotes mutual understanding and appreciation in the dyad. High-quality LMX partnerships (and by extension all the partnerships dyads shared with the common leader) exist in a space of high maturity, trust, and obligation (Graen & Uhl-Bien, 1995). Members can promote a mutually supportive climate that provides the affective benefits of loyalty, encouragement, and empowerment while also offering functional career benefits.

LMX has been conceptualized as developing over three important stages (Graen & Uhl-Bien, 1995; Dansereau, Graen & Haga, 1974), each of which may have different implications for nonbinary individuals in the workplace. In the role-taking stage (the first of these stages), a new member joins a group and the leader engages in an overall assessment of their subordinate's fit and capacity to enter a high-quality relationship. More importantly, in this stage the new relationship emerges as the leader and subordinate develop an understanding of each other's views and desires respect. Cisnormativity may present some specific challenges in this area. Both the prevalence of stereotyping, as well as powerful binarism compounded by gender role expectations, may become daunting to the development of a high-quality relationship.

The second of these stages in the LMX relationship involves role-making, that is trust must be developed between the supervisor and subordinate. Again, it is reasonable to hypothesize that the frailty of the novel trust relationship will be complicated by stereotyping and other forms of confirmation bias against gender nonconfirming individuals. Because trust is extraordinarily critical for strengthening and committing to high-LMX relationships, authentic conversations about the cisnormativity will be especially serious in forging the new relationship. Moreover, violations of trust will likely be easy to commit for reasons that range from genuine ignorance about the experiences of transgenders to an overt bias against challenging cis-supremacy in the workplace. Dyadic relationships that reach this stage are likely to be working through their understanding of discriminatory behavior and their experiences with them. Trust as well as perseverance will likely be factors in fostering LMX.

The third and final stage of LMX is role-routinization. At this stage, a mutual obligation between the supervisor and subordinate has crystalized. Arrival at this stage implies that role-making has succeeded. More importantly, though, any pertinent issues about cisnormativity and gender nonconformity have likely been addressed. It seems reasonable to suggest that dyadic partnerships that arrive at this stage have likely already addressed the negative categorizations and stereotyping. The role-routinization stage would likely be a period of relative stability, and the consequences of exposing and addressing cisnormativity have all likely been addressed. While acknowledging and addressing cisnormative barriers may continue to strain and challenge the dyadic relationship, trust should be sufficiently strong and stable enough that the relationship has a far less chance of becoming unstable or decompensating.

Certainly, then, a central hypothesis of this chapter is that LMX will positively moderate the implementation of inclusive policies and strategies in organizations. The mechanism of trust that is embedded in the LMX construct can be an effective facilitator of inclusivity. Thus, LMX can become an avenue—through the relationship linkages—for promoting expansive and permanent change.

LMX, TRANS INCLUSIVITY, AND RECOMMENDATIONS

Inclusivity is a process, and LMX brings, bluntly, nothing unique toward creating transgender specific inclusivity. But as a mechanism that emboldens the presence of trust in the workplace, LMX has the potential for being a powerful vehicle for promoting inclusivity generally and transgender inclusivity specifically. First of all, the construction of a trans-inclusive space will not occur through dictates alone, but they are an obvious and important start. Table 11.3 provides a brief list of opportunities to create trans-inclusive organizations that maximize the potential of their employees and stakeholders. However, one can certainly argue that an immediate supervisor is a particularly critical player in promoting inclusivity and mitigating organizational effects of discrimination, particularly to sexually marginalized individuals (Tejeda, 2008).

While LMX has no bearing, per se, on the writing of such policy, LMX may play an important role in its implementation. Supervisors have the opportunity to leverage their trust networks to facilitate implementation. As the group leader, an immediate supervisor shapes not only the local group

TABLE 11.3 Basic Elements of a Trans Inclusive Workplace

1. Develop, adopt and promote clear, conspicuous and explicit policies that promote a *safe* environment for transgenders.
2. Reinforce organizational values that promote inclusion.
3. Recognize that inclusion is a process.
4. Empower the community of organizational allies through personal networks.
5. Identify cisgender spaces and re-orient them to promote inclusive spaces based on identity rather than birth-assignment.
6. Promote inclusive language in forms, pronouns and policy document.
7. Protect confidentiality.
8. Train employees on issues and inclusivity.

culture, but also filters the organizational impact of organizational policies (Erdogan, Liden & Kramer, 2006). LMX quality influences not just the perception of role fulfillment, but the execution of the implied psychological contract of work (Henderson, Wayne, Shore, Bommer, and Tetrick, 2008). Psychological contract theory (Rousseau, 1995) denotes the structure and arrangements of the beliefs around fulfilling the employee-employer exchange agreement. These beliefs range from pre-employment factors to specific in-job experiences including socialization practices (Aselage & Eisenberger, 2003; Dabos, 2004).

At its core, LMX shapes how employees evaluate their success at work through the supervisory relationship and as a result are motivated to materialize the expectations of high achievement. And there trust is a primary psychological factor. LMX is grounded in the concept of differential treatment of direct reports while also operating at multiple levels (Henderson et al., 2008). This is an advantage of the LMX theory in promoting changes, such as inclusivity, through the direct exchange of behavior and the supportive psychological mechanisms like trust that build safe spaces for inclusivity.

Furthermore, the loyalty and professional respect cultivated by high-LMX relationships can serve as a means to subdue concerns about implementing new policies promoting inclusivity. As Wayne, Shore, and Liden (1997) noted, although LMX has been positively related to perceptions of organizations being supportive, future research attention can certainly explore these conjectures more fully.

One last point of conjecture about LMX is as a vital mechanism promoting inclusivity and specifically a climate supportive of transgenders. The construction of trust, loyalty, and respect, which are all outcomes of high-LMX relationships, is also a relevant mechanism in suppressing aggression and advancing a climate of safety in the workplace. While little research has looked at safety and LMX, some research has addressed retaliation and LMX (Townsend, Phillips, & Elkins, 2000). Indeed, managers who are abusive have little capacity to build and maintain LMX relationships. As Tepper (2000) observed, subordinates experiencing abusive supervision experience workplaces that are significantly less supportive while also reporting increases in psychological distress and work-family conflicts. Furthermore, individuals who are targets of abusive supervision tend to report passive or avoidant coping strategies reducing their engagement of both their supervisor and ostensibly the workplace itself (Tepper, Moss, & Duffy, 2014; Tepper, Moss, Lockhart, & Carr, 2007).

It is equally important to underscore the issue of safety and the possibility that LMX may serve an important function in solidifying a climate of security and respect, because vulnerable populations (like transgenders) routinely, consistently, and emphatically note clinical, consulting, and research venues where safety is a paramount concern. Truly inclusive workplaces must not only address the issue of safety, but become committed to institutionalizing a climate of security as well as patrolling its success. No workplace can be inclusive without the elimination of all forms of interpersonal violence. While again conjecture, there is evidence that LMX can become an important variable for promoting climates of safety.

Recommendations

Leaders are in critical positions to promote those changes at the organizational level. At the individual and group levels, leaders can leverage the trust they cultivate and invest in their followers to expose their support of inclusivity. While leaders may not necessarily have the legitimate power required to enact organizational changes in support of inclusivity, they are competent and capable advocates for it. Demonstrating that advocacy—and competency and genuineness in that advocacy—supports the valuing of belongingness and the valuing of uniqueness.

The evolution toward implementing policies that are supportive of transgenders and gender nonconfirming individuals presents a set of unique challenges that have straightforward implications and solutions. Policies promoting transgender inclusivity also challenge the nexus of gender stereotyping, heterosexism, and the organizational role expectations that link them. In addition, they expose not only individual resistance toward and discomfort with gender role ambiguity, but also organizational social structures that support the discomfort and limit the genuine expression of a person's authentic self.

One cannot underestimate the importance of legitimizing with an organization that discrimination against transgenders or on the basis of any gender nonconformity is unacceptable. Even in jurisdictions where such discrimination is illegal, organizations can still offer their affirmations against discrimination by codifying them into policy. Equally, organizations can offer aspirational and practical statements about their inclusivity and invoke the terminology of belonging and uniqueness as valuable and central elements of their organizational culture. A public commitment to inclusive values is essential to promoting inclusivity.

In addition, organizations should consider the revocation of policies that serve to police gender-centered behavioral expectations, such as policies on the choice of bathrooms. Some establishments have succeeded in creating full gender-inclusive restroom facilities. While the challenge may be more complicated in other facilities that have locker rooms or areas where nudity may occur, policies that entrust employees with their personal judgment regarding the expression of their authentic selves will promote inclusivity far better than statements that lead toward segregation and concern about gender expression.

Organizations should be equally encouraged to expand access to benefits. While marriage equality has now eliminated the restriction of spousal benefits in many parts of the world, it is not a universal privilege. Organizations involving themselves in jurisdictions where such equality is not present can demonstrate their incisive practices by promoting these benefits regardless of location. Furthermore, the continued expanded access to benefits such as bereavement leave, employer-provided supplemental life insurance for partners, adoption assistance, joint/survivor annuity for partners, retirements benefits, and even access to employee discounts are continuing affirmations of inclusivity.

But to promote specific inclusivity for the entire community, organizations are encouraged to enact health insurance coverage that focuses specifically on the health needs of transgenders. Specifically, organizations would be encouraged to promote policies that have blanket coverage with no exclusions from care based on gender nonconformity. Furthermore, organizations can examine their policies to ensure they are consistent with the World Professional Association for Transgender Health (WPATH) Standards of Care, while also including appropriate mental health benefits, pharmaceutical benefits, and reconstructive surgery benefits associated with sex reassignment and other services around sex transition.

Finally, opportunities for continued training, merit access, and dialogue should be obvious and present. These would include the formation of a diversity council with a clear and specific charge to examine issues around trans inclusivity. Moreover, organizations can offer not only continued training on matters related to gender nonconformity, but also embed that training during the socialization at the time of hire. Involvement in continued training should be equally required of individuals at all levels. And for organizations wanting to demonstrate a full commitment, linking merit and pay increases to the documented participation in diversity seminars broadly and seminars on trans inclusivity and gender conformity more specifically, in essence, organizations desiring to maximize their obvious support for inclusivity, will demonstrate an overall leveraging of their resources to sustain an accountable and measureable commitment to diversity.

CONCLUDING REMARKS

History has already documented the progressive stance of businesses regarding inclusivity. On the question of sexual diversity, Fortune 500 businesses were part of the vanguard that adopted protections for gay and lesbian employees in the early 1970s. The same remains true today. The number of employers with transgender inclusive policies continues to expand. The Human Rights Campaign's annual Corporate Equality Index

(2016) identified 511 large employees with trans*[1] inclusive policies, nearly 10 times more employers that had such policies than in 2009. Moreover, there is a growing demand that managers and other administrative professionals be reasonably literate on transgender discrimination.

A critical assertion of this chapter is that LMX can be an important and possibly overlooked mechanism for promoting and supporting inclusivity. LMX may prove to be an important relational variable to reduce inclusivity resistance as well as shape workplace environments that leverage the benefits in diversity. Besides, there's little downside risk in cultivating high-quality LMX relationships. The benefits secured by high-quality LMX relations worth every effort to promoting that managers adopt the skills needed to engage in high-quality relationships. The climate of trust cultivated by LMX is not just vital for inclusivity it must be a hallmark of effective leadership.

NOTE

1. This term is sometimes written as trans* with the asterisk denoting a wild card for all variations. Leaders in the transgender community have criticized the presence of the asterisk noting that it is redundant, unnecessary, and unwelcome, commenting that the asterisk has other uses inconsistent with the wildcard.

REFERENCES

Acquavita, S. P., Pittman, J., Gibbons, M., & Castellanos-Brown, K. (2009). Personal and organizational diversity factors' impact on social workers' job satisfaction: Results from a national Internet-based survey. *Administration in Social Work, 33*, 151–166.

Aselage, J., & Eisenberger, R. (2003). Perceived organizational support and psychological contracts: A theoretical integration. *Journal of Organizational Behavior, 24*(5), 491–509.

Ashforth, B. E., & Mael, F. 1989. Social identity theory and the organization. *Academy of Management Review, 14*, 20–39.

Becker, H. S. (1963). *Outsiders: Studies in the sociology of deviance.* Chicago, IL: University of Chicago Press.

Bornstein, K. (1994). *Gender outlaw: On men, women, and the rest of us.* New York, NY: Routledge.

Brewer, M. B. (1991). The social self: On being the same and different at the same time. *Personality and Social Psychology Bulletin, 17*, 475–482.

Brewer, M. B. (2007). The importance of being we: Human nature and intergroup relations. *American Psychologist, 62*, 728–738.

Brewster, M. E., Velez, B., DeBlaere, C., & Moradi, B. (2012). Transgender individuals' workplace experiences: The applicability of sexual minority measures and models. *Journal of Counseling Psychology, 59*, 60–70.

Budge, S. L., Tebbe, E. N., & Howard, K. A. S. (2010). The work experiences of transgender individuals: Negotiating the transition and career decision-making processes. *Journal of Counseling Psychology, 57,* 377–393.

Burns, C., & Krehely, J. (2011). *Gay and transgender people face high rates of workplace discrimination and harassment.* Retrieved October 1, 2016, from https://cdn.americanprogress.org/wp-content/uploads/issues/2011/06/pdf/workplace_discrimination.pdf

Butler, J. (1999). *Gender trouble: Feminism and the subversion of identity* (10th ed.). New York, NY: Routledge.

Carli, L. L. (2001). Gender and social influence. *Journal of Social Issues, 57,* 725–741.

Cialdini, R. B., & Trost, M. R. (1998). Social influence: Social norms, conformity, and compliance. In D. Gilbert & S. Fiske, (1998). *Handbook of social psychology* (Vol. 2, pp. 151–192). Boston, MA: McGraw Hill.

Crocker, J., Major, B., & Steele, C. (1998). Social stigma. In D. Gilbert & S. Fiske, *Handbook of social psychology,* (Vol. 2, pp 504–553). Boston, MA: McGraw Hill.

Dabos, G. E., & Rousseau, D. M. (2004). Mutuality and reciprocity in the psychological contracts of employees and employers. *Journal of Applied Psychology, 89*(1), 52–72.

Dansereau, F., Graen, G. B., & Haga, W. J. 1975. A vertical dyad linkage approach to leadership within formal organizations: A longitudinal investigation of the role making process. *Organizational Behavior and Human Performance, 13,* 46–78.

Dispenza, F., Watson, L. B., Chung, Y. B., & Brack, G. (2012). Experience of career-related discrimination for female-to-male transgender persons: A qualitative study. *The Career Development Quarterly, 60,* 65–81.

Dunegan, K. J., Duchon, D., & Uhl-Bien, M. (1992). Examining the link between leader–member exchange and subordinate performance: The role of task analyzability and variety as moderators. *Journal of Management, 18,* 59–76.

Erdogan, B., Liden, R. C., & Kraimer, M. L. (2006). Justice and leader–member exchange: The moderating role of organizational culture. *Academy of Management Journal, 49,* 395–406.

Foucault, M. (1994). *An archaeology of the human sciences.* New York, NY: Vintage Books.

Gamson, J., & Moon, D. (2004). The sociology of sexualities: Queer and beyond. *Annual Review of Sociology, 30,* 47–64.

Garfinkel, H. (1967). *Studies in ethnomethodology.* Englewood Cliffs, NJ: Prentice-Hall.

Gates, G. J. (2011, April). *How many people are lesbian, gay, bisexual, and transgender?* Los Angeles, CA: The Williams Institute at UCLA School of Law. Retrieved August 15, 2016, from http://williamsinstitute.law.ucla.edu/wp-content/uploads/Gates-How-Many-People-LGBT-Apr-2011.pdf

Gedro, J., & Mizzi, R. (2014). Feminist theory and queer theory: Implications for HRD research and practice. *Advances in Developing Human Resources, 6*(4), 445–456.

Gonzalez, J. A., & DeNisi, A. S. (2009). Cross-level effects of demography and diversity climate on organizational attachment and firm effectiveness. *Journal of Organizational Behavior, 30*(1), 21–40.

Graen, G. B., & Cashman, J. (1975). A role-making model of leadership in formal organization: A developmental approach. In J. G. Hunt & L. L. Larson (Eds.), *Leadership frontiers*. Kent, OH: Kent State University Press.

Graen, G. B., & Uhl-Bien, M. (1995). Relationship-based approach to leadership: Development of leader–member exchange (LMX) theory of leadership over 25 years: Applying a multi-level multi-domain perspective. *Leadership Quarterly, 6*(2), 219–247.

Grant, J. M., Mottet, L. A., Tanis, J., Harrison, J., Herman, J. L., & Keisling, M. (2011). *Injustice at every turn: A report of the national transgender discrimination survey*. Washington, DC: National Center for Transgender Equality and National Gay and Lesbian Task Force.

Harding, S. (1986). *The science question in feminism*. Ithaca, NY: Cornell University Press.

Hausman, B. L. (2001). Recent transgender theory. *Feminist Studies, 27*, 465–490

Hawkesworth, M. (2006).Gender as an analytic category. In M. Hawkesworth (Ed.), *Feminist inquiry: From political conviction to methodological innovation* (pp. 145–175). New Brunswick, NJ: Rutgers University Press.

Henderson, D. J., Wayne, S. J., Shore, L. M., Bommer, W. H., & Tetrick, L. E. (2008). Leader–member exchange, differentiation, and psychological contract fulfillment: A multilevel examination. *Journal of Applied Psychology, 93*(6), 1208–1219.

Herek, G. M. (2004). Beyond "homophobia": Thinking about sexual stigma and prejudice in the twenty-first century. *Sexuality Research and Social Policy, 1*(2), 6–24.

Herman, J. L. (2013). Gendered restrooms and minority stress: The public regulation of gender and its impact on transgender people's lives. *Journal of Public Management & Social Policy, 19*, 65–80.

Jagose, A. (1996). *Queer theory*. Melbourne, Australia: Melbourne University Press.

Kimmel, M. (1996). *Manhood in America: A cultural history*. New York, NY: Free Press.

Landström, C. (2007). Queering feminist technology studies, *Feminist Theory, 8*(1), 7–26.

Lennon, E., & Mistler, B.J. (2014). "Cisgenderism." *Transgender Studies Quarterly, 1*(1/2), 63–64. doi:10.1215/23289252-2400136

Levitt, H. M., & Ippolito, M. R. (2014). Being transgender: Navigating minority stressors and developing authentic self-presentation. *Psychology of Women Quarterly, 38*, 46–64. doi: 10.1177/0361684313501644

Lewicki, R. J., Wiethoff, C., & Tomlinson, E. C. (2005). What is the role of trust in organizational justice? In J. Greenberg & J. A. Colquitt (Eds.), *Handbook of organizational justice* (pp. 247–270). Mahwah, NJ: Erlbaum.

Liden, R., & Graen, G.B. (1980). Generalizability of the vertical dyad linkage model of leadership. *Academy of Management Journal, 23*, 451–465.

Maccoby, E. E. (1988). Gender as a social category. *Developmental Psychology, 24*, 755–765.

Miller, F. A. (1998). Strategic culture change: The door to achieving high performance and inclusion. *Public Personnel Management, 27*, 151–160.

Mor Barak, M. E. (2000). Beyond affirmative action: Toward a model of diversity and organizational inclusion. *Administration in Social Work, 23*(3/4), 47–68.

National Center for Transgender Equality. (2016). *National transgender discrimination survey*. Retrieved on August 14, 2016, from http://www.transequality.org/issues/national-transgender-discrimination-survey

Pelled, L. H., Ledford, G. E., & Mohrman, S. A. 1999. Demographic dissimilarity and workplace inclusion. *Journal of Management Studies, 36,* 1013–1031.

Riordan, C. M. (2014, June 5). Diversity is useless without inclusivity. *Harvard Business Review.* Retrieved from https://hbr.org/2014/06/diversity-is-useless-without-inclusivity/

Roberson, Q. M. (2006). Disentangling the meanings of diversity and inclusion in organizations. *Group and Organization Management, 31,* 212–236

Roccas, S., & Brewer, M. B. 2002. Social identity complexity. *Personality and Social Psychology Review, 6,* 88–106.

Rousseau, D. (1995). *Psychological contracts in organizations: Understanding written and unwritten agreements.* Newbury Park, CA: SAGE.

Rudman, L. A., & Fairchild, K. (2004). Reactions to counterstereotypic behavior: The role of backlash in cultural stereotype maintenance. *Journal of Personality and Social Psychology, 87,* 157–176.

Ruggs, E. N., Law, C., Cox, C., Roehling, M. V., Wiener, R. L., Hebl, M. R., & Barron, L. (2013). Gone fishing: I-O psychologists' missed opportunities to understand marginalized employees' experiences with discrimination. *Industrial and Organizational Psychology: Perspectives on Science and Practice, 6,* 39–60. doi:10.1111/iops.12007

Sadjadi, S. (2013). The endocrinologist's office-puberty suppression: Saving children from a natural disaster? *Journal of Medical Humanities, 34,* 255–260.

Scandura, T. A., Graen, G. B., & Novak, M. A. (1986). When managers decide not to decide autocratically. An investigation of leader–member exchange and decision influence. *Journal of Applied Psychology, 71,* 579–584.

Scandura, T. A., & Lankau, M. J. (1996). Developing diverse leaders: A leader–member exchange approach. *The Leadership Quarterly, 7*(2), 243–263.

Scandura, T. A., & Pellegrini, E. K. (2008). Trust and leader–member exchange: A closer look at relational vulnerability. *Journal of Leadership and Organization Studies, 15,* 101–100.

Schein, V. E. (2001). A global look at psychological barriers to women's progress in management. *Journal of Social Issues, 57,* 675–688.

Schilt, K. (2006). Making gender visible: Transmen as "outsiders-within" in the workplace. *Gender & Society, 20*(4), 465–90.

Schilt, K. (2010). *Just one of the guys? Transgender men and the persistence of gender inequality.* Chicago, IL: University of Chicago Press.

Schilt, K., & Connell, C. (2007). Do workplace gender transitions make gender trouble? *Gender, Work & Organization, 14,* 596–618. doi:10.1111/j.1468-0432.2007.00373.x

Schilt, K., & Westbrook, L. (2009). Doing gender, doing heteronormativity: Gender normals, transgender people, and the social maintenance of heterosexuality. *Gender & Society, 23*(4), 440–464. doi:10.1177/0891243209340034.

Schilt, K., & Wiswall, M. (2008). Before and after: Gender transitions, human capital, and workplace experiences. *Contributions in Economic Analysis & Policy, 8*(1), 1862–1862

Schriesheim, C. A., Neider, L. L., & Scandura, T. A. (1998). Delegation and leader–member exchange: Main effects, moderators, and measurement issues. *Academy of Management Journal, 41,* 298–318.

Schyns, B., & Day, D. (2010). Critique and review of leader–member exchange theory: Issues of agreement, consensus, and excellence. *European Journal of Work and Organizational Psychology, 19*(1), 1–29.

Scott, J. W. (1986). Gender: A useful category of historical analysis. *The American Historical Review, 91,* 1053–1075.

Seidmen, S. (1996). *Queer theory sociology.* Oxford, England: Wiley-Blackwell.

Shore, L. M., Chung, B., Dean, M. A., Ehrhart, K. H., Jung, D., Randel, A., & Singh, G. (2009). Diversity and inclusiveness: Where are we now and where are we going? *Human Resource Management Review, 19,* 117–133.

Shore, L. M., Randel, A. E, Chung, B. G., Ehrhart, K. H., & Singh, G. (2011). Inclusion and diversity in work groups: A review and model for future research. *Journal of Management, 37,* 1262–1289. DOI: 10.1177/0149206310385943

Stryker, S. (1994). My words to Victor Frankenstein above the village of Chamounix: Performing transgender rage. *GLQ: A Journal of Lesbian and Gay Studies, 1,* 237–254.

Tejeda, M. J. (2004). Egalitarianism and self-esteem as correlates of hate ideation against gay men and lesbians. *Journal of Multicultural Nursing and Health, 10*(1), 42–50.

Tejeda, M. J. (2006). Non-discrimination policies and sexual identity disclosure: Do they make a difference in employee outcomes? *Employee Rights and Responsibilities Journal, 18,* 45–59.

Tepper, B. J. (2000). Consequences of abusive supervision. *Academy of Management Journal, 43*(2), 178–190.

Tepper, B. J., Moss, S. E., & Duffy, M. K. (2011). Predictors of abusive supervision: Supervisor perceptions of deep-level dissimilarity, relationship conflict, and subordinate performance. *Academy of Management Journal, 54*(2), 279–294.

Tepper, B. J., Moss, S. E., Lockhart, D. E., & Carr, J. C. (2007). Abusive supervision, upward maintenance communication, and subordinates' psychological distress. *Academy of Management Journal, 50*(5), 1169–1180.

Townsend, J., Phillips, J. S., & Elkins, T. J. Employee retaliation: The neglected consequence of poor leader–member relations. *Journal of Occupational Health Psychology, 5,* 457–463.

Uhlmann, E. L., & Cohen, G. L. (2005). Constructed criteria: Redefining merit to justify discrimination. *Psychological Science, 16,* 474–480

Walls, N. E., & Costello, K. (2010). Head ladies center for teacup chain: Exploring cisgender privilege in a (predominately) gay male context. In S. Anderson & V. Middleton, *Explorations in diversity: Examining privilege and oppression in a multicultural society* (pp. 81–94). Florence, KY: Brooks Cole.

Wayne, S., Shore, L. M., & Liden, R. C. (1997). Perceived organizational support and leader–member exchange: A social exchange perspective. *Academy of Management Journal, 40,* 82–111. doi:10.2307/257021

Weinberg, F. J., & Cleveland, A. O. (2017). Gender as a deep-level, communicated, and interactional construct: Implications for leaders, subordinates, and teammates. In T. A. Scandura & E. Mouriño (Eds.), *Leading diversity in the 21st century* (pp. 27–54). Charlotte, NC: Information Age.

Yarovsky, J. E. (2016). Cisgendered organizations: Trans women and inequality in the workplace. *Sociological Forum,* 1–22. doi:10.1111/socf.12291

CHAPTER 12

SOCIAL MEDIA, INNOVATION, AND DIVERSITY IN THE 21ST CENTURY

Pamela McCauley
University of Central Florida

Edwin Nassiff
InfoSec Intelligence, LLC

ABSTRACT

Due to dynamic changes in technology and accessibility, collaboration is evolving such that it no longer demands that a person or group be physically present to have a meeting, share research, thoughts, or ideas. As a result, teams focused on innovation and collaboration have broader opportunities to engage stakeholders and enhance diversity to support organizational goals. This chapter provides an in-depth look at the scientific communities' response to social media tools, the criticality of innovation, and how a social media platform can be used to promote innovation, diversity, and collaboration. Specific details are provided about the ongoing development of Algonite as a social media platform to connect scientists for the purpose of innovation and diversity.

WHY INNOVATION IS SO CRITICAL IN THE CURRENT SCIENTIFIC GLOBAL COMMUNITY

Innovation is essential in all phases of scientific development, particularly in the creation and diffusion of technologies, which are essential for financial development and welfare throughout all economies. Various kinds of innovation play a role at different stages. True innovation is also a product of collaboration, team effort, and representation from all stakeholders on the innovation team.

In the context of global competition, there are cumulative societal difficulties in regards to the scientific, environmental, demographic, social, and financial sustainability. Nations need to urgently improve their innovative capacity and should promote a culture of development that enables and motivates all people, research organizations, firms, the entire public sector, and other actors of society to actively promote innovation in science. Innovation is not just the subject of the moment, the future of science depends on it.

According to Gerschenkron (1962), the differences in a nation's ability to innovate, develop, and adjust to their specific situations was the main reason for differences in per capita income among nations, and the ability to utilize the innovations of others is of essence. However, innovative activities emanating beyond "knowledge-intensive" sectors can offer considerable opportunities for success. Examples consist of the effective exports of fish from Uganda, wine from Argentina and Chile, and medicinal plants from India. In the initial phases, innovation adoption with small developments is rewarding and successful (Acemoglu, Aghion, & Zilibotti, 2006). Innovations in established countries like Korea, China's Taipei and Hong Kong, and Singapore began with an initial phase of advancement based upon technology know-how and by maintaining a strong focus on structure innovation capacity, which led to more innovations.

Innovation matters even in the most underdeveloped countries with backward economies. Their adoption of foreign innovations has had high rewards since innovation adoption requires adjustment to regional financial, technological or ecological conditions. This can cause the advancement and build-up of innovation capabilities. There is proof that domestic innovation played a larger role than importing knowledge when the emerging Asian economies began to explode (Ang & Madsen, 2011).

What Innovation Means in Science

According to the Frascati Manual of the Organization for Economic Cooperation and Development (OECD, 2013), scientific and technological innovation encompasses the transformation of an idea into a new or improved saleable product, an operational process in industry or commerce, or into a new approach in social service. Thus, it consists of those scientific, technical, commercial, and financial steps that are necessary for the successful development and marketing of new or improved manufactured products, the commercial use of new or improved processes and equipment, or the introduction of a new approach to a social service (Semolic, 2008).

The term innovation can have different significances in various contexts, and the one chosen will depend upon the particular goals of measurement or analysis. Scientific and technological innovation may be thought of as the change of an idea into a new or enhanced product presented on the market, into a new or improved functional procedure utilized in industry and commerce, or into a brand-new method for a social service (Semolic, 2008).

The use of innovation in science can offer numerous insights over the technological management of any economic activity, market, or particular organization, and their performance on innovation can assist in shaping tactical decisions. For example, policymakers may see a declining innovative capacity in some sectors or markets, which may indicate the need to develop brand-new policies. For example, these policies may lead to the improvement of educational facilities for certain technological fields that are closely associated to how an innovation in science can be enhanced (Semolic, 2008).

In addition, organizations enhancing their innovation in science might depend on designating more resources for research and advancement (R&D), participating in research study alliances along with other organizations, promoting first-mover research, or contracting out nonresearch activities. Preferences in all of those elements can be informed by analyses of innovative capability over time. Comparisons of the stages of innovativeness between markets or between companies in any sector can also offer indications of sound technological management (Semolic, 2008).

Why Diversity Matters in Development

Today, most managers agree that organizations benefit from a diverse workforce; however, the idea can be hard to quantify or prove particularly when it pertains to determining how diversity affects an organization's ability to innovate. However, new research provides engaging evidence that diversity opens innovation and drives market development, a finding that should enhance management's interests in ensuring diversity at various levels of the organization.

Decades of research by organizational researchers, sociologists, psychologists, financial experts, and demographers reveal that socially varied groups (that is, those with a diversity of race, ethnic culture, gender, and sexual orientation) are more innovative than homogeneous groups (Phillips, 2014).

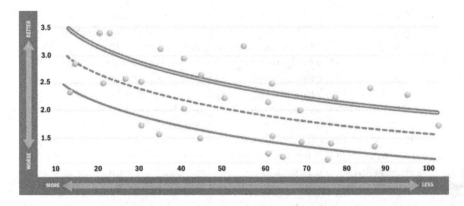

Figure 12.1 Proof that diversity drives innovation (Fan, 2011).

A study by Fan (2011) addressed the importance of diversity in innovation. In an empirical study conducted by Ron Burt of the University of Chicago, it was found that individuals with more diverse sources of information consistently created better ideas. (Figure 12.1).

On the graph, the vertical axis shows management evaluations of a series of employee concepts connected to supply-chain management. The horizontal axis measures the level of diversity in a worker's internal connection. As you move to the right, the concepts become less diverse, which results in a lower level of ratings of the concepts. The study also suggests that the lack of diversity in connections is representative of the lack of diversity in their daily interactions, which negatively impacts the level of innovation. Finally, the chart illustrates that greater diversity of connections means the development and presentation of better quality ideas and concepts, which is a basic component of innovation (Fan, 2011).

We found that many companies today are becoming more deliberate about leveraging diversity to stimulate innovation. For example, the U.S. based multinational retailer Walmart continues to develop a diverse worldwide workforce by engaging world-class skills through innovative techniques, such as their Women in Retail initiative and their Junior Military Officer hiring program through community and school outreach efforts. This is clearly an example of the sensitivity and efforts of this company to engage, support, and promote diversity within their organization.

How Collaboration and Connecting With Others Facilitates Innovation and Diversity

Collaboration is an increasingly common mode to organize work within and between companies (Chen, Rainie, & Wellman, 2012). Current advances in information and communication technologies (ICTs) make it possible for people to engage in collaborative work by linking and working together much more efficiently and effectively with their coworkers and clients. Thus, collaboration has made it possible to facilitate innovation. Collaborating workers can communicate quickly and frequently through space and time utilizing various types of ICTs, while allowing organizations to be more versatile and team based, as well as utilizing a flatter, decentralized structure (Gladwell, 2000).

Such networks hold the promise that ICTs will lead to better sharing and usage of information, and for that reason individuals and teams will be more effective in accomplishing innovative tasks (Barta, Kleiner, & Neumann, 2012; Burt, 2010; Wu, Lin, Aral, & Brynjolfsson, 2009). This quality of collaboration is especially essential given the fact that innovation is critical to attaining competitive advantages and organizational sustainability. Furthermore, collaboration applies to virtually every industry ranging from scientific research to entertainment productions to entrepreneurial ventures (Taylor & Greve, 2006; Wuchty, Jones, & Uzzi, 2007).

In Williams & O'Reilly's (1998) 40-year evaluation of diversity, it was observed that diversity of knowledge works best in idea generation and workgroup efficiency. It was shown that greater cognitive diversity created more efficiency from an informational and decision-making perspective (Taylor & Greve, 2006). For example, when specific team members had varied backgrounds, skills, capabilities, information, and understanding, they were most likely to look for solutions and options that helped to connect disconnected ideas that may not have been previously connected. This in turn generated more innovation (Guimera, Uzzi, Spiro, & Amaral, 2005)).

How Social Media Is Changing the Way We Connect and Collaborate

Social media is an umbrella term used to refer to a group of online and electronic tools that may include blogs, social networking websites, and video sharing websites (CDC, 2012).

Social networks have actually significantly changed how we receive information, connect with others, and monitor a situation and share information. Prior technologies included landline telephones, regular mail service, and more recently electronic mail, Skype, and other information based electronic modes of communication. However today, we are migrating to more advanced technologies such as text messaging, mobile phones, earphones, and online video chats as well as other resources found on the web. The next wave of connectivity will emphasize access for larger groups for the purposes of professional networking and personal communications as well as discovery and innovation. Through these means of social media, the approach, expectations, and intention of electronic communications is being redefined.

Such a redefinition has actually had an enormous impact. The whole paradigm of social media has changed the fundamental guidelines of communication, especially between organizations and their audiences. The one-way communication methods of the past (i.e., business-to-customer and business-to-business) have actually been replaced by a more dynamic multidimensional interaction model. This social media model promotes exchange of information between organizations/individuals and their audiences by inviting involvement. In turn, this leads to broader user engagement; however, the full impact of this engagement is not yet fully understood. What is understood is that there is a broad interest in connecting to these social media sites among individuals and organizations, and that the sites that are most successful provide fast access along with a collaborative platform that is intuitively organized and easily distributes information.

According to Perrin (2015), 65% of American adults have friends and other connections such as followers on their social network accounts. The nature of connecting with multiple individuals and sites can produce synergism within a social media environment. This is because individuals' connections can grow not only on their own network, but through links to other sites and individuals as well as other resources such as automatic feeds.

THE RISE OF SOCIAL MEDIA

The Internet and Social Networking

It is estimated that there are 3.6 billion Internet connections worldwide (Stats, 2016) and 2.3 billion social media users (Smith, 2016). In terms of information passed through the Internet, Cisco predicts there will be 1,000 exabytes or one zettabyte of Internet global IP traffic by the end of 2016 and 2.3 zettabytes by 2020 (Cisco, 2016). In terms of online activities, social networking clearly surpasses the use of email, news, and online shopping as reasons why people use the Internet (Ribia-García, Elichc-Qucsada, Rus-Casas, & Aguilar-Pena, 2016).

Cheung, Lee, and Chan (2015) revealed that people spend much more time on social networking than any other online activities. In fact, much of their privacy information is revealed when a social network requires the user to create a social profile including such personal information as photographs, current status, and personal preferences or experiences (Cheung, Lee, & Chan, 2015).

Why People Use Social Networking

Research performed on 405 social networking sites indicated that social influence was the greatest reason why people use social media, and that has an overriding effect in terms of disclosing any of their privacy information (Cheung, Lee, & Chan, 2015). In another study, it was indicated that 93% of students connected to the Internet have one or more active accounts in social networks. Not only did the students use their social networks for gaining information, but also used them for building an identity and establishing personal and professional relationships. In essence, social networking was used to establish and reinforce relationships and to feel a part of a community or a group (Ribia-García, Elichc-Qucsada, Rus-Casas, & Aguilar-Pena, 2016).

Over the years, researchers have attempted to build theoretical models to explain how networks have the ability to impact both individual and organizational capabilities (Sherif, Munasinghe, & Sharma, 2012). The term "social capital" is used to mean all of the resources and benefits bestowed to an individual or group of individuals when linked in a durable network with institutionalized relationships of shared acquaintance and recognition (Bourdieu & Wacquant, 1992). Social capital leads to knowledge sharing and helps facilitate the creation of new knowledge (Sherif, Munasinghe, & Sharma, 2012).

There are three recognized dimensions of social capital: structure, relationship, and cognition (Sherif, Munasinghe, & Sharma, 2012). The structure dimension refers to the information channel that connects individuals or groups on a network, as well as the extent to which members are linked to others in the group (Sherif, Munasinghe, & Sharma, 2012).

The second dimension of social capital is relational and it refers to the resources embedded in relationships that are usually developed over time, such as the trust and the trustworthiness of all of its members. A strong relational membership between members enhances the evolution of social norms, which can engender obligations and responsibilities as well as cooperation in transforming and exploiting new knowledge (Sherif, Munasinghe, & Sharma, 2012).

The last dimension of social capital is cognition, i.e., the shared meanings that develop among network members that result through social interaction. Shared meanings lead to knowledge transfer, understanding, and assimilation of knowledge (Sherif, Munasinghe, & Sharma, 2012).

Social capital can be simply stated as the relationship between people and the outcomes of those relationships. It is an element of social life that may be used to explain the logical behavior of people in most any society (Sander & Lee, 2014).

Community Networking

Community networking links people with diverse members and has three common aspects: residential commonality, performance of daily activities of "like-minded" individuals, and a sense of being included in a larger social entity. These technology mediated networks create a sense of community. An online virtual community represents a group who has common interests without actual residential proximity (Chewar, McCrickhard, & Carroll, 2005).

Although there are many uses of social networking, two types of community networks exist for learning, working, and sharing knowledge. One is the community of practice (a tightly knit network engaged in a shared practice where members personally know each other) and the other being a network of practice (members are geographically dispersed, loosely knit, but are still engaged in a shared practice; Wasko, Faraj, & Teigland, 2004). As with a community of practice, members of a network of practice may not personally know each other, but are generally engaged in the sharing of knowledge via electronic means for a purpose that focuses on the interests of a given community (Wasko, Faraj, & Teigland, 2004).

Community networks are technology mediated and contain a set of common characteristics that include multiusers, persistent contexts of activity, linkage between the real world and the virtual world, and real-time communications. These characteristics lead to a user network where members are free to identify themselves as opposed to maintaining anonymity, participation is preserved over the long run, a sense of membership exists, and a greater level of trust ensues (Mynatt, 1997).

In the research performed by Sherif, Munasinghe, and Sharma (2012), two types of networks affecting researchers were studied, which included electronic open networks as well as closed networks, and the researchers concluded that there are significant social capital benefits to be gained when relationships are built. The more competency that network participants displayed in different contexts, the more likely they would accumulate more social capital to exploit. Furthermore, the interaction of people with dissimilar backgrounds, expertise, and status did facilitate the acquisition and assimilation of new knowledge.

Social Media and the Scientist

Scientists are often perceived as not being the most social individuals in the world, and in many cases, the scientific community has been reluctant to engage the social media environment for interaction. As this stereotype suggests, many scientists would prefer to be in their laboratories trying to make the next huge discovery than using social media where virtual chats with unknown individuals often occur. However, this landscape is changing.

Social media networking websites like Facebook, Twitter, and LinkedIn with all of its 24/7 interactions can seem daunting for the unexposed scientist or any other type of professional. Nonetheless, online communities are best for people to reflect and become more deliberate prior to commenting on any position. Social networks likewise offer extroverts a channel for real-time intercommunication globally. Regardless of the personality type, career consultants recommend that postdocs use online networking tools to exchange scientific ideas, make connections, and advance their careers (Tachibana, 2014).

Through the web, social network tools present a powerful method for scientists to enhance their expert profile and act as a public voice for science. Although the kind of online discussions and shared content can differ widely, scientists are progressively using social networks as a way to share journal posts, post updates from conferences and meetings, market their thoughts and scientific opinions, and distribute information about professional opportunities and future events.

Google is a powerful tool that has now also become a verb. Google searches now symbolize an approach for finding extensive details regarding virtually any subject, location, or individual. This includes from people in all ages, backgrounds, and socioeconomic status; information that previously required hours or days to collect is available within seconds. Conversely, the inability to identify useful information on a subject can be viewed negatively. Subsequently, in today's technology driven world, the absence of an online presence can impact or limit a scientist's exposure.

Social websites promote engagement with online scientific colleagues, which can motivate and provide paths to those with interest but who have insufficient expertise to acquire adequate expertise to contribute sufficiently. This includes collaborations between professional scientists. Social media provides a single click-through access to available online scientific objects, which makes it easier to gather references into the user's individual space or stream (Lackes, 2009)

Generally, scientists have stacks of papers, procedures, and notes that they circulate as web documents. In fact, many social networking websites were designed as a document management system that enabled scientists and students to quickly upload those documents, organize them, and browse and share them. Scientists can develop groups, and invite other scientists in their line of research to create a common depository of works and concepts that can be accessed from anywhere by group members.

However, some scientists remain unconvinced of such openness, especially in the hyper-competitive fields of biomedical science where patents, tenure, and promotion can depend upon being the first to publish a new discovery. From that point of view, social networking can appear dangerous because utilizing blogs and social networks for vital work is perceived as an open invitation to have online lab notepads vandalized, or even worse have innovative concepts stolen and released by a competitor (Horrobin, 2001). However, secured networking tools can offer the benefits of collaboration while still protecting a scientist's idea. With greater interaction among scientists, one would expect the greater distribution of new knowledge. Science would become more of a partnership where scientific socials media would assist in and enhance the way scientists work together.

WHY INNOVATION MATTERS

Innovation Defined

Kao (2007) defines innovation "as the ability of individuals, companies, and entire nations to continuously create their desired future. Innovation depends on harvesting knowledge from a range of disciplines besides science and technology, among them design, social science, and the arts." Kao adds that innovation is manifested by more than just products, services, and experiences, as a unique and creative process can also be considered an innovation. Innovation is a team activity as the work of entrepreneurs, scientists, software experts, and various like-minded individuals contributes to innovation. It also includes those individuals who know how to realize and illustrate the value of ideas to the end user. Innovation flows from shifts in mindset that can generate new business models, recognize new opportunities, and weave innovations throughout the fabric of society. It is about new ways of doing and seeing things as much as it is about the breakthrough idea.

What Does Innovation at Work Look Like

Innovation begins with creativity. In the world of organizations such as universities, corporations, small businesses, or government agencies, the lack of creativity leads to stagnation and leaves an organization unable to perform and respond to the dynamic needs of its stakeholders (Serrat, 2009).

More evidence of the importance of innovation is that this process does not happen in a vacuum and needs reliable methods and structures along with encouragement and incentives for a willingness to think outside of the box. Creativity flourishes in organizations that motivate workers through open concepts and environments. Those that do not flourish generally suppress creativity through rigid rules and provide little or no opportunity for any organizational modifications (Serrat, 2009).

In our observation and review of the literature, we have found that when people are faced with a problem, their instinct is to fix it with the least disruptive solution. This means they may analyze and evaluate the situation by applying logic until they are confident that they know and understand enough of the problem to formulate a viable solution. The process of attaining most solutions is better realized when the solution is developed by a group or team. In other words, a collaborative solution is generally better than any individual solution.

Most managers today are not lacking in ideas, information, or theories, and display extraordinary knowledge and competence. They are competent specialists utilizing traditional business or technical thinking. Business thinking is based upon deep research, logical facts, and formulas. Inductive and deductive reasoning are favored tools as we try to find precedent or proof to base decisions on. Business thinkers are typically quick to make choices while searching for the best answer among the least favorable responses. Business thinking has to do with eliminating obscurity and driving results.

However, often what is needed is innovative thinking, which often is not dependent on past experiences or recognized facts. It envisions a desired future state and determines ways to get there, and requires being instinctive and open to new and different possibilities. Rather than relying on previous correct answers or wrong answers, the goal is to discover better methods and explore multiple possibilities. In this situation, ambiguity is a benefit, not an issue. It enables you to ask: Exactly what if? Innovative thinking is an important addition to conventional business thinking. It enables individuals to bring new ideas and energy to their role as a leader and to resolve their challenges. It likewise leads the way to bringing more innovation into a company.

IMPACT OF INNOVATION ON BUSINESSES, COMMUNITIES, AND INDIVIDUALS

The United States economy for the last few centuries has benefited from research and innovation that have provided a competitive edge in many industries. Without innovation, no development would be possible. One of the factors that has continuously pushed the American system forward is strength of mind that both promoted and demanded innovation at the same time. People have used their imaginative abilities to create things that would benefit society and which have grown to a point where new innovations are nearly elementary.

In the globalized age, individual innovation in the workplace is the foundation of high performance (Carmeli, Meitar, & Weisberg, 2006; Janssen, Van de Vliert, & West, 2004). It has actually been considered a crucial source of most organization's innovation that advances organizational competitiveness and promotes long-term achievement (Hill, Ball, & Schilling, 2008).

A crucial factor in interjecting innovation into any organization is a consciousness need to transform knowing the benefits innovation can bring. In order for innovation to be achievable, individuals and organizations must continue to believe and maintain an open mind and receptive environment that is welcoming to varied issues and perspectives. When companies and innovators believe they have achieved most everything they need, they cease improving. The impact can quickly spread to communities, states, and nations. In the worst case, without innovation the economy can become stagnant, businesses will not grow, and communities as a whole suffer.

Types of Innovation

Innovation is more than just new products and flashy designs. They include:

- Product innovation: new and better products that an organization provides to customers
- Service innovation: new and better service offerings and delivery of those services to customers
- Process innovation: better ways of doing things that save time and/or money
- Business model innovation: improving the way an organization creates, delivers, and extracts value for customers
- Organizational innovation: improving the way one manages and engages employees
- Brand and communication innovation: new and better ways of representing an organization (Australian Psychological Society, 2012)

Wang and Ahmed (2004) defined organizational development as the "public capability to present brand-new items to market or opening brand-new markets through innovative procedures and behavior." Innovation is not a quick-fix solution to the challenges of an organization. While it is true that organizations need to innovate to stay profitable and current, developing an innovation process requires time, dedication, and incremental shifts in the culture. Leaders must be genuinely committed in their efforts to drive innovation at all levels and be cognizant of how their own behavior and actions influence and shape the desired corporate innovation culture.

Diversity and Innovation

> *Diversity is the key to creativity. Not just diversity in your workforce, but in your personal life, the teams you form, and the managers whom you hire and promote.*
> —Jeffrey Baumgartner

In the fast-moving business world of today, the competence to take decisions rapidly that everybody agrees with is admired. However, business boardrooms and teams of similar thinkers can act quickly, but oftentimes lack the diversity of opinions, perspectives, and backgrounds, and do not regularly get the best results. While there is a sense of fulfillment when everybody agrees, there is a good deal to be said regarding diversity of ideas and constructive disputes. According to a McKinsey & Company report, U.S. public businesses with executive board diversity (Figure 12.2) have a 95% better chance to reap a greater return on equity (Barta, Kleiner, & Neumann, 2012).

Many organizations are likely missing opportunities for the development of creative ideas, innovation, and success due to the fact that they are made up of individuals who think similarly. The bottom line is diversity drives innovation and creativity from every aspect and in all kinds of businesses including startups, marketing agencies, and Fortune 500 companies.

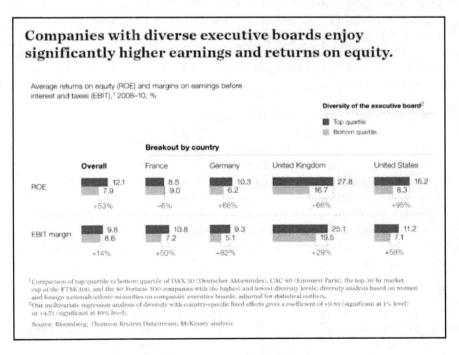

Figure 12.2 Is there a payoff from top-team-diversity?

Diversity also develops a better understanding of an organization's client base, specifically in areas such as marketing where the objective is to reach, connect, and secure a diverse audience or customer base. The present society represents new levels of diversity in the workplace, home, and community. It is now common to see baby boomers sitting at the very same table with fresh-out-of-school Millennials who have totally diverse skillsets, expectations, and experiences. For an organization seeking to secure loyalty from these diverse groups, it is essential to have a broad range of diverse minds, experiences, and cultures to successfully reach these varied audiences.

How Social Media Can Support Innovation

Social media tools can be used as the bond that brings together incomplete knowledge, deficient groups, inadequate concepts, and insufficient capability. The social network can be used as a community of individuals with common interests. Ultimately, it is an instrument that can be used to link diverse individuals and information.

Social networking can incubate new ideas that would otherwise have been abandoned or neglected. Just as easily as social network tools can propel innovation, they can also be an obstacle when participants succeed in making the less active majority feel that innovation is not appropriate for them. Thus, it must be approached in a manner that considers these risk factors as well. Social media systems today have been used in positive ways to achieve the following:

- To allow people to have discussions
- To build a community
- To ease information exchange
- To help people enlighten themselves
- To link people to others who share their passion
- To make innovative ideas noticeable and obtainable
- To make it possible for knowledge sharing
- To power partnerships on idea development
- To bring out insights and techniques that people can use to develop concepts

The better individuals and organizations utilize and gain confidence in social media, the better and stronger their organization's innovative potential. This is a result of a more engaged team of workers, a developed sense of community, and a more prepared organization that can be positioned to engage effectively in open innovation.

To comprehend how social networks are affecting product innovation, Kalypso surveyed more than 90 product and service companies (Kenly & Poston, 2016). The objective of their research was to better comprehend how the worlds of social media and product innovation are coming together to offer new business value in the form of social product innovation. Research surveys indicate that:

- Over half of surveyed companies are utilizing social media in product innovation at some level.
- Although most of responding companies have taken some action, most of them have only used social media for a small number of their product innovation efforts.

Those using social media for product innovation gained organizational advantages consisting of more and better product ideas and requirements at a much faster item adoption rate, lower product development and product costs, and a faster time to market. Table 12.1 provides a summary of the average improvement in these key areas of innovation for companies using social media in this study.

WHY DIVERSITY MATTERS

What is Diversity?

"Diversity is the presence of people from a wide range of backgrounds and possessing different traits. Differences in age, race, ethnic origin, culture, physical abilities, religion and sexual orientation are just some possible contributors to diversity" (Kokemuller, 2016). True diversity includes a regard for and an appreciation of differences in gender, ethnicity, and age as well as special needs, national origin, sexual preference, faith, and education. It

TABLE 12.1 Tangible Benefits of Social Media in the Front End of Innovation

Metric	Average Improvement
Faster time to market	16%
Faster product adoption	20%
Higher market share	6%
Improved product revenue	5%
Lower product cost	12%
Lower product development cost	15%

Source: Kenly & Poston, 2016

also extends to include diverse viewpoints, job experiences, lifestyles, and cultures. Diversity is a "big concept" in business and in society that is a driver and a source of innovation. Diversity implies more than just acknowledging and enduring differences, it is a mindset of practices that involve:

- Acknowledging that personal, cultural, and institutionalized discrimination develops and sustains opportunities for some while producing and sustaining disadvantages for others
- Appreciating and understanding human connections, cultures, and the natural environment
- Appreciating the fact that diversity is a way of understanding
- Building collaborations across differences to enable everyone to work together and do away with all forms of discrimination
- Practicing mutual respect for experiences, values, and qualities that are different from our own

Impact of Diversity on Business

A number of essential advantages are recognized in a well-managed diverse workplace. Offices where staff members represent the basic composition of the community population are generally better received by customers and the public. In addition, many times diverse work groups have more and better concepts because they emanate from more comprehensive backgrounds and experiences. Ethnicity and multiculturalism typically assist businesses that operate worldwide to better understand international markets.

Years of study by organizational scientists, sociologists, psychologists, demographers, and economic experts show that socially diverse groups (that is, those with a diversity of race, gender, ethnic, culture, and sexual preference) are more ingenious than homogeneous groups (Phillips, 2014).

It appears apparent that a group of people with diverse specific expertise would be better than a homogeneous group at fixing difficult, nonroutine problems. It is less apparent that social diversity works in the same way; nevertheless, according to Phillips (2014), science shows that it does. Not only do people with different backgrounds bring new information, they engage with people who are different from them or a different work group, and they are motivated to better prepare, to consider different perspectives, and to anticipate that reaching agreement will take effort (Phillips, 2014).

In Germany, scientists studied 28 teams with a varieties of diversity distinctiveness and discovered that highly diverse groups performed much better on highly intricate tasks than homogeneous groups. The authors speculated that this outcome was connected to the diverse group's broader diversity of perception and increased creativity, (Higgs, Plewnia, & Ploch, 2005).

Another study discovered that simple exposure to numerous cultures boosted creativity. It also revealed that substantial multicultural experiences were positively connected to creativity that supported cognitive processes such as retrieval of exceptional understanding, recruiting of ideas from unfamiliar cultures, expansion, and creative efficiency like remote association, insight learning, and idea generation, (Leung, Maddux, Galinsky, & Chiu, 2008). Finally, recent research by McKinsey & Company makes it obvious that companies with more diverse labor forces perform much better financially (Hunt, Layton, & Prince, 2015). These are some of their specific findings:

- Companies in the top quartile for racial and ethnic diversity are 35% more likely to have financial returns above their respective national industry medians. Companies in the top quartile for gender diversity are 15% more likely to have financial returns above their respective national industry medians (Figure 12.3).
- Companies in the bottom quartile both for gender, ethnicity, and race are statistically less likely to achieve above-average financial returns than the average companies who are bottom-quartile companies.
- In the United States, there is a linear relationship between racial and ethnic diversity and better financial performance. For every 10% increase in racial and ethnic diversity on the senior-executive team, earnings before interest and taxes (EBIT) rise 0.8%.

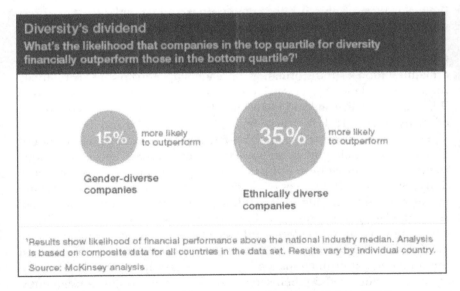

Figure 12.3 Diversity's dividend. (*Source:* Hunt, Layton, & Prince, 2015)

- Racial and ethnic diversity has a stronger impact on financial performance in the United States than gender diversity. This may be attributed to previous efforts to increase women's representation in top levels of business that have yielded some positive results.
- In the United Kingdom, greater gender diversity on the senior-executive team corresponded to the highest performance; i.e., a 10% increase in gender diversity corresponded to a rise of 3.5% in EBIT.
- While certain industries performed better on gender diversity and other industries on ethnic and racial diversity, no industry or company was in the top quartile on both dimensions.
- The unequal performance of companies in the same industry and the same country implied that diversity is a competitive differentiator that shifted market share toward more diverse companies (Hunt, Layton, & Prince, 2015).

The Ability to Impact Customers on a Global Level

Cultural diversity in the workplace has increased in conjunction with the rise of world globalization. "Cultural diversity is when differences in race, ethnicity, language, nationality, religion, and sexual orientation are represented within a community" (Amadeo, 2016) There is a new age of diversity management today. Globalization has transformed many things including politics, the economy, and societies, which have significantly influenced demographics within communities and workplaces. Workforces today are more diverse with minorities making up as much as 40% of the United States labor force in 2009. In addition, heads of state, such as Barack Obama, Nicolas Sarkozy, Angela Merkel, and Ellen Johnson Sirleaf indicate a manifestation of transformation in leadership perceptions. A multicultural, worldwide workforce, including leadership is leading to new ways of thinking about diversity and inclusion efforts. Nations have varied levels of ethnicity (Figure 12.4).

The general population today understands that cultural backgrounds have a considerable impact on how consumers express their service experiences. Different cultural influences normally equate to various expectations resulting in differences of experiences encountered. With more and more people traveling abroad organizations are experiencing difficulties in accommodating these foreign cultural influences. With this diversity in clients comes various perceptions and expectations of exactly what makes up good service. Because of this, it is necessary for organizations to understand the fundamental distinctions among cultures and have a better consideration of specific needs in their services or product offerings. Consequently, organizations should offer more customized global services.

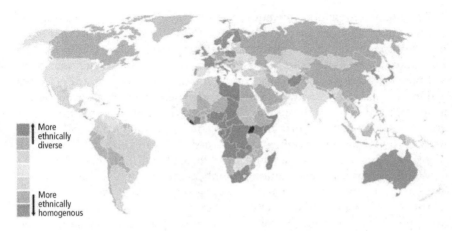

Figure 12.4 Level of ethnic diversity in countries. (Source: Harvard Institute for Economic Research, Washington Post, 2015)

Workers who emigrate from various cultures have different experiences that can be useful in providing an organization with a reliable and large knowledge base. Al-Jenaibi (2011) studied the effect and range of cultural diversity in organizations in the United Arab Emirates. The study showed that the majority of the workers agreed group work with culturally diverse people helped "to overcome cultural differences through shared experiences when working within a team" (Al-Jenaibi, 2011).

Research studies conducted on 13 leading law firms in the United Kingdom found that all of them have faced demand-side diversity pressure. When bidding for potential private sector customers, the law firms reported that they received requests for details about their diversity policies and efforts. This practice is becoming more common as customer interest in diversity is moving past the recruitment process and continuing even when a firm is retained (Braithwaite, 2010).

> Leading companies know it's essential to consistently maintain diversity as a top business imperative over a period of, at minimum, five years before diversity can gain traction and become part of the way those companies do business. True diversity is not just about the mix that constitutes the workforce, it's also about a company's customers and business partners. (Andrade, 2014)

Diversity of Thought: Better Product Development

New product development is the transformation of a market's need into a set of product technology characteristics that are built into a product that eventually becomes available for sale (Higgs, Plewnia, & Ploch, 2005).

To enhance their innovativeness and competitiveness, organizations often assemble new product development (NPD) teams that are made up of interdisciplinary and cross-functional employees. The combined understanding and abilities of team members from various functional backgrounds will have a variety of individual ideas, views, and experiences that will increase a team's creativity and innovativeness (Gebert, Boerner, & Kearney, 2010). Diverse staff members who bring a broader range of thoughts and points of view can produce greater innovativeness than a homogeneous group. For that reason, greater diversity within NPD teams can result in greater innovativeness (Amabile T., 1998; Milliken & Matins, 1996).

When groups interrelate among members, every member benefits from ideas or arguments that are shared and the group becomes more productive. Through interaction and consultation, their innovative output will normally avoid problems requiring diverse solutions. Innovation is not a product of everyone's understanding, but an outcome of interactions between everybody. Communication acts as a crucial facilitator to enhance creativity and stimulate individuals to share concepts from different point of views.

In literature that examined cognitive ability (intelligence) and cross-functional knowledge, it was shown to have a direct effect on NPD efficiency. Hall and Ellis (2010) presented three dimensions of knowledge that directly influenced NPD efficiency: supplier knowledge, technical knowledge, and supply market knowledge. Knowledge is crucial for cross-functional integration, which helps with communication, information processing, knowledge transfers, and provides a platform of interaction through diverse functions (Hall & Ellis, 2010).

HOW TO PROMOTE AND DIVERSIFY IN AN ORGANIZATION

Activities that promote internal diversity provide an organization with the opportunity to broaden its cultural horizons, expand its customer or membership base and become a better reflection of the communities it serves. Successful activities that promote diversity in organizations focus on education, participation and communication. (McQuerrey, 2016)

Additionally, cultural change is necessary for sustainable diversity within any organization. Strategies for advancing diversity include:

- Effective interaction: Managers and supervisors are often the ones on the front line when it comes to executing new policies and procedures. Those in management positions should determine essential messages and recognize effective channels that can be used to receive

the communication of diversity. It should flow from the highest levels of leadership to human resources to line managers at every level of the organization. Effective interaction should be predetermined to make sure the right messages are sent out to the right individuals.
- Include diversity in the framework of organizational policy: Diversity needs to be woven into the fundamental policies of the organization. This should include recruitment and promotion policies and practices.
- Create leadership commitment: Just as the management of organizations are concerned about safety programs, they should also assert and actively encourage diversity in their organizations. As pointed out earlier, this will help ensure success and effectiveness, which is necessary to derive all the benefits of diversity. Organizational managements can accomplish this by crafting policies that command equal and reasonable treatment of workers based on ethnic background and gender. They must also serve as good examples by considering and promoting diversity in all of their actions.

It's very important that diversity efforts are strengthened by the CEO and vigorously supported by other leaders. One cannot underestimate the effect of staff involvement. Engaging staff members at all levels is the most efficient way to collaborate and communicate the significance of diversity.

HOW SOCIAL MEDIA CAN SUPPORT DIVERSITY

We utilize social networks as the forefront of voicing our viewpoints, sharing information about our lives, and coming together to converse about issues as a community. However what about the issue of diversity? Can we actually speak about diversity on social networks? With the record speed and the ability to broadcast, tweet, and share our written thoughts and ideas just as fast as we can say them, individuals align themselves with their technological devices for hours ready to defend ideas, opinions, and beliefs.

Is social media, therefore, a good channel to discuss diversity? Yes, it is. Social media is a great avenue to discuss and support diversity since it gives a chance for thousands and even millions of people to be part of a conversation that can change individual perspectives and even alter their lives. More specifically, social media can support diversity in the following ways:

- Support is now observable. Individuals support diverse people, concepts, and things they like on sites like Digg and Reddit.
- Learn more from each other. Social media enable people to learn from each other. Anybody can search for and find diverse information

and answers to most any question. There are countless videos available on YouTube, Facebook, and other social media to teach people anything from how to cook to how to be successful in business.
- Crowd sourced wisdom. People share their wisdom, knowledge, and experiences on social media. Quora is a platform where anyone can ask any question in the world and anticipate a sensible response.
- Innovation and inspiration are given free rein. People share diverse, innovative ideas and inspirations through social media. Pinterest, for instance, has redefined the digital catalog/portfolio.
- Enhanced positive reception of the unique and handmade. Social media enables people to still have a healthy respect for the special and the handmade. Etsy, for instance, has empowered many diverse entrepreneurs and infuses a diverse culture with an amazing richness of creativity and innovations.
- Anyone can contribute. What better way can social media support diversity than the ability for anyone to contribute to issues and ideas and freely express their views and opinions? When people make use of social media to have discussions, everyone is instantly invited since it is public. Not everyone will be open minded and ready to have a natural conversation. It is necessary to approach discussion in a way not to mock others, but to inform and pay attention to others' perspectives. Overall, people have to be cautious with how they approach conversations of diversity and the platforms they use in exploring them.

It is good to have these discussions, but it is essential to comprehend that change and new ways of thinking will not come through mocking others, but through listening to other perspectives, asking questions, and aspiring to understand others' points of view.

Social media and the Internet create exceptional possibilities for establishing and expanding diversity efforts for one basic reason: They do not inherently discriminate. People from essentially every age and every walk of life around the world can be found online making use of numerous social networking platforms. The ways that businesses are leveraging this tool as a way to reach their clients demonstrates the numerous possibilities.

The statistics of social networking alone provide a concrete case for the possible reach of various online platforms. Facebook reports more than 1.79 billion monthly active users (Statista, 2016). In addition, LinkedIn has more than 450 million members with 25% who are active monthly (Yeung, 2016).

According to YouTube statistics (YouTube, 2016):

- There are more than a billion users who represent almost one-third of all people on the Internet. Everyday people spend hundreds of millions of hours on YouTube and generate billions of views.

- YouTube has launched local versions in more than 88 countries and is presented in a total of 76 different languages (covering 95% of the Internet population).

Since social networking drives outcomes for diversity activities, smart businesses are investing money and time into it. They are using it for staff member recruitment and retention, internal interactions, client satisfaction, and sales outreach.

INTRODUCTION TO ALGONITE (ALGORITHM THAT UNITES)

What is Algonite?

Algonite is currently in development as a niche social media tool for the virtual collaboration community of STEM professionals. It can foster research, discovery, innovation, and product development. The secure platform intelligently matches collaborators based on collaboration style, desired level of engagement, technical focus areas, and desired outcomes of collaboration. In essence, it provides a social network for innovation, research, and patent production.

A Newly Developing Product to Promote Collaboration

In recent years, scientists have become highly engaged in social media sites for the purpose of connecting, collaborating, and disseminating scientific information or perspectives. Presently 4.5 million scientists are signed up for ResearchGate and another 10,000 arrive daily (Van Noordan, 2014). While this pales in comparison to the 1.3 billion users of Facebook, ResearchGate is a site specifically for researchers.

Algonite is open to researchers, STEM professionals, and anyone seeking collaborations for technical purposes. While multiple social media tools and collaboration environments exist today, there does not currently exist a site that provides a matching feature, the opportunity to give technical ideas while ensuring secure collaboration, and the use of the virtual research community that includes a mobile app for video chats between collaborators.

Algonite facilitates the collaborative process by providing an accessible, easy to use platform for advancing the collaborative process in a secure environment and allowing consistent access for collaborators. This compatibility pairing and infrastructure feature allows a higher likelihood of success for all collaborative endeavors (Barta, Mancha, & Ashcraft, 2014).

A secondary benefit of Algonite is to provide scientists with relevant and current information on commercially available R&D innovation as well as product development opportunities with private companies, investors, and federal agencies. There are free postings for desired collaborations, innovations, R&D, funding, and commercialization opportunities, which are tailored and disseminated to users. By providing users with productive team structures and targeted funding opportunities, Algonite offers secondary benefits as it address this disparity and key components of innovative pathways.

PROVIDES AN APPROACH THAT PROMOTES DIVERSITY THROUGH THE ONLINE SOCIAL MEDIA PLATFORM

Algonite is compatible with existing social media sites and allows a user to sign up by linking his/her Algonite profile with existing social media sites (e.g., ResearchGate or LinkedIn). However, unlike existing networking sites for scientists such as LOOP, academia.edu, ResearchGate, and LinkedIn, Algonite is able to automatically populate a researcher's profile with additional information when a user completes registration using the PARSA (Personalized Algorithm for Research and Scholarly Activity) data collection model.

To initiate the PARSA profile development approach, a user completes a personal technical profile in PARSA (e.g., name, institution, etc.) and uploads a representative set of publications from the last 5 years and a current curriculum vita or resume. PARSA then searches the text for patterns and self-generates a technical user profile. Upon creation of the PARSA user profile process, the individual is presented with the output and allowed to edit any details. Finally, the user will be required to do a final review and approve the profile before it is incorporated and released to the site.

How Does It Work?

Algonite's innovation is built around the PARSA algorithm where users have the benefit of a system that efficiently matches researchers with desired competencies, expertise, and personal profiles that are expected to be compatible for the purpose of applicable collaborations.

Algonite is not just another social media site; however, it utilizes the benefits of this powerful medium to connect scientists and innovators based on professional, technical, and personal characteristics with a focus on identifying and matching STEM collaborators for essential partnerships and facilitating the collaborative process. This is accomplished through the use of an algorithm to make "high-probability" matches using select sources of information. The objective is to identify individuals who focus on a particular innovation or project and who have the necessary professional backgrounds, technical experience, and personality profiles for a collaborative team effort. The soundness of the algorithm will be a key rating point in the establishment and engagement of the collaboration process.

After collaborative exchanges in Algonite, the system allows users to engage in a rating poll to provide their opinions of the success and outcomes of their collaborations. Open-ended responses are collected from users about the quality of the PARSA match, the value of the current collaborative activity, and key outcomes that have resulted from their collaborative endeavors. Additionally, future versions of Algonite will offer incentivized quarterly survey completions to seek longitudinal feedback on the quantity and quality of the collaborations.

The structure of Algonite is compatible with existing social media sites allowing a user to sign up by linking their Algonite profile with existing social media sites (i.e., ResearchGate or LinkedIn). However, unlike existing networking sites for scientists such as LOOP, academia.edu, ResearchGate, and LinkedIn, Algonite is able to automatically populate a researcher profile with additional information when a user completes registration using the PARSA data collection model.

To initiate the PARSA profile development approach, a user completes a personal technical profile in PARSA (e.g., name, institution, etc.) and uploads a representative set of publications from the last 5 years and a current curriculum vita or résumé. PARSA then uses a deterministic approach to search the text for patterns that will self-generate a user's technical profile. Upon creation of the PARSA user profile, the user is allowed to edit any aspect of the details. Finally, the user is required to do a final review and approve the profile before it is officially incorporated and released on the website.

THE FUTURE OF INNOVATION AND DIVERSITY ARE GOING TO BE CONTINUOUSLY IMPACTED BY TECHNOLOGY AND SOCIAL MEDIA

Due to the dynamic changes in technology throughout the world, collaboration will evolve such that collaboration will no longer demand a physical presence in order to have a meeting or to share research, thoughts, or ideas. Additionally, the identification of collaborators will also change to allow more rapid formation of teams to address global challenges facing our engineering and scientific communities.

As communicated to the principal investigator during customer discovery for Algonite, there is a "window of opportunity" open to address this need. Algonite could be the platform that answers this opportunity by intelligently connecting STEM professionals worldwide

In an era of growing open-access of resources and at the same time growing security concerns, the need for a tool that allows access to individuals worldwide for sharing of information in a secure environment is increasingly necessary. According to a review of the scientific and business literature, the development of a social media system that connects researchers and seeks to establish diverse teams for STEM related innovations has not yet been accomplished. The development of such an innovation is challenging due to the interdisciplinary nature of the requirements and the dynamic nature of human interaction.

To accomplish this goal will require technical expertise not only in computing, but also an understanding of social science about team behaviors and the innovation process. However, Algonite has a plan to accomplish this daunting task. The concept for this research social media site with intelligent algorithms, data mining, and membership profiles can facilitate the development of high-probability collaborative teams. In achieving this goal, Algonite intends to lead the way as a dynamic and adaptable platform that engages the global STEM community.

CONCLUSION

Social media present a game-changing opportunity for individuals and organizations who become skilled at how to take advantage of it. However, taking advantage of social media's diversity necessitates more than just having a Facebook account with a loyal base of friends.

Social media can be much more than a channel where likeminded individuals connect, it can be a game changer for individuals, organizations, and communities. It can promote conversations, enlighten people, and facilitate goals that lead to innovation while creating communities that are both inclusive and diverse. However, this will not happen automatically or without planned initiatives to promote these objectives. Algonite represents a promising technique to support the realization of global collaborations in order to support innovation, diversity, and inclusion while positively impacting the global society.

REFERENCES

Acemoglu, D., Aghion, P., & Zilibotti, F. (2006). Distance to frontier, selection, and economic growth. *Journal of European Econonmic Association*, 4(1), 37–74.

Al-Jenaibi, B. (2011). The scope and impact of workplace diversity in the United Arab Emirates: An initial study. *Journal for Communication and Culture, 1*(2), 49–81.

Amabile, T. (1998). How to kill creativity. *Harvard Business Review, 76*(5), 76–87.

Amadeo, K. (2016, September). *Cultural diversity in the work place.* Retrieved from https://www.thebalance.com/cultural-diversity-3306201

Andrade, S. (2014, June). *6 advantages to workplace diversity.* Retrieved from https://www.linkedin.com/pulse/20140606233540-35065017-6-advantages-to-workplace-diversity

Ang, J., & Madsen, J. (2011). Can second-generation endogenous growth models explain the productivity trends and knowledge production in the Asian miracle economics? *The Review of Economic Statistics, 93*(4), 1360–1373.

Australian Psychological Society. (2012). Innovation in organisations. *Illuminations,* 6–10. Retrieved from http://www.inventium.com.au/wp-content/uploads/2013/03/Innovation-in-Organisations-APS-Shelley-Logan.pdf

Barta, T., Kleiner, M., & Neumann, T. (2012, April). *Is there a payoff from top-team diversity?* Retrieved from http://www.mckinsey.com/business-functions/organization/our-insights/is-there-a-payoff-from-top-team-diversity

Barta, T., Mancha, C., & Ashcraft, C. (2014). *What is the impact of gender diversity on technology business performance? Research Summary.* Retrieved from https://www.ncwit.org/sites/default/files/resources/impactgenderdiversitytechbusinessperformance_print.pdf

Bourdieu, P., & Wacquant, L. (1992). *An invitation to reflexive sociology.* Chicago, IL: The University of Chicago Press.

Braithwaite, J. (2010). The stategic use of demand-side diversity pressure in the solicitors' profession. *Journal and Law and Society, 37*(3).

Burt, R. S. (2010). *Neighbor networks: Competitive advantage local and personal.* New York, NY: Oxford University Press.

Carmeli, A., Meitar, R., & Weisberg, J. (2006). Self-leadership skills and innovative behavior at work. *International Journal of Manpower, 27*(1), 75–90.

CDC. (2012). *CDC's guide to writing for social media.* Retrieved from http://www.cdc.gov/socialmedia/Tools/guidelines/pdf/GuidetoWritingforSocialMedia.pdf

Chen, W., Rainie, L., & Wellman, B. (2012). Networked work. In H. Rainie & B. Wellman (Eds.), *Networked: The new social operating system* (pp. 171–196). Cambridge, MA: MIT Press.

Research paper (PDF): The Effects of Diversity and Network Ties on Innovations: The Emergence of a New Scientific Field. Available from: https://www.researchgate.net/publication/273740564_The_Effects_of_Diversity_and_Network_Ties_on_Innovations_The_Emergence_of_a_New_Scientific_Field [accessed Apr 6, 2017].

Cheung, C., Lee, Z. W., & Chan, T. K. (2015). Self-disclosure in social networking sites : The role of perceived cost, perceived benefits and social influence. *Internet Research, 25*(2), 279–299.

Chewar, C. M., McCrickhard, S., & Carroll, J. M. (2005). Analyzing the social capital value chain in community network interfaces. *Internet Research, 15*(3), 262–280.

Cisco. (2016). *The zettabyte era: Trends and analysis*. Retrieved September 20, 2016, http://www.cisco.com/c/en/us/solutions/collateral/service-provider/visual-networking-index-vni/vni-hyperconnectivity-wp.html

Fan, D. (2011). *Proof that diversity drives innovation*. Retrieved from http://www.diversityinc.com/diversity-management/proof-that-diversity-drives-innovation/

Gebert, D., Boerner, S., & Kearney, E. (2010). Cross-functionality and innovation in new product development teams: A dilemmatic structure and its consequences for the management of diversity. *European Journal Of Work And Organizational Psychology, 15*(4), 431–458.

Gerschenkron, A. (1962). *Economic backwardness in historical perspective*. Cambridge, MA: Belknap Press.

Gladwell, M. (2000). *Designs for working*. Retrieved from http://gladwell.com/designs-for-working/

Guimera, R., Uzzi, B., Spiro, A., & Amaral, L. (2005). Team assembly mechanisms determine collaboration network structure and team performance. *Science, 308*, 697–702.

Hall, D., & Ellis, S. (2010, May). *Core and overlapping knowledge, cross-functional integration, and process*. POMS 21st Annual Conference, Vancouver, Canada.

Higgs, M., Plewnia, U., & Ploch, J. (2005). Influence of team composition and task complexity on team performance. *Team Performance Management, 11*(7/8), 227–250.

Hill, H., Ball, D., & Schilling, S. (2008). Unpacking pedagogical content knowledge: Conceptualizing and measuring teachers' topic specific knowledge of students. *Journal for Research in Mathematical Education, 39*(4), 372–400.

Horrobin, D. (2001). Something rotten at the core of science? *Trends in Pharmacological Sciences, 22*(2), 51–52.

Hunt, V., Layton, D., & Prince, S. (2015, January). *Why diversity matters*. Retrieved from http://www.mckinsey.com/business-functions/organization/our-insights/why-diversity-matters

Janssen, O., Van de Vliert, E., & West, M. (2004). The bright and dark sides of individual and group innovation: A special issue introduction. *Journal of Organizational Behavior, 25*, 129–145.

Kao, J. (2007). *Innovation nation: How America is losing its innovation edge, why it matters, and what we can do to get it back*. New York, NY: Free Press.

Kenly, A., & Poston, B. (2016). *Social media and product innovation*. Retrieved 2016, from http://viewpoints.io/uploads/files/Kalypso_Social_Media_and_Product_Innovation_1.pdf

Kokemuller, N. (2016). *What is diversity and how does it impact work?* Retrieved from http://smallbusiness.chron.com/diversity-impact-work-15985.html

Lackes, R. (2009, January). Social networks as an approach to the enhancement of collaboration among scientists. *International Journal of Web Based Communities, 5*, 577–592.

Leung, A., Maddux, W., Galinsky, A., & Chiu, C.-y. (2008). Multicultural experience enhances creativity: The when and how. *American Psychologist, 63*(3), 169-180.

McQuerrey, L. (2016). *Activities to promote diversity in organizations*. Retrieved from http://smallbusiness.chron.com/activities-promote-diversity-organizations-20563.html

Milliken, F., & Matins, L. (1996). Understanding the multiple effects of diversity in organizational groups. *Academy of Management Review, 21*(2), 402–433.

Mynatt, E. A. (1997). Design for network communities. In proceedings of the *ACM conference on human factors in computing systems* (pp. 210–217). New York, NY: ACM Press.

OECD. (2013). *Glossary of statistical term* (F. Manual, Ed.). Retrieved from https://stats.oecd.org/glossary/detail.asp?ID=2314

Perrin, A. (2015, October). *Social media usage: 2005–2015*. Retrieved from http://www.pewinternet.org/2015/10/08/social-networking-usage-2005-2015/

Phillips, K. (2014, October). *How diversity makes us smarter*. Retrieved from https://www.scientificamerican.com/article/how-diversity-makes-us-smarter/

Ribia-García, D., Elichc-Qucsada, C., Rus-Casas, C, & Aguilar-Pena, J. D. (2016). The social media networking tools for the promotion of the entrepreneurship. In *2016 technologies applied to electronics teaching (TAEE;* pp. 1–6). Seville, Spain: IEEE.

Sander, T., & Lee, T. (2014). A concept to measure social capital in social network sites. *International Journal of Future Computer and Communications, 3*(2), 105–107.

Semolic, B. (2008). *PM research journal:Project overload*. Retrieved from http://www.ipma.world/assets/rs-PM-Research08.pdf

Serrat, O. (2009, September). *Harnessing creativity and innovation in the workplace*. Retrieved from https://www.adb.org/sites/default/files/publication/27596/harnessing-creativity-and-innovation-workplace.pdf

Sherif, K., Munasinghe, M., & Sharma, C. (2012). The combinative effect of electronic open networks and closed interpersonal networks on knowledge creation in academic communities. *VINE, 42*(2), 277–294. doi:http://dx.doi.org.ezproxy.net.ucf.edu/10.1108/03055721211227291

Smith, K. (2016, 03 07). *Marketing: 96 amazing social media statistics and facts for 2016*. Retrieved September 19, 2016, from https://www.brandwatch.com/2016/03/96-amazing-social-media-statistics-and-facts-for-2016/

Statista. (2016). *The statistics portal*. Retrieved from https://www.statista.com/statistics/264810/number-of-monthly-active-facebook-users-worldwide/

Stats, I. W. (2016, June 30). *Internet users in the world by regions*. Retrieved September 19, 2016, from http://www.internetworldstats.com/stats.htm

Tachibana, C. (2014, Febuary). *A scientist's guide to social media*. Retrieved from https://www.sciencemag.org/careers/features/2014/02/scientists-guide-social-media

Taylor, A., & Greve, H. (2006). Superman or the fantastic four? Knowledge combination and experience in innovative teams. *Academy of Management Journal, 49*(4), 723–740.

Van Noorden, R. (2014). Scientists and the social network. *Nature, 512*(7513), 126–129.

Wang, C. L., & Ahmed, P. K. (2004). The development and validation of the organisational innovativeness construct using confirmatory factor analysis. *European Journal of Innovation Management, 71*(4), 303–313.

Wasko, M. M., Faraj, S., & Teigland, R. (2004, December). Collective action and knowledge contribution in electronic networks of practice. *Journal of the Association for Information Systems, 5*(11–12), 493–513.

Williams, K., & O'Reilly, C. (1998). *Demography and diversity in organizations: A review of 40 years of research.* Retrieved from https://www.researchgate.net/publication/298960487_Demography_and_diversity_in_organizations_A_review_of_40_years_of_research

Wu, L., Lin, C., Aral, S., & Brynjolfsson, E. (2009). *The value of social network.* Retrieved from http://smallblue.research.ibm.com/projects/snvalue/

Wuchty, S., Jones, B., & Uzzi, B. (2007). *The increasing dominance of teams in production of knowledge.* Retrieved from http://science.sciencemag.org/content/316/5827/1036

Yeung, K. (2016, August). *LinkedIn now has 450 million members, but the number of monthly visitors is still flat.* Retrieved from http://venturebeat.com/2016/08/04/linkedin-now-has-450-million-members-but-the-number-of-monthly-visitors-is-still-flat/?utm_source=tuicool&utm_medium=referral

YouTube. (2016). *Press statistics.* Retrieved from https://www.youtube.com/yt/press/statistics.html

ABOUT THE CONTRIBUTORS

Vincent Bagire is an associate professor in the department of Business Administration at Makerere University Business School, Kampala–Uganda. He holds a PhD in Strategic Management from the University of Nairobi. He has been a faculty member for twenty years and involved in both academic and administrative roles. He is currently the Deputy Dean in the Faculty of Graduate Studies and Research. His teaching and research areas are management, strategy, organizational theory and corporate strategy. He has published on management practices and strategic management in the African context. He is currently engaged in studies on practical experiences of management and strategy as practice in the public and civil society sectors with particular interest on NGOs operating in the less developed economies. He is also involved in several community based activities in the urban and rural settings of Uganda. Vincent is an Alumni of the Africa Academy of Management faculty development workshop, a former Global Representative for Africa of the Business Policy and Strategy division of the Academy of Management and currently a member of the Research committee of the same division.

Ghada Baz (MBA, Georgia State University) is an instructor of management at the College of Business Administration and a doctoral student in the Industrial and Organizational Psychology program at the University of Central Florida. She is also a partner at OpenPublic Networks, an Orlando, FL, based consulting firm assisting startup, small, and medium businesses in establishing their professional presence through technology, telecommunication, branding, and consulting services. Baz is a member of the

Small Business Development Center's Business Advisory Council, and is a certified Project Management Professional (PMP) with international experience in the management consulting industry, mainly with Ernst & Young.

Cynthia A. Bulley is a senior lecturer in marketing and organizational research with the Central University, Ghana. She has had a varied career in industry and academia. She has facilitated workshops and training program for organizations in Ghana. Her considerable research, teaching and consulting activities focus on the application of marketing practices and organization capacity building. She is interested in organizational management, experiential marketing and international business.

A. O'Shea Cleveland is a doctor of veterinary medicine candidate at the Louisiana State University. She received her degree in women's studies from the University of Maryland with a concentration in gender and sexuality. Her research specializations include gender, diversity, and communication. She has published, and has conducted numerous seminars on the topics of gendered communication and communication diversity.

Claudia C. Cogliser is Associate Dean for Student Affairs in the Graduate School and Associate Professor of Management in the Rawls College of Business at Texas Tech University. She received her PhD from the University of Miami, and previously held faculty positions at the University of Oklahoma and Oregon State University. Claudia teaches courses in organizational behavior, leadership, and research methods and was inducted into the Texas Tech Teaching Academy in 2013. Her research interests include leader-follower relationships, entrepreneurial orientation, scale development, and multi-level analysis. With over 30 publications, Claudia's research appears in scholarly outlets such as *The Leadership Quarterly, Journal of Management, Journal of Organizational Behavior, Entrepreneurship Theory & Practice, Organizational Research Methods,* and *Educational and Psychological Measurement.* In 2013 she received the Texas Tech Chancellor's Distinguished Teaching Award and the President's Excellence in Teaching Award. Claudia serves on the editorial boards of The Leadership Quarterly and Group and Organizational Management. She is a member of AOM, APA, SMA, and SIOP, and serves currently as the treasurer of SMA.

Nancy DiTomaso is Distinguished Professor of Management and Global Business at Rutgers Business School—Newark and New Brunswick. Her research addresses issues of diversity, culture, and inequality. Her PhD is from the University of Wisconsin–Madison. Her 2013 book, *The American Non-dilemma: Racial Inequality without Racism* (Russell Sage) won the C. Wright Mills Award from the Society for the Study of Social Problems; the Inequality, Poverty, and Mobility Section Distinguished Book Award from the American Sociological Association (ASA); received Honorable Mention for the Max Weber Award for Best Book given by the Organizations, Occupations, and Work Section of the ASA; and was Runner Up for the George R. Terry Award given by the Academy of Management for the Best Book in Management over a two-year period. Professor DiTomaso won the 2016 Sage Award for Lifetime Scholarly Achievement in Gender and Diversity given by the Academy of Management Division on Gender and Diversity.

Barbara A. Fritzsche (PhD, University of South Florida) is Associate Chair of the Department of Psychology and Director of the MS Program in Industrial and Organizational Psychology at the University of Central Florida. Her research interests include workplace diversity, successful aging at work, and employee health and wellness. She serves on the editorial board of the *Journal of Organizational Behavior* and has recently published papers in *Work, Aging, and Retirement, Organizational Psychology Review, Human Resource Management Review*, and *Journal of Managerial Psychology*.

Bella L. Galperin holds a PhD, Concordia University (Canada) and is Professor of Management/Senior Associate Director of TECO Energy Center for Leadership, University of Tampa. Research interests include international organizational behavior, leadership, and workplace deviance. Published in a variety of journals including, the Journal of Business Ethics, International Journal of Human Resource Management, Journal of Applied Social Psychology, Leadership Quarterly, and International Business Review, as well as edited volumes. She recently co-authored a book on leadership in Africa and the African diaspora.

Cristina M. Giannantonio is an Associate Professor of Management in the Argyros School of Business and Economics at Chapman University. She is an Associate at the Thompson Policy Institute on Disability and Autism at Chapman University. She served as the president of the Chapman University Faculty Senate in 2015–2016. She received her PhD from the Smith School of Business at the University of Maryland, College Park, MD. Dr. Giannantonio's research interests include extreme leadership, image norms, and high tech entrepreneurial careers. Her research has been published in academic journals, including the *Journal of Management, Personnel Psychology*, and *The Journal of Business Leadership*. She was the co-editor of the *Journal of Business and Management* from 2005–2016. In 2012 Drs. Giannantonio and Hurley-Hanson's Academy of Management symposium Staying Hungry, Staying Foolish: Academic Reflections of the Life and Career of Steve Jobs was designated an AOM Showcase Symposium. Dr. Giannantonio and Dr. Hurley-Hanson's book *Extreme Leadership: Leaders, Teams and Situations Outside the Norm* was published by Edward Elgar Publishing in 2014. The book is part of the New Horizons in Leadership Studies series. *Extreme Leadership* was selected as a finalist for the 2014 Outstanding Leadership Book Award by the Department of Leadership Studies at the University of San Diego.

Lucy Gilson (PhD, Georgia Institute of Technology) is a Professor and the Management Department Head at the University of Connecticut. Her research examines teams in different organizational settings performing a diverse range of jobs to understand how creativity, empowerment, leadership, and virtual communication influence effectiveness. She is the Senior Associate Editor of *Group and Organization Management*, and her work has been published in the *Academy of Management Journal, Journal of Management, Leadership Quarterly*, and other top international journals. Professor Gilson has consulted with multinational companies as well as state and national agencies in the areas of leadership, women and leadership, managing virtual teams, managing change, and leading for creativity.

Caren Goldberg (PhD, Georgia State University) is an Associate Professor at Bowie State University, whose research focuses on diversity and sexual harassment. Her work has been published in a variety of management and women's studies journals, including *Journal of Applied Psychology, Journal of Organizational Behavior, Human Relations, Human Resource Management, Journal of Business and Psychology, Group and Organization Management, Sex Roles*, and *Psychology of Women Quarterly*. She is currently serving as Treasurer of the Gender and Diversity in Organizations Division of the Academy of Management and is on the editorial boards of several journals. Dr. Goldberg has testified in over a dozen employment law matters.

Carolina Gomez is a full professor at Florida International University. Her research interests within organizational behavior lie in motivation and the factors that affect critical constructs such as organizational commitment and organizational citizenship behaviors. In addition, she does research on control and coordination in MNCs. Finally, she has looked at how country institutions affect levels of entrepreneurship across countries. Her papers have been published in journals such as *Academy of Management Journal, Strategic Management Journal, Group and Organization Management, Journal of Business Ethics, International Journal of Human Resource Management, Journal of Management Studies, Journal of World Business, Journal of Business Research*, and the *Journal of Experimental Social Psychology*. In the private sector, Dr. Gómez worked with Nortel and subsequently, completed a leadership development program within General Electric Capital.

Daniel P. Gullifor is a PhD student in the Rawls College of Business at Texas Tech University. He obtained his Bachelor of Science and Master of Business Administration from the Foster College of Business Administration at Bradley University. He conducts research in the field of organizational behavior and human resource management. Specifically, he studies leadership, the leader's relationship with her or his self, and how the dynamics of this relationship affects their leadership ability.

Courtney A. Henderson holds an MA in Literature (University of Toledo); an MS in Linguistics (University of Hawaii at Manoa), a Higher Education Professionals Certification from Harvard and is working on an EdD in Higher Education Administration and Leadership. She has taught at the University of Miami, Barry University and Pharos University. She also served as the Director of the Writing Center with the international study abroad program Semester at Sea. She gave seven presentations during the voyage as both a professor and Writing Center Director. Henderson earned grants to create a Hawaiian/English book and game to help with Hawaiian language revitalization and it was distributed at Hawaiian language immersion preschools on Oahu. Henderson has also presented at conferences around the world speaking on linguistics, leadership, writing and literature. Henderson is currently a mentor for undergraduate students and an Academic Advisor at Berkeley College.

Amy E. Hurley-Hanson is an Associate Professor of Management in the George L. Argyros School of Business and Economics at Chapman University. She is an Associate at the Thompson Policy Institute on Disability and Autism at Chapman University. She received her PhD in Management from the Stern School of Business at New York University. She is the co-editor of the recent book *Extreme Leadership: Leaders, Teams and Situations Outside the Norm*. She was the co-editor of the *Journal of Business and Management* from 2005–2016. Dr. Hurley-Hanson was chosen as an Ascendant Scholar in 2000 by the Western Academy of Management. In 2008 Drs. Hurley-Hanson and Giannantonio received the Best Symposium Award from the Management and Education Division of the Academy of Management. Her areas of research are organizational decision making, image norms, high tech entrepreneurial careers and the application of behavioral decision theory to strategic aspects of executive succession. Her work on these topics has appeared in numerous journals including the *Journal of Vocational Behavior, Journal of Applied Psychology, Women in Management Review, Journal of Organizational Behavior, Group and Organization Management, Journal of Leadership and Organization Development, Organizational Dynamics*, and the *Journal of Psychology*. She was selected as a Research Fellow at the Center for Leadership and Career Studies at the Goizueta Business School of Emory University.

Terri R. Lituchy has her PhD in International Organizational Behavior from University of Arizona. Dr. Lituchy is the PIMSA Distinguished Chair at CETYS Universidad in Mexico. Dr. Lituchy taught on Semester at Sea spring 2016. She has also taught around the world including: United States,

Mexico, Canada, Trinidad, Barbados, Argentina, France, UK, Czech Republic, Japan, China, Thailand, and Malaysia. She teaches courses on Organizational Behavior, Cross-Cultural Management, International Negotiations, and Women in International Business to name a few. Terri's research interests are in cross-cultural management and international organizational behavior. Dr. Lituchy's current project, LEAD: Leadership Effectiveness and Motivation in Africa, the Caribbean and the Diaspora has received many awards as well as grants from SAMS, the SHRM Foundation, Emerald Publishing, McMaster University, University of the West Indies, Concordia University, and SSHRC; and has been published as *LEAD: Leadership Effectiveness in Africa and the African Diaspora* (2016). Terri has published several other books on *Successful Professional Women of the Americas* (Elgar Publishing, 2006), *Gender and the Dysfunctional Workplace* (Elgar, 2012) and *Management in Africa* (Routledge, 2014), and *LEAD: Leadership Effectiveness in Africa and the African Diaspora* (Palgrave, 2016). Dr. Lituchy has over 35 published journal articles and many research awards and grants. In her spare time, Terri enjoys traveling, photography, bird watching, and learning about other cultures.

Patricia G. Martínez is an associate professor at the College of Business Administration at Loyola Marymount University. Her work has been published in *Human Resources Management Review, Personnel Review, Employee Responsibilities and Rights Journal, Nonprofit Management and Leadership, Management Research* and the *Business Journal of Hispanic Research* and she contributed to *Managing Human Resources in Latin America: An Agenda for International Leaders*. She received her doctoral degree from the University of California, Irvine. Professor Martínez's research interests link human resources management research with organizational behavior topics particularly in the areas of paternalism as a leadership style, how human resource management practices can lead to the creation of psychological and legal contracts, and whether "overqualification," possessing experience or education beyond job requirements, affects applicants' likelihood of being selected for job interviews and hiring.

Pamela McCauley, PhD, CPE is an ergonomics and biomechanics expert, an internationally acclaimed keynote speaker, a Professor and Director of the Ergonomics Laboratory in the Department of Industrial Engineering and Management Systems at the University of Central Florida where she leads the Human Factors and Ergonomics in Disaster Management Research Team. She previously held the position of Martin Luther King, Jr. Visiting Associate Professor of Aeronautics and Astronautics at the Massachusetts Institute of Technology.

She is the author of over 80 technical papers, book chapters, conference proceedings and the best-selling ergonomics textbook, *Ergonomics:*

Foundational Principles, Applications, and Technologies. Many of her leadership, diversity, innovation and STEM education related keynote talks draw from her research-based book: *Transforming Your STEM Career Through Leadership and Innovation: Inspiration and Strategies for Women*, which examines the growing need for leadership and innovation, particularly among women and STEM professionals.

Her newest book, *The Essentials of Engineering Leadership and Innovation*, is underpinned by years of applied experience in engineering settings, and is designed to develop and prepare engineers as leaders to accept the technical and managerial challenges that they will face as professionals. To inspire students, particularly minorities and females, to consider careers in STEM she authored, *Winners Don't Quit... Today They Call Me Doctor*, in which she shares her challenging yet inspirational journey to engineering success despite financial, academic, and personal difficulties.

Dr. McCauley has the distinction of being a 2012 U.S. Fulbright Scholar Specialist Program Awardee for her U.S.–New Zealand Human Engineering and Mobile Technology in High Consequence Emergency Management Research Program. Due to her extensive expertise in biomechanics, human factors, and ergonomic design, Dr. McCauley is a highly sought Certified Professional Ergonomist (CPE) and Expert Witness.

Lemayon L. Melyoki holds a PhD, University of Twente (Netherlands) and is a lecturer at the University of Dar es Salaam Business School and a member of the Institute of Directors of Tanzania. His current research interests include corporate governance and leadership and entrepreneurial ecosystems. Lemayon has also recently been involved in governance issues of the petroleum sector in Tanzania and has informed various legislations, which stimulated efforts to transform the Tanzanian National Oil Company. His recent article on the governance of the petroleum sector in Tanzania has been accepted for publication in the *Journal of Extractive Industries and Society*. In addition, Lemayon is currently the Operations Research Advisor for a USAID-funded Project focusing on Public Sector Systems Strengthening representing the Urban Institute based in the United States.

Elham Metwally is an Adjunct Assistant Professor in the School of Business, the American University in Cairo. She earned her doctorate of business administration degree from Maastricht School of Management in the Netherlands, and her dissertation explored "The effect of managing change through information technology to achieving strategic competitiveness for private banks in Egypt." She earned her MBA and her bachelor degree in Economics from the American University in Cairo. Elham is a founding member of the Africa Academy of Management, an affiliate of the Academy of Management, and was the Co-chair of the Africa Academy of Management 2016 Conference in Nairobi, Kenya. She serves on the editorial review board of the *Africa Journal of Management*, and she is a member of the Academy of Management in USA, the European Academy of Management (EURAM), the European Institute for Advanced Studies in Management (EIASM), the Middle East Council for Small Business & Entrepreneurship (MCSBE), and Holland Alumni Network in the Netherlands Organization for International Cooperation in Higher Education (NUFFIC). She is an active participant in the Academy of Management annual conferences. She has several publications and her research and teaching interests include strategic management, organizational behavior, human resources management, organizational development, banking, entrepreneurship and small businesses. Her current research interests include research on Leadership effectiveness, motivation, and culture in Africa, diversity management, informal settlements, and human resources management in North Africa. She has published a number of book chapters, a book review, and authored and co-authored several articles that appear in several journals and books including the *Canadian Journal of Administrative Sciences, Journal of International Finance and Economics,* the *International Journal of Strategic Management,* among others. Elham made more than a dozen years of experience in the realm of banking, namely in the Hong Kong and Shanghai Banking Corporation (HSBC), and she had and extensive managerial experience of around twenty years in an educational setting where she worked as the Director of Scholarships at the American University in Cairo.

Edwin Mouriño-Ruiz (PhD, Barry University) is a Assistant Professor of Management and Human Resources in the School of Business at Rollins College. He has both Air Force and Corporate Industry experience. He is a graduate of the Department of Defense (DOD) school of diversity, Defense Equal Opportunity Management Institute (DEOMI). His current research interests center on leadership, diversity (in particular Latino growing workforce), human capital trends and its implications for organizations, leaders, and human resources. His book, *The Perfect Human Capital Storm: Workplace Challenges and Opportunities in the 21st Century* was published by CreateSpace in 2014.

Clive M. Mukanzi holds a PhD, Jomo Kenyatta University of Agriculture and Technology, Kenya. Dr. Mukanzi is lecturer at the College of Human Resource Management Jomo Kenyatta University of Agriculture and Technology. His research interests include Human resource management, organizational behavior, leadership, culture and motivation. Dr. Mukanzi has presented his research work at various professional workshops and conferences in multiple countries. His current research is on responsible leadership in mission driven organization in Africa and establishment.

Sarah Nesci is an undergraduate student at the University of Connecticut. She is a senior studying Business Management and Communication. Sarah is researching how gender effects communication styles and leadership for her Honor's Senior Thesis. This will be her first published work.

Edwin Nassiff is co-founder of InfoSec Intelligence, LLC, an information technology security consulting company, an adjunct professor in the Computer Science department of the University of Central Florida (UCF), a mentor in UCF's I-Corps program which trains and assists start-up ventures, and is a member of Florida Angel NEXUS, an organization that helps power angel investment groups statewide. He has a BS in Math, MS in Computer Science, and a PhD in Information Systems and served in numerous senior IT management positions for the U.S. Department of Defense as well as the Lockheed Martin Corporation.

Noble Osei-Bonsu is a highly self-motivated individual and a team player. He holds MPhil degree in Psychology from the University of Ghana, Legon, with a specialization in Industrial and Organizational Psychology. Currently, he is a senior lecturer in the Department of Human Resource Management, Central Business School, Ghana. His research interests and publications focus on downsizing, organizational justice and career guidance.

Catrina Palmer is a doctoral student in the Management and Global Business department at Rutgers Business School–Newark and New Brunswick. She is majoring in Organizational Behavior and pursuing a minor in Social Psychology. Her research interest include diversity, inequality, and networks. She received her Bachelor of Business Administration and Master of Business Administration with a concentration in Human Resources Management at Kent State University with honors.

Betty Jane Punnett holds a PhD, New York University and is Professor Emerita, University of the West Indies (Cave Hill). Research on the impact of culture on management, particularly the Caribbean. Published extensively in international journals, books and encyclopedias. Recently authored *Management: A Developing Country Perspective*, co-authored book on leadership in Africa and the African diaspora. An active member of AOM, AIB, and AFAM, and founding editor of AIB Insights.

Cort Rudolph is an assistant professor of industrial and organizational psychology at Saint Louis University. He received his BA from DePaul University and his MA and PhD from Wayne State University. Rudolph's research program focuses rather broadly on issues related to aging at work, including issues of aging and occupational health and well-being, and applications of lifespan development models to further the understanding of work, aging, and retirement. His research is published in journals such as the, *Journal of Occupational Health Psychology, Human Resources Management Review,* and the *Journal of Gerontology*. He currently serves on the editorial boards of the *Journal of Occupational and Organizational Psychology*, *Journal of Vocational Behavior*, and *Work, Aging and Retirement*.

Thomas Senaji holds a PhD, Kenya Methodist University (Kenya) and is a Senior Lecturer in Strategy and Knowledge Management and the coordinator of doctoral and postgraduate studies at Kenya Methodist University. He is an adjunct professor at Jomo Kenyatta University of Agriculture & Technology and Africa Nazarene University. Dr. Senaji has over 35 publications comprising refereed journal articles, conference proceedings, and workshops. His current research focuses on leadership, organizational development and change and spirituality in Africa. He is also an international consultant on broadband communications.

Terri A. Scandura (PhD, University of Cincinnati) is a Professor of Management in the School of Business Administration at the University of Miami. From 2007-2012, she served as the Dean of the Graduate School. Her current research interests center on leadership, leader–member exchange, and mentorship. Her book, *Essentials of Organizational Behavior: An Evidence-Based Approach* was published by SAGE Publications in 2016.

Jacqueline H. Stephenson, PhD is a lecturer with the University of the West Indies, based in the Department of Management Studies. Dr. Stephenson read for a doctoral degree in Human Resource Management at the University of Nottingham, U.K. and her research interests include fairness and equality at work, age discrimination, diversity, inclusion within organisations and discrimination in the Caribbean.

Manuel J. Tejeda is a professor of management and psychology at Barry University in Miami, Florida. He has served in numerous administrative roles and currently serves as the executive director for the Barry Institute for Community and Economic Development which focuses on capacity building and entrepreneurship education in underserved neighborhoods and nations. He has served on several editorial boards as well as grant review boards for national governmental institutes. His research on leadership, spirituality, diversity and social justice has been features in numerous journals and technical reports. He has served on healthy workplace initiatives and international development activities. Dr. Tejeda is also the recent president of Alliance for GLBTQ youth, that is focused in youth in Miami-Dade County and is the largest and most comprehensive provider of mental health services and care coordination for LGBTQ youth in the Southern United States.

Lori L. Tribble is a PhD student in the Rawls College of Business at Texas Tech University. She obtained her Bachelor of Science at the University of

Georgia. She received her MEd and MBA from Georgia Southern University. She conducts research in organizational behavior and strategic management. Her research interests include authentic leadership, ethical leadership, leader–member exchange, family business, and organizational ethics.

Frankie J. Weinberg is an associate professor of management and holds the Chase Minority Entrepreneurship Distinguished Professorship in the College of Business at Loyola University, New Orleans. He received his PhD from the University of Georgia. His scholarly interests include dyadic and team-level interactions at work, including mentoring, leadership, communication, and social networks as well as team and organizational diversity.

Hannes Zacher is a professor of work and organizational psychology at the University of Leipzig in Germany. He received his MS from the Technical University of Braunschweig and his PhD from the University of Giessen. In his research program, Hannes investigates aging at work, career development, and occupational well-being; proactivity, innovation, leadership, and entrepreneurship; and pro-environmental employee behavior and organizational climate. His research is published in journals such as the *Journal of Organizational Behavior, Journal of Management,* and *Psychology and Aging.* He is an associate editor of the *Journal of Occupational and Organizational Psychology* and currently serves on the editorial boards of the *Journal of Occupational Health Psychology, Journal of Vocational Behavior, Group & Organization Management,* and *Work, Aging and Retirement.* He is a research fellow at the Sloan Center on Aging & Work at Boston College, an adjunct researcher at the Research Center for Innovation and Strategic Human Resource Management at Jiangxi University of Finance and Economics, and an adjunct professor at Queensland University of Technology.

CPSIA information can be obtained
at www.ICGtesting.com
Printed in the USA
LVHW041802151121
703328LV00002B/17